Insult and the Making of the Gay Self

Edited by Michèle Aina Barale,

Jonathan Goldberg, Michael Moon,

and Eve Kosofsky Sedgwick

Insult

and the Making of the Gay Self

Didier Eribon

TRANSLATED BY Michael Lucey

DUKE UNIVERSITY PRESS   DURHAM AND LONDON   2004

© 2004 DUKE UNIVERSITY PRESS

All rights reserved. Printed in the United
States of America on acid-free paper ∞
Designed by Amy Ruth Buchanan. Typeset in
Quadraat by Keystone Typesetting, Inc. Library
of Congress Cataloging-in-Publication Data
appear on the last printed page of this book.

DUKE UNIVERSITY PRESS GRATEFULLY
ACKNOWLEDGES THE SUPPORT OF
THE GILL FOUNDATION, WHICH PROVIDED
FUNDS TOWARD THE TRANSLATION AND
DISTRIBUTION OF THIS BOOK.

OUVRAGE PUBLIÉ AVEC LE CONCOURS
DU MINISTÈRE FRANÇAIS CHARGÉ DE
LA CULTURE—CENTRE NATIONAL DU LIVRE.
THIS WORK WAS PUBLISHED WITH THE
HELP OF THE FRENCH MINISTRY OF
CULTURE—CENTRE NATIONAL DU LIVRE.

English translation © 2004 Duke University Press.
Réflexions sur la question gay by Didier Eribon
© Librairie Arthème Fayard, 1999.

For Marie Ymonet

To know how to get free is not so hard;
what is arduous is to know how to be free.

ANDRÉ GIDE, *The Immoralist*

Contents

Preface

This book was published in France in 1999, but I began writing it in 1996 and had been thinking about it since 1995. It was conceived at the intersection of a number of different theoretical and political preoccupations, and its development is closely linked to the specific context of the mid-1990s in France.

First of all, this book is one of a series of works I have written on Michel Foucault. The notable discrepancies between the French and American receptions of my biography of Foucault provided an initial impulse to think at greater length about the links that existed between Foucault's gay subjectivity and his thought—from his formative years to his final projects. When the biography appeared in France in 1989,[1] a number of Foucault's disciples (in a way that is all too familiar) took upon themselves the role of guardians of the temple and protectors of the orthodox interpretation of the work. They criticized me rather harshly for having tried to "explain Foucault's work by way of his homosexuality," which, for them, somehow implied a betrayal or a devaluation of that work. One of them even suggested that I should "go take a flying leap [aller me rhabiller]." It was nearly impossible in France at that moment to speak of a philosopher's homosexuality. Sexuality was never supposed to leave the private sphere, and to claim that a person's homosexuality could be related to his or her work was viewed as an attack on the integrity of that person's thought itself.

Strangely enough, when this same book was translated into English two years later, the American intellectual field was so different from the French one that people reproached me for not having perceived the important place sexuality had, or that Foucault's sexual politics had, in the elaboration of his work.[2] Yet, to my mind, I had used my biographical investigations to show to what an extent Foucault's career could also be read as a "revolt against the powers of normalization," to cite a phrase from the opening of my preface to that book. I tried to do this without neglecting Foucault's position in a cultural, intellectual, and philosophical space that determined to a large extent his theoretical interventions. I showed that Foucault's interrogation was partly linked to his homosexuality—or, more precisely, to the place homosexuality occupied in France in the 1940s and 1950s—and to Foucault's troubled relationship to his own sexuality during those years. It was also linked to what I described as a slow process in which Foucault became reconciled with himself and his sexuality in the 1970s and the early 1980s. The biography I wrote was published in 1989, and while I certainly would not write it the same way were I to write it today, it still seems to me that it radically transformed the way Foucault was considered and read, both in France and elsewhere, and opened the way to a new understanding of his work. In 1994, I published a second book on Foucault, *Michel Foucault et ses contemporains*,[3] which in many ways can be read as a second biography, this time organized principally around an investigation of the relations between Foucault's thought and that of a number of other philosophers or theoreticians, such as Dumézil, Lévi-Strauss, Sartre, Beauvoir, Lacan, Althusser, and Barthes. In this book I also returned at some length to the question of the relation of Foucault's work to his homosexuality and to his relation to the French gay movement. The French intellectual climate continued to evolve. To write about such questions was no longer so scandalous, and so I undertook to write a third book that would contain yet a third biography of Foucault. This time the starting place would be the question of gay sexuality, and it would show how both Foucault's evolving relation to his own homosexuality and the historical transformations in the situation of homosexuality in France between 1940 and 1980 could help us to understand the evolutions and the transformations in the most theoretical elaborations of Foucault's works, from *Madness and Civilization* up to the final volumes of *The History of Sexuality* by way of *La Volonté de savoir*, the first volume of that *History*. Foucault does not only help us think about the history of sexuality and the history of homosexuality; he is a part of that history.

In any case, the Foucault presented in the following pages is quite different from the one constructed in the United States. For I take special care to show to what an extent *The History of Sexuality, Volume 1* [*La Volonté de savoir*], far from containing any definitive truths about the history of homosexuality, is simply one moment among many in Foucault's thought, one closely linked to a specific point in time; it is rooted in Foucault's own personal, political, and theoretical difficulties. This small volume from 1976, far from representing a radical or radically modern theoretical gesture, might—to the contrary—better be interpreted as part of the persistence and the resistance of an identity linked to the "closet" when it is confronted with the eruption of the new gay movements of the 1970s, with their insistence on the necessity of speaking out and affirming oneself in the broad light of day. (In this, Foucault's text might be read alongside certain astonishingly similar declarations made by Barthes.) By putting forth this hypothesis, I do not mean in any way to minimize the richness that Foucault's remarks from this time might contain. Nor do I mean to lessen the importance of Foucault's thought (or of Barthes's). Rather, my intention is to remind us that Foucault reflected on and reacted to problems that were most contemporary to him, to questions that were posed to him, to the kinds of uneasiness he felt when confronted by the theoretical or political moment in which he was obliged to participate. We should not decontextualize or dehistoricize his work. The Foucault I present here, restored to a human dimension, down-to-earth, reinserted into his historical moment, is, it seems to me, thereby rendered all the more moving and his work all the more powerful. For from this point of view we can see how Foucault, in his own manner and in a nearly ideal-typical fashion, lived through all the phases that have marked twentieth-century gay lives (just as his books would have confronted and found ways to give expression to them): from the intense experience of the violence exercised by norms and by the forms of exclusion they produce to the reinvention of oneself in the context of what he would call, toward the end of his life, an "ascesis" or an "esthetic of existence." The theoretical and political gestures Foucault made, the path he followed, are woven tightly together with his personal experience. The model of the philosophical life that he proposed is equally a response to that same experience.

⊁ It has always seemed to me that the first volume of Foucault's *History of Sexuality* was on one hand a book whose daring intellectual inventiveness totally changed the way people thought, yet on the other a book whose hypotheses and whose claims regarding historical periods were at the least freewheeling, even problematic. Moreover, it seems—especially in the United States, where what were for Foucault simply working hypotheses have been transformed into veritable dogmas—that it has not been sufficiently noticed that Foucault himself rapidly abandoned those hypotheses and quickly reformulated his entire project, almost before the first volume had even been published. I wanted to work on texts (notably those of John Addington Symonds) in which one can find already in place a way of thinking about oneself that Foucault thought was only possible once certain psychiatric categorizations were in place. This would amount to a critique of the notion of the performative production by psychiatric discourse of what had in large measure been elaborated elsewhere in a movement of autoproduction, in popular culture (as historians have amply shown), and in philosophical and literary culture. I think that to a great extent Symonds's texts undermine Foucault's demonstrations. My goal was thus to trace the history of people coming to speak for themselves. Yet I also wanted to show how, in fact, it would be possible to think of Foucault as belonging to this history, a tradition that runs from the Oxford Hellenists (such as Walter Pater and Symonds) to the final volumes of Foucault's *History of Sexuality*, by way of such figures as Oscar Wilde and André Gide. It would have been possible to follow a different path, one that seems to me today to be of equal importance: a specifically French history of homosexuality in popular culture and in literature. (But there is still a shortage of published work on these questions in France, where lesbian and gay studies are still in their infancy.) For in fact, both male and female homosexuality were omnipresent in late-nineteenth- and early-twentieth-century novels (those of Catulle Mendès, for example, or Jean Lorrain, Liane de Pougy, Renée Vivien, and many others whose names are not well remembered today). Gide, Colette, and Proust thus need to be read not so much as authors who enabled sexual realities that had remained unspoken until they wrote of them to find literary representation. Rather, they are writers who worked to provide different images, different approaches to these realities than the ones that had proliferated before them and around them, especially in the field of literature.[4] But Jean Lorrain's writing, like that of certain others, is rooted in a relation to popular culture, which is to say in relation to a gay and lesbian subculture present in the less salubrious neighborhoods of Paris (such as Montmartre, with its bars, cabarets, balls, and so on) at the end of the nineteenth century. There is no way such a culture can be understood in Foucauldian terms as a "reverse discourse" that creates itself in reaction to psychiatric discourse by reappropriating and reversing it, while thereby also necessarily ratifying it.

» Studying the constitution of a gay "identity" in a certain group of texts then led me to a more general analysis of the contemporary mechanisms of gay subjectivation, an analysis not only in terms of the transmission of an inheritance—a cultural filiation—but also in terms of those subjectifying mechanisms that construct an individual as well as a collective psyche, designating certain people as destined for shame. Such mechanisms then become the launching pad for a process (again both individual and collective) of re-subjectivation or of the reconstruction of a personal identity.

My intention was also to use a set of sociological, historical, and theoretical reflections as a way of reacting to the hostile discourse directed at the gay and lesbian movement and found in the French media (in a highly centralized nation, where, unlike in the United States, a small number of national newspapers play a preponderant role in the circulation of ideas and in intellectual life in general) and the French intellectual world of the mid-1990s. (That world has, in the past twenty years, undergone an incredible evolution toward the right, toward a neoconservatism that is sometimes astonishingly reactionary, most notably among those people who go on claiming to be leftists even as they recite some of the most traditional themes from the repertory of reactionary thinking.) The mid-1990s were a moment in which Lesbian and Gay Pride celebrations, which had previously only attracted a few thousand people, became, in the space of two or three years, immense parades of up to three or four hundred thousand people. They garnered media attention that was as hostile as it was sudden. In 1995, the year of the first enormous French Gay Pride, editorials in the press, from the right and from the left, gave free reign to sentiments that can only be qualified as phobic. Gay Pride, they said, was a danger to democracy; the homosexual "separatism" that such events revealed threatened to "destroy the architecture of the nation," to destroy "common life" and the very "republican principles" on which French society was based. Newspapers went on to worry about the growth of a gay neighborhood in Paris, exhibiting ridiculously extravagant fantasies about it; they insulted the field of lesbian and gay studies, which apparently represented a danger to knowledge, to culture, to thought, and to the university. Anything that tried to define itself as lesbian or gay was systematically and viciously attacked in order to invalidate it. The time-worn rhetoric of an "interior menace" was trotted out yet again by newspapers, journals, and many intellectuals who communed together in this obsessional denunciation of a homosexual plot against society and culture. Of course homosexuals should be "accepted," but only as long as they made no effort to be different, to exert any kind of collective force—only (according to the demands of one television philosopher) as long as they continued to be "discreet" citizens within a nation that recognized people only as individuals, never as members of a group.[5] All these same people, from the right or from the left, would later forget all their loud declarations regarding the equality of individuals when they turned to struggle against any legal recognition for same-sex couples, a recognition that, according to them, would once again threaten the very foundations of civilization.

(In a somewhat bizarre way, at a moment when the French Socialist government then in power was obliged by powerful grass-roots activism, and despite many forms of reticence and hesitation on its own part, to pass a law establishing the PACS [Pacte civil de solidarité, France's national domestic partnership legislation], numerous so-called leftist intellectuals [anthropologists, psychologists, and sociologists of the family] began churning out an endless series of proclamations [published in newspapers and journals—even academic ones] in which they expressed their opposition to the horrifying threat represented for the future of society and of civilization by "the abolishment of sexual difference" and by same-sex parenting. I am fully aware that these outbursts of academic homophobia—doubtless linked to some kind of crisis in French heterosexuality at the threshold of the twenty-first century—are entirely different from the kinds of homophobia one finds in the United States, where until recently sexual relations between men were illegal in certain states and where gay men and lesbians are not uniformly protected from discrimination. Still it is worth insisting that what one finds written in France by putatively left-wing academics in the name of "reason" and of "scientific inquiry" would only be imaginable in the United States from the pens of religious conservatives or right-wing thinkers.)

Faced with this wave of attacks, all of which seemed to me to be simply more or less well-disguised insults, I felt some kind of counterattack was called for. I wanted to offer gay men and lesbians some resources with which to resist this organized campaign of denigration, this insistent call to toe the line. At the very least, I wanted to show that another approach, another discourse was possible. Everything from my past, everything about who I was, objected to this injunction addressed to gay men and lesbians—the injunction to get back into the closet, once again to silence oneself, to submit to heteronormative demands. Along with these injunctions there was an equally objectionable effort to devalorize anything gay men and lesbians might do, anything they might say, in the end, anything they might be. So I undertook to write this book, destined not only to an academic audience, but to a larger public as well. (That will explain why it is sometimes deliberately pedagogical in nature.) It was, for me, a political gesture. In the end, I might even say that in many ways this book—at least the first part—could be read as a kind of autobiography. One cannot write such things without drawing on personal experience. When I look over the table of contents and the titles of the chapters, it seems to me that I find the signposts of my own journey, and doubtless that journey was what more or less unconsciously guided and inspired me as I wrote. Yet the almost unimaginable number of letters I received in the months after the book was published (in which men and women wrote that "you have described my life," that "you have given words to what I experienced," that "I lived through what you wrote about without being able to analyze it") would seem to justify my claiming that this personal autobiography is also simultaneously, to paraphrase one of Gertrude Stein's titles, a kind of "everybody's autobiography," or, in any case, the autobiography of a good number of people. This is not to say that my intention was to universalize my own particular experience. Rather, I wanted to make use of that experience, to combine it with sociological studies, literary texts, and theoretical reflections and thereby come up with a number of theoretical models for thinking about a collective minoritarian experience. Moreover, it is precisely this relation between an individual and a group that is at the heart of the book: individual subjectivity is always "collective," we might say, because an individual is always socialized—socialized within a social realm traversed by hierarchies and divisions. A minority subjectivity is always that of a group of people assigned to the same place within the social order and, in this particular case, within the sexual order.

So this book was a political intervention, but also a theoretical one, intended to formulate new questions and elaborate new answers. Given that the hostile discourse I mentioned was found not only in the least intelligent and most vulgar newspapers, not only in the most conservative ones, but also in those with the most elevated intellectual pretension, often claiming to be left-wing; and given that the same discourse could also be found in the mouths of the representatives of most academic disciplines—all these voices united in some bizarre and obsessional way in order to ward off the threat of lesbians and gay men—I wanted to show that a theoretical discourse on homosexuality need not necessarily be a discourse from the outside on an object considered and judged from a hostile, wary, and often scornful distance. Such a discourse could be produced from inside gay experience, through the mobilization of a variety of intellectual and theoretical resources. A critical way of thinking should construct its own questions and problems, rather than simply accepting them as they had been constituted by previous kinds of knowledge or simply being content to take them as they are offered in doctrines that merely rehearse old heterosexist thematics. I think, for example, that one dramatically and decisively shifts the kind of analysis one offers when the starting place becomes the role of insult in the lives of gay men and lesbians, something that is never taken into account by psychoanalysis or by philosophies of communication or communicative action—for these are only the expression of the dominant point of view regarding the social life of language, the point of view of "decent folk," as Sartre would have said about those people who have been empowered to give names, the point of view of the majority. In my subsequent book, *Une Morale du minoritaire: Variations sur un thème de Jean Genet*, I take this analysis even further, examining insult as a social structure of inferiorization, examining the power of name-giving, the role of shame as a kind of inscription of the social order into the subjectivity of "pariahs" and as a factor in one's subsequent recomposition of oneself—that is, the dual processes of the constitution and reinvention of minority subjectivities.[6]

❥ This is all part of an effort to put together an approach that leaves behind those normative concepts of psychoanalysis that so predominate in our culture and that impose themselves and the grids through which they perceive the social and sexual world on everyone. Whether it be the texts of Lacan that are so blatantly and fundamentally homophobic (see, for instance, the fifth volume of his seminar, the volume on the "formations of the unconscious") or those of most of his followers today, whether it be those of the large majority of practicians and ideologues of any of the other branches in the analytic corporation, psychoanalysis often seems to be nothing other than a long heterosexual discourse on homosexuality. (This can be seen in the unbelievable crusade on which various squadrons of analysts, irrespective of their doctrinal allegiances, have set out and continue to set out—in

newspapers and journals, on television programs, at professional meetings—to fight against the idea of same-sex domestic partnership legislation,
against gay and lesbian marriage, against gay and lesbian parenting, and so
on. For certain among them, it remains a question of a crusade against
homosexuality itself, which they still work to "explain" or, as a recent issue
of the *Revue française de psychanalyse* proudly proclaimed, to "cure.") It is
urgent and necessary to think outside the limits of psychoanalysis, to work
to elaborate a sociological and anthropological theory of subjectivity and of
the unconscious. ("The unconscious is simply history," Durkheim said, in a
sentence Pierre Bourdieu was fond of citing, adding that it is also the forget-
ting of history.)

My emphasis on the mechanisms of production of gay subjectivities and
on the practices and politics of resubjectivation might seem to some people
to be slightly incompatible with the place I give to works that came out of the
current of thought known as queer theory. I make frequent reference in this
book (at least in the first part) to such American authors as Judith Butler,
David Halperin, Eve Kosofsky Sedgwick, and others. I was writing in a
country in which, until a very recent date, lesbian and gay studies basically
did not exist, and in which any attempt to encourage them resulted in thun-
derous insults from the media as well as from institutions of higher learning. (This indeed remains the case, as can be seen in the active and permanent—and sometimes nearly ridiculous—hostility that is still directed
from within the institution at the seminar Françoise Gaspard and I run at the
École des hautes études en sciences sociales in Paris.) I wished not only to
help these American works become better known in France, but moreover to
import an entire field of discussion to where that field was absent and even
unknown. I wanted thereby to transform in some way the kind of thinking
that could take place in France. The colloquium that I organized at the
Pompidou Center in June 1997 on lesbian and gay studies (and in which Leo
Bersani, Monique Wittig, Eve Kosofsky Sedgwick, George Chauncey, David
Halperin, Pierre Bourdieu, and others all participated) created such excitement and attracted such large crowds that a long article on the front page of
Le Monde was devoted to it—an article that was scandalized and indignant
that a public institution would dare invite authors of such a "separatist" and
"identitarian" (and any other perjorative -ist, -ian, or -ism that one could
imagine) bent. Particular ire (indeed, particularly *vulgar* ire, for a newspaper
ordinarily so intent on preaching to people about the appropriate way to
conduct oneself in democratic debates) was directed at Pierre Bourdieu for

the support he had lent to these American insanities, to this project that was apparently so destructive of knowledge and of culture.[7] The works of the American authors I mention had not yet been translated into French, and today translations are still quite incomplete. (At the moment I write, two of Halperin's books have been translated, only two of Butler's, none of Sedgwick's.) It is perfectly clear why I would have wanted to help these works become better known and, in presenting their theoretical contributions to a French readership, to integrate them with a whole set of other references, thereby demonstrating that it is possible to make intellectual traditions that might seem different and heterogenous work together in a productive way. Reflections on questions such as these, I am quite convinced, can only be collective and international.[8]

Yet to wish to import a certain field of inquiry and of research, to open a space of discussion that crosses national boundaries, to bring important books to peoples' attention is not thereby necessarily to be in total agreement with the various theses of the authors with whom one chooses to enter into dialogue. Indeed, I would be tempted to say that in many ways I wrote as much *against* queer thought as *with* it—especially to the extent that I try in this book to use the terms of a social anthropology of domination to reintroduce an analysis of the specificity of gay subjectivation. This is a type of analysis that seems to me precisely to have been in large measure proscribed by queer thought—perhaps not in the books of those authors I have already mentioned,[9] but in the kind of academic vulgate that has been inspired by it, a vulgate in which all that was rich and innovative has little by little become a kind of doctrine that can be summed up in a few simple notions that are endlessly repeated and then reduced to a set of injunctions as to what research "should" or "should not" be. Such a reduction is obviously an extremely effective way of drying up thought and limiting intellectual and political innovation. All this is not to say that I wish to return to a concept of identity that is either fixed or unifying. Rather, I want to claim that it is by way of the analysis of the processes of subjectivation and of the reinvention of oneself that we can attempt to reflect upon the noncoherence of the self, on retrospective or momentary forms of coherence, on cultural identifications (and on multiple identifications or on disidentifications), on political engagements, and on ideological allegiances. I am currently working on the question of "trajectories" and of minority "ascesis" (this by the way of rereadings of Gide, Genet, Jouhandeau, Julien Green, Dumézil, Barthes, Foucault, and others), on literature and theoretical thinking as fields of struggle in which "heretics" invent strategies in order to let their voices be heard, on the persistence of identities beyond the historical moments in which they predominated, and on their coexistence with new ways of being or thinking. I am also interested in "bad homosexuals" (those of whom one cannot be proud, notable those on the far right) and in revisiting the theoretical and political heritage of the 1970s in order to better appreciate what went on at that moment (a critique of psychoanalysis, ways of thinking about difference, the connection between theory and politics, and so on) and what we can make of it today. All these projects continue the avenues of research opened up for me by this book, which is appearing today in an American edition under the title *Insult and the Making of the Gay Self.*

I would like to close this preface by paying homage to Pierre Bourdieu, who died in January 2002. His work, one of the most important intellectual contributions of the twentieth century, is, along with that of Sartre, the major theoretical reference of this book. It has always been difficult for me to understand why those involved in lesbian and gay studies in the United States (and elsewhere) have made such little use of Bourdieu's work, especially when his work seems to offer (and to have offered for quite some time) so many tools for the analysis of, and indeed so many decisive elements of the answers to, questions that are at the center of those studies today. From his *Outline of a Theory of Practice* in 1972, which contains his magnificent ethnological studies of Kabylia, to his *Pascalian Meditations* of 1997 and *Masculine Domination* in 1998, Bourdieu situated at the center of his inquiry the way in which the social order, via a long "apprenticeship by way of the body" that begins in infancy in the daily contact with the world, comes to be inscribed in the bodies and minds of individuals; the way in which social or gender hierarchies are thus able to perpetuate themselves; but also the ways in which certain "heretical" ruptures in the doxical adherence to the world-as-it-is come to be able to subvert the logic of the reproduction of social "orthodoxy." My goal was to transpose his analyses onto a domain that his work does not deal with at any length (but which he nonetheless mentions from time to time) and to inquire into the way in which the inscription of the sexual order as a matrix of inferiorization happens in those bodies and minds that contravene the norms. In that way could I reflect upon the constitution of particular types of subjectivity.[10] Thus I made an effort to use the sociology of domination as elaborated by Bourdieu as regards social classes or as regards gender for an analysis of domination in the sexual order. This was a way of posing a question to Bourdieusian sociology about the relations between what Bourdieu calls "symbolic violence," the notion of habitus, and the idea of the incorporation of the social into schemas of thought and of perception and even down to the level of the folds and the gestures of a given body: what would a class of individuals be that is collectively destined to domination in spite of all of the differences—social, ethnic, sexual—that separate and sometimes oppose its members? How is the habitus of individuals constructed by way of the inscription of the sexual order into minds and bodies in the forms of schemas of perception? In short: how does the sexual order function, and how is it possible to resist it as one works to create and to hold open new social and cultural possibilities?

Acknowledgments

I wrote this book in Paris, Boston, and Berkeley, between the autumn of 1996 and the winter of 1999. It wouldn't exist were it not for the help, the advice, the comments, and the suggestions of a large number of people. I dare not give the list here, however great my debt to these people. No matter how long a list I made, it would, I fear, be incomplete. I would surely forget someone who, sometimes with just a word or a suggestion of something to read, helped direct my thinking and my work on these pages.

I hope I may be excused for mentioning only a single name, that of John Tain, who one day while walking in Boston spoke to me about Walter Pater.

Abbreviations

The following abbreviations are used in citations.

Aesthetics   Michel Foucault. *Aesthetics, Method, and Epistemology.* Ed. James D. Faubion. Trans. Robert Hurley and others. Volume 2 of *Essential Works of Foucault, 1954–1984.* Series ed. Paul Rabinow. New York: The New Press, 1998.

Dits   Michel Foucault. *Dits et écrits, 1954–1988.* Eds. Daniel Defert and François Ewald. 4 vols. Paris: Gallimard, 1994.

Ethics   Michel Foucault. *Ethics: Subjectivity and Truth.* Ed. Paul Rabinow. Trans. Robert Hurley and others. Volume 1 of *Essential Works of Foucault, 1954–1984.* New York: The New Press, 1997.

FL   Michel Foucault. *Foucault Live (Interviews, 1961–1984).* Ed. Sylvère Lotringer. New York: Semiotext(e), 1996.

HF   Michel Foucault. *Histoire de la folie à l'âge classique.* 1961. Paris: Gallimard [Tel], 1972.

HS1   Michel Foucault. *The History of Sexuality. Volume 1: An Introduction.* [*La Volonté de savoir*]. Trans. Robert Hurley. New York: Vintage, 1990.

MC   Michel Foucault. *Madness and Civilization: A History of Insanity in the Age of Reason.* Trans. Richard Howard. New York: Vintage Books, 1973.

MIP   Michel Foucault. *Mental Illness and Psychology.* Trans. Alan Sheridan. Foreword by Hubert Dreyfus. Berkeley: University of California Press, 1987.

Power   Michel Foucault. *Power.* Ed. James D. Faubion. Trans. Robert
              Hurley and others. Volume 3 of *Essential Works of Foucault, 1954–
              1984.* Series ed. Paul Rabinow. New York: The New Press, 2000.

Recherche   Marcel Proust. *A la recherche du temps perdu.* Ed. Jean-Yves Tadié. 4
              volumes. Paris: Gallimard [Pléiade], 1987.

RTP   Marcel Proust. *Remembrance of Things Past.* Trans. C. K. Scott
              Moncrieff, Terence Kilmartin, and Andreas Mayor. 3 vols. New
              York: Vintage, 1982.

StG   Jean-Paul Sartre. *Saint Genet: Actor and Martyr.* Trans. Bernard
              Frechtman. New York: George Braziller, 1963.

Introduction:
The Language of the Tribe

Our point of departure will be the following passage from Proust's *The Captive*:

> M. de Charlus did not care to go about with M. de Vaugoubert. For the latter, his monocle stuck in his eye, would keep looking round at every passing youth. What was worse, shedding all restraint when he was with M. de Charlus, he adopted a form of speech which the Baron detested. He referred to everything male in the feminine, and, being intensely stupid, imagined this pleasantry to be extremely witty, and was continually in fits of laughter. As at the same time he attached enormous importance to his position in the diplomatic service, these deplorable sniggering exhibitions in the street were constantly inter-rupted by sudden fits of terror at the simultaneous appearance of some society person or, worse still, of some civil servant. "That little tele-graph messenger," he said, nudging the scowling Baron with his elbow, "I used to know her, but she's turned respectable, the wretch! Oh! that messenger from the Galeries Lafayette, what a dream! Good God, there's the head of the Commercial Department. I hope he didn't notice anything. He's quite capable of mentioning it to the Minister, who would put me on the retired list, all the more so because it appears he's one himself."[1]

How can one not recognize, in this scene written nearly a century ago and so precisely linked to the time of its writing (by, for example, the reference to the "telegraph messenger"), something that might just as well be taking place today, a scene that perhaps many gay people will have experienced, or whose equivalent they will have witnessed? How many of them speak in the feminine, about themselves or about boys passed on the street, yet police their gestures and language as soon as they cross the path of a colleague or an acquaintance? It might seem that there is nothing to be done but applaud the genius of the writer who managed to provide this characterization that seems to transcend its time. Yet all of the elements that come together in these lines from Proust to create such a truthful portrait also work precisely to encourage a deeper look at what they have to say about homosexuality.

Let us begin with this crucial observation: two homosexuals are speaking with each other here, and they are speaking about homosexuality. This presupposes that they are each aware of the other's tastes[2] and indicates that their complicity is based upon what we can only call a shared affiliation. We might also note that both of them are insistent about hiding their homosexuality from those who do not belong to their "race."

What, one might ask, is so extraordinary about that? About the fact that two homosexuals are speaking together about their homosexuality while making sure not to let anything be noticed by any outside observers? There is something in this scene that is less obvious than one might at first think: Is not the question of affiliation somehow the central point in so many of the discussions of homosexuality of the past one hundred years? Do homosexuals form a particular group, a specific minority, or are they merely individuals like everyone else, except that they have different sexual practices? Are they "different than the others," as suggested by the title of Richard Oswald's 1919 film (Anders als die Anderen)? Or are they the same as anyone else? If one accepts the second hypothesis, how do we account for the rapport that has been established between these two characters in Proust? Why would Charlus choose to speak to Vaugoubert about his love life—for that is the reason they go for a walk together—unless it is because he feels the need to speak to someone, and that person must necessarily be another homosexual? What would form the basis of such a bond? Is it not the sheer multitude of bonds of this kind that forms the network Proust described as the "freemasonry" of the "sodomites," and that we today would call gay subculture?

Charlus does not much care for Vaugoubert. He finds him too flashy and exuberant. Charlus strives to appear virile and detests effeminacy. He aims for discretion and worries about the possible effects of Vaugoubert's exuberance. Here too we find a characteristic trait of (male) homosexuality: the polarity of masculinity and effeminacy. The scorn, the hatred, of those who prefer to think of themselves as masculine or virile for those they deem "effeminate" has been one of the major dividing lines in the self-representations of gay men. And not only in their self-representations, but also in all of the discourses accompanying these images, even in the theories proposed by certain gay advocates—in Germany at the beginning of the twentieth century, for example. More generally, one often finds that the kinds of discourses offered up by gay men harbor the desire to disassociate themselves, to distinguish themselves, from other gay men. Think of the story Christopher Isherwood tells of visiting Magnus Hirschfeld's Institute in Berlin in the early 1930s. On seeing the photographs on display, he first feels a certain repugnance, and only then takes a moment to reflect and accept that he too belongs to the same "tribe."[3] By what odd conscious or unconscious mechanisms does a gay man come to associate himself with the other members of his "tribe" (Charlus and Vaugoubert) while spending enormous amounts of time denigrating those other members and finding detestable, even revolting, those who exemplify other manners of living out one's homosexuality?

What Charlus finds annoying in Vaugoubert's behavior is first and foremost that he speaks of other gay men in the feminine. This linguistic particularity, we also know, extends across time and has lost none of its appeal today. But where does this shared culture—which allows Vaugoubert to express himself in this way and still be understood by the nonetheless exasperated Baron de Charlus—come from? Proust speaks of an "identity . . . of vocabulary" (*RTP*, 2:639–40) that unites individuals coming from different backgrounds and different social conditions. How are these linguistic codes, these specific kinds of slang, learned—the ones that allow gay men, like members of any "professional organization" (Proust's term), to understand each other without having to spell things out, to grasp jokes, allusions, aspersions, and so on? How are these forms of humor—like "camp" or what in French is referred to as "*l'humour folle*"—passed on from one generation to the next? And what can be said about codes of dress, or of gesture, ways of speaking, postures and attitudes, and all the other "cultural" reference points of which so many examples—including the "inversion" of language—could be provided for today or for yesterday?

Vaugoubert cuts himself off when he sees the director of the Commercial Department passing by, resuming his ordinary social image. Thus gay people, or, as Proust puts it, "inverts," know how to play with what Erving Goffman has called "the presentation of self." In different social situations they present different self-images.[4] Of course, this is the case for everyone. You are not the same person in your employer's office that you are dining with your friends. But it is especially true for gay people. Goffman speaks of their "double biography."[5] Gay lives are often dissociated lives, producing dissociated personalities.

Notice the final remark of Vaugoubert's peroration. It emphasizes how this disassociation within gay lives, together with the necessity of self-concealment, leads to shame and self-hatred. It also shows that it leads to a hostile and repressive attitude toward other homosexuals—in order to safeguard one's own secret and ward off any suspicions on the part of other people. If Vaugoubert is fearful of how the minister would react, it is because "it appears he's one himself."

One more observation about this passage. It is impossible to read it without being struck by the structure of class relations that it reveals: two aristocrats are chatting while taking a stroll. It is noteworthy that they are speaking of telegraph boys and delivery boys as sexual objects. Even more noteworthy is the transgression of these class boundaries: these "men of society" spend their time seeking out liaisons with the youthful members of what are called in Paris "les petits métiers." The literature of the second half of the nineteenth century and the early twentieth attests to the fact that heterosexual men from the monied classes had no hesitation about establishing relationships with milliners, florists, and shopgirls. Still, the social mixing seems more systematic and more clearly marked among homosexuals. It has even been described as one of the characteristics of their way of life, both in order to praise and to condemn it. (This was one of the aspects of Wilde's life that most scandalized his judges.) The forms of sociability, meeting-places, literary and journalistic representations, private imaginings—all the different modes of existence of the "gay subculture"—gave a large place to this abolition of class barriers. However artificial it may have been, however detestable it may have sometimes proved in what it implied about social exploitation and domination by money, it nonetheless remains one of the invariants of gay life of at least the past two centuries (and perhaps earlier ones as well).

⇥ So many cultural changes, so many social transformations, so many shifts in sexuality and in homosexuality have taken place since Proust that it is a bit disturbing to come across, in a text already quite old, situations, codes, ways of being, and identities that have scarcely changed. Why might contemporary experiences seem so close to those described by Proust? Is it merely an optical illusion?

Joan Scott, in a well-known article, has called into question exactly this, the "evidence of experience" that leads one to recognize oneself in this or that aspect of a past moment whose whole cultural configuration is in fact unknown. The same words, gestures, or characteristics can have different meanings in different contexts, and thus can only be understood if they are reinserted into their proper historical "sites." "It is not individuals who have experiences," Scott writes, "but subjects who are constituted through experience."[6]

A "subject," then, is always produced by the social order that organizes the "experiences" of any individual at a given historical moment. This is why the temptation to see oneself in those past facts and gestures runs the risk of obscuring the reality of the complex systems that governed experience at that time. Today those facts and gestures might stir up in us a sense of the obvious, whereas we should rather inquire into the social, ideological, and sexual mechanisms that gave them their meanings in their own moment and that produced the "subjects" that enacted them. A "subject" is always produced in and through "subordination" to an order, to rules, norms, laws, and so on. This is true for all "subjects." To be a "subject" and to be subordinated to a system of constraints are one and the same thing.[7] This is even more the case for those "subjects" assigned to an "inferiorized" place by the social and sexual order, as is the case for gay men and lesbians.[8] Reading the passage from Proust, we are led to ask: what could this description of homosexuality teach us about its society, about the ways in which that society shaped the categories of gender and sexuality, about the relations between people of the same sex, about the ways those relations were perceived and lived out by people from different social milieux (M. de Vaugoubert and the delivery boy from the Galeries Lafayette). What might we learn about the imbrication of each of these levels with wider social realities? In short, we would do well to ask this essential question: Is not the act of spontaneously recognizing oneself in these categories a way of ratifying their "self-evidence," when in fact we should be looking at them critically? Would that not be to naturalize them at exactly the moment when we should be historicizing them?

Given that we are here undertaking a reflection on "subjectivation," by which I mean the production of "subjects," might we not begin the analysis with a look at this feeling of self-evidence?[9] That feeling would tend to suggest that, whatever transformations have occurred over the course of the last century, the systems of the sexual order have maintained a certain continuity. Pierre Bourdieu asks a similar question about women in *Masculine Domination*: How have structures of domination managed to reproduce themselves across time despite all the changes that have so altered the relations between the sexes?[10] Could we not pose an analogous question about homosexuality? Of course, things have changed since Proust wrote this description, and one should even be wary of imagining that a single situation could be taken to characterize a given historical moment. There have been marvelous studies done of the differentiated modes of existence of "homosexuality" at this or that moment in the nineteenth or twentieth centuries, in this or that country, in this or that city. They have shown ways in which each time and place is singular and incomparable. We have learned from all these studies of the past that the notion of "homosexuality" is more recent than one might have thought, and that even for periods not so very far in the past that notion is too massive, too unwieldy, too normative, to take into account all these multiple and heterogeneous experiences. Figures of "homosexuality" are always specific to a given cultural situation. There is no reason to deny any of this, and it is in no way my intention—this should go without saying—to challenge the value and the importance of all this historical work. Yet it remains the case that there is a particular type of symbolic violence that is aimed at those who love members of the same sex and that the schemas of perception, the mental structures, that underlie this violence (doubtless largely based on an androcentric worldview) are more or less similar everywhere, at least in the Western world, and have been so for at least the past century and a half.[11] This explains the sense that gay men and lesbians might have of their relation to gay or lesbian experiences from another country or another historical moment when they read works that reconstruct those experiences. We need therefore to investigate the perpetuation of this symbolic violence, its effects, and the forms of resistance to it.

⊮ This is the double task I have set myself here: first, to study the gay experience of "subjectivation" today, and second, to study how, in many ways and despite many changes, it is not so different from what it was a century ago. I have made use of work in the social sciences (contemporary work as well as work from ten or twenty years ago) as well as of works of contemporary or older literature, especially Proust. My heavy reliance on Proust is in part to avoid endlessly multiplying references, thereby giving the reader easier access to the works I am citing; but it is also and more importantly because his work seemed to me, despite what is often said of it, astonishingly modern in regards to gay issues.

I begin with the question of insult, so important in gay and lesbian lives, today as previously. I try to reconstruct the ways in which gays are "subjugated" by the sexual order, as well as the ways, different in different moments, in which they resist domination through the production of ways of life, spaces of freedom, a "gay world." My attention is therefore drawn to those processes of subjectivation or resubjectivation, by which I mean the possibility of recreating a personal identity out of an assigned identity. This implies that the acts through which one reinvents one's identity are always dependent on the identity that was imposed by the sexual order. Nothing is created out of nothing, certainly not subjectivities. It is always a question of reappropriations, or, to use Judith Butler's term, "resignification."[12] Yet this "resignification" is an act of freedom par excellence, in fact the only possible one, for it opens the door to the unheard of, the unforeseeable.

In the second part of this book, "Specters of Wilde," I examine how, this time on the historical level, a form of gay "speech" was invented by way of a vast process in which a literary and intellectual discourse emerged with the goal of legitimizing something that had been forbidden. From the "homosexual code" in the writings of the Hellenists at Oxford in the mid-nineteenth century through André Gide's *Corydon* in 1924, by way of certain writings by Oscar Wilde, a wide range of discourses strove to give same-sex loves access to legitimate public expression. This will-to-speech always took the form of what Foucault called "reverse discourse": it always formulated itself by way of a strategic response to the values, norms, and representations that of course condemned it in advance, but that also more fundamentally shaped it from within. Historically speaking, the repression of homosexuality has nourished the determination toward self-expression. But inversely, that expression has shaped itself to the modes of thought that despised it. My attempt here is to study the imbrication of gay speech and homophobic discourse.

If today's gay culture is still haunted in many ways by the ghosts of Wilde and of Gide, if its inventions are attached via numerous threads to a subterranean history, if today (as Neil Bartlett has shown so well) gays write their biographies while reading the biographies of those who preceded them, it is surely necessary to sift through this heritage in a critical fashion.[13] To inherit, Jacques Derrida has said, is to choose.[14] A selection must be made between what it is possible to keep and what must clearly be rejected. After all, however important the figure of Wilde has been, nothing could be more detestable than his elitism, his aristocratic aestheticism. Yet how could we do without his praise of self-fashioning: the idea that one could create oneself, make of one's life a work of art?

The evocation of this very theme calls to mind immediately the name of Michel Foucault. In a whole series of texts, Foucault offered numerous reflections on the gay question. He insists, for example, on the idea that a process of self-fashioning must proceed by way of the invention of new kinds of relations between individuals and by the development of what he called a "gay culture." It has seemed to me that often he was simply reproducing, in modern garb, discourses that had preceded him—those I have just mentioned, that must be critically sifted through before they can be reappropriated. I have therefore tried to engage with Foucault's arguments—not always perfectly coherent ones—in order to clarify both their promise and their limitations.

Foucault's name is inevitably associated, as regards the questions we are dealing with here, with the radical dissolution of the notion of homosexuality that he undertook in La Volonté de savoir, the first volume of his History of Sexuality.[15] In that volume he describes the invention by psychiatric discourse—toward the end of the nineteenth century—of the "personage" of the "homosexual." Before that time, he says, there were only condemnable "acts"; after that time, people who practiced those acts were assigned a psychology, a set of feelings, a particular kind of childhood, and so on. Foucault has thus become a powerful antidote to John Boswell and his "essentialist" conception of gay history. Foucault's analyses have become the Bible of "constructionist" historians, which is to say that he is the source of inspiration for almost everything written in the United States and for almost everything written elsewhere as well. The idea that there is no invariant reality to homosexuality, that Greek love is not a prefiguration of modern homosexuality, has become widely accepted. The case has been won. Still, it equally remains the case that the Hellenists in Oxford in the mid-nineteenth century thought of themselves as different kinds of "personages" than those around them and that they had this sense of being different from childhood onward. They wrote well before psychiatric discourse got hold of "sexual inversion" as a concept, before that discourse pigeonholed acts between persons of the same sex in their large nosological table of perversions and "identities."

There is another difficulty that has, to my knowledge, never been brought up before. It is the case that Foucault himself, in *Madness and Civilization*, fifteen years before *La Volonté de savoir*, suggested a different date for the invention of the "personage" of the "homosexual": the seventeenth century.[16] In the earlier book he describes a process through which "homosexuality" is invented that is nearly the opposite of the one described in *La Volonté de savoir*: it is only because the "homosexual" and the "mad person" have already been constituted (notably through a profound transformation of "sensibility" of which the internment of the insane and the debauched is the most visible symptom), it is only because these objects are now readily available that psychology, which will take hold of them for its own purposes, can appear and develop in the nineteenth century.

I do not juxtapose these two books by Foucault with their contradictory presentations merely out of a sense of the need for exactitude and precision in commentary on his work and its evolution. Many other cultural and political matters are at stake here as well. In *Madness and Civilization*, Foucault gives us an analysis cast in the terms of prohibition and repression: his project is to make audible the speech of those who had been reduced to silence. In *La Volonté de savoir* he describes the act of speech as one of the constitutive elements of an apparatus of power that incites individuals to speak. It is easy enough to imagine how different the political perspectives implied by these two analyses would be. Yet I have the impression that in his interviews from the 1980s Foucault was trying to integrate these two positions and to go beyond them through the idea of an "aesthetics of existence" that would involve the creation of new subjectivities.

There is thus an astonishing intellectual kinship between Foucault and Wilde, seen in the manner in which they both sought to invent gestures of resistance, to take their distance from instituted norms. Foucault should be placed within a history of the coming to speech of gay people and in the line of authors who, from the end of the nineteenth century onward, have tried to create spaces—practical spaces as well as literary and theoretical ones—in which to resist subjection and in which to reformulate oneself.

Thus the three distinct sections of my book are organized around a single idea: I have tried to reconstruct, in lived experience, in literary history, and in the life and the work of Michel Foucault, the movement that leads from subjection to the reinvention of the self—from a subjectivity shaped by the social order to a chosen subjectivity.

⯈ The French title of this book is *Réflexions sur la question gay*. French readers will have little difficulty noticing the reference to Sartre.[17] It is more than a passing reference. Sartre is not read as much nowadays as he used to be. When he is read, it is usually not with an eye toward finding tools for thinking about politics. Yet perhaps it is time to return to Sartre, whose thought—both its practical and philosophical sides—contains a great conceptual richness for those who wish to understand struggles for cultural recognition or minority movements. His work, along with that of Bourdieu, Goffman, and Foucault, constitutes one of the major points of reference for the reflections I offer here.

I owe a great debt to certain American authors, such as Eve Kosofsky Sedgwick, Judith Butler, David Halperin, and a few others. Their works have provided me with endless inspiration. The polemics against gay and lesbian studies that have flourished in France in recent years in a certain sector of cultural journalism as well as in academic circles have had a certain absurd quality about them—offering us nightmarish visions and waving banners saying "You must not read this." Of course those waving the banners *haven't* read anything and are merely asking others to follow their example. Who has ever had the idea of "reducing Proust to his homosexuality," to cite the phrase used over and over again? The point is to analyze what Proust said about homosexuality, which is something quite complicated. Would one say of George Chauncey that he wanted to reduce New York to its homosexuality, in recreating for us the "Gay New York" of the end of the nineteenth century and the beginning of the twentieth?[18] Should we refuse to read this masterwork of historical analysis? Refuse to learn? To pursue knowledge?

Of course that would be ridiculous. Important works have been published (even if most of them are not translated into French). Perhaps in France a different name will be chosen for gay and lesbian studies, given how many misunderstandings have occurred around this expression, one which seems to call for the establishment of a new discipline. Whereas it is in fact much more a question of opening a whole group of disciplines to new approaches and new objects of study. But gay and lesbian studies, which is to say, the whole set of works published and of research projects undertaken in this area, have at their best always first and foremost been about adding to knowledge, inciting thought, provoking reflection. I will often take my distance from the authors I refer to; I will sometimes oppose them. But in many ways this book is my acknowledgment of all I have learned from them.

I use the word gay for the simple reason that it is the word the people who are in question in this book today use to designate themselves.[19] Language is never neutral; acts of naming have social effects: they provide definition for images and representations. The choice of the word "gay" is a recognition of both the legitimacy and the necessity of the movement of self-affirmation that mobilized the word. In this regard, this book is an engaged act.

I am not unaware of certain problems resulting from the choice of the word gay, and I do not wish to minimize them. I will be criticized, given that I am talking about "gay questions," for remaining silent about lesbians. This is a deliberate choice, but not because I am uninterested in lesbian questions. It is not my intention to reproduce the classic gesture of leaving out women when speaking of homosexuality in general. Far from it. To the contrary, I am convinced that, as far as contemporary politics are concerned, lesbians and gay men are quite close to each other, and for very good reasons. Their common enemies (as we have seen frequently in France in the past few years) make no distinction between them, denouncing them with the same gesture and fighting against them without distinction.

My choice is also not due to any belief that certain fields are reserved for specific people, inaccessible to those who do not belong to the group that is the focus of the work or the research. Just as I have never thought that one had to be gay to write about homosexuality—be it historically, sociologically, or theoretically—I do not think that one must be a woman to write about women or a lesbian to offer thoughts on lesbians. The richness of intellectual labor suggests that anyone can intervene in any debate, and that works cannot be disqualified ahead of time by those who imagine they possess the monopoly over a given field. The quality of the work is what matters, not the sex or the sexual orientation of the author.

Yet, given that I wanted to pose the problem of "subjection-subjectivation" (what is a gay subjectivity and how is it constituted?), it seemed to me that the analyses would rarely be able to apply both to men and to women. To evoke socialization in the family, at school, in relation to professions, and, of course, in relation to sexuality and to the construction of "gender" would require very different approaches for boys and for girls, for men and for women. From this point of view it seems impossible to approach the question of gay men *and* lesbians as if they were a homogenous group.

Still, when it seems to me that my analyses bear with equal validity on men and on women, I indicate this. The process of subjection-subjectification may not always be the same for gay men and lesbians, but it sometimes is.

⇥ This is, then, a book on the gay question. Yet there will be no theory of homosexuality to be found in it, not even of male homosexuality. I want merely to present a set of reflections, sometimes incomplete, provisory, and hypothetical. They will perhaps provoke further reflections; in fact they are intended to do so, without regard for borders—be they national, disciplinary, or sexual. This is an open book, open to debate, discussion, dialogue.

POSTSCRIPT

At the moment that I am finishing this introduction, I read in the newspapers that a young gay man was murdered in a small town in Wyoming. He was tortured by his two attackers and left to die, tied to a barbed-wire fence. He was twenty-two. His name was Matthew Shepard. I know he is not the only gay man to have had such a tragic fate in the United States in the past few years, just as I know that numerous gays, lesbians, bisexuals, and transsexuals are regularly and systematically victims of such violence. A report by Amnesty International recently provided a terrifying list—one that was, alas, far from complete.[20] But it is Matthew Shepard's photograph that I have in front of me today, along with the account of what he suffered. How can I not think of him as I prepare to publish this book? How can I not ask the reader to remember, in reading it, that there are more than just theoretical problems at stake?

PART 1

A World of Insult

Dominated individuals make common cause with discourse and consciousness, indeed with science, since they cannot constitute themselves as a separate group, mobilize themselves or mobilize their potential power unless they question the categories of perception of the social order which, being the product of that order, inclined them to recognize that order and thus submit to it.

PIERRE BOURDIEU, "Description and Prescription: The Conditions of Possibility and the Limits of Political Effectiveness"

1

The Shock of Insult

It all begins with an insult. The insult that any gay man or lesbian can hear at any moment of his or her life, the sign of his or her social and psychological vulnerability.

"Faggot" ("dyke")—these are not merely words shouted in passing. They are verbal aggressions that stay in the mind. They are traumatic events experienced more or less violently at the moment they happen, but that stay in memory and in the body (for fear, awkwardness, and shame are bodily attitudes produced by a hostile exterior world). One of the consequences of insult is to shape the relation one has to others and to the world and thereby to shape the personality, the subjectivity, the very being of the individual in question.

As Marcel Jouhandeau wrote in his extraordinary short treatise on homosexuality from 1939, *On Abjection*, to be insulted is to be branded on the shoulder by a red hot iron.

> What a revelation it is to be insulted, to be scorned in public. We become familiar with certain words that up to that point had only been heard in classical tragedies, but that now become our own accouterments, our own burdens. We are no longer what we thought ourselves to be. We are no longer the person we knew, but the one others think they know, the one others take to be this or that. If someone could think that of me, then in some way it must be true. At first we pretend that it is not true, that this is only a mask, a costume for a play in which someone has clothed us, and that we could take off. But no. These garments adhere so tightly that they have already become your face, your flesh. To take them off would be to rend your own being.[1]

The insult lets me know that I am not like others, not normal. I am *queer:* strange, bizarre, sick, abnormal.[2]

❧ The insult is a verdict. It is a more or less definitive sentence, for life, one that will have to be borne. A gay man learns about his difference through the force of insult and its effects—the principal one being the dawning of the awareness of a fundamental asymmetry instantiated by that particular linguistic act: I discover that I am a person about whom something can be said, to whom something can be said, someone who can be looked at or talked about in a certain way and who is stigmatized by that gaze and those words. The act of naming produces an awareness of oneself as other, transformed by others into an object. Sartre puts it nicely in an observation about Genet, tagged as a thief by the gaze of the other: "It is as if a page of a book suddenly became conscious and felt itself *being read aloud* without being able to *read itself*" (*stG*, 41). Insult is thus a way of looking me over and a way of dispossessing me. My consciousness is "beleaguered by others" (57) and I am disarmed by this aggression. To cite Sartre on Genet a bit more: "A dazzling spotlight transpierced him with its beams." Alone, powerless, all he could do was struggle "in that shaft of light" that is the gaze of the other, its power to name (136).

Insult is more than a word that describes. It is not satisfied with simply telling me what I am. If someone calls me a "dirty faggot" (or "dirty nigger" or "dirty kike"), or even simple "faggot" (or "nigger" or "kike"), that person is not trying to tell me something about myself. That person is letting me know that he or she has something on me, has power over me. First and foremost the power to hurt me, to mark my consciousness with that hurt, inscribing shame in the deepest levels of my mind. This wounded, shamed consciousness becomes a formative part of my personality. An insult can thus be analyzed as a "performative utterance," according to J. L. Austin's definition. In a well-known work, that English philosopher distinguished between constative and performative utterances.[3] The former describe a situation and can be true or false. The latter produce an action and thus are neither true nor false—for example, "I call this meeting to order." In fact, Austin defines two kinds of performative utterances, illocutionary and perlocutionary. In the first kind, the utterance itself constitutes the action it announces. To say "I name this ship the *Queen Elizabeth*" or to respond "I do" (meaning: "I do take this woman as my lawful wife" or "I do take this man as my lawful husband") during a wedding ceremony is to make an utterance of this kind.[4] In the second kind of performative utterance, the action is not produced by the utterance per se; rather it is one of the consequences (the fear, the emotions, or the thoughts produced by words like "I am warning you") of having said something. At first glance, one would include insult in this latter category. Insult is a linguistic act—or a series of repeated linguistic acts—by which a particular place in the world is assigned to the person at whom the acts are directed. This assignment determines a viewpoint on the world, a particular outlook. Insult profoundly affects the consciousness of an individual through what it says: "I assimilate you to this," "I reduce you to that." And so I am this or that. Insult can be found anywhere: linguists have expanded this category of performative utterances to include allusions, insinuations, irony, metaphor, and so on. Given that at the end of his book Austin himself comes to dissolve the distinction between performative and constative utterances, we might say that many of the utterances of everyday life can be described as injurious speech acts.

In any case, insult is a performative utterance. Its function is to produce certain effects—notably, to establish or to renew the barrier between "normal" people and those Goffman calls "stigmatized" people[5] and to cause the internalization of that barrier within the individual being insulted. Insult tells me what I am to the extent that it makes me be what I am.

2

The Flight to the City

All of the studies done in homosexual populations (of either sex) show that the experience of insult (not to mention of physical violence) is one of the most widely shared elements of their existence—to different degrees, of course, according to which country, and, within any country, according to where they live and in what environment they grow up. But it is a reality experienced by almost everyone. This tells us that even those who feel the most freedom these days, in large Western cities, need to know how to deal at every instant with the surrounding world: to know whether it is possible to hold hands with a partner or to show signs of affection to someone of the same sex, or whether those actions should be avoided. This practical knowledge, so deeply interiorized that one seldom even notices it, does not need to be made fully conscious in order to have effects, to organize successful forms of behavior. Mistakes can have painful consequences. The experience of physical violence or the obsessive awareness of its threat are so common in gay lives that they are mentioned in almost every autobiography and in numerous novels with gay male characters.[1] Sometimes no gesture is even necessary: one's appearance or clothing suffice to provoke an act of hatred. For the most openly gay, as for those who are less so or are not open at all, for those who are "flaming" as for those who are "discreet," the possibility of being the target of verbal or physical aggression is never absent, and has in any case often been a determining factor in the way a personal identity has been constructed (including the ability to sense danger) or in the way strict controls on words and gestures have been internalized.

The phrase "moral harassment" has recently been used to describe what certain salaried employees experience in the workplace.[2] The experience has notable psychological consequences. Is not the whole life of gay people entirely defined by permanent "moral harassment," be it direct or indirect, a harassment present in every situation in which they find themselves, a social harassment? And are not the personalities that they construct and the identities that they shape determined by the psychological consequences of the "harassed" social position they occupy in daily life (produced by ambient insults, mockery, aggression, hostility)? It is not hard to understand why one of the structuring principles of gay and lesbian subjectivities consists in seeking out means to flee insult and violence, whether it be by way of dissimulation or by way of emigration to more hospitable locations.

This is why gay lives are oriented toward the city and its social networks. Those who seek to leave their birthplaces and the places where they spent their childhoods in order to live in more welcoming cities are numerous. Marie-Ange Schiltz writes, speaking of recent studies, that "in comparison to studies of the general population, it seems that the departure from the family household and the attainment of economic independence are much more precipitous among young homosexuals."[3] This flight surely leads, in most cases, to large cities.

Cities have always been the refuge of gay people. At the end of the 1960s, a gay activist described San Francisco as a "refuge camp" that had attracted gay people from all over the country—people who were running from the impossibility of living out gay lives in the hostile, hate-filled atmosphere of small-town America.[4] One sees clearly, reading the works of Allan Bérubé or John D'Emilio, that the history of the construction of gay "enclaves" within large cities is closely tied to the history of discrimination and homophobia. Allan Bérubé shows that during World War II, soldiers dismissed from the U.S. armed forces because of their sexual orientation often stayed in the city in which they were demobilized (San Francisco for the navy, for example). It was hardly possible to return to one's small town having been dismissed from the armed forces. For others, the simple fact of having been able to build up a set of relations with other gay men during the time spent in uniform led them to decide not to return home, where a heterosexual marriage seemed inevitably to await them.[5] For his part, John D'Emilio reminds us that during the McCarthy era, at the beginning of the 1950s, it was not only communists who were being hunted, but homosexuals as well, many of whom were removed from public functions at the time. What else could a person rendered infamous in this way do but seek out a large city? There gay men and lesbians had some chance of warding off a hostile environment, even given the extreme difficulty of organizing a gay or lesbian milieu at that time, due to the unrelenting repression brought to bear on bars and other social spaces.[6]

Yet even well before that, from at least the beginning of the century, even from the end of the nineteenth century, certain cities such as New York, Paris, or Berlin had reputations that attracted waves of "refugees" from a wide area, even from abroad, refugees who thereby helped to consolidate the reason for their coming: the existence of a "gay world" that they joined and to which they brought the enthusiasm that characterizes new arrivals.[7]

This explains why a true mythology of the city developed within gay culture, within the collective homosexual imaginary, from the end of the nineteenth century onward (and perhaps even earlier). Paris, London, Berlin, Amsterdam, New York, San Francisco: these became wonderful symbols of a certain freedom; they nourished the dreams of anyone reading books or newspapers (even when the images given by these sources were pejorative or even insulting) or hearing reports brought back by luckier travelers, those who had been able to visit a capitol or a major metropolitan area. (George Chauncey cites the accounts of gay men who decided, on the basis of a story told by a friend of a stay in New York, to leave behind the small town in which they had been living.)[8]

This mythology of the big city—and of migration to it—coexisted for a long time with a more general mythology of travel and exile, not to the city in this case, but to a foreign country, another continent. There was—and doubtless still is—a phantasmagoric "elsewhere" for gays, an "elsewhere" that offered the possibility of realizing your hopes and dreams—ones that seemed impossible for so many reasons, unthinkable even, in your land of origin.[9] Among possible examples, one might mention the appeal of Italy at the end of the nineteenth century and the beginning of the twentieth (von Platen) or Germany in the 1920s (Isherwood, Auden, Spender, etc.), trips to the colonies or distant lands (Gide in North Africa, Forster in Egypt and India), or expatriation for career reasons (Dumézil in Turkey, Foucault in Sweden).[10]

But the pull—real or imaginary—exercised by the city seems the more general phenomenon. Even today, the migration of gays and lesbians to large cities continues. Homosexuality is intimately connected to cities. As Henning Bech, a Danish sociologist, puts it, "The city is the social world proper of the homosexual, his life space; it is no use objecting that lots of homosexuals have lived in the country. Insofar as they wish to be homosexual, the vast majority must get out into 'the city' one way or another."[11] That is not to say that there can be no gay life in small towns or in the country. To the contrary:

there, as elsewhere, there exist (and have existed for a long time) meeting places, circles of friends who get together regularly, organizing evening parties, and so on. The forms of sociability found in these urban or semirural subcultures are little known and little studied by historians and sociologists, doubtless because documents are rare and hard to come by (often being private diaries or personal correspondences), but also because the "invisibility" of these clandestine ways of life has been better protected (for obvious reasons) than in big cities: it is difficult to find out in which bar or which restaurant gays get together—even more difficult to know in which private homes. Perhaps a systematic review of police records and court archives would allow one to discover lives and ways of life that are less well known than those that have been recently studied by historians of urban culture.

It remains the case that it was in large cities that gay ways of life found the possibility of full development. The city is a world of strangers, which allows a certain anonymity to be maintained. Such anonymity is hardly possible given the stifling constraints created by the acquaintance networks that characterize small town or village life, where everyone knows everyone else and any breach of normal behavior must be all the more well hidden. As Magnus Hirschfeld wrote in his 1904 book about "homosexuals in Berlin," the city is a "desert of men" where an individual "evades the controlling influence of those around him better than in any provincial location, where everything, the senses and the mind, reduces itself to a narrow horizon. In provincial places people know—quite consciously—when, where, and with whom their neighbor has eaten and drunk, has gone walking or gone to bed . . . whereas here, people living in a given street do not even know who lives on the other side of the building, and thus even less so what those other lodgers might be doing."[12]

Of course the city is also a social world, a world of possible forms of socialization. Along with anonymity, it provides the possibility of surmounting loneliness. A gay person who decides to move to a big city plans to join others who have done the same thing previously, who have helped create the world that provides the city's attraction, that has made it an object of dreams long before the move could be undertaken. This is why there is a sort of exaltation, mixed with fear, that characterizes the arrival in the city and the discovery of all its possibilities.[13] Magnus Hirschfeld gives a wonderful description of gay and lesbian culture at the beginning of the century, of cabarets, restaurants, taverns and cafes, balls, nightlife, and everything else that makes up what we would call today gay subculture—a culture whose richness, whose evolutions, whose chance developments, even, have recently been reconstructed for us by George Chauncey's book on New York. That book shows how widespread that culture already was at the end of the nineteenth century, in spite of the repression brought to bear on it.[14] We are speaking of the city as it was lived, loved, dreamed, and fantasized by millions of gay people of both sexes throughout this century, a city in which what Hirschfeld called the "web" of homosexual life causes changes: "Through its own specific action, [it] alters every nuance of the scene, inflects in an essential way the physiognomy of the whole."[15]

It is quite likely the case that the interaction between gay and lesbian culture and the city as a whole was much more wide-ranging in the early years of the century and in the 1920s than it would be in the 1940s and 1950s. Chauncey shows this to be the case for New York: huge drag balls drew crowds of heterosexual spectators. Newspapers wrote articles about them that were accompanied by photos. Moreover, places for meeting or socializing (bars, saloons, restaurants) were rarely exclusively gay. The border between the gay world and the heterosexual city was not as marked as it would become after World War II, even if police raids and arrests and various other kinds of controls of course kept up a constant pressure on this semiclandestine, semiopen subculture. The fluctuations in the degree of openness to the exterior world can be thought of as one of the most striking aspects of the level of general awareness of gay people and of the level of self-awareness of gay people throughout this period—and also of the ability of gay people to affirm their identities and their ways of life, to resist hostile forces when those identities and ways of life came under attack. During this period one moved from a time of surprising audaciousness to one of almost total self-concealment, in which the doors to the gay world were almost locked shut from the inside. One finds a perpetual give and take between secrecy and visibility, between silence and public openness, between fear and daring.[16]

Clearly then, a "gay world" did not burst into existence suddenly with the Stonewall riots in 1969, those riots set off by a police raid in New York, and whose annual commemoration, beginning a year later, would become the starting point for the contemporary Gay Pride movement. To the contrary, it is only because a subculture had already existed for quite a long time that any such riot was possible. It is the case that in almost every Western country the 1950s and 1960s (and before them the 1940s and the wartime period) had been a period in which gay subcultures were forced to become more rigorously clandestine than in the 1920s and 1930s. Repression became much more intense than it had been before the war. (In France, in 1960, the parliament approved an amendment that defined homosexuality as a social illness alongside alcoholism and prostitution.)

Consequently, the upsurge at the beginning of the 1970s, one that continued to develop in the 1980s and 1990s, forms part of a longer history of urban culture, a history including the ways of life that made cities famous in the Belle Époque and the Roaring Twenties.[17] It seems quite noteworthy that we are witnessing today a reopening of this world to the exterior, if only in that it is again suddenly extremely visible. There are now few who do not know about the existence of gay bars, gay cafes, or gay neighborhoods: the subculture is once again in permanent contact with the city as a whole. For even if the bars are exclusively gay (and this is not necessarily the case for all of them), the cafes and restaurants are open to all, and the neighborhoods are obviously not private enclaves, but areas in which gay visibility is affirmed in relation to and interaction with other "communities" (the gay quarter in Paris, for example, adjoins the historic Jewish neighborhood) and with the city more generally. The boundaries of these gay enclaves within large cities are in any case quite fluid and subject to change according to the openings and closings of bars, cafes, and restaurants. Gay businesses usually remain in the minority, and, in any case, the streets are open to all. A mix is the normal state of affairs.

We also see that, far from being adequately understandable through terms sometimes invoked with hostile intent, such as "identity politics" or "separatism" (in French, one speaks of communautarisme or of communautarisme à l'américaine, which is always unfavorably juxtaposed with a putatively more French universalisme), such phenomena as Gay Pride festivals or the growth of gay neighborhoods in major European cities are indicators of the reopening of doors of the "gay world," doors that had shut themselves of necessity for a good number of years. What seems to upset so deeply those observers who wax indignant about the growth of a gay neighborhood (I am thinking of the many articles in recent years in French newspapers devoted to the development of the Marais neighborhood in Paris) is that this new gay visibility allows an entire culture to open onto and interact with the exterior world, with the rest of the city—as was already the case, on a smaller scale, of course, in the 1920s and 1930s. Think, for instance, of the participants in the costume balls of those years making their way toward the entrance of the dance hall through a crowd of perhaps applauding, perhaps hissing, bystanders who had made their own way there on purpose to watch. . . .

3

Friendship as a Way of Life

The city is first and foremost a means of escape, to the extent that this is possible, from the rule of insult, in which it is impossible to live out one's homosexuality without constant dissimulation. When Erving Goffman studies the strategies used by those he refers to as "stigmatized," he mentions in speaking of homosexuals the act of leaving for the big city. But he also insists that it is not simply a matter of going to live "somewhere else" in the search of "anonymity." Such an act involves a serious break in one's biography.[1] Much more than a simple geographical displacement or a quest for potential partners, it also creates the possibility of redefining one's own subjectivity, reinventing one's personal identity. Eve Kosofsky Sedgwick, in a suggestive formulation, speaks of the psychological as well as geographical trajectory that leads from small towns to big cities, as the "more than Balzacian founding narrative of modern identity of numerous American and European gays," a story that unfolds with the passage from an isolated childhood and adolescence in a small town or some other hostile environment, to the freedom offered by city life.[2] A small town is a place where it is difficult to escape from the only available mirror, that offered by family life and by school, difficult to escape from the "interpellations" that enforce conformity to the affective, cultural, and social models of heterosexuality, to escape from what Adrienne Rich has called "compulsory heterosexuality."[3] A personal identity in fact takes shape through the degree of acceptance or refusal of this "interpellation" and through the often difficult and painful evolution, over years, of this relationship of submission or of rebellion. Such an identity assembles itself step by step, necessarily remaining a conflicted one, no matter which alternative one chooses: in one case, there will be conflicts between the submission to the heterosexual order and the internal pressure for relations with people of the same sex; in the other case, there will be conflicts between the refusal to submit and the calls permanently emitted by every social agency to return to the heteronormative order, be they in the form of the ordinary violence produced by the most banal situations of family or school life or the traumatizing brutality of insult and attacks.[4]

⋈ Gay as well as lesbian sociability is founded on a practice, even a "politics," of friendship, on the necessity of making contacts, meeting people who could be friends, and slowly building a circle of chosen relationships. As Henning Bech puts it, "Being together with other homosexuals allows one to mirror oneself in them and find self-affirmation. It allows one to share and interpret one's experiences. . . . The network of friends and the association [various kinds of gay social organizations—clubs, lodges, coalitions, choirs, and so on], together with the pub or bar, are the most important social institutions in the homosexual's life. Only through these is it possible to develop a more concrete and more positive identity as a homosexual."[5] One can here grasp the decisive importance such places hold: their primary function is to make encounters possible. (Thus one can also understand the necessity of guides to inform new "arrivals" of their existence and their whereabouts.)

Proust, at the beginning of Cities of the Plain, makes a distinction between, on the one hand, "the solitaries" among homosexuals, who suppose "their vice to be more exceptional than it is" and who have "retired into solitude from the day on which they discovered it, after having carried it within themselves for a long time without knowing it," and, on the other, those who have built up circles of friends with whom they meet in cafes, circles Proust compares to "professional organisations." Yet he immediately adds that "it is, in fact, very rarely that the solitaries do not eventually merge themselves in some such organisation, sometimes from simple lassitude, or for convenience" (RTP, 2:642, 646). This literary snapshot might seem a bit faded with age, the reflection of a bygone time. But if one brackets what Proust says of the necessity for discretion to which these "organisations" and groups of friends in cafes submit themselves (to a greater or lesser degree, it is true), and if one sets aside the particular vocabulary used by Proust, his entomological (even teratological) point of view, then it might seem that the structures of individual itineraries and of collective ways of life he describes are not so different from what we know today.[6]

For today, as yesterday, a set of friends will form the center of a gay life, and the gay person's psychological (and also geographical) journey moves from solitude to socialization by means of meeting places (such as bars or parks). The gay way of life is founded on concentric circles of friendships as well as on the continually renewed effort to create these circles, to form these friendships. Chauncey's book is a wonderful demonstration of this: while, from the beginning of the century onward, political authorities and the guardians of the social order described urban development as a "disorganizing" influence on traditional social bonds and a "destructuring" influence on individual psychologies, it was, for gays—and continues increasingly to be—an opening to social reorganization, the creation of new social bonds, and new forms of sociability, rendering possible a psychological restructuration around these bonds.[7] A shared participation in a stigmatized sexuality and the marginalization and exclusion implied by that sexuality form the basis for a specific world, inscribed just as much in the topography of cities as in the personalities of the individuals who have congregated in that world. Such individuals foster its existence and ensure its perpetuation from generation to generation. Michael Pollak described the gay world as "a group one is fated to join [un groupe de destin]," yet it seems preferable to me to speak of an invention, both collective and individual, of oneself.[8]

» It thus makes little sense to speak of the "community" or of the "ghetto" and so forth (these are all notions defined in regard to other categories—ethnic or religious—and are most often transposed to the gay and lesbian context without care or method) without linking them to the process of migration and the effects it produces, without linking them to the entire history of the departure for the big city and of the construction of a "gay world" produced by that history. The city, as the sociologist Robert Parks wrote in 1916, brings together a "mosaic of little [social] worlds."[9] This overlapping set of small worlds offers individuals the chance to belong to several universes simultaneously and, therefore, to have several social identities—professional, ethnic, religious, sexual—which are often sharply separated from each other. Thus a gay man can participate in the "gay world" without losing his place in the heterosexual world: he will have two (or more) identities, one attached to his professional insertion in the social world (or to his ethnic origin) and another attached to his leisure time—one identity for the daytime, another for the night and the weekends. This often produces the tensions inherent in a difficult "double life," but it also permits a good many gay men to resist oppression and marginalization.[10]

Today's gay visibility should not be taken as a sign that a certain number of people have only in recent years decided to define themselves by their sexuality. It is a sign that a larger and larger number of gay people have ceased hiding the "nocturnal" part of their life. If the "gay world" in which people had participated in more or less clandestine fashion is now more openly visible, this is not due to the fact that gays have suddenly decided to leave behind their previously homogenous and coherent social identities in order to affiliate solely with their sexual identity. Rather, large numbers have ceased to hide the sexual identity that was just as defining for them as was their professional identity. Bars that open out onto the street with crowded terraces and windows displaying rainbow flags have taken the place of bars hidden in small streets with heavy doors equipped with a peep hole to allow the establishment to protect itself against unwished for invasions or attacks.

If one wishes to analyze what the gay "community" is today—the simple evocation of which seems in France to provoke shivers of horror from upright-thinking people of all persuasions—all of this history of the sociability and of the "world" that gays constructed for themselves throughout the past century must be taken into account. For that very sociability, whose increasing commercialization or whose uniformity it is so easy to denounce these days, initially had and still has an emancipatory value, offering the possibility to young gays and lesbians to speed up the process of self-acceptance.[11]

The liberating effect of gay visibility probably extends even to those who do not participate in this "culture," either because they are unable to (they do not live in a big city) or because they do not wish to (they choose to avoid the gay "scene"). There is no doubt that the lives of gay men and lesbians as a whole have, over the past twenty years, evolved in a shared direction due to the visibility of a certain number of them, but evolved also in a way that is differentiated based on the degree of proximity to or distance from the central locations of subcultural life.[12] What counts is that homosexuality be sayable and showable. A gay man—or a gay couple—does not need to belong to the "gay scene" to profit from what has been gained through gay visibility and affirmation. A growing number of them can live more serenely, no longer entirely dissimulating who they are.

If, as all of Foucault's work insists (at least the early Foucault), a society defines itself by what it finds sayable and thinkable, we can assert that gay and lesbian visibility has had the effect of transforming the whole of society by the ways it has modified what can be seen, said, and thought. The gay movement, the opening outward and the intensification of "subcultural" life, surely represents (along with feminism) one of the most intense questionings of the instituted order—the sexual and social order, but also the epistemological order—of the contemporary world.

4

Sexuality and Professions

Gay lives often begin in a state of deferral. They only really begin when someone reinvents himself, leaving behind, at least partially, his ashamed secrecy and his silence, when he makes choices instead of merely putting up with things—for example, when he assembles a family for himself, made up of friends, former lovers, and friends of former lovers, thereby reconstructing his identity and leaving behind the stifling, narrow field of his family of origin with its tacit or explicit injunctions to be heterosexual. Such a flight does not, of course, necessarily entail a total rupture with one's family, but rather the necessity of taking one's distance from it. Before that, gay lives are only lived by proxy or in one's imagination; they are lives in the offing, both feared and longed for.

Doubtless it is all of the wounds experienced during what Eve Kosofsky Sedgwick has splendidly described as "that long Babylonian exile known as queer childhood"[1] that nourish the energies through which gay people create or recreate personalities for themselves—the same energies through which gay "culture" and "community" are created. It is a creative energy that begins by creating itself through flight. The capacity and the will to transform oneself and the necessary energy to do so are produced by the memories, but also by the permanent traces, the persistence of the feelings experienced during childhood and adolescence, feelings that have deeply structured the personal identity of many young gay people. Sedgwick rightly insists on the way in which the feelings of shame experienced in childhood form "a near-inexhaustible source of transformational energy" (4). How can the intensity of this shame be understood by those who have never experienced it? How can they understand the strength of the motivations produced by the desire to escape from it? And there are many other feelings or behaviors produced by the sexual "dissonance" within a family that might be mentioned for the subsequent roles they play as "sources of energy" for someone's project of self-restructuration. Take, for instance, the vague sentiment of being different or marginal, of being "separate"; take the investment in literary or artistic models in the place of family or society-based models, because the former represent the only available recourse. The gay child—we need to be able to think here of "gay childhoods"—first of all turned in on himself and organized his own psychology and his rapport with others around his secret and his silence. It is from this inner life that he draws the ability to transform himself. Perhaps this can help to explain the peculiar relation—one that has often been described—between gay men and books, between gay men and the world of culture. In a draft for *Cities of the Plain* (*Sodome et Gomorrhe*), Proust evokes as a paradigmatic figure the "young boy made fun of by his brothers and friends" who

> walks alone for hours on the beach, sitting on boulders and questioning the blue sea with a melancholy eye, an eye already full of worry and persistence, wondering if perhaps in this marine landscape with an azure sky—the same that already glittered in the days of Marathon and Salamis—he might not see advancing toward him on a rapid skiff and ready to whisk him away, the very Antinous that he dreamed of all day long, and all night, as well, when any passerby could see him in the moonlight at the window of his villa, gazing out into the night, but hiding himself as soon as he was noticed—still too pure to imagine that a desire such as his could exist anywhere other than in the pages of a book.[2]

But what book would Proust be speaking of? He also gives a description of the mechanism by which a particular relation to reading is established for gay men and by which they are led to identify with female characters: such is the only way for them to live out, by proxy, an emotional relation with another man: "Through an unconscious transposition, they associate with their bizarre desire everything that literature or art or life has contributed throughout the centuries to the effort to widen the notion of love as one would the bed of a river. . . . They await faithfully—as would a heroine in a novel by Walter Scott—the arrival of Rob Roy or of Ivanhoe."[3] Perhaps this is the source of the importance for gay men of culture in the large sense and of the fascination so often noted for "divas" and "stars," whether of films, the press, literature, books, the arts, and so on.[4]

❧ The flight from "heterosexual interpellation" of which I spoke in the previous chapter can even help to interpret a choice of profession as a fundamental component of one's self-construction, of one's personal identity. A certain number of studies, notably the recent article by Marie-Ange Shiltz, have put forward the hypothesis of a form of upward social mobility specific to gay men. It would seem that the migration to the big city is statistically linked to the effort of young gay men from more working-class backgrounds to escape from manual occupations and to orient themselves toward professions in which it is possible to imagine that they will benefit from a greater degree of tolerance, or, at least, which will enable them to live out their sexuality more easily. It would also seem that, more generally, there is an orientation toward "artistic" professions, or toward the more "artistic" poles of other professions. This allows one to understand, as Michael Pollak suggested, the orientation toward occupations such as that of hairdresser, which would be situated at the most artistic pole of manual occupations.[5] In any case, migration to the big city seems to lead to rising educational or social trajectories, at least statistically speaking. Of course, given that the studies by Marie-Ange Schiltz (and those she conducted earlier with Michael Pollak) are based on the analysis of replies to questionnaires that were published in the gay press, her results rely on a spontaneously produced sample, which necessarily creates certain significant biases. (Only people who have already self-identified as gay are likely to take the step of buying a gay magazine, not to mention taking the further step of responding to a questionnaire found in that magazine.) This would explain the over-representation in the responses of men living in large cities and better circumstances. It is clear, in effect, that gay men in more working-class environments, in small towns, in rural areas, and in ethnic suburbs often find it impossible to acknowledge themselves as such and thereby to be taken into account in statistically based sociological studies. Yet, as Marie-Ange Schiltz has emphasized, the divergence between the voluntary response from the gay sample and responses obtained from the general population by other means is so significant that one can assume that the bias in the sample is not sufficient in and of itself to explain the phenomenon.

What conclusions shall we draw from what the statistical information reveals? There is doubtless some kind of intergenerational solidarity (even if it is not lived or experienced as such) between older gay men and the younger ones they may help to escape from their social or familial surroundings, providing them with the occasion or the impulse to leave. (This phenomenon may well nourish the old myth about a gay free-masonry—"they all help each other out." But above all it reveals that the invisible chain of solidarity between gay people is created first and foremost through the aggregation of thousands of individual gestures.)[6] This undeniable reality (whose effects are of course somewhat limited) could not on its own explain the phenomenon revealed by the sociological studies, which perhaps encourage us to wonder about a kind of pre-knowledge of oneself as homosexual before even entering into one's sexuality. One is obliged to think that the observed tendency toward a scholastic achievement higher than the norm, the choice of certain kinds of professions ("artistic" rather than manual), or, within certain kinds of careers or occupations, the difference that encourages gay people to become, for example, cultural rather than economic journalists or lawyers who specialize in the rights of authors rather than in business law, must come into play very early, even at the youngest of ages. One might also recall, among other possible givens, the penchant for reading (a more "feminine" activity), which is associated with a penchant for interior as opposed to exterior spaces (staying home to read rather than going out to play soccer, when reading is considered by the masculinist ideologies of working-class milieux as an activity for "fairies" or "fags"), and so on.[7]

An anthropology of homosexuality would need to concern itself with this particular aspect of personal accounts, which one often comes across in autobiographies (even if it is not explicitly thematized). It is not enough simply to tabulate the distance from statistical averages of certain trajectories and certain incomes. Perhaps one should compare educational, social, and professional trajectories within a given family, those of a gay man and his heterosexual siblings. There is a crucial question to be asked that quantitative and qualitative studies often leave to the side (it is, of course, not their central concern): what exactly is a social trajectory, and, in particular, what is an upward social trajectory—more exactly, what does it signify in particular for this or that individual? At what moment does such a thing come into play, at what age, and what are the signs of such a trajectory, what are its components? The point is not to establish some overly simplistic causality (being gay—even before the fact—somehow producing a will to succeed at school); rather it is a question of inquiring into the relation between the dispositions associated with a certain kind of sexuality (and a kind of psychology that goes along with it) and the dispositions that orient someone toward educational and professional courses of action that could be understood as having to do with upward mobility. What would be the genesis of this kind of relation, unless, in fact, we are talking about what are basically the same dispositions?

Proust was already, in his own way, writing about what seemed to him the obvious and yet mysterious link between a sexual orientation and artistic dispositions: "I thought with curiosity of this combination in a single person of a physical blemish and a spiritual gift. M. de Charlus was not very different from his brother, the Duc de Guermantes. . . . But it had sufficed *that nature should have upset the balance of his nervous system* enough to make him prefer, to the women that his brother the Duke would have chosen, one of Virgil's shepherds or Plato's disciples, and at once qualities unknown to the Duc of Guermantes and *often linked to this lack of equilibrium* had made M. de Charlus an exquisite pianist, an amateur painter who was not devoid of taste, and an eloquent talker" (*RTP*, 2:985–86, my emphasis, translation modified). Let us set aside for the moment the Proustian explanation by way of an "imbalance in his nervous system" and the link between a psychological imbalance and an artistic temperament. Doubtless Proust owed such explanations to his readings of psychiatrists: is this not exactly the thesis presented by Max Nordau in his book, *Degeneration*, which devotes a number of pages to Wilde, or by Cesare Lombroso in *The Man of Genius*? Despite all that, Proust is clearly posing the question of the relation between certain dispositions which are linked in no self-evident way, and yet which are sufficiently frequently found together so that their relation seems noteworthy.

This imbrication of the feeling of being "different" with a yearning for an "artistic" life can be discovered in many an autobiography—for instance in that of Guy Hocquenghem, who wrote in 1988: "One's childhood years are somewhat undefined; there's the inspiration of a desire to differentiate yourself and an aspiration (a frenetic one) toward other atmospheres that together cause one's chest to swell with unsatisfied regrets. It's something like a cross between the promise to become a genius, to start a revolution, to become a saint or a great artist, or else to kill yourself at the first sign of adulthood."[8]

This brings to mind the quandary Bourdieu points to in *Distinction*, when he wonders why there is such a strong correlation between the frequency with which one visits museums and the amount of time one has devoted to one's schooling, given that there has been almost no time devoted to artistic education in those schools. We can recall how Bourdieu works to find an explanation for this correlation by studying the common genesis both of a happy and lasting relation to the educational system and of a love of art. He shows how the positioning of individual subjects within the established social order determines—even on the deepest levels of a given personality—the concomitant acquisition of aesthetic and educational dispositions, thereby reinscribing singular cases within a general pattern. We have posed here a question of the same order: how is this correlation between sexual and intellectual dispositions, one Proust ascribed to an anomaly of nature, produced? Doubtless, we must consider the entire process (both conscious and unconscious) of the formation of gay subjectivities, which means considering the effects that the established sexual order exercises on gay people and the place that they occupy in that order, in order to account for the individual forms of differentiation or divergence that awakened Proust's "curiosity." It is as if the process of subjection itself brought into being a will (already present prior to any conscious decision) to resist that process, to escape from it—to choose oneself the shape of one's own subjectivity.[9]

5
Family and "Melancholy"

If friendship networks are crucially important for young gay men newly arrived in a city, they are equally so for older gay men, especially when they stop participating in bar life or cruising. The well-known theme of the "loneliness" of the aging gay man is not merely the product of a homophobic imagination: it corresponded for a long time to the lived experience of numerous individuals. "Gay culture" has allowed for the creation of lasting bonds of friendship. Friends are thus for gay men what we might call a "substitute family," except that such an expression would seem to recognize what rather should be put into question: the legitimacy and "naturalness" of the heterosexual way of life. It is undeniable that the quasi-necessity to break away from the family milieu (or, more exactly, to give up a harmonious place within that family) obligates individuals to undertake the serious work of establishing friendships—and also provides them the occasion and the energy to devote to that work. Friends who have been met in gay locales replace both family relations that have been abandoned to a greater or lesser extent and relations in the workplace, which are so difficult for gay men and lesbians to establish and maintain, especially if they are trying to keep their sexuality secret.

This project of substituting chosen or constructed bonds for "natural" and familial ones is far from easy. It presupposes a simultaneous project of mourning, often a long and painful one, which, like all mourning processes, as Jacques Derrida rightly reminds us, is never finished.[1] One has to give up— to a greater or lesser extent—life within the family circle; further, one has to accept, as constitutive of one's own self, this more or less obligatory renunciation. Perhaps this explains, *a contrario*, why a certain number of gay men and lesbians experience such a strong desire to be recognized as legitimate couples or families by those close to them (notably by their families) and by society at large (and thus by the law). In such cases it is not simply a question of adopting heterosexual "models," as is sometimes asserted ("imitating the hets," as would say those who prefer to remain outside any recognized institutional framework), but, more fundamentally, of recovering a grounding in a lost family and perhaps thereby of restoring the bonds with the family one has left, or of reentering "normal" life by joining once again the sequence of generations. Of course, this break with or distancing of the family (more or less fierce, more or less complete) is often initially felt as a moment of true liberation. Often (although not always) individuals, far from suffering from the break with their families (except perhaps in specific kinds of moments, as in an illness), see in it a necessary precondition to their self-realization as gay or lesbian. But with the passage of time, especially once the most intense period of one's sexual life (and thus the ways of life associated with it) is over, this separation becomes harder and harder for many to endure. The same is doubtless true for many heterosexuals who have broken with their family for any number of reasons, including upward social mobility, diverging political opinions, living as an unmarried couple in circles that do not accept such arrangements, or having as a partner someone from a stigmatized category (black, North African, Jewish, and so on). But this experience seems almost consubstantially attached to homosexuality.

One day it becomes time to try to reestablish family ties. This may be the beginning of a long process of reconciliation and reintegration, one that will take a lifetime. These attempts at reconciliation usually involve concessions on both sides—for example, the decision to leave sexuality in the realm of the unspoken: even if parents "know," they act as if they do not. Sometimes the situations allow for more explicitness, when, for example, a gay man or a lesbian get their parents slowly to recognize the reality of their relationship with a partner, who is finally admitted into the family.

» Surely there exists a specifically homosexual "melancholy." ("Melancholy" is meant here in the psychoanalytic sense of a never-ending process of mourning, one impossible to finish, and which, as Freud tells us, marks the process of ego-formation by way of a set of refused identifications.[2]) Judith Butler mentions this idea of a melancholy specific to homosexuals in regard to the "choice" of a sexual object. She discusses the process of mourning of the rejected heterosexual object, one integrated as a rejected possibility into the process of ego-formation.[3] I would like to modify her analyses (which in my view are too dependent on the theoretical schemas of psychoanalysis) in order to shift to a more general sociological approach to the question of the relationship of individuals to family structure and to their social insertion.

This "melancholy" arises from the unending, unfinishable mourning of the loss homosexuality causes to homosexuals, that is to say, the loss of heterosexual ways of life, ways that are refused and rejected (or that you are obliged to reject because they reject you). Yet the model of social integration attached to these rejected ways of life continues to haunt the aspirations and the unconscious of many gay men and lesbians. Bergson says that an individual's life is haunted by choices not made. In this case, the life of gay men—and of lesbians—is unquestionably haunted by ways of life and forms of relations to others that have been set aside or done without, willingly or not, because of their sexuality. This "melancholy" is linked to the loss of family ties (with parents, brothers, the family circle), but also to the sometimes unavowed dream of a family life, a dream certain people cannot bring themselves to give up, endeavoring as much as possible to create such a life for themselves over time, living as long-term couples, raising children (who may be the offspring from a previous heterosexual existence or, in the case of women, the result of artificial insemination or the more "natural" intervention of a friend).

This "melancholy" is closely tied, for a certain number of gay men and lesbians, to the idea that they cannot have children. Such an idea is often offered in responses to the questionnaires of sociologists as an instance of an obstacle to self-acceptance as gay or lesbian, the idea of admitting that one is "permanently" gay or lesbian being perceived as synonymous with the obligation—an unimaginable one for certain people—to give up the hope of having children. One might wonder if this sensitive issue does not represent one of the most deeply rooted aspects of psychological "suffering" in homosexuals of both sexes. Or perhaps one could choose to think of it as one manner of expressing a diffuse form of suffering difficult to express in any other way than by reference to conventional situations. In The Weight of the World, Pierre Bourdieu and the sociologists who worked with him have shown how "suffering" is not linked merely to economic "conditions" but also to what they call the "positions" within the specific space in which one lives. In order to explain what he means by "positional suffering," Bourdieu mentions Patrick Süskind's play, The Double Bass, which "presents an especially striking image of how painfully the social world may be experienced by people who, like the bass player in the orchestra, occupy an inferior, obscure position in a prestigious and privileged universe."[4] Surely homosexuality (even though, oddly enough, it is not considered in Bourdieu's book) is one of those social "positions" that engenders a particular form of psychological "suffering." Moreover, it seems symptomatic that one of the problems encountered by the sociologists in conducting this huge project—a project that resembles a form of social psychoanalysis—grew out of the difficulty in transforming the weight of this suffering into speech. There was the further problem, within the speech produced, of grasping what is really being said among all the remarks that tend to obscure matters and all the things that are said so as to avoid saying what is crucial. This can help us to understand why the current demands of the lesbian and gay movement find themselves publicly expressed with such vehemence. It is not only because they express the legitimate desire to put an end to certain forms of discrimination or because the demands encounter discourses of such violent hostility, such hatred, such scorn, that reactions of anger and revolt seem inevitable. It is also because these demands stir up for many the deepest fibers of consciousness and of the unconscious, marked by all the wounds of childhood and adolescence of which I spoke above. They contain within themselves all of the passion produced by the "melancholy" from which the demands are meant to help one escape.[5]   .

One might well think that this "melancholy" is constitutive of the gay ego to such an extent that it is present even in those who feel no inclination to recognize anything lacking in themselves simply because they do not participate in a family, and who, far from seeing in the family an ideal to strive for, rather hold it in contempt. The aggression that often characterizes this discourse of radical rejection of the family shows that the relation to the family is never simple and certainly never neutral. Mourning for the family is "interminable" for those who recognize the process. Even for those who refuse the entire process, it cannot be said that such mourning can simply be done away with, for it is finally in this "mourning" that a personality is constituted. The gay man or lesbian with the most hostility toward family models is still defined precisely by the rejection of an identification with those models. One might even think, given the social omnipresence of these models, that they even manage to shape the way in which one defines oneself against them. Judith Butler is certainly correct when she writes (in a somewhat different context) that "what is repudiated and hence lost is preserved as a repudiated identification."[6]

This is why it seems to me worth one's while to avoid creating an opposition between those gay men affiliated with a way of life outside of any institutional or juridical recognition (many of them affiliated with a free sexuality that welcomes multiple partners) and those gay men who prefer to live as a couple and who aspire to have this union legally recorded. Such an opposition, accepted by many gays in one or the other of these two "camps," is one of the most pernicious traps set by a liberal form of homophobic discourse—a discourse that makes use of the fact that there are those who do not want to hear marriage spoken of in order to justify refusing that right to others who would like to obtain it. The dividing line between the two camps is far from clear and seems to disappear the closer one looks. First of all, the demand for gay marriage is not simply the expression of the aspiration of certain gay people to enter into the matrimonial institution—this would be a simple abdication of will in the face of heterosexual ways of life. Were gay marriage to become a reality, it would profoundly and permanently alter the institution itself. Indeed, if gay people today are able to demand the right to marriage, it is because the institution has already changed. The desacralization of marriage is what makes possible the claim that it should be open to same-sex couples.[7]

One might also point out that what might seem to be two irrevocably opposed ways of life (sexual freedom on the one hand, marriage on the other) can sometimes simply be different stages in the life of the same individuals. Those who participate in the former during a more or less lengthy period may as the years pass move toward the latter, as did the Baron Charlus, who, "tiring of the strangers whom he picked up, had gone to the opposite extreme, to what he used to imagine that he would always loathe, the imitation of conjugal life or of fatherhood" (RTP, 3:207). Or, alternatively, persons who had set up as couples at a young age may, after a breakup, discover the pleasures of multiple partners. This leaves unmentioned those who live as lasting couples without feeling obliged to give up multiple encounters. But the real reason one might think that these two ways of life are not mutually opposed, but rather mutually reinforcing, is that they are produced by the same set of determining factors, by the same set of "sufferings," and are both "solutions" invented to escape from that suffering. Sartre spoke on several occasions of homosexuality as a "solution" [issue] invented by an individual to escape from an unbearable situation. (This is why he compares homosexuality to literature, his model being, as usual, Genet.)[8] The idea that one "chooses" to be homosexual makes, of course, little sense and was refuted by Genet himself, who always replied that being homosexual was for him on the same order as having two feet and two hands. But, on a different level entirely, one might recuperate this idea of homosexuality as a "solution" or a "way out" as a description not of the "choice" to be homosexual, but of the choice that a gay person makes of a certain way of life, the choice to aspire to a way of life that gives a way out of an unbearable "positional suffering" and the "melancholy" that is its psychological expression.

6

The City and Conservative Discourse

Certainly the city represents an aspiration to freedom and self-realization, yet it can also be a place of misfortune. In certain ways condemned to city life, gay people are also forced to live with all the forms of violence that come with the city: gay bashings, police harassment, communicable diseases, and so on. Of course all of this exists in smaller towns as well, and it is even in order to escape physical violence and harassment that many gay people have taken refuge in larger cities.[1] In the big cities violence takes on other forms, and methods to resist it are better developed, yet social control of the subculture and various manifestations of hostility find ways of flourishing as well. This is perhaps one of the prominent characteristics of gay history and of the gay city, especially as George Chauncey describes it. He emphasizes the effort given to the social control of sexuality and of gender, something he labels a "street-level policing of gender."[2] Unless one understands this phenomenon it will be difficult to grasp how contemporary gay identity emerged via the installation of specific ways of life and specific freedoms. The city is thus both the place in which gay culture comes to exist and the place in which that culture is subject to social surveillance in its most basic and quotidian forms. In the city these two phenomena interact. Throughout history, homosexuality and the vice squad have formed a strange couple, whose divorce, alas, seems still to be nowhere in sight, even if the couple has gone through some changes and even modernized itself over the years.

❧ The city is also a place of illness. In Western countries it was the "ecological niche" of the AIDS epidemic.[3] The marvelous names that had figured in the dreams of generations of gay people (San Francisco, New York, Paris . . .) were darkened by the specter of death as well as by the infinite sadness of the repeated acts of mourning experienced by those who survived and yet lost so many friends. Yet the city also became at that time the locus for new forms of solidarity and bonding: new organizations to fight the epidemic, newsletters to provide information about it, demonstrations, and so on. Sociological studies have shown that even if certain "activists" (though obviously not all of them) were slow to realize the gravity of the growing epidemic at the beginning of the 1980s, it was in any case those gay people most fully integrated into and involved in their communities (thus those living in the big cities) who reacted the most rapidly to the epidemic, adopted preventive measures (once they had been recommended by doctors), and founded organizations. At the outset, the prime movers of the struggle against AIDS were, along with some former activists from the 1970s, gays from the urban subculture.[4]

The city has thus been both a place for new forms of solidarity and a place for new forms of abjection. Those who had fled from shame and insult would encounter them anew in this new place and have to learn to live with them again—supplemental forms of aggression attacking an immune system already threatened by illness. AIDS has often forced those who had previously chosen to remain silent about their homosexuality to come out, bringing on the hostility of neighbors, colleagues, and family. For many infected people, it has been not only their seropositivity or AIDS that has been difficult to speak of, but also, of course, their homosexuality. The shame of being gay was reinforced by the shame of being ill—and with an illness that reinforced the shame of being gay.[5]

The abjection could extend even further when those who had sought to escape their families were, on many occasions, literally retaken by them: families who would sometimes go as far as refusing hospital access to a partner, not notifying the partner of his lover's death, evicting the partner from the apartment the couple had lived in for years, denying the partner all rights to his lover's personal belongings—even clothes, records, books. . . . Indeed, this is hardly a new phenomenon: is it not exactly the theme of Balzac's *Cousin Pons?* This "queer cousin" (as Michael Lucey has called him), who lives with another man and seems to have strange tastes (in his way of life as well as in his artistic passions), is held at a distance by his family until the moment that family conceives of the project of laying their hands on the marvelous collection of art objects that he has amassed over the years. At a distance from their families, exterior to the order of generations and filiation, such people "have no heirs." They seem to have "sprung up like mushrooms on this earth," as the concierge of Pons and Schmucke's building says of them. (Similarly, Miss Wade, in Dickens's *Little Dorrit*, is an orphan who comes from nowhere.) But these "queers" are caught up by the family order again when Pons dies. One sees how, at the end of the novel, Schmucke, to whom Pons has left everything, is entirely dispossessed by the family. Michael Lucey has referred to this event as "a final revenge of heterosexuality on a queer attempt to wrest some of society's wealth to its own ends."[6] The deceased "queer" is reinscribed into the heterosexual family order as soon as the transmission of an economic patrimony—or even some simple inheritance, however small—comes into question. But this is accomplished only through the effacement of the queer aspect of the person who has died, thereby implying a radical exclusion of the surviving partner. Schmucke, driven to misery and death, is a paradigmatic instance of this.

With AIDS, it has become more clear than ever that the relation of exteriority that gay people maintain with families and with the family order carries with it numerous juridical consequences that can lead to spoliation and systematic discrimination. It has come to be increasingly unbearable to be deprived of the most elementary of rights. The city has thus become the battleground for these rights, just as it has been, on numerous occasions throughout the century, the place in which gay movements were born and developed.[7]

⊁ Even before AIDS, the city was always considered by conservative discourse as an exemplary place of perdition, the cauldron of sexual freedom, and thus of the corruption of bodies and souls. Chauncey cites a text from 1895 that asserts that the growth of big cities and the influx of foreigners would "lead to an increase in inversion and similar vices."[8] Similarly, the earliest practitioners of urban sociology (who cooperated closely with social reformers and faithfully repeated all of their worries) did not fail to call attention to the fact that urbanization had a destructive effect on families and the other kinds of social bonds that, in smaller towns, allowed for controls on individual behaviors. As Walter Reckless wrote in 1926, this "personal disorganization" caused people to stray from "socially approved channels" and could end "not merely in prostitution, but also in perversion."[9]

One could even go so far as to say that Proust's work (without, of course, exhibiting such foul ideological tendencies) is also haunted by the opposition between the city and the countryside. On one side there is Françoise, the feeling of nostalgia for childhood and family life, the traditional rhythms of the works and the days, the rural landscape and its church towers. On the other there is Charlus, the breaking down of class boundaries, cafes filled with gay people, and male bordellos in which all forms of "vice" are allowed.

The cities mentioned above as symbols of a freedom that was either lived or dreamed of (Berlin, Paris, Amsterdam, London, San Francisco, New York . . .) have thus at the same time, and in symmetrical fashion, represented everything that the guardians of social and moral order—the apostles of religion, familialism, and oppression of women and homosexuals—held (and continue to hold) in horror. The city's atmosphere is vicious and deleterious. The city is sick and also a place of sickness. In all the discourses of traditional ideologies, as in those of conservative revolutions or restorations, of nationalisms and fascisms (which are nonetheless linked to the city by the very structure of political mobilization upon which they rely), the idea of the city has always been associated with the threat of decadence (as opposed to health) and of mixity (as opposed to purity—of race, for example). Nazism and fascisms prospered from the denunciation of everything that made cities into paradises for gay people. It must not be forgotten that Nazism presented itself as a project of "purification" that was sexual as well as racial.[10] And who could deny that today the French National Front also draws sustenance from the televised images of Gay Pride?

At the beginning of the twentieth century, as in the 1920s and 1930s, Berlin was continually denounced as the international capital of decadence. Octave Mirbeau described this "Berlin-Sodom" in 1907.[11] One wonders what image or phantasm of the city all the conservative revolutionaries of pre-Nazi Germany had in their minds, leading them to preach the return to an authentic life—that is to say, the life of the countryside. Surely it was the same image, but reversed, that Hirschfeld provided in his description of Berlin in the early years of the century. The story Ernst Jünger tells of a stay in Hamburg at the end of the 1930s can be read as supporting this idea.[12] And how can one not think of Hirschfeld's exalted descriptions upon reading the text Heidegger wrote in the autumn of 1933, in order to explain why he turned down the offer of a Chair at Berlin University? In these few pages, titled "Why We Are Remaining in the Provinces," pages that constitute a veritable resume of the entire right-wing ideology of the metropolis that flourished after Spengler, Heidegger opposes the Black Forest, contact with nature, an anchoring in the soil and in peasant memory to the evil spells of the city and its "pleasure haunts."[13]

Still today the city is denounced as the place of luxury and of the loose morals that eat away at the nation and lead it to its downfall. Imprecations against modern-day Sodoms and Gomorrahs are one of the structuring principles of the discourse of the American religious right (or even the American right *tout court*), and this is merely an exaggerated version of what is found in most French right-wing discourse (and even in that of many on the Christian "left" in France). These same schemas of thought were found, at the beginning of the AIDS crisis, in many remarks made about New York, San Francisco, or Paris as gay cities or cities of debauchery. Today's mobilization of the right and the extreme-right against the legal recognition of same-sex couples shows sufficiently clearly the degree to which the horror of homosexuality is active and violent in the more retrograde sectors of society.

Is it not the barely dampened echo of this out-of-date hatred for the modern city, its turpitudes and its "abnormal" and suspect inhabitants, that one still hears in the discourse of all those who denounce the gay "community" and its visibility, as well as Gay Pride and its "excesses"? Surely the horror provoked by this gay "community" is colored, in the fantasy that lurks behind it, by a certain disgust at promiscuity, and at sexual promiscuity in particular. In his denunciation of "Berlin-Sodom," one of Mirbeau's characters was already speaking out against the phenomenon that so many editorialists in the "liberal" Parisian press of the 1990s also found repugnant: "Can you imagine that such men have actually formed an organization?"[14] The denunciations of "identity politics" by those who seem today finally to have noticed that cities contain people with minority identities (which are consubstantial with the very existence of cities, one might note), their fright at the sight of the "gay menace" that threatens the "unity" of society, recalls the accusation (one already leveled at Oscar Wilde and André Gide) that homosexuals represent a corrupting element in the heart of society, a gangrene that threatens the strength of the nation. It is hardly surprising that one finds in those homophobic ideologists with the widest media exposure today a kind of watered-down Heideggerianism (Heidegger without the philosophy): a discourse that invokes a nation's roots, that refers to the "immemorial" order in which the family guarantees the transmission of a spiritual heritage, that repeats in incantatory fashion how these days everything is going to the dogs. Thanks to all this, such a discourse seems nothing more than a repetition in a minor mode of all of the main themes of the founders of conservative, nationalist, and fascist ideologies.

7

To Tell or Not to Tell

I realize that heterosexual readers may have a hard time believing my assertion that insult is a constitutive part of gay identity. They may never have
thought about these questions before. More importantly, especially if they
are men—white, Christian men of the Western world (women or black,
Jewish, or Arab men may see things differently)—if they have never been
confronted by the violence of insult, they may find such an assertion exaggerated. I also know that certain gay men might also deny my assertion. Even
if they have themselves experienced what I am writing about, they may make
a point of insisting that it has had no effect on their lives, behaving as if the
fact of having been called, perhaps even repeatedly, a "faggot," could have
no importance, could leave no trace, could remain an isolated and insignifi-
cant event within the context of a given existence.

Perhaps certain gay men will assert that they have in fact never been the
target of a verbal attack. One might respond that there are many who would
make that assertion without it being true. But further, it needs to be pointed
out that insult is only the extreme form on a linguistic, cultural, and social
continuum that also includes malicious gossip, allusions, insinuations,
spiteful remarks, and jokes that are more or less explicit, more or less nasty.
An insult can be heard or understood merely in the inflection of a voice or in
an amused or a hostile glance. All of these attenuated or displaced forms of
insult together form the linguistic horizon of the hostility within which gay
people lead their lives.

Moreover, even those who are the most resistant to the idea that insult
could be an important aspect of their relation to the world will concede that,
even if they have no concrete experience of it, they are nonetheless fully
conscious of the fact that such a verbal attack is possible at any moment, that
it is a threat forever present in their social life, that there is a risk it will

plunge that life into an unimaginable and even unbearable future. One has only to read the interviews conducted by Régis Gallerand with the members of the Christian organization David and Jonathan, one of the largest gay and lesbian organizations in France. Consider the remarks of one small-town secondary-school teacher. He confides that every morning, as he enters his classroom, he worries about whether he will find the two letters "PD" written on the blackboard.[1] To him it seems impossible even to imagine the consequences of any such labeling, any such definitive accusation and stigmatization.[2] Such a story reveals a great deal about the reality of gay and lesbian existences outside of the big cities, and even within them. One book from the United States designates the teaching profession as the "last closet."[3] This deft title is nonetheless probably inexact, for the list of professions in which it is impossible to cease hiding one's homosexuality remains quite a long one. It certainly includes the more "advanced" sectors of the workforce (computer science, for instance, or international banking), sectors in which one is nonetheless quite likely to hear complaints about other kinds of "resistance to change." But certainly the teaching profession is high on the list. It would be interesting to be able to read the stories of teachers—or laborers, employees, bureaucrats, salespeople, and so on—who are obliged to lead a double life, often conducting their "sex life" in the big city nearest to their workplace. Such a situation decreases the likelihood of any satisfactory intimate relationship, makes any such relationship difficult to manage; it limits many people (for there are many who are obliged to lead a "clandestine" second life) to a dissociated and unhappy existence. Such people must devote large amounts of energy to preserving the barrier between their two lives, trying to avoid being seen by a colleague near a gay bar or cruising area or in the company of someone a little less closeted, and therefore more compromising, than they are.[4] Gide recounts an exemplary scene of this nature, one whose equivalent any gay person will doubtless have experienced. Walking along a Parisian boulevard one day, he bumps into Oscar Wilde, who has just been let out of prison, and to whom he had demonstrated the faithfulness of his friendship by going to visit him in Normandy as soon as Wilde arrived in France:

> I heard my name called. I turned about: it was Wilde. Ah! how changed he was! . . . Wilde was sitting at a table on the terrace of a café. . . . I was going to sit down facing him, that is, in such a way as to turn my back to the passers-by, but Wilde, perturbed by this gesture,

which he thought was due to an absurd shame (he was not, alas! completely mistaken):

"Oh! sit down here, near me," he said, pointing to a chair beside him; "I'm so alone these days!" . . .

"When, in times gone by, I used to meet Verlaine, I didn't blush for him," he went on, with an attempt at pride.[5]

The fear of being caught may have as a consequence a generalized attitude of reserve, something like an obligation to remain on the sidelines of social life within one's professional world in order to avoid the risk of discovery. Goffman gives a good description of the way "stigmatized" people, especially those whose "stigma" is invisible, can be reticent about establishing real relationships of friendship with "normal" people (especially in the workplace) in order to avoid being drawn into an exchange of confidences or simply to avoid being found out.[6]

As numerous studies have shown, this also implies that gay people often find themselves developing a repertory of different behaviors to be used in the context of the different publics in which they find themselves, moving from one set of gestures or bodily positions to another as the situation requires. Thus, for instance, those who may be quite "campy" when among a small group of other gay people will limit their vocabulary, their expression, and their intonation to the most strictly normal in the workplace.[7]

In such situations of a "double life" and with much more frequency than those who live in big cities might imagine (and indeed, quite frequently within big cities themselves), it goes without saying that, for the gay man who has been "uncovered," insult will no longer just be something on the horizon, an ever-present potential menace; it will be a daily hell. As the example of the schoolteacher and the blackboard reveals, insult and personal identity are intimately related (personal identity being a relation to one's self, a self-presentation to other people, one's ways of being and of managing one's cultural habits, sexual desires, and emotional preferences). Yet even for those who live in big cities and who benefit from the freedom offered by gay subcultures and neighborhoods, more often than not it is necessary to hide their homosexuality in the workplace. For certain people in managerial positions, career advancement could be severely compromised were they to be open about it. And for laborers or employees, life could become unbearable. And then there are athletes, psychoanalysts, soldiers, politicians, and even academics . . .

❧ Two remarks need to be added to the preceding.

First, the obligation to secrecy and clandestinity has been (and continues to be) a place or a structure in which a certain number of gay men have taken (and continue to take) a certain kind of pleasure: the hidden life, secret meetings, clandestine social networks, all the delights of a kind of free-masonry . . . One can find regularly, in the words of gay men who lived a part of their sexual life before the 1960s and therefore before "liberation," a certain amount of regret at the passing of an era in which secrecy was required, at the passing of the games that one had ceaselessly to invent to pull the wool over people's eyes and to create the necessary complicities. It is the case that the closet was also a location of resistance against oppression, a way of living out one's homosexuality in times and places where openness was not possible. The closet has so often been denounced by gay activists as a symbol of shame, of submission to oppression, that we have forgotten or neglected the extent to which it was also, and at the same time, a space of freedom and a way—the only way—of resisting, of not submitting to norma-tive injunctions. And for many gays it is that still. In a certain sense, it was a way of being "proud" when everything pointed toward being ashamed—even if this pride was secret, intermittent, even transient. Perhaps it is this extraordinary sentiment of a hard-earned, constantly maintained, secret pride and freedom, one that was shared with a small group, that gay men from preceding generations find lacking in the openly asserted pride of today—a pride that perhaps seems to them too easy, too faded, having lost its flavor with the disappearance of the play with prohibition. This contempo-rary pride might seem to some coercive, an obligation imposed upon them as though being out of the closet were the only acceptable path for being truly gay today.

We should also mention here the recurring remarks by gay men from French literary circles to the effect that the repressive situation, the obliga-tion to be in the closet, allowed literature to flourish. It is doubtless the case that a good deal of the energy that sustained literary creation and gay literary expression came from the divided psychological configuration that gave rise to the opposition between the desire to speak of oneself and the obligation to be silent. Gide and Julien Green said this so frequently that we need not dwell on it here. But the idea that therefore today there can no longer be interesting literature (because it was the prohibition that fostered literary creation) seems to me ludicrous. It represents nothing but an interiorization of the kind of social homophobia that tolerates homosexuality in literature but not in the street, or else a kind of aesthetic elitism that arises out of a regret for those repressive times when literary types could claim for themselves, and could even imagine monopolizing, the audaciousness of transgression.

Second, we need to ask more precisely what a personal identity is, or even what it is that defines someone as homosexual. Let's come back to the case of the small-town schoolteacher frightened of someday seeing the two letters "PD" written on the blackboard. Obviously there is no need for him to have had sexual relations with another man in order to fear this symbolic violence. It suffices for him to know—or perhaps not to know or not to want to know—that he desires to do so. It is possible, as well, that all of his psychological characteristics (and perhaps even his physical ones: his mannerisms, his way of speaking, of walking, and so on) seem to manifest such a desire or such a personality.[8] To affirm that there are no "homosexual persons" but only "homosexual acts" amounts to leaving aside all those intensely lived individual experiences in which there is no necessity that any acts have been practiced in order for a certain identity to be constructed—sometimes unconsciously—around their very possibility, around the impulses that lead to them, around fantasies that have been nourished by images and models perceived since childhood, and even around the fear of being recognized as one of those people we know are likely to be called a "faggot." Similarly, such a fear might be found in someone who once had a gay sex life, yet no longer has any sexuality. In short: there is such a thing as a homosexual "person," and homosexual "acts" are only one of the elements that permit such a person to be defined.

All of this can be seen clearly in the polemics that have surrounded the presence of gays in the military in the United States. Military leaders, by declaring that gay people could serve in the military on the condition that they not say they are gay (for to do so would be to announce their intention to engage in homosexual sex acts), have put forth a definition of homosexuality that gives a considerable degree of importance to self-declaration. To say "I am gay" would mean "I intend to engage in homosexual sex acts." Thus, to say is to do. But it thereby becomes possible to "be" gay, as long as one does not say so and therefore does not create the expectation that one will be engaging in homosexual sex acts. That the potential act is determined by the statement implies that what is being refused is the possibility of the homosexual "act"—which would apparently imperil the military community. The homosexual "person" is not being refused, which admits that his simple presence is not prohibited by the demands of masculine life, as long as that "homosexual" does not declare himself openly and does not practice that very sexuality that one might have thought defined him as "homosexual." "Homosexual identity" would therefore be possible as long as sexuality itself is (at least fictively) unmentioned and excluded.

How striking that this same way of dissociating "homosexual persons" from "homosexual acts" can also be found in texts put out by the Vatican. On the one hand there are the "persons" who must be welcomed with pity as those who have been "wounded by life" (for it is not their "fault"); and on the other hand there are the "acts," which must be condemned as crimes against nature (for they have to do with individual responsibility and therefore might be avoided).

Without dwelling at greater length on the United States military or the Catholic hierarchy—astonishing and exemplary machines for the production of guilty consciences or neuroses as well as hypocrisy and repression—we might just insist that both institutions are in agreement that there exist "homosexual persons" and that their entire discourse is tied up in the acknowledgment of the existence of such persons. Otherwise, if it were simply a question of "acts," there would be no need for such convoluted argumentation. Acts could simply be forbidden. Yet no such interdiction would solve the problem of all those who, independently of such acts, perceive themselves as, and are perceived to be, "homosexual."

It is, in any case, perfectly clear that this is simply rhetoric aimed at legitimating the status quo: homosexuals engage in homosexual practices, but must do so in silence and secrecy. If they are caught, they must be thrown out of the military (or the church). And the real problem is not so much *being* homosexual as *saying* that one is. For if the possibility of saying so were officially allowed, then all the vulnerability and inferiority attached to being gay or lesbian, all the means of control wielded against them, would be invalidated. The control over homosexuality rests on this imposed silence and this forced simulation, as it does on the feelings of guilt and inferiority inevitably produced in individual psyches by the division between what one is and what one is allowed to do, between what one is and what one is allowed to say. Pierre Bourdieu forcefully reminds us that it is impossible to write a history of "masculine domination" without taking into account those institutions that work to perpetuate the established "sexual order."[9] Similarly, there is no sense in writing a history of homosexuality without studying all those agencies (the same ones, in fact, given that we are dealing with the same "order") that not only produce homophobic discourse, but also create "inferiorizing" representations of homosexuality and work to inscribe them in both minds and laws—the church and the army, of course, but also, in different registers, businesses and organizations linked to the workplace, lawyers, psychiatrists and psychoanalysts, conservative or traditional organizations linked to universities, "intellectual" journals, journalists, and so on.

᠉ So it is that the question of "telling" is so central to the experience of gays and lesbians. Must one reveal one's homosexuality, and when? To whom can one imagine telling this? It is first through meeting other gay people that the possibility of speaking presents itself, in the discovery of a context in which one can be what one is without hiding, even if only for a few hours a week, if only with a limited number of people. This is the function that bars, clubs, and organizations have always fulfilled. It is, however, much more difficult to speak to "others." Here again, studies done of gays and lesbians prove quite helpful. Almost all those who respond to requests for information (little, of course, can be known of those who do not respond, but we might imagine that those people speak of themselves even less) say that they have spoken of their sexual orientation or identity with a friend or with several friends, more rarely with their parents, and, when this is the case, more frequently with their mother than with their father. A much smaller percentage have ceased to conceal their identity in their workplace or in professional circles. (Often one colleague—rarely more than one—will be "in the know" but sworn to secrecy.)

In any case, one thing that characterizes a gay man is that he is a person who, one day or another, is confronted by a decision to tell or not to tell what he is. A heterosexual man will not need to do this, being presupposed by the world to be what he is. One's relation to this "secret" and to the different ways of managing it in differing situations is one of the characteristics of gay life. It is, of course, one of the things at stake in the struggle for visibility and affirmation being conducted today, the struggle to show that homosexuality exists and thereby to interrupt the process by which the self-evidence of heteronormativity is reproduced. This will certainly not alter the fact that a gay man will always, at one moment or another in his life, have to tell or at least let it be known what he is. But perhaps that act can be made easier and that *telling* less painful.[10]

Let us go even a bit further. The gay man who is obliged (or who chooses) to attempt to hide what he is can never be sure that the person from whom he is hiding this "secret" does not know it anyway, or at least suspect it, while pretending to know nothing.[11] We can turn to Proust again here, in particular to the pages in which the members of the Verdurin circle quietly make fun of Charlus after one of them has revealed his homosexuality, while he remains persuaded, to cite his own expression, that no one is "in the know [fixé sur son compte]" (*RTP*, 2:1076). For example, during a train ride, the doctor Cottard says to the sculptor Ski (who was the first, during a dinner party, to make an allusion to Charlus's "vice"): "You see, if I was on my own, a bachelor . . . but because of my wife I wonder whether I ought to allow him to travel with us after what you told me" (*RTP*, 2:1071 and, in general, 1070–77). Mme Verdurin herself casts many more or less explicit aspersions: "You must know far better than I do, M. de Charlus, how to get round young sailors," she says to him when she asks him to organize a charity event in which the sailors of Balbec-Plage are to participate. On offering him a certain book, she makes this commentary: "Look, here's a book that has just come which I think you'll find interesting. . . . The title is attractive: *Among Men*" (*RTP*, 2:1079). Thus is it possible for the baron to believe that his "vice" is perfectly hidden while in fact his "secret" is known by everyone and leaves him open to sarcastic and cruel remarks that he is unable to perceive as such and to which he is unable to reply, remaining under the illusion that he is protected by his own discretion. It is an "open secret," to use Eve Kosofsky Sedgwick's expression, that well reveals how *Remembrance of Things Past* is structured by the "spectacle of the closet," that is to say, the public gaze into an interior that is supposed to be unknown to all who are outside of it.[12]

A gay man is thus placed in a situation of inferiority because he can be the object of the discourse of others, who can toy with him and draw profit from the privilege they gain not only from what they know, but also from the knowledge that the person in question believes they know nothing and fears precisely that they may find out what in fact they already know.

When, on the other hand, a gay man insists on affirming what he is, a heterosexual person, who is never obliged to say what he or she is, still has a certain privilege—the ability to claim that he or she does not want to know, is not interested, cannot see why it is necessary to say anything, and so on. This is what Eve Kosofsky Sedgwick calls the "privilege of unknowing," the faculty not of being ignorant but of not wanting to know, of acting as if there was nothing to be known. Doubtless this is because when a gay person claims to be gay, a heterosexual person is obliged to think of him or herself as heterosexual, whereas previously there would have been no need to ask oneself any questions about one's identity or the social order that enables it. That is a state of absolute privilege. Thus arises the indignation when a loss, even a partial one, of that privilege is threatened. And thus arises the demand that gays recover their "discretion," a discretion that would allow the reassertion of peaceful certitudes, of the comfort of a normalcy built on the silence of others. Or perhaps heterosexuals consider such gay people to be badly behaved, excessive, flagrant, overly provocative. Gay people should be only the objects of discourse, and they become unbearable as soon as they assert their right to be subjects. Proust conveys this quite well when he writes that the faithful members of the Verdurin circle "who so longed to hear the avowals he would always evade," would doubtless not have accepted, were he to have become more loquacious, that he then speak in his own right. They "would in fact have been unable to endure any real display of his mania; ill at ease, breathing with difficulty as one does in a sick-room or in the presence of a morphine addict who takes out his syringe in public, they would themselves have put a stop to the confidences which they imagined they desired" (RTP, 3:814).

It is an insurmountable paradox: the gay man who decides to speak openly leaves himself open to ironic remarks or condescension, or sometimes to rebuffs, whereas the gay man who prefers to remain silent finds himself in an uncomfortable, impossible situation. The former gets lectured; the latter is made fun of. The heterosexual is privileged over the homosexual; this dissymmetry is always in play. The heterosexual decides what kind of attitude to adopt, what kind of meaning to give to a gay man's words and gestures. The heterosexual will always have a point of view on what gay men should or should not do, should or should not be, should or should not say. The heterosexual will understand more about homosexuality than the gay man, will always have an explanation (more often than not a psychological or a psychoanalytic one) to give, and will always be ready to dismiss scornfully anything a gay man might say of himself. The heterosexual is in an "epistemologically" dominant position, having control over the conditions of production, circulation, and interpretation of anything that might be said about this or that gay person, about gay people in general—having control, as well, over the conditions of reinterpretation and resignification of anything gay men and lesbians might say about themselves, ready to deny it, devalue it, subject it to ridicule, or simply reduce it to the state of an object within the categories of dominant discourse.

8

Heterosexual Interpellation

Thus do gay people live in a world of insults. They are surrounded by a language that hems them in and points them out. The world insults them; it speaks of them and of what is said about them. The words of day-to-day life as well as of psychiatric, political, and juridical discourse assign each of them individually and all of them collectively to an inferior place within the social order. And yet this very language preceded them: the world of insults preexisted them, and it takes hold of them even before they know what they are.

At the outset of the book she devoted to hate speech, Judith Butler considers the question as to whether a given individual's social being is not fundamentally dependent upon being the object of someone else's speech— even before that speech is expressed. One does not exist because one is "recognized," but because one is "recognizable." An address is, in its possibility, prior to any specific actualization. Butler writes: "If we are formed in language, then that formative power precedes and conditions any decision we might make about it, insulting us from the start, as it were, by its prior power."[1] Insult, as we usually understand it, would then only be a particular case of this constitutive and "insultive" power of language.

Butler thus confers on language the role that Louis Althusser, in elaborating the notion of "interpellation," gave to "ideology." For Althusser writes, in a famous article devoted to "ideological state apparatuses," that "ideology interpellates individuals as subjects." To elucidate this idea of interpellation, Althusser makes recourse to what he calls a "little theoretical theatre," imagining a scene in which a police agent yells to someone: "Hey, you there!" Althusser continues: "Assuming that the theoretical scene I have imagined takes place in the street, the hailed individual will turn round. By this mere one-hundred-and-eighty-degree physical conversion, he becomes a *subject*.

Why? Because he has recognized that the hail was 'really' addressed to him, and that 'it was *really* him who was hailed' (and not someone else). Experience shows that the practical telecommunication of hailings is such that they hardly ever miss their man."[2]

Althusser in fact specifies that in the real functioning of ideology there is no temporal succession (first the interpellation, followed by the fact of self-recognition as the person interpellated): "The existence of ideology and the hailing or interpellation of individuals as subjects are one and the same thing" (175). Consequently, given that ideology precedes the birth of the very individuals it interpellates, Althusser can claim that "ideology has always-already interpellated individuals as subjects" and that individuals, even before being born and therefore from the very moment of birth, are "always-already" subjects constituted by the ideology that shapes the world into which they come (175).

We may well want to leave behind this rather massive notion of "ideology," which, however suggestive, surely does not account for the diversity of processes that are at work. There is no *one* ideology, and it would doubtless be preferable to speak (as does Bourdieu, basing his remarks on his ethnological work in Kabylia) of cognitive structures, or, more exactly, of schemas of perception. We could then investigate the rather miraculous concordance of individual cognitive structures with social cognitive structures and with social structures themselves—that is to say, the construction of an individual unconscious or *habitus* in its adaptation to the surrounding world, the incorporation within a given brain (through the very process of being in the world) of a collective history and of the social and sexual structures that are the product of that history. We could investigate the very processes by which such a concordance is created.[3] But Althusser's idea that the "subject" (a subjectivity) is "subjected" by the "interpellation" that ideology (or language, according to Judith Butler) throws its way seems particularly useful and pertinent in the context of a reflection on insult and on the social forces carried by insulting words. For certainly insult is one of the most remarkable (or most concrete) forms of what Althusser has (abstractly and metaphorically) designated as "interpellation." He recalls, in fact, that the word "subject" has two meanings. It is at one and the same time "a free subjectivity, a center of initiatives, author of and responsible for its actions," and "a subjected being, who submits to a higher authority, and is therefore stripped of all freedom except that of freely accepting his submission." Thus he is able to say that "the individual is interpellated as a (free) subject in order that he shall submit freely to the commandments of the Subject, i.e. in order that he shall (freely) accept his subjection. . . ." There is thus no subject except in a fundamental relation to subjectivation. This is why Althusser can assert that subjects "work all by themselves [marchent tout seuls]."[4]

We should note that Althusser is here first and foremost speaking of the division of labor between classes and of the role given to individuals in that division by ideology—as if they were naturally assigned to their place, attaching them to the social function to which they have been designated. Yet clearly these remarks can be transposed to other social realities, such as sexual divisions and hierarchies between the sexes and between sexualities. This analysis can thus provide a theoretical framework for understanding the efficaciousness of insult: it—just like the interpellation by the police agent—fulfills the function of an injunction that assigns someone a place in a sexualized social space. But in the real working of language and of social life there is no temporal succession (I am insulted, and thereafter I recognize myself as the person at whom the insult was aimed). The insult preexisted me. It was there before I was, and it has *always-already* (as Althusser puts it so well) subjugated me to the social and sexual order that it simply expresses and recalls. If subjects "work all by themselves," that is, if people seem to accept the roles given to them in the division of the sexes and of sexualities, just as in the division of classes, it is not because insult has been granted some police-like power to imprison me in some devalued place. Similarly, the police are not required to guarantee that laborers turn up each morning to be exploited at the workplace. Insult and its effects are only the most visible components of a deeper interpellation that has already, indeed always-already, been performed upon me by social, mental, and sexual structures. Insult and what it produces within me are two faces of the same phenomenon, the same reality, of what we might call the social and sexual order. Insult sets loose within me a spring whose tension had been built up by the processes of socialization, the very processes that guarantee that an insult means something to me. Insult sets loose the built-up tension in the spring, and it rebounds upon me in its violence.

The social and sexual order that language carries within it, and of which insult is one of the most pointed symptoms, produces the subject simultaneously as subjectivity and as subjection-subjectivation—that is to say, as a person adapted to all of the socially instituted rules and hierarchies. Gay subjectivity is thus an "inferiorized" subjectivity, not only because of the inferior social position in which gay people find themselves in society, but also because that very society produces those subjects: it is not a question of, on the one hand, a preexisting subjectivity, and, on the other, a social imprint that comes along later to deform it. The subjectivity and the social imprint are one and the same: the individual "subject" is produced by the interpellation, that is to say, by the cognitive (and therefore social) structures of which it is the vector.

Thus "homosexuality" does not simply designate a class of individuals defined by sexual preferences and practices. It is also a set of processes of "subjection," processes as much collective as individual to the extent that there is a common structure of inferiorization at work, and it is all the stronger to the extent that it is the same for all, and yet at the same time specific to each individual—who might even at moments in his or her life believe that he or she is the sole victim.

The "homosexual" subject thus always has a singular history, yet this history is itself always in relation to a collective history constituted by other "subjects" being subjugated by way of the same process of "inferiorization." A homosexual is never simply an isolated individual, even when he or she believes himself or herself to be alone in the world or when, having understood that not to be the case, he or she attempts to dissociate himself or herself from all the others precisely to evade the difficult recognition of belonging to this stigmatized "collective." For it is only by way of becoming critically and reflectively conscious of one's belonging to such a group that one can, to whatever extent it may be possible, liberate oneself from it. The "collective" exists independently of any individual's consciousness of it and independently of any individual will. Only by accepting and assuming this belonging can an individual come to constitute himself or herself as the "subject" of his or her own history.

⊮ If every homosexual is subjected-subjugated by way of identical processes that operate with reference to the same social and sexual norms and that produce the same effects in minds and in bodies, and if, as a consequence, a gay man is always-already inscribed in a collective that includes him even before he belongs to it or knows or wants to belong to it, then clearly every gay gesture, every kind of participation—even the most reticent or distant or secretive—in gay life will place any gay men into relation with all the others, with the entire history of homosexuality and its struggles. No sooner does he walk into a bar, cruise in a park or some other meeting place, or visit a gay social space, no sooner does he open a book that evokes kinds of experience or feelings in which he can recognize himself to some extent (and certainly it is often for that very reason that he chooses to read this book or that: how else are we to understand why gay men who never read literature still sometimes read Proust or Wilde?), than he finds himself linked to all the others in his same moment who make the same kinds of gestures. But he also finds himself linked to all those who, in the past, created those spaces, visited them before him, to all those tenacious individualities and collectivities that imposed them and maintained them in the face of oppression, to all the effort and all the courage that was necessary so that gay literature and gay thought might exist.[5]

Walking through London at the beginning of the 1980s, Neil Bartlett gazes at all the nineteenth-century facades and thinks of all the men who walked these same streets before him. He notices that the city has a history, that that history is his own: what he is today, others have invented for him.[6] Nicole Brossard says much the same thing about lesbian experience when, in her poem, "My Continent," she evokes the manner in which she associates herself with all those women who have written before her: "My manifold continent of those who have signed themselves: Djuna Barnes, Jane Bowles, Gertrude Stein, Natalie Barney, Michèle Causse, Marie-Claire Blais, Jovette Marchessault, Mary Daly, Adrienne Rich, Colette and Virginia, other drowned women. . . ."[7]

Consciously or unconsciously, willed or unwilled, accepted or not, gay subjectivity is haunted by a world and a past of which it is perhaps unaware (but never totally so, except in childhood), yet which provides the basis for a collective belonging that today's visibility only brings into the light of day. It brings this world and this past into the light of day by affirming it, remaking it, reformulating it, organizing it, and also by defending it against all the efforts to erase it, efforts that struggle to recreate older situations—ones in which it would nonetheless be incorrect to believe that this "collective" did not exist. It was simply less visible and, perhaps, less conscious of itself as a "collective." (Although even that is not absolutely certain.)

❧ If all that has been said so far about the way insult defines the relation of a certain group of individuals to the world is indeed correct, this is evidently because there is a general validity to this structured relation to language.

(Judith Butler emphasizes this point.) Language is "already there" for every-one, and it imposes on everyone and on every group the cognitive structures and perceptual schemas that it carries with it, just as it imposes the subjuga-tion to those schemas and structures and to the psychological identities that they help to determine and reproduce. Language is already there when I arrive in the world, as are the social roles that words—and, in particular, insults—designate. As Sartre puts it so well, and here he is remarkably close to Althusser (or the other way around), "processes" [techniques] and "roles" take hold of us from childhood onward. "When the young Gustave Flaubert emerges from his childhood years," Sartre says at the outset of The Family Idiot, "processes lie waiting for him. As do roles to be played."[8] We do not create the world into which we arrive. In it we find gestures to be made, social roles, beliefs, professions, mental habits, and so on. They are all there before we are. Among all the materiality that we find, there is language: a language that carries with it representations, social and racial hierarchies, forms of "character" and "identity" made by history and preexisting any individual. Within language we find insults which mark out, make known, and reinforce the hierarchy between various "identities." All the "processes" and the "roles" of which Sartre speaks are clearly hierarchized—socially, culturally, racially. The world is "insulting" because it is structured accord-ing to hierarchies that carry with them the possibility of insult. One can see this exemplified in the film by the videographer Marlon T. Riggs, Tongues Untied, in which he narrates the itinerary that led him to assume his identity as both gay and black. In his case, the "formative" insults of his personal identity designate two relationships of belonging to two stigmatized groups: the black adolescent subject to insults from white people who call him "nigger" and the gay adolescent subject to the insults from both black and white people who call him "faggot."[9]

It is more or less certain that the majority of gay people will have heard homophobic insults spoken before they ever enter into sexuality themselves, before they could have been the target of those insults, before reaching the age at which one might know oneself to be a potential target. This, we should note, distinguishes sexual insults from racist insults. The latter, when, for example, they deal with skin color, are directed at a visible "stigma," whereas the former are directed at a "stigma" that is not given, or at least not actu-alized, from the moment of birth and that can therefore be disguised. It is possible to hide the fact of being gay, and in all moments of ferocious repression of "sexual deviance" many such people have managed to escape persecution by hiding or even obliterating their "homosexual being." More simply, and more commonly, marriages of "convenience" have been for many gay people a means of evading suspicion and stigmatization. In contrast, it is much more difficult to hide the fact that one is black. More tellingly, at the age of ten or even fifteen, one may not know that one is (or will be) gay, but at the age of ten one knows that one is black. From earliest childhood one has the experience of the meanings that takes on in Western societies, from which racism is rarely absent. Yet, however fundamental this distinction is, it is not absolute. For a black youth might not know that he or she is black before being confronted with the violence of racial prejudice.[10] But also, inversely, for many gay people (at least for those who are gay from their youth) there is a correlation between their apprenticeship in the use of insults and the confused awareness that they themselves are that which is in question in the insulting word. A child can know at ten—without knowing it completely, but knowing something of it in any case—that the word "faggot" just about designates him and will do so entirely one day. (From this comes the discomfort, or even the horror, of having to understand one's situation more and more clearly as the years go by and of having to understand that others know this as well.)

There are other differences that can be mentioned. A black youth will most likely live in a black family, and thus, to the extent that he or she is subjected to racism, will likely be supported by his or her family through that experience. A gay youth is rather unlikely to live in a gay or lesbian family, and the insult and stigmatization found in the exterior world are likely to be found in the family as well. Such young people will frequently be obliged to disguise themselves from their "own" as well as from "others," and the kind of "racism" they are subjected to is as inherent in family life as in the outside world. In a famous passage Proust speaks of "a race upon which a curse is laid and which must live in falsehood and perjury because it knows that its desire, that which constitutes life's dearest pleasure, is held to be punishable, shameful, an inadmissible thing . . . sons without a mother, to whom they are obliged to lie all her life long and even in the hour when they close her dying eyes" (*RTP*, 2:637). This creates a practice of silence and dissimulation in gay youths and perhaps produces those peculiar psychological characteristics by which gay people have been identified in literature and in film (deceitful, mendacious, traitorous)—characteristics that, of course, refer back to the homophobic image of homosexuality, yet also to certain realities that there is no point in denying, ones produced by homophobia and by the self-dissimulation it necessitates. In any case, gay and lesbian childhoods have a strong connection to secrecy, and this will inevitably have profound and lasting effect on personalities.[11]

9

The Subjected "Soul"

At the same time that someone is learning how to look at the world, learning how to occupy a place in that world, how to relate to others, it also happens that—in the deepest mental structures of that person—the fact is recorded that there are insults used to designate certain people. These people are presupposed to have certain characteristics in common (in this case, certain sexual practices and a certain psychological identity), whether those characteristics be real or imaginary, natural or produced out of a shared history. All this training is almost consubstantial with training in language. One learns early on that there are people who can be called "faggot" or "dyke," and one of the most formidable and effective aspects of this insult is the way it operates as a kind of censorship, the formulation of a prohibition addressed to everyone in the way that it decrees, guarantees, and reinforces the heterosexual norm, barring access to that which is stigmatized by language. Of course, this prohibition's effect is more deeply imprinted on those who, in some confused way, know from their earliest years that they are one of these "abnormal" beings designated by such words of hatred. We should add that it is not the case that everyone who will become homosexual is privy to this confused knowledge about themselves. To the contrary, insult itself prevents a good number of individuals from gaining access to this information about themselves, to this consciousness of themselves; it "slows down" their life in the dimension of the sexuality that will later be their own.[1]

Of course, the insult "faggot" is not exclusively directed at those who are suspected of being one. It has a sort of universal applicability. Anyone of the male sex, of any age, can be subjected to this insult at any time—on a school playground or in a traffic jam, for instance. Bourdieu has quite accurately remarked that the expression "faggot" often refers to nothing more than the perception by the popular classes of bourgeois ways of speech or bodily habits that are thought of as too refined and therefore not virile. In this context, the insult would have no necessarily sexual connotation in the strict sense of the term, given that it does not necessarily attribute to the person being addressed a particular sexual orientation.[2] Still, even here the insult makes clear reference to an implicit hierarchy—one experienced as if self-evident—between what is perceived as masculine and what is perceived as feminine. Moreover, the insult here also links (in the case of men, of course) masculinity to heterosexuality and femininity to homosexuality. Thus even in this case one cannot finally assume that the insult is entirely free from sexual signification, for this is the very hierarchy on which is based not only the social "inferiority" of women but also the stigmatization of homosexuals.

In any case, whatever the motivation of the person wielding the insult, it undeniably functions as a call to order, sexually speaking. Even if the person at whom the insult is being directed is not homosexual, the insult makes clear not only that being homosexual is worthy of condemnation, but that everyone considers it shameful even to be accused of being so.[3]

⊁ To the extent that insult defines the horizon of one's relation to the world, it produces a fateful feeling in a child or an adolescent who feels himself or herself to be contravening the world's order as well as a lasting and even permanent feeling of insecurity, anxiety, and even terror and panic. Numerous studies have shown that the rate of suicides or attempted suicides among gay youth is considerably higher than among young heterosexuals.[4] It is the terror faced with one's impossible fate that all gay people (I mean those who feel themselves to be such from their youth, those who discover themselves to be so much later, or those who fight against themselves in order not to know or admit that they are so) must overcome at some moment of their lives if they want, once they have decided no longer to resign themselves—as so many do—to hiding what they are, to be able to live out a life that would include what they are. To choose to be what you are can attenuate or annul the weight of "deviance" that is lived as a personal drama. The recomposition of one's own subjectivity, inscribing oneself in "practices of friendship" and of visibility, are all factors that can help to efface the heavy sense of fate.

An entire gay cultural tradition has fostered the belief that visibility would encourage hostile attention and even further oppression. This tradition, handed down from periods when social repression was much more intense, is still lively today. It can be found in the appeals of certain gay people for a kind of "assimilation" that could be taken as a form of "discretion," which is more often than not merely another way of advocating dissimulation, here envisioned as the simplest way to avoid the forces of alienation and the violence of stigmatization. Yet it seems quite obvious that oppression can take a much more intense hold on what remains invisible or secret, especially to the extent that oppression is understood as an interiorization of domination in the mind of the dominated that guarantees submission to the sexual order and its hierarchies.

This is perfectly clear in the case of insults: for their stigmatizing effects to work it is not necessary that the stigmatized characteristic be apparent for all to see. Stigmatization works even before I become its direct victim. A given individual does not need to be actually "discredited" if he is already "discreditable." The very fact of being "discreditable" (and of knowing that one is, and of fearing being "discredited") acts on individuals both consciously and unconsciously as a subjectivizing force, a force of interiorized domination, all the more effective given the fear of being discovered and the self-censoring necessary in order to avoid being so.[5] "Visibility" does not, of course, disable oppression, and it is not capable of thwarting the subjugating processes of surveillance, of policing, of the norm, for it cannot in and of itself cause insult or the social dissymmetry of which it is the symptom to disappear. But, despite appearances, insult does not have a more violent effect on someone who is "visible" than on someone who is not, even if someone who is identifiably gay may more frequently be directly insulted than someone who keeps his or her sexuality hidden. For visibility, insofar as it is a manner of assuming and laying claim to an identity that has been stigmatized by insult, partially defuses the charge of social violence that insult carries. It offers no foothold to insult; on the contrary, it is perhaps a reflective surface that wards off insult and destroys, even if only partially, its terrible effectiveness.

In insult, it is one's inner sanctum that is threatened, one's heart of hearts, what the spiritual tradition calls the "soul." If a well-targeted insult provokes such a strong echo in the consciousness of the person at whom it is directed, it is because this "soul" has been created through socialization in a world of insult and inferiorization. One could even say that the soul is nothing other than the effect of this socialization. As Foucault put it, the "soul" is the "prison of the body" and it is of no use to dissimulate one's bodily gestures from the inquiring gaze of a homophobic society in an effort to protect the soul from subjectivation. For the soul is not simply the *object*, the target, of a training process, it is also, and primarily, the *effect* of that process. And so it remains its tool.[6]

It is therefore this "soul" that must be reinvented, refashioned. Certainly no such process can take place under the sign of "discretion," for the obligation or the will to discretion, to hide oneself, are nothing but the products of the subjected soul, inferiorized and conscious of its inferiorization. I am, of course, aware that the majority of gay people hardly have a choice in this matter. They are required to disguise themselves in their hometown or at work; they must lie to their family and friends (to their parents certainly, but sometimes also, for gay men who married before knowing what they were or before assuming their identity, to their wives, or to their husbands for certain lesbians, and sometimes to their children). But the discourse that would transform this obligation to dissimulate and this real alienation into a political choice, the discourse that has as its corollary the denunciation of any and all manifestations of collective visibility, merely ratifies such situations and helps perpetuate them instead of contesting the social order that sets them up.

▸▸ The result of the inculcation of structures of domination into the minds of the dominated is that an insult can even be used by those at whom it will later be directed—or who already know that they are potential or even real targets. What "faggot" has not one day or another called someone exactly that, or referred in passing to someone as "that faggot," perhaps during his childhood, his adolescence, or even much later? This is simply because we are as much spoken by language as we are speakers of it and also most certainly because making such an accusation, assigning that stigma to someone else, is a way—certainly an illusory one—of guarding against it for oneself. Self-hatred, interiorized homophobia—these are clearly among the strongest effects of the structural relation to the world that is created by the preexistence of insult.

But self-hatred is not merely an unhappy relation to oneself, one which forces a person into a double life filled with the fear of discovery. It also leads to behaviors based on hatred and hostility toward those others in whom one sees, and wishes to refuse the sight of, an image of oneself. Here we could think of the remarks Proust makes about "Sodomites" who "are so readily admitted into the most exclusive clubs that, whenever a Sodomite fails to secure election, the black balls are for the most part cast by other Sodomites, who make a point of condemning sodomy, having inherited the mendacity that enabled their ancestors to escape from the accursed city" (*RTP*, 2:655). Or one could think of the story told by Christopher Isherwood of his failed attempt in 1934 to bring his German companion Heinz (who wanted to flee from the growth of Nazism in his country) to England, passing him off as an employee of his mother. The immigration agent, after making a perfidious comment about the true nature of the relation between Isherwood and his lover, a relation the agent had had no trouble understanding, refused Heinz entry onto British soil. Here is what W. H. Auden, who was with Isherwood, had to say about the painful scene: "As soon as I saw that bright-eyed little rat, I knew we were done for. He understood the whole situation at a glance—because he's *one of us*."[7] Precisely because he is himself homosexual the agent understands the situation, and precisely because he is homosexual he refuses to admit the young German man to Britain, in a characteristic demonstration of hatred of oneself in another and the desire to disassociate oneself from that other.

I have always read this episode from Isherwood's wonderful book as a kind of parable, and every time I hear or read of a gay man who, in order to prove his conformist credentials and his submission to the heteronormative order, denounces the very existence of a gay movement, I cannot avoid thinking of the expression Auden uses in order to make clear his disgust when faced with that British immigration official.

So many other examples could be provided of this hatred of gays by other gays, and there is no point in recalling that depressing list one more time here. Let it suffice to mention the two menacing figures of Roy Cohn, advisor to Senator McCarthy, who led the witch hunt against gay men in the early 1950s (and who died of AIDS thirty years later), and of J. Edgar Hoover, longstanding director of the FBI, who relentlessly kept track of the homosexuality of various politicians the better to control them, yet who we now know himself lived with a man and on occasion dressed in drag to welcome guests to dinner parties he gave at his home.

Such a characteristic is not specific to gays. Self-hatred and the concomitant hatred of others who are like you have been the subject of many studies. Kurt Lewin has provided a great deal of surprising material in his study of Jewish antisemitism.[8] It seems to be a question of a will to wipe out that which one is. We could include here the desire of many gay men to become heterosexual—and some make an enormous effort in this direction (marrying, undergoing a psychoanalytic "cure"). In any case, there are many who regret or deplore as a kind of curse the fact of being gay. Generations of gay men have been obsessed by the idea that they would need to change in order to be happy or simply to be able to live. Lionel Ovesey and Abram Kardiner, in their classic work on African Americans, have shown how the "mark of oppression" is inscribed in the conscious and unconscious minds of the oppressed not only as a difficulty in living out what one is, but also as a radical rejection—one that can take many forms—of what one is. They report, for example, that blacks in their dreams imagine that they or their children have become white.[9] And clearly the fantasy or the illusion that it is possible to "change" is all the more likely to be more widespread among gays than among blacks. It is thus perfectly comprehensible why political movements that take up the task of struggling against these forms of oppression—and their interiorizations—choose as slogans "Black is beautiful" and "Gay is good."

▸▸ Insult and its effects are not simply limited to defining an exterior horizon. Insult creates an interior space of contradiction in which are found all the difficulties a gay person will meet before being able to assume his or her identity, before being able to accept being identified with or identifying with other gay people. It is this identification which is first rejected; but then it must, as a place from which to start, be constructed or at least accepted— even if later its importance or its signification may lessen.

10

Caricature and Collective Insult

Insult is intensified and reinforced through images and caricature. Throughout the ages, homosexuality has given rise to a proliferation of devalorizing and degrading images, especially caricatures (but also images from film or television, which often simply provide in different ways images close to those from the tradition of caricature).[1] Caricature is, of course, closely related to insult, as Ernst Kris and Ernst Gombrich, inspired by the Freudian analysis of jokes, have noted.

Freud defines a joke as a sort of outlet for hostile impulses, an "allusion" to an unspoken insult that forms the background of the joke.[2] Kris and Gombrich interpret "caricature" as the equivalent of such a mechanism in the visual realm. It is a veritable form of symbolic aggression; it enacts violence, and places itself, according to Kris and Gombrich, in the lineage of the "defamatory images" of the Middle Ages.[3] Homophobic caricature (like antisemitic caricature) is a "defamation"; it "alludes" to insult; it places itself within the horizon of insult and draws upon the mental schemas that produce laughter at the sight of gay people. It expresses the inferiority assigned to homosexuality within society and perpetuates the mental structures that ground that inferiority. It "alludes" to the immemorial condemnation of homosexuality and is thereby an acknowledgment of all the social, cultural, political, and juridical violence of which gay people are the object. But it is not directed merely at a given individual, who is made fun of personally (the joke often relying on a representation of that person as effeminate). It claims to reveal the objective "truth" about an entire group by way of a magnifying glass offered to the reader or the spectator by the humorous image.[4]

Caricature always offers a "group portrait." It is the portrait of a collective, of a "species" defined by a set of traits that anyone can immediately recognize. A drawing of an effeminate man "represents" male homosexuals—all of them—even when one knows this has no basis in reality. It is rather striking to remark, for example, among all the caricatures and derogatory images that flourished at the moment of the Eulenburg affair in Germany, how much of the humor relied on decking out soldiers with handbags and lace handkerchiefs, as if to heighten the contrast between the assumed masculinity of the soldier and the supposed effeminacy of the homosexual.[5]

There is a certain historical invariability to this theme, as if the homophobic image always draws on some common and ancient set of representations and insults. At the beginning of the nineteenth century Cambacérès was a favorite target for caricaturists. He can be found, for instance, represented turning his back to three women, which signifies that he takes no part in reproduction from generation to generation, and that he therefore embodies the death of society. Yet he is also without fail accompanied by a turkey that has in its anus the finger of a hand that would seem to be an appendage of its body. The lesson of these images is blindingly clear: Cambacérès is a Sodomite who is leading society to its ruin.[6] When Foucault, in an article published in the newspaper Libération in June 1982, critiques the idea that one could think of homosexuality as an "anthropological constant" and emphasizes that there is no permanence across time in what is designated by the term, he mentions Cambacérès in a list of those who should not be lumped into this category, one which had not yet been constituted in the period in which he lived.[7] I will come back to Foucault's article in the third part of this book. Here I will only claim that a certain invariance does exist, even an astonishing stability, in homophobic discourse, whether it be caricature used as a defamatory image or insult used as a vehicle for the derogatory representation of those who have relations with persons of the same sex.[8] As Barry D. Adam comments, a gay man finds himself confronted with a "composite portrait" of himself, proposed by a set of images, representations, and discourses, all providing him with a degrading or inferiorizing image of himself. Not only are the inferior categories presented without fail as ridiculous or devalorized, the particular people categorized in them are always brought back by dominant or "legitimate" discourses to a set of general attributes and "discrediting" associations with crime, immorality, mental illness, and so on.[9] The inferiorized individual is thus refused the status of an autonomous person, for the dominant representation of the individual is always as an example of a particular species (one that should be condemned, one that is always to some degree monstrous or ridiculous).

So it is that insult is both personal and collective. It aims at a particular individual by associating that individual with a group, a species, a race; and at the same time it targets a whole class of individuals by aiming at a particular member of the class. Insult works by way of generalization rather than by particularization. It globalizes more than it singularizes.[10] It works by attributing to a category (treated as a whole or treated through the example of one individual) a group of characteristics that are conceived of as derogatory and that are considered applicable to each and every member of that category. Thus an insult can reach a person who is not its direct target, for in fact that person is *also* targeted.[11]

This is why the effects of insult ceaselessly perpetuate and reproduce themselves, along with the wounds they provoke, and along with the submissions and the revolts that follow (sometimes both at the same time within the same person). But this is also why individuals who belong to a given stigmatized category do everything they can to dissociate themselves from the "group" that insult constitutes. Even though they unavoidably belong to a "collective," constituted as such through the effects of insult (which is to say through the entire process of subjectivization and the constitution of personal identities), the members of the said "collective" work hard to escape from it in order to be able to see others in that group through the eyes of those doing the insulting or the mocking. The gay man who wishes to hide that he is a "faggot," or the gay man who is known as such but wishes to gain his credentials of normalcy, will laugh along with those making tasteless or rude jokes about "fairies." Perhaps he will delude himself into believing that he is spared the insult if he speaks it himself, or if he laughs along with the others who speak it; perhaps he believes that the others will perceive him differently than those at whom they are laughing. (Imagine all the effort that will go into one's clothing, one's speech, one's gestures in order to persuade oneself and others of one's conformity to normalcy.) That effort notwithstanding, insult will still be directed at such people—even should they take it upon themselves to insult others—simply because insult is speaking of them too. They are constituted by it. That is its social function. Given that the principle of insult is to globalize, to do away with the singularities of any individual, its constitutive power will have outwitted in advance, and will forever outwit, all individual strategies aimed at dissociating oneself from the group that insult addresses collectively. *Volens, nolens*, you will belong to it, however hard you try not to. When he laughs at other gay men, a gay man laughs at himself. And those with whom he laughs at the "fairies" and the "silly queens" will laugh at him as soon as he turns his back. ("We all know," Truman Capote is reported to have said, "that a fag is a homosexual gentleman who just left the room.") Yet this internalized shame, the will to dissociate from the group, to demonstrate that one does not belong among those laughable folk who become the object of insult— these forces are so strong that for a long time they blocked any chance of establishing even a minimal degree of "solidarity" among the stigmatized. "Shame isolates," writes Sartre, speaking precisely about the absence of "solidarity" and "reciprocity" among those whom he refers to, in the vocabulary of the 1950s, as "pederasts" (a word synonymous at that moment with male homosexuality).[12]

To summarize: because it is always collective in nature, because it writes an individual into a group, one of the effects of insult is that it encourages the individuals in question—or those who wish to avoid being brought into question—to find any means to separate themselves from the "species" to which the social and sexual order would have them assigned. Precisely because it collectivizes, insult encourages individualism.

The power of insult and stigmatization is so great that it brings an individual to the point of doing almost anything to avoid being included in the group being designated and constituted by insult. It thus becomes possible to understand why, as a result, only the decision to accept oneself as a member of that targeted "collective," and only the minimal solidarity found as a gay man with other gay men and with lesbians can serve as a point of departure for an effective resistance to insult and to the process of stigmatization socially performed on gay people. Such a struggle has to do not only with political mobilization or with the creation of a culture. It is also a self-transformation and a change in the world, experienced in each gesture one makes, each word one says, in order to free oneself as much as possible from the weight of interiorized homophobia. It is the accumulation of all of these tiny moves, microscopic actions that begin to take the place of, or at least begin to counteract, the ongoing accumulation of small acts of cowardice, microscopic acts of resignation or renunciation, innumerable silences, which, in their totality, make up the lived reality of domination. Yet such a process could never be brought into existence by an individual will unless that will were supported by the awareness that it was acting as part of a collective enterprise—one of self-reconstruction—in which people as group recover their status as autonomous and free individuals. This is why collective visibility is so important. And this is why, on the other hand, all those who work to perpetuate the current sexual order find it necessary to condemn this visibility.

To recover one's personal autonomy and become a full individual implies in the first place the reconstruction of a collective image so that it offers different models. It may be by challenging or bypassing those "portraits" made available by the spokespersons of social and sexual norms or by relieving those portraits of their derogatory force (effeminacy only being ridiculous because of the effects of a decree that can be overturned, even if such a rejection of the norm might only be sustainable within the confines of a counterculture). This is why individual autonomy and individual freedom can only be won and built up through collective battles, battles that must be ongoing.

>> Day-to-day language (like the language of images) is everywhere traversed by power relations as by social relations (of class, sex, age, race, and so on), and it is by and through language (and images) that symbolic domination works, by means of the definition—and the imposition—of socially legitimate ways of perceiving and representing the world. Dominance, as Pierre Bourdieu puts it, belongs to the person who imposes a way of being seen. A person is dominated who is defined, thought, and spoken of by someone else's language and/or who is unable to impose his or her own self-perception.[13] Only through periods of social or cultural crisis or by way of the emergence of political or cultural organization can the symbolic order be brought into question. The linguistic representations tied to that symbolic order find their principle power in their claim to arise from some unchanging natural order. Sometimes people sympathetic to that order pretend to analyze it in order to be able to reaffirm it in all its arbitrariness, presenting it as if it has always existed.[14]

Political organizing and political action are always struggles for representation, for language, for words. They are struggles about ways of perceiving the world. It is a question of who is to control the ways a group is perceived and defined, indeed the way the world is perceived and defined. Political organization and action often consist in a group trying to validate, to impose, its own way of perceiving itself, thereby escaping from the symbolic violence being done by the dominant representation. But it is worth specifying that there is hardly any one way in which gay men "perceive themselves." (And the situation is only more acute when one speaks of gay men and lesbians.) Thus we have the necessary complexity of the gay and lesbian movement. And thus, as it is often pointed out, the definitions it provides will be only provisional constructions, fragile ones, often necessarily in contradiction with themselves. So it is that younger gay men come to the big city and, even as they establish a relation to the long tradition that precedes them there, they will reinvent for themselves, in their own way, the very history that has itself provided for more than a century the conditions for its own recreation. No wonder that one often experiences the contradictory feelings that "it has always been this way" and that "things are always changing."

⊮ It is necessary and essential that gay men and lesbians be able to provide their own images of themselves to escape from the images that have been so long produced of and on them. In doing so they will offer more positive models (or at least more neutral ones or ones closer to reality) to those who have at hand only strongly negative images. The project is to produce one's own representations for oneself and thereby to produce oneself as a discursive subject who refuses merely to be the object of the Other's discourse. Yet, given that the ways in which gay men and lesbians perceive themselves and wish to speak of themselves are so eminently multiple, it is inevitable that any definition produced by some of them will not please others. Many things are at stake between gay men and lesbians themselves in the project of collective self-definition. "Identity" is therefore neither a reality nor a program, neither a past nor a future nor a present, but a contested space, a space of political and cultural conflict. This implies that that space can never be completely stabilized by any unitary discourse that would claim to provide a fixed way of apprehending identity.

One thing, we should insist, is very clear: for young gay men and lesbians who are obliged to construct their personal identities with no other models than those provided by caricatural and insulting images, and with no other schemas for thinking about their sexuality and their emotions than the insulting words by which they are surrounded—even if those words haven't been directly addressed to them—the mere fact that other images are being produced, that other models of identification can be located in their society, that all the phenomena that make up a "gay culture" can be visible, all this generates freedom. For it is through these other identifications that the affirmation of one's own singularity in the face of the identity shaped from the exterior by the social order becomes possible. It was that exterior social order that instituted gay people as a collective and then isolated them from each other. It is amusing then, or maybe frightening, to notice that every time non-devalorizing images of homosexuality are produced, this or that guardian of the heteronormative order will be there to decry the "proselytism" behind them. We should note, in passing, how ludicrous this notion of proselytism is. It imagines that someone could be incited to become homosexual by way of representations of homosexuality. But it thereby brilliantly reveals the absolute dissymmetry between a desirable heterosexuality and a regrettable homosexuality: no one ever speaks of "heterosexual proselytism," yet images of heterosexuality have a positively hegemonic distribution. The omnipresence of the image of heterosexuality rather serves to make clear that representations do not entice people to become this or that: a gay man can be exposed to images of heterosexuality during his entire childhood, adolescence, and adult life without thereby becoming heterosexual. Gide had already pointed this out, when he put these words in the mouth of his character, Corydon:

> Just think how in our society, in our behavior, everything predestines one sex to the other; everything teaches heterosexuality, everything urges it upon us, everything provokes us to it: theater, literature, newspapers, the paraded example set by our elders, the ritual of our drawing rooms and our street corners. . . . Yet if a young man finally succumbs to so much collusion in the world around him, you refuse to grant that his decision was influenced, his desire manipulated if he ends up making his choice in the 'right' direction! And if, in spite of advice, invitations, provocations of all kinds, he should manifest a homosexual tendency, you immediately blame his reading or some other influence; . . . it has to be an acquired taste, you insist; he must have been taught it; you refuse to admit that he might have invented it all by himself.[15]

⊁ To those who today reproach gays and lesbians for constructing themselves as a group, as a "mobilized minority," and who consistently insist that they return to the values of free and independent individuals, one can of course respond that in fact it is the social and juridical order that has already constituted "homosexuals" as a collective—as an ostracized minority that has been deprived of rights. But one should go even further and add that the very possibility of personal autonomy is denied to them given the structural impossibility for them to identify with positive images of their own feelings, their own sexuality, and therefore of their own personalities—given, further, the impossibility of accepting a relation of "reciprocity" (in the Sartrian sense of the word) with other gay people. They are limited by an external constraint; their consciousness has literally been invaded by discourses and images (in short, by a social order) that rejects them.

And if someone who is heterosexual can think of him or herself as free and autonomous as regards his or her psychological and sexual characteristics, is this not precisely because everything that such a person feels and is corresponds to the demands and the impositions of the sexual order? The feeling that heterosexuals possess of their own free will and personal autonomy in fact exists only as a surface effect of the supposed naturalness and self-evidence that they gain by belonging to the majority. Their "individuality" and their "freedom" are made possible, sustained (as a pure illusion) by their conformity with values that are hardly universal. How could they be when they deny the right of first-person existence to a certain number of individuals who have been reduced to the status of discursive objects, of negative signs to be manipulated by dominant culture. One could even say that the stability of heterosexual identity is only assured by way of the delimitation and exclusion of "homosexuality," of a homosexual "identity" defined by a certain number of devalorized characteristics assigned to an entire "category" of persons. Heterosexuality defines itself in large measure by what it rejects, in just the same way as, more generally, a society defines itself by what it excludes. (This was Foucault's point in *Madness and Civilization*.) It seems likely that as gays and lesbians affirm their multiple and heterogeneous identities, thereby destabilizing an imposed and inferior homosexual "identity," they also contribute to the undoing—for heterosexuals themselves—of the seamless adhesion to things taken for granted. For those things taken for granted would depend on the exclusions and demarcations that are being undone. Thus, as the Foucault of the 1980s would say, "gay culture" is capable of generating new ways of life, new forms of relations between individuals, as much for heterosexuals as for gay men and lesbians.

A veritable autonomy can only see the light of day through the construction of a "collective" that is conscious of itself as such and conscious of the fact that personal autonomy is never a given but always something that must be fought for. This concrete autonomy is to be won in the first place from those who always plead for an abstract autonomy as a way of demanding that gay men and lesbians continue to accept a situation in which autonomy is refused to them or somehow rendered impossible. It is only in becoming conscious of the determinisms that shape conscious and unconscious minds that individuals can come to constitute themselves as "subjects," as their *own* subjects.

11

Inversions

To say that insult is already present, that it preexists the arrival into the world of this individual or that who will become its victim, is also to say that it preexists the person who will wield it. As Judith Butler has put it so well, insult is always a citation.[1] It merely reproduces words that have already been heard. The person who flings an insult draws from an available repertory in order to declare his or her hatred or disgust of someone. Insult's power arises from the fact that it preexists the two persons caught up in it—the one who flings it, the other who receives it—and that it has a prior history that exceeds that of the two people in question.

So we need to understand insult over the long term: it has been shaped by its history, and its present-day possibilities are the fruit of that history. An insult that is actually or potentially spoken, or an insult that is feared or assumed by someone who may be or already has been its victim, is only a symptom. If it is efficacious, this is not only due to the performative force of language. Judith Butler asks: why do words hurt, why is the body susceptible to them? Language is performative only because it is supported, traversed, and given direction by the various powers that organize society and patterns of thought. This is the deepest reason why insult works.

As Pierre Bourdieu has shown in his critique of Austin, language is historical, social, and political in every way. It would require a thorough exploration of the anthropological structures that shape the unconscious of our societies in order to understand why it is insult that establishes the horizon on which homosexual identity is formed, as it would to understand why it turns out that gay identity is always forced to remember its origins in insult as soon as it makes an effort to forget them.

Insult is really just the verbal leading edge of the symbolic violence that organizes sexuality according to extremely precise hierarchies and exclusions and that confers on homosexuality its inferior status in our societies. Doubtless this symbolic violence is anchored in what Bourdieu calls "masculine domination," which can be understood not only as the domination of men over women, but also, more generally, the domination of a "masculine principle" over a "feminine principle," and thus of a heterosexual man (which is to say, a man!) over a homosexual one (who is not considered to be a man) to the extent that homosexuality is filed under "femininity" in the unconscious of our societies.[2]

This would not, of course, account for all the representations of relations between people of the same sex throughout history. One would also have to take into consideration, for example, the masculinist valorization of relations between men in certain past societies, as part of the basis of military excellence. Homosexuality has not always and everywhere been associated with effeminacy. Or perhaps we should say that this image has sometimes coexisted alongside other representations. But it is certainly the case that sexual "deviance" has been perceived, at least since the end of the nineteenth century, as first and foremost a kind of "gender inversion," a perception that has been applied to both sexes. The male homosexual is someone who has renounced his masculinity, just as the lesbian is someone who has renounced her femininity. We could also add, however, that "inversion" often has another meaning. It is understood and denounced as the simple fact of not looking for a partner of the opposite sex. Effeminate men and masculine women are not the only people who incur the accusation of "inversion." So do any men who love men and women who love women. The confusing admixture of heterogeneous themes in the notion of inversion can be seen clearly in the list of terms by which doctors have claimed to diagnose this "illness": "inversion (or perversion) of the genital sense," "inversion (or perversion) of the sexual instinct," "contrary attraction," and so on.[3] Within homophobic discourse then, inversion will take on two distinct meanings: an interiorized inversion of gender (a woman's soul in a man's body or a man's soul in a woman's body) and an exteriorized inversion of the desired object (another man instead of a woman, or another woman instead of a man). The Italian psychiatrist Arrigo Tamassia had already noted this double meaning of inversion at the very moment it was being thematized in medical discourse.[4] And in a note added in 1920 to his *Three Contributions to the Theory of Sex*, Freud mentions the "important points of view" of Ferenczi, who proposes abandoning the word "homosexuality" in favor of "homoerotic" in order to account for the "very marked differences at least between two types of subject-homoerotics, who feel and act like women, and the object-homoerotic who is masculine throughout and has only (mistakenly) exchanged a female object against one of the same sex." Freud accepts such a distinction between two possible meanings of the word "inversion," yet also immediately comments that there are many people in whom one finds a mixture of these two types of homoeroticism.[5] We might even go so far as to say that the majority of discourses on homosexuality have for ages done nothing other than recite and recombine these two meanings of inversion— the same two meanings around which, in the second half of the nineteenth century, in psychiatric, medical, and police discourses, the definition of homosexuality that we know today crystallized.

Current discourses are an inextricable mixture of these two themes, to be found in variable proportions. It is the particular dosage, one might say, that gives to each discourse its particular physiognomy, that apparently differentiates it from all the other discourses. Yet one only has to read through some psychoanalytic texts—classic ones or ones from today—to see that we have not moved far from the generative principle of this double meaning of "inversion." A legitimate distinction can be made between two large discursive types, the ones that favor one meaning of inversion or the other, either the interiorized inversion of the person in question or the exteriorized inversion of the desired object. In the first case, one will insist upon the pathological character of an individual and his or her psychology; in the second case, one will turn to the "deviant," "perverse," or simply inferior (and therefore, in that case as well, "abnormal") character of a relation with someone of the same sex. While it is necessary for the sake of clear understanding to distinguish between these two large discourses, in practice they are never totally separate from each other. Yet they are in fact logically contradictory: if the homosexual is "inverted" in the interior sense, that is to say if he is truly a "woman" in a man's body, one cannot also accuse him of an "inversion" of the object of desire and therefore consider him a man who, instead of being attracted to women, is attracted to men.

Proust, greatly influenced by the psychiatrists he read, never ceased struggling with these difficulties. After having described the "invert" as a man who is not really a man and who therefore can only be attracted by a man who is not like him, by a man who is really a man, that is, by a heterosexual, he then had to explain that such an invert was obliged, for lack of a better choice, to content himself with those of his own race, making a huge imaginative effort in order to see other "inverts" as real men.

In fact, one finds in Proust, at least in his theorizing, neither "homosexuals" nor "homosexuality." In a draft in which he poses the question as to what name to use to designate those he will (in the opening of *Cities of the Plain* [*Sodome et Gomorrhe*]) sometimes call "Sodomites," he chooses the word "invert" while expressing his regret that he cannot use the only word that really suits his purpose: the word "*tante*" (literally, aunt, but used similarly to the English slang sense of "queen"), which one finds in Balzac. Proust in any case declines to use the word "homosexual," writing:

> According to the rather fragmentary theory that I am sketching here, in reality no homosexuals would exist. However masculine in appearance the *tante* might be, his taste for virility would arise from a fundamental femininity, even if it is disguised. A homosexual would simply be that which an invert earnestly claims to be. (*Recherche*, 3:955)

The homosexual believes he is a man who loves other men, whereas he is a woman who loves other men. This is not a love for the same sex or for the same gender, but rather a love for the opposite sex or gender. Thus Charlus "seeks out essentially the love of a man of the other race, that is to say a man who is a lover of women (and incapable consequently of loving him)" (*RTP*, 2:654).

And given that this "theoretical" love is nearly impossible to enact in the real world, an invert turns to other inverts: "It is true that inverts, in their search for a male, often content themselves with other inverts as effeminate as themselves. But it is enough that they do not belong to the female sex" (2:653). In his draft from 1909, Proust said the same even more clearly: "An accursed race, for [its members can] only love a man who has nothing of a woman about him, a man who is not 'homosexual,' and it is only with such a man that they could satisfy a desire that they should not be experiencing for him and that he should not be experiencing for them, were it not that the need for love proved trickster enough that the most infamous *tante* could take on for them the appearance of a man, a real man just like all the others, who, through some miracle, would have fallen in love with them or at least deigned to take them into consideration" (*Recherche*, 3:924).[6] Thus Proust ends up comparing inverts to flowers or hermaphroditic animals, like snails, "which cannot be fertilised by themselves, but can by other hermaphrodites" (*RTP*, 2:653).

Consequently, we can see that this theory of interior inversion—of (given that it is really the desire of a "woman" for a man) the fundamental heterosexuality of homosexual desire—can only lead, once we have faced up to the quasi-impossibility of an interracial union between a man-woman and a man-man, to a theory of love among the inverts. They are all snails! The element of humor that inspires Proust to come up with these considerations should not be forgotten. That humor can be found generally throughout his description of homosexuality.[7] Yet we should also note that his allegiance to the theory of "inversion"—the invert is a woman looking for a man—caused him to make profound changes in the character of Morel between the drafts and the published novel. In one of the drafts, Proust writes, at the moment that Charlus meets Morel at the Saint-Lazare train station, of a "small *tante* disguised as a soldier."[8] In the published version, Morel is no longer a *tante*: he has become more masculine (so that the baron can authentically be in love with him). And so that this sexual transformation can take place, it is necessary that he no longer be "homosexual," but rather bisexual or perhaps heterosexual, yet willing to have relations with men when there is money to be gained.[9] In fact, the inverts' desire "would be for ever unappeased did not their money procure for them real men" (*RTP*, 2:638).

The Proustian theory takes as its point of departure that the homosexual man is in fact a woman and is looking for a heterosexual man who would be a real man. But to the extent that for Proust, definitionally speaking, the heterosexual man cannot take a sexual or emotional interest in the homosexual, because he only loves real women, the invert must generally content himself with other inverts, trying to imagine them to be real men—the exception being when money can gain the invert access to real men. While the invert may be under the illusion that he is the same as the heterosexual man he desires, under the illusion of being a man desiring another man (just as "a snob believes himself to be noble"[10]), he is in fact identical to other inverts, to whom he is necessarily drawn. This would be a meeting of two "women," but not real women, rather hermaphroditic beings possessing the organs of both sexes, as in the earliest moments of time, before the general division of all beings—according to the Platonic myth to which Proust is referring.[11]

Not truly resembling a woman because he has the body of a man and not truly resembling a man because he has the psychology of a woman, the invert is simply like other inverts—for Proust acts as if it would be possible to subsume all the representatives of this race that is so "numerous" into one category, a category simultaneously biological and psychological. Even if his way of describing certain of his characters (such as Saint-Loup) clearly does not accord with his general theory of inversion,[12] nonetheless what we have here is a condensed representation of all the discourses on homosexuality available at the time—discourses on which he draws heavily in order to give to his individual characterizations a kind of universal value. Charlus is not simply an "old queen" (une vieille Tante) as he puts it in a letter to Paul Souday.[13] He is, in many ways, the paradigmatic queen. I will come back in the second part of this book to the theory of inversion one finds in Proust. It is clearly quite close to the theory of the third sex that was developed in Germany by Hirschfeld, who had himself drawn on Karl Heinrich Ulrichs, the first great advocate of the gay cause.

In fact, as early as the beginnings of the 1860s (doubtless thanks to a certain number of medical works that had already been published at the time), Ulrichs had already forged a theory of interiorized gender inversion in men who were attracted to other men, explaining it as "the soul of a woman in a man's body."[14] In his fight on behalf of those he called "Uranists," he did not hesitate to demand for them the right of marriage. But, as he did not imagine that a "Uranist" (a word coined in reference to Plato's Symposium) could marry another Uranist (what would two such women have done together?), he conceptualized this "homosexual" marriage on the model of a "heterosexual" marriage between a real man—heterosexual—and a man-woman, the Uranist. He considered such a union as comparable to a marriage of convenience. Still, far from imagining relations between Uranists as a kind of last resort, as Proust would, Ulrichs also elaborated a theory that distinguished between two poles: at one pole were masculine Uranists who seemed to be drawn to more or less effeminate younger men, and at the other were effeminate Uranists who loved more virile young men. For this reason, and perhaps also because he had foreseen the kind of objections that Proust would raise many years later as to the improbability of sexual relations between homosexuals and heterosexuals, Ulrichs did also allow for the possibility of a marriage between two Uranists, as long as they came from the two separate poles he had laid out.[15] Of course this contradicted the underlying idea of his general theory of Uranism as a form of love that was basically feminine in nature. (He wrote, for example, that "we are all women in spirit."[16]) If he proved unable to abandon his point of departure, doubtless this was because in his eyes any sexual desire directed toward a man had to be thought of as a feminine form of desire. So on some deep level Ulrichs's way of thinking may still be coherent. If one is attracted by the "same," it is because on some deep level, one is "different." To love the same sex must mean that one is of a different "sex." Yet, strangely, having defined Uranists as men-women, he is obliged, in order to have his theory coincide with what he observes in the world, to reduplicate gender difference inside the category of men-women, producing masculine men-women who love feminine ones, and feminine ones who love masculine ones. Ulrichs offers the clarification that these are manifestations of the extremes, and that numerous intermediate possibilities exist. And all of this may show how the desire to produce an apologia that anchors homosexuality in nature, that makes it into a different sex, a "third sex," produces insurmountable kinds of conceptual incoherence which Ulrichs, and Proust after him, deal with as best they can—trying to hold together possibilities that seem rather to cancel each other out.

Ulrichs considered himself to be an effeminate Uranist, and he had a pronounced liking for soldiers. To those who disparaged him for crossing class boundaries in this way he replied that he saw no harm in it, noting that "opposites" attract and that similarity in intellectual levels hinders rather than helps sexual love: "Let's stop once and for all confusing love and friendship," he wrote.[17] What is unthinkable for Ulrichs is that someone should love the "same." Love and sexuality are always thought of as a meeting of opposites, a complementarity between sexes or genders, as well as between social classes. This is why he is obliged to come up with so many different levels so that in every relation an insurmountable difference between the masculine and the feminine remains. In a couple, in love, in sexuality, there is always a "man" and a "woman," or, in any case, masculinity and femininity.

If Proust did not invent the problems that he takes up in his novel—far from it—still we can see that his enormous originality consists not so much in his lively mixture of the two meanings (interior gender and exterior object) of the word inversion (for others did the same), as in the way he integrated them, rendered them indistinguishable, and then justified this fusion: the interior inversion of gender and the love for someone like you become one and the same: inverts can only love inverts. Having begun by excluding the idea of "homosexuality" from his theory—for it is only in a state of delusion that an invert can believe that he loves the "same sex," the sex to which he does not in fact belong, Proust reintroduces "homosexuality" on another level, as an effect of practical necessity, the necessity of "queens" finding sexual partners. Men belonging to the "race of queens," which is to say to the "third sex," are certainly not attracted to each other. In fact they detest each other, as Proust never stops pointing out. They are

horrified by the effeminacy that they find in the others. But either by necessity or by love they reciprocally choose to forget that the person they are
sleeping with is not a real man but an "infamous queen." Yet what should
one call a member of the "third sex" who sleeps with another member of the
"third sex," a "hermaphrodite" who sleeps with another "hermaphrodite,"
if not, precisely, "homosexual"?[18] In spite of himself, in spite of everything,
the invert can only love one who is like him, while imagining him to be
different.

≽ There is an important difference between Ulrichs and Proust. The first
intended to defend homosexuality. His was a militant project. He produced
an entire theory of the "particular" nature that characterized a certain number of individuals, in order to enable himself to request the decriminalization of homosexuality. If "inversion" is "natural," it can no longer be a
"vice" or a sin. Proust's intention, on the other hand, is to build his novelistic project around the revelation of a truth whose appearance he knows
might seem monstrous, and he does nothing to make that appearance more
palatable.[19] He will even say to Gide that he transposed into the "*shades of
young women* all the attractive, affectionate, and charming elements contained in his homosexual recollections, so that for *Sodom* he is left nothing
but the grotesque and the abject."[20] Doubtless this is the reason why he was
praised by critics for a good number of years for his way of showing, as a
good "moralist," the abjection of this infamous race.[21]

In Ulrichs we find an astonishing mixture of gay activism and of homophobic thought, and in Proust an equally astonishing mixture of an un-
daunted will to speak of homosexuality and the necessity to present it in an
inglorious light. In both of them together we find a mixture of a careful
affirmation of the existence of homosexuals and an eternal obligation to
portray them in reference to heterosexuality, to describe them in terms of
inversion and the relationship between masculinity and femininity. All of
this, as we shall see in the pages ahead, is a formative part of the history
of homosexuality since the mid-nineteenth century, and part of the struggle
for gay peoples to begin to speak for themselves.

But what interests us at this point is to see to what an extent homosexual
subjectivity is subservient to heterosexual modes of representation and to the
normative violence exercised by them. Homosexuality is always referred
back to a norm, even when it is homosexuals who speak. The word "queen"

(*tante*) is not only an insult. It is also a social image and a psychological type that have been defined by the sexual order and by the inferiorization of homosexuality. In this context, the notion of inversion is nothing other than an insult dressed up in pseudo-scientific clothing. In its double meaning, it refers, on the one hand, to the idea that the masculine is superior to the feminine (and therefore to the idea that the man who loves women is superior to the man who loves men, who might be suspected of being a woman in any case). On the other hand, it refers to the idea that a relation that unites "differences" is superior to one that brings together things that are the same. Which amounts to saying, in both cases, that a heterosexual is superior to a homosexual—because he is heterosexual.

Moreover, the way of thinking that sets up the difference between sexes as a norm, and same-sex love as a form of deviance or perversion, or, at best, a "special case"—a way of thinking that has at certain times in history taken on the face of totalitarian violence and sometimes takes on today the face of liberal tolerance—is simply the expression of the social and sexual order that set up the world of insult in which gay people must live. As a way of thought, it is sufficiently powerful that it often imposes itself on gay people themselves.

The gay unconscious is also structured by the rules of heterosexual language. Only the political and cultural work of the collective reinvention of gay people by themselves could manage to perturb the immemorial cycle in which this unthought social heteronormativity reproduces itself.

12

On Sodomy

With Proust and Ulrichs, one sees clearly how a reflection on homosexuality is inevitably and deeply marked by homophobic representations and often imprisoned in the very structures of the heterocentrist unconscious—for which sexuality is only possible when it involves the difference between and the complementarity of masculinity and femininity. This domination of the heterocentrist unconscious, from which Proust and Ulrichs, in their historical moments, probably did not have the tools to escape, has been given legitimacy by psychoanalysis, which provided it with a foundation that it claimed was scientific. From Freud to Lacan and on to Lacan's disciples, this idea of the "difference of the sexes" has prospered and has imposed itself as an ideological principle that is never subjected to interrogation in all that is written about sexuality, and, obviously, about homosexuality. Homosexuality can only ever be seen as a sexuality or an affectivity from which something is missing; it is always confronted with the normality of "difference." It is a "perversion," an "arrested development" of an individual and his or her desires. It is an "incapacity" to recognize the "other." And so on ad nauseam. All these heterocentrist discourses, all these scientific mythologies which make heterosexuality into the norm and the point of view from which every situation must be viewed (aided by all the implausible ideological constructions that have been produced out of the theory of the "Oedipus complex"), all contribute to the ongoing processes by which homosexuality is rendered inferior. They all contribute to the perpetuation of this inferiorization (even if Freud's intentions had something admirable about them— given that he always wished to struggle against the repression inflicted on homosexuals). It is worth noting that there is not a single instance of a political position being taken against social and legal recognition for couples of the same sex, against equal legal treatment, that does not sooner or later invoke in its argument for continuing discrimination the great principle of the "differentiation of the sexes" and of its "institution" by the social order, providing thereby the very basis of culture, civilization, and so on.

Clearly a specifically sexual kind of racism exists, one that refuses to consider love for the same sex as equivalent to love for the other sex. This racism is not directly or explicitly the product of an analysis in terms of the "inversion of genders," even if that particular thematic is always lurking in the shadows of the homophobic unconscious, ready to jump back into play in any given paragraph. In this context, what is rejected or treated as inferior (for many nuances are possible) is simply "the love of the same." In order to declare an opposition to the right to marriage, to adoption, to reproductive technologies, or simply to any kind of legal recognition for same-sex couples, it is sufficient to call upon the idea or the presupposition that there is some kind of natural, biological, cultural, or ethical superiority of a couple that involves sexual duality over a couple that unites two who are "the same." Or one can simply denounce homosexuality as a refusal of "alterity," a rejection of "difference," and an "exclusion" of the opposite sex.

Certainly the existence of this sexual racism directed at the inversion of the object is incontestable. It is even sometimes today the dominant note in homophobic discourse, notable in its liberal and most euphemistic versions. Yet it remains true that it is in the condemnation of "interior" inversion, that is to say of a failure to conform to conventionally defined roles, that the most violently homophobic fantasies and the greatest hostility toward homosexuality find themselves constructed in Western societies. The constant and brutal hatred of effeminacy in men, be it real or supposed, is doubtless matched by the hostility directed at women who are too "masculine." The reactions to the "garçonnes" of the 1920s and 1930s would be good evidence of this.[1]

One might say that all of the transformations that, over the course of the past thirty or forty years, have affected the image that gay men seek to provide for themselves—notably the processes of bodily or gestural "masculinization," the masculinization of codes of dress, and so on—have yet to successfully challenge the traditional representation of the gay man as a "fairy," "queen," "fruit," "nelly," or "nancy-boy," all those feminizing words that signify homosexuality as gender inversion in a man. ("Butch" or "bull dyke" or "diesel dyke" are perhaps equivalents for women.) It might occur to one to wonder about the illusion under which gay men may have been operating in imagining that it would suffice for them to wear boldly on their sleeves the signs of their masculinity in order to transform stereotypes of homosexuality. George Mosse notes that, as early as the 1920s, the majority of gay magazines sought to provide "masculine" images to gay men. "The continuity of the normative ideal among homosexuals through a time of change can be illustrated by examples . . . taken from German gay love stories written between 1924 and 1979, in which 'beautiful young men' are invariably lithe, muscled, and blond, with faces hewn in stone. . . . Here, there was no difference between normative masculinity and its foes."[2] Yet despite all that, gay men were in all those years still perceived and still rendered in caricature and in homophobic discourse as effeminate. In television sitcoms today, the requisite gay character may be buff, but he is also still effeminate. Little has changed since the time when Proust described gay men as women wearing a man's body. Consequently, however that body chooses to present itself, however "manly" it has made itself, indeed even if it has constructed itself as a masculine body to the point of caricature, still nothing has changed in the social perception of the person inhabiting that body, whose psychology, seen according to normative categories, could only be feminine. For homosexuality between men implies a desire for a man, and therefore a necessarily feminine psychology. It hardly suffices to demonstrate the absurdity or the incoherence of such representations (two gay men who are attracted to each other are, in fact, difficult to perceive simultaneously as women attracted to a man) in order to make them disappear.

Thus it is not hard to understand the force with which many gay men reject "femininity" and "effeminacy." Those men work so eagerly to distance themselves from such aspects of gay identity precisely because others, to the contrary, continue to take up such roles, to "camp it up." (This is made clear by the permanence of a specific trait in the subculture which has endured across many periods and which consists in men speaking of themselves and other men in linguistically feminine forms.) Perhaps Michael Pollak was revealing his own wishes when he wrote, in an astonishingly prescriptive manner for someone usually so careful as regards scientific rigor, that this play with the feminine form and with femininity was the product of oppression and would disappear with it.[3] The idea that visibility and "emancipation" would bring with them an "end of oppression," of repression, and of homophobia is already quite surprising in its own right. Yet beyond that, Pollak's claim is still astounding, given that it seems to choose to ignore that a good portion of contemporary gay culture takes its very form from an attraction to femininity. Certainly there is another part of that culture that might be described in opposing terms as arising from a strong allegiance to masculine values. Still, one need not go all the way back through all the centuries in which this attraction to the feminine is found (it was already being denounced by the canonical authors of classical Greece and Rome and has more recently provoked anger from feminists when they take it to be an attraction to the most caricatural images of femininity) in order to suppose that this cultural trait is sufficiently omnipresent that it cannot simply be the fruit of the interiorization of homophobic representations.

Camp and drag humor can certainly be described as a strategy of resistance to or reappropriation of the accusation of effeminacy.[4] But above all, camp and drag express the creativity and inventiveness of a minority culture and the ways in which such a culture, through its own irony, offers the best critique of itself and of others. It is hard to see why this play with femininity should be described as the interiorization of a constraint. Why should it not be seen as one—and certainly it is only *one*, but, whether you like it or not, it certainly *is* one—of the characteristic traits of male homosexuality, of the ways in which a certain number of gay men like to think of themselves, like to carry themselves. Would it not rather be through an *inability* to think in these terms—which do not fit with normative conceptions of masculinity and femininity—that one would reveal oneself to be trapped by some kind of interiorized constraint?

In any case, we can now see that the obsession with masculinity that has imposed itself throughout the past twenty years as one of the most visible features of an affiliation to "gay culture" has hardly caused a play with femininity or even simply effeminacy to disappear. Far from it. These two aspects can inhabit the same bar, the same nightclub, the same demonstration, and even the same individual.

Despite all the efforts of certain gay men to put an end to the "feminine" image, despite their impatience with and their anger at those who renew or perpetuate this "bad image" in Gay Pride parades (as if the only "good" image acceptable to the agents of the established order were not precisely that of a total submission to their norms, and therefore a renunciation of homosexuality), it seems obvious that, in the regard directed at gay men, there continues to be the idea that a gay man is someone who renounces his virility by accepting or being always susceptible to accepting the "passive" role in the sexual act. Our most frequent insult makes that so blatantly clear that we need not dwell on the matter.[5] And if psychoanalytic studies show that the homophobia of male heterosexuals is often tied to the fear of (or the fantasy of) anal penetration, it will not be sufficient, in order to overcome this hostility, as deeply anchored in the archaic region of the masculine brain as it is, indeed, as deeply anchored as it is in the very definition of masculinity, to point out that not all gay men practice sodomy. It will not suffice to let it be understood that many gay men are "tops." (After all, if there are "tops" there are "bottoms," which simply renews the stigmatization of homosexuality.)

It might be more useful to reject the entire dichotomy of active/passive or top/bottom and then to analyze its ideological function as the structural principal of masculine domination of women, and, by extension, of heterosexual domination of homosexuals.[6] For example, Bourdieu analyzes the opposition between "front" and "back" as a structuring principle of the Kabyle cosmology. The front is the noble (and masculine) part, the back the shameful (and feminine) one. Now it is striking to find that it is always the "rear" that becomes the focus of jokes and insults regarding gay men. In the caricatures published in the newspapers during the Eulenburg affair, one sees the most high-ranking army officers reviewing a lineup of soldiers who turn their backs to them and stick out their rumps.[7] How could one not think of these images when one reads in Proust of the comment made by the sculptor Ski in reference to Charlus during a train ride to La Raspelière: " 'Oh!' the sculptor would whisper, seeing a young railwayman with the sweeping eyelashes of a dancing girl at whom M. de Charlus could not help staring, 'if the Baron begins making eyes at the conductor, we shall never get there, *the train will start going backwards. Just look at the way he's staring at him: this isn't a puffer-train but a poofter train* [ce n'est plus un petit chemin de fer, où nous sommes, c'est un funiculeur]' " (*RTP*, 2:1075; my emphasis). We might just note in passing that the description of the young employee does anything but indicate that he might be "virile." It thereby contradicts the idea so forcefully expressed in the opening pages of *Cities of the Plain* according to which the Baron, a case-study of the invert, is really a "woman" looking for a "man." Perhaps this means that neither the phobia around sodomy nor the important place this fantasy occupies in the ritual jokes about gay people has much to do with "roles" (top or bottom, real or imagined) that the people about whom such jokes are made (here Charlus and the railway employee) might actually enact in any hypothetical sexual relation. Specifically regarding the sculptor's expression, and treating it more directly, if the little train is no longer a "*chemin de fer*" (railway) but a "*funiculeur*" (a deformation of *funiculaire*, funicular railway, to make it rhyme with *enculeur*, buttfucker), we have really no way of knowing who would be the *enculeur* and who would be the *enculé*, if, in fact, that sexual practice would take place were the two to meet.

But the spiciness in this example of what Proust calls a "malicious witticism" (*mauvaise plaisanterie*) lies in its implication that there necessarily would be an *enculeur* and an *enculé*, for the perfidious aspect of the remark about the train going *backwards* refers explicitly to a backside, to an inversion of the proper direction. The joker thus has no reason to be precise, no reason to provide any details about the stigmatized relation: for him to succeed in making people laugh it suffices that he suggest that two inverts together will in fact practice sodomy and that consequently one of them will necessarily be a bottom. What makes the joke work is the idea that the "homosexual" is potentially and fantasmatically passive in a sodomitical relation. Given that he wants to present Charlus as the paradigmatic invert, Proust is obliged to attribute this sexuality to him, despite the incoherence that this induces in the psychological description of the character. (How, for instance, given this context, are we to take his attraction for very young fellows such as the sons of Mme de Surgis, by whom he is so captivated at one point in *Cities of the Plain*?) Yet there is no end of remarks that intend to suggest to the reader the type of sexuality the baron is supposed to practice. Consider, for example, this exclamation of Jupien's after his sexual encounter with the baron at the outset of this volume: "What a big bum you have" (2:632). Now this is the very moment at which the narrator discovers that the baron, given that he loves men, is a "woman": "I now understood, moreover, why earlier, when I had seen him coming away from Mme de Villeparisis's, I had managed to arrive at the conclusion that M. de Charlus looked like a woman: he was one!" (2:637). Either Proust or his narrator insists, of course, on bringing this observation into contradiction with the self-proclaimed virility of the baron: "I could not help thinking how angry M. de Charlus would have been could he have known that he was being watched; for what was suggested to me by the sight of this man who was so enamoured of, who so prided himself upon, his virility, to whom all other men seemed odiously effeminate, what he suddenly suggested to me, to such an extent had he momentarily assumed the features, the expression, the smile thereof, was a woman" (2:626). We should notice, as I have already suggested, that this text is peppered with contradictions. For Charlus is described, a few lines further along, as a "male" bird attracted to a "female" one.[8] Yet what at this moment might seem to be only temporary, that is, Charlus's true feminine nature here coming to the surface, is slowly going to reveal itself to be a more durable and ongoing inscription on his body. This is why, later, at the same time as he mentions how much Charlus has aged, Proust is able to describe him as a man covered in makeup and powder, "waddling along" with an "almost symbolic behind," as if, with the coming of age, the truth about a man revealed itself—not only regarding the virility he had been able to lay claim to earlier (when he could still hide his "femininity"), but also regarding his "inversion" and the practices it implies (2:890).

⋈ Precisely because the "passive" role, real or imagined, is always considered degrading, it becomes impossible in certain cultures to think of relations between men as "homosexual"—for this would imply that either of the partners might be passive. Rather, these relations are thought of as like the relation of a "man" and a "woman," the active man playing the truly masculine, dominant role, and the false man/real woman, playing the passive, dominated, feminine role. One can see, in reading George Chauncey's book on New York between the end of the nineteenth century and the 1930s, how, among the popular classes and in certain immigrant cultures, only those who performed the "passive" role were considered homosexual or, more exactly, "inverts" or "fairies." The active partner, on the other hand, was not obliged to think of his sexuality in relation to the sex of his partner, only in relation to the role he played and the gender persona he displayed. Thus it was not the sex of one's partner that determined sexual identity, but one's role within the sex act. The so-called active partner was not homosexual, but a man. Here there is strictly speaking no "homosexuality," for that notion implies, precisely, that both partners are to be considered homosexual and that the relationship is to be thought of as bringing together two people attracted to the same sex. Whereas in the cultures that Chauncey describes, one finds not a homosexual relation, but a relation between a "normal" and an "effeminate" man, between a "wolf" and a "fairy," between what in French would be called a jules and a tante, a mec and a folle.

This way of representing roles and the identities assigned to them can be found, even more extremely, in the relations studied by Annick Prieur between Mexican transvestite prostitutes and their clients.[9] These transvestites from the Mexican popular classes define themselves as "homosexual" (jotos or jotas) and dress as women to seduce "men" who doubtless would not be able to have relations with persons of the same sex were it not arranged in such a way that sexual difference was to be, and would continue to be, maintained. It is precisely this exacerbation of the difference in roles, this differential construction of "gender," that enables homosexual relations in certain social sectors—for, as Prieur, like Chauncey, emphasizes, things are different for the middle classes. In the popular classes homosexual relations are possible to the extent, and only to the extent, that they take on the appearance of heterosexual ones. But it is obviously not only sexual difference that is at stake here—or gender difference. It is also sexual or gender hierarchy, the domination of masculinity over femininity. This is why, while they are rather well integrated into their own world, the *jotas* nonetheless live surrounded by insults, attacks, and repeated dramas that can even go so far as violent deaths. They are permanent victims of aggression because they are men who dress as women or who pretend to be women. (A very particular case of aggression arises when they have been attempting to make a partner believe that they really are women, and he then discovers the truth.) But Prieur also emphasizes that some of the macho "men" who have relations with the *jotas* sometimes engage in the passive role in sodomy (the *jota* taking the active role). This, of course, can only happen as long as it is agreed that no one will know of it. What is important is not so much what happens in bed as what is known of what happens in bed. Appearances must be kept up.

↠ There can be little doubt, however disagreeable the idea might seem, that even today for certain gay men, even in those countries where the phenomenon of gay emancipation has developed, there persists a vague idea that those who are "tops" are not really gay, or are less so than those who are "bottoms." This is the case even if, in those societies and in those periods where the category of "homosexuality" has established itself, there turns out to be no difference for either of the partners as regards the stigmatizing gaze—which considers any and all homosexuals as potentially *enculés*. It is even possible to find, when one considers certain discourses or certain images circulating in the gay world, that there persists the more or less conscious, more or less explicit idea that the partner who takes the "active" role might as well be bisexual or heterosexual. (Even though studies show that frequently a bisexual man seeks the role of "bottom" in homosexual encounters, which turns out also to be the case for heterosexual men who seek out a homosexual experience.)[10]

It is surprising to discover how permanently, how systematically, the "passivity" of a man is situated at the extreme end of the continuum of stigmatized practices. It demonstrates how old modes of perception and categorization, such as the ones Chauncey describes, survive and retain a certain durability within the contemporary mental structures of gay men themselves. As they do within the whole of the population: this is confirmed by the continually recurring surprise (this is already a theme in Gide's *Corydon*) upon discovering that this or that man who had seemed so "masculine," so "virile," is, in fact, *despite all that*, gay.

Pierre Bourdieu suggests that the cognitive structures of the traditional world of the Mediterranean that he studies in his work on Kabylia can offer a kind of magnifying glass view of the statutory situation of women in our own societies, and, in any case, a "hyperbolic realization of all male fantasies."[11] In the same way, the structuring of roles and identities in the societies described by Annick Prieur or George Chauncey (which are not all that dissimilar to the one studied by Bourdieu—all of them call to mind the antique Mediterranean world as it is analyzed by Dover, Veyne, or Foucault) accentuate traits that can be found in more or less attenuated form in societies as differentiated and heterogeneous as our own. This may explain the seemingly congealed permanence of the repertory of insults directed at gay men, notably that one referred to in Proust's novel, concerning the direction in which the little train is moving.

13

Subjectivity and Private Life

Numerous stories—even if we shouldn't assume them to account for the totality and the full multiplicity of gay and lesbian experience—recount how for many gay men and lesbians, the sense of one's "sexual orientation" dates from earliest childhood. The American psychoanalyst Richard Isay emphasizes that both his clinical work and his research lead him to believe that while homosexuality, like heterosexuality, may have different ways of manifesting itself, it is nonetheless "present from earliest childhood."[1] Cocteau declares something similar in 1928, in the first lines of The White Book: "As far back as I can remember and even at the age when the mind still has no power over the senses, I find traces of my love for boys."[2] Christopher Isherwood remembers his school years when he "had fallen in love with many boys."[3] And, still limiting ourselves to literary testimonies, we could also cite Jean Genet's remarks, in an interview from 1964: "Do we know why we are homosexuals? Homosexuality was, in a manner of speaking, imposed on me, like the color of my eyes, or the number of feet I have. As a child, I was aware of being attracted by boys." And, in an interview for the BBC in 1985, "I have always been different [J'ai toujours été à part]."[4]

This feeling of being "different," of not fitting in, is surely a determinant part in the construction of a personal identity, in the construction of one's self. Here we can perhaps find a key to one of the problems brought up earlier: the question of an orientation toward literary or artistic professions or toward the literary or artistic aspects of other professions. These professional choices permit one to continue to live out a kind of marginality familiar since childhood, providing in any case a little distance or difference. They also allow for a kind of loosened relation to social time, by which I mean the possibility of a kind of perpetual adolescence created by the reproduction of this constitutive marginality. Perhaps there is also in play an identification that dates from very early childhood (when it may not even have been conscious) with persons who offered models of free lives that escaped from certain norms, whereas the social roles offered by the family or "professional life" seemed rather what needed to be resolutely avoided.

In *Becoming a Man*, the story of his childhood and adolescence, the American writer Paul Monette also describes himself as having been a "fag" from his earliest days. He too mentions the extent to which he felt different: "I was such a cipher in prep school, so out of my league in every way."[5] It is telling that he opens his book with the discovery, upon entering adulthood, that he was not alone, that many other gay men shared his experiences, men who had also believed themselves to be unique. Monette's childhood experiences include insults and physical attacks by his classmates on another boy deemed to be "effeminate." He recounts the constant fear of being discovered himself and his constant strategizing to avoid discovery. What is most striking in the scene of violence that he describes (in which he struggled to appear indifferent, not to watch, not to pay attention) is the cowardly relief he feels once it is over. At that point he was able to tell himself that, given that he himself had been passed over, it meant that he was capable of carrying off his disguise and of passing as a "regular boy" (34–35). Monette calls this double game "ventriloquism": a game that consists of a gay man pretending that's not what he is, that leads him to speak the "legitimate," dominant language, a language which, in fact, is not his own. This is why he can write, at the outset of his book, more than twenty years after the experiences in question: "I still shiver with a kind of astonished delight when a gay brother or sister tells of that narrow escape from the coffin world of the closet. *Yes yes yes*, goes the voice in my head, *it was just like that for me*" (2).

What is described in Monette's troubling pages is an entire psychological structure in which can be discovered a kind of phenomenology of the lived experience of gay people (at least gay men). These pages brilliantly portray how a gay subjectivity is formed through a process of self-education, through a severe self-discipline that can never be relaxed, that must scrutinize every move, with the goal of appearing to be "as normal as everyone else." The long-term effects of insult and hatred (here in the form of physical violence) write themselves into the body; they act by way of your own submission to the injunction they carry, your own consent to the order they enforce— that your personality and your desires must remain hidden, that the line must be toed. They command you always to act "as if." They necessitate a permanent effort to ensure that none of your emotions, feelings, or desires are ever revealed. "Such obedient slaves we make," Monette exclaims, when he is speaking of the years of his youth, but also of the years leading up to the great emancipation movements of the late 1960s and early 1970s (2).

Goffman accurately describes the necessity for an individual who belongs to a stigmatized category but who wishes to hide his "failing," to be "alive to the social situation as a scanner of possibilities." Such a person is "therefore likely to be alienated from the simpler world in which those around him apparently dwell," because "new contingencies always arise, making former concealing devices inadequate."[6] Such an effort at disguise, such an obligation to lie, even to those to whom one is close, to one's relatives, produces an "intolerable" strain, which cannot fail to have profound effects on an individual personality, on a given subjectivity (90). Goffman emphasizes the fact that "the stigma and the effort to conceal it or remedy it become 'fixed' as part of personal identity" (65). One should add that this is an *essential* part of that identity, providing both its interior and its exterior physiognomy.

Understandably, a gay man who decides to identify as gay and to accept himself as such will be much less marked in his daily life by the strain that Goffman evokes—and much less dependent on the identity produced by that strain. The self-identified gay man is freer, less imprisoned by a homosexual identity than is the individual obliged to be attentive to every moment and every situation for fear of "betraying" what he is to those around him. To say that one is gay is thus to free oneself from the weight that bears down on those who struggle to conceal that identity. Thus one is less dependent on or less enclosed in that "identity" and freer in one's relations to other people (to other gay people as well as to people in general).

The obligation to lie effectively involves keeping a large segment of yourself enclosed in secrecy. It amounts to setting up a psychological ghetto in which to conceal your sexual and affective identity—a good portion of that which defines your personality—preserving it from any exterior gaze and from the threat of insult, injury, and devalorization. But, as we have seen, the closet only offers a tenuous form of security, one that is always under threat and frequently only fictive. The gay man who secludes his "secret" in a corner of his consciousness can never be sure that others will not discover it. The secret might already be known to a certain number of people who already make fun of him when he is not around—as the example of Charlus and of the public spectacle of his private secret makes clear. The obligation to enclose one's private life in the interior ghetto of a divided mind leaves an individual open to public speculation, gossip, rumor, insinuation, and mockery. This rendering private is thus truly a structure of oppression for gay men and lesbians. More often than not it is imposed upon them, and more often than not they also choose to submit to it. They shape their personalities and their behavior according to it.

To shake off this interiorized yoke of domination implies, along with the decision no longer to tolerate it, a serious effort at getting rid of old mental and behavioral habits: to be able to say that one is gay involves an unlearning of all the pretenses that had been so assiduously learned and practiced with such vigilance and for so long.[7] Every gay man starts off learning to lie.[8] He now has to learn a new language, a new way of speaking, new forms of self-presentation.[9] Here we can clearly see that there are no such things as "universal structures" of communication, of intersubjective reciprocity between subjects supposed to be equal. After all, some subjects are required to learn *not* to communicate (or to rig the way they communicate), to try to create ignorance or error through their communication, until such time as they are ready to relearn how to use language, to relearn their ways of relating to others through language. A gay man learns to speak twice.

» We can see, then, that a communication theory such as the one proposed by Habermas is incapable of accounting for these kinds of realities of everyday language. When Habermas takes as a point of departure for his reflections the idea that any exchange is necessarily oriented toward intersubjective communication, that behind any dialogue necessarily runs the will to reach an agreement with someone else (which involves some kind of reference to the universal norms of language), he leaves out of the picture all the violence language carries with it and all the effects of this violence. He writes: "Fundamental to the paradigm of mutual understanding is, rather, the performative attitude of participants in interaction, who coordinate their plans for action by coming to an understanding about something in the world. When ego carries out a speech act and alter takes up a position with regard to it, the two parties enter into an interpersonal relationship."[10] This is a theory of "communicative action" that sets up rational exchange and the transparency of consciousnesses as the regulating ideals that should organize concrete interactions. How could any such theory account for situations in which a certain number of interlocutors are obliged to scramble communications, to avoid mutual comprehension? Language, in the real world, is not regulated by universally accepted moral norms, but rather by the structural inequalities in the social and sexual order. An injurious speech act is obviously not subtended by the search for intersubjective communication. It does not inaugurate mutual comprehension between two abstract subjects with equal entitlements. When one is dealing with insult, it is not a question of "opening up a relation," but, to the contrary, of establishing and per-petuating breaks between different classes of social and sexual beings. There is no equality; rather there is dissymmetry. This very dissymmetry organizes all linguistic situations and is reproduced by them.

⋫ To decide that you are going to free your speech from the constraints im-posed by permanent self-surveillance means not only that you have chosen to oppose an identity that has been imposed and hidden with one that has been chosen and affirmed. It also implies that you will have to reconstruct yourself and find the means and the support structures to enable such a transformation. Today, a socialization in the "gay world" is doubtless one of the most effective methods for this.

Those who denounce the "ghettoization" of gays and lesbians in big cities (of course this is often nothing more than a disguised insult produced by a phobic reaction to the collective visibility of gays and lesbians) need to be reminded that this visible "ghetto" is above all a way of escaping from an invisible one, the mental ghetto—that is to say, the act (performed by many of those people who cannot or dare not live their homosexuality openly) of shadowing a goodly segment of their existence and their personality in secrecy. Visibility is an escape path from the terrible interior ghetto that is experienced by a soul that has been subjected by shame. What the discourse of liberal tolerance would recommend is nothing other than the perpetua-tion of precisely that interior ghetto: its recommendations amount to a suggestion that this inferiorized identity be maintained within the "invis-ible" space of private life, the space conceded to gay people by heterosexuals, to the minority by the majority.[11] This call for discretion would annihilate the historical victories that today allow one to leave behind the psychological ghetto. It would also thereby contribute to the perpetuation of the sexual racism of homophobia and would also permit (as a kind of class privilege) a small number of gay people living in easier circumstances to act out their sexuality without (too many) problems. All the others, denied the objective

occasion to realize themselves, would be sent back to live within the interiorized borders of private life—a life that is obligatorily kept secret.

When gays and lesbians are reproached for displaying their private lives
in public, for crossing the line between public and private, we are again
dealing with the protection of privilege—of heterosexual privilege. That such
arguments can still be mounted these days after so many years of feminist
critique attests to the fact that ideology will never be overcome through
argument. It also attests to the fact that there will always be people around
who are overly eager to defend the structures of oppression and of the
established order. Feminism (I think in this case it is permissible to speak of
feminism as a homogeneous phenomenon, for we are dealing with a kind of
common denominator) has shown that not only the categories of public and
private but also the reality of public and private spheres function to assign
roles; as places, they create a division of labor between the sexes (the public
sphere for men, the private sphere for women—although within it they will
find a private life of their own denied to them).[12] Similarly for the division
between sexual orientations: public space is heterosexual and homosexuals
are to stick to the space of their private lives. One might notice, for instance,
that all the forms of masculine sociability (the life men lead with other men),
along with being fundamentally misogynist, are also based on the exclusion
of homosexuality. All the fantasies regarding communal showers that proliferated in newspapers and in official texts during the debate about gays in the
military in the United States show quite clearly that this masculine sociability
(this homosociality that might sometimes seem so close to homosexuality,
or to a sort of generalized homoeroticism) is in fact based on an abrupt and
radical exclusion of any possibility of sex between the men who participate in
this common life. Eric Dunning, in his study of English rugby, reports that
the themes that occur with the most frequency in the songs sung in rugby
clubs have to do with brutality toward women and derision directed at gay
men (who are not "real men").[13] Homosexuality is thus *proscribed* from the
prescribed relations between men.[14] Masculinity publicly constructs and affirms itself against homosexuality. This, of course, engenders a permanent
threat of violence ready to burst forth, especially when men are together as a
group (for instance, the attacks by bands of soldiers in military towns or by
young suburban youths on gay cruising places and the various forms of
mistreatment, even rapes, in barracks and prisons).

Inside these groups, those who are homosexual or who experience some
kind of homosexual physical desire must behave so that no one else suspects

it. This is so in almost every social situation. At school, in the workplace, men (from adolescence onward) speak (ceaselessly) among themselves about their sexuality, about their real or imagined feminine "conquests."[15] We are talking about words spoken in public, and whose public nature is crucial, for the stories are often the products of bragging or exaggeration. Bourdieu notes that, in North African societies, "virility" or "manliness" is "subject to a more or less masked form of collective judgment" and that, consequently, every man has "the duty to assert his manliness in all circumstances."[16] Yet, as his entire book makes clear, this masculine "point of honor" of Mediterranean societies is nothing other than the "magnified image" of the way in which masculine identity is affirmed in a society such as our own. And all of the repeated stories men tell each other (that adolescent boys tell each other) about their sexual prowess, to the extent that they are intended to display and highlight their virility, also consolidate the (often violent) rejection of whatever is thought of as a renunciation of this "virility." All these communicative situations, where the point is the obligatory public recounting of sexual relations (heterosexual ones), effectively and purposively repress and obfuscate homosexuality. In all these situations, in all these exchanges, those whose sexuality is homosexual (or those adolescents who do not yet have a sexuality but who are attracted by persons of the same sex) are obliged to silence and to hide the reality of their desires or their practices. Sometimes they even invent fictive heterosexual relations (to the point where it frequently happens that two gay men discover years later that they had both been lying to each other).

In all such conversations the gay man will feel excluded. He will have the experience of being "different," but will be obliged to hide this difference on pain of being excluded from the group. In fact, he will often manage to exclude himself from those situations and those groups in which his position is always false and in which he cannot help but feel deeply uneasy. Solitude and withdrawal (perhaps with a corresponding turn toward books and culture, to recall our earlier discussion) will be a way of coping with a stigmatized identity, managing it from day to day. (The subtitle of Goffman's book *Stigma* is *Notes on the Management of Spoiled Identity*.) The process of rendering homosexuality private, of forcing it into the most secluded interior space, begins in childhood and at school. And the deliberate and liberating gesture by which, one fine day, someone decides to break with secrecy, the act by which that person makes his or her homosexuality public, marks the refusal to submit even a moment longer to the (interior) violence ex-

ercised by the intensely experienced dichotomy between what can be said in
public and what must remain part of private life, what must never leave one's
heart of hearts.

‡ For many gay men the break between public and private life is, we can see,
imposed by structures of oppression. These structures define the contours of
ways of being or ways of life that require a radical dissociation between one's
hidden self and one's presentable self. Expressions such as "dissociated
lives" or "double lives" remind us that one's "private" life is kept secret,
hidden from the eyes of those with whom friendly or social or professional
relations are conducted. The public sphere requires one to wear a mask of
heterosexuality and to hide any "abnormal" identity; public life is fundamentally linked to heterosexuality and excludes anything that deviates from it. We
might even say that heterosexuality is one of the major, foundational characteristics of what is referred to as public space. In that space, heterosexuality is
displayed, recalled, manifested, at every moment, in every gesture, in every
conversation—as any trip to the cinema, to a cafe, to a restaurant, any bus
ride, any conversation at work can attest. The public sphere is the place in
which heterosexuals can choose to display their affection and their sexuality.
Every day, at any time, any place, the street offers the *spectacle* of heterosexual
couples of all ages kissing, holding hands, or with their arms around each
other's shoulders. And young gay men and lesbians—along with those not so
young—have, for many, many years, no other image of couples or of affection
between two people, than the image provided by the public representation of
heterosexuality. For, in inverse fashion, the "public sphere" is precisely that
place where gay people may not display affection or hold hands or kiss—on
pain of insult or violence. They may not and, in fact, they do not, except at
night, as they say goodbye, at the door of the building where one of them
lives, after having made sure no one is there to see what should not be made
public. And except, of course, in the neighborhoods called "ghettos," because it is precisely there that they feel authorized to do so, because they are
present in sufficient numbers to feel safe. Surely that suffices to justify, or at
the very least to explain, the existence of such neighborhoods.

‡ It is, in fact, insult—its power of intimidation—that establishes the frontier between public and private for gays and lesbians. Thus the public and

private spheres are not materially or physically distinct spaces for them (public being the street, work, politics; private being the home and personal relations). Rather it is a matter of a binary structure that reproduces itself in homologous fashion in every lived situation and in every social relation. Goffman remarks that "the general identity-values of a society may be fully entrenched nowhere, and yet they can cast some kind of shadow on the encounters encountered everywhere in daily living."[17] This "shadow" of normalcy is what always and everywhere imposes, even in the slightest conversation, the border between the public and private spheres. It creates for some (heterosexuals) the possibility of fully inhabiting public space, and for others (gay people) the obligation to leave a part of their personality in the private space. Those who carry a "normal identity," to use Goffman's expression, can speak publicly of what they are. Those with a "discredited identity" (even more so for those who have a "discreditable" one) do their best to remain silent, to leave behind in the private space anything that might recall their stigma, any and everything about which they should not or cannot speak. The public/private structure is mobile, constantly in motion, being recreated at every moment of daily life, with the effect of excluding homosexuality from every "public" scene, even if that "public scene" takes place within a limited and "private" circle (in the family, among friends).

The opposition between public and private is so taken for granted that as soon as any gay man fails to respect it (or decides to respect it no longer—given that most of them have respected it for a certain part of their life), as soon as he makes his sexuality public (and speaks about it in the workplace), he is immediately accused of flaunting his sexuality. He will hear others complain (those very people who have spoken incessantly about their sexuality since they were teenagers): "Why do gay people always have to be so open about it?" There is a very simple answer to this question: a man comes out as gay so that he will no longer be thought to be straight.[18] For that is what always happens if he does not insist that he is gay: heterosexuality is taken for granted, assumed to be the case for everyone, for the simple reason that most gay people do not come out openly. (Thus the never-ending claims to be astonished when someone does come out, or, for example, during a Lesbian and Gay Pride parade, remarks like "they're everywhere" or "I never guessed there were so many of them," as if one had lived in total ignorance prior to the recent discovery.) Someone might also come out after realizing that a certain number of people around him already know it or suspect it and are gossiping or making tasteless jokes about it. Perhaps the very same people who, when he was not around, would say "I think he's a fag," or "the queen has stepped out for a minute" will be the ones to wax indignant as soon as he ceases to hide his sexuality: "Why does he have to flaunt it? This exhibitionism is hardly normal."

The gay man who speaks about his "private" life breaks with "normal" practice. Normal practice is defined as normal because "normally"—as we say in everyday speech—homosexuality cannot be spoken, or, what amounts to more or less the same thing, is rarely spoken of. Anytime one speaks of homosexuality, then, it can only be heard as an attempt to affirm it, to flaunt it; it can only be seen as a provocative gesture or a militant act. Leaving shame behind is always perceived to be a declaration of pride. (As, indeed, it is. A person who comes out as gay and thus brings homosexuality into discourse not as the object of a joke, or not simply as an object, but as belonging to the speech of a subject knows that what he or she has to say will be heard in this way.) It is never possible simply to say that one is gay. It is always an affirmation, in the face of everything, in the face of everyone. An affirmation not only against those who would have prevented you saying it, but also against those who would insist that there was no real need for you to say it. Thus coming out as gay or lesbian always has a certain theatricality about it.[19] Sartre has said, "Since we are merely playing at what we are, we are whatever we can play at" (stG, 324), but that does not seem satisfying in this particular case. Rather, it is because a gay man must for so long play at being what he is not that he can later only be what he is by playing at it. Exhibitionism is apparently shame's opposite. How could it be otherwise?[20]

As we have seen, there is a kind of energy born out of shame, formed by and in it, that can act as a force for transformation. This energy finds its expression in a theatricalized identity, in performance, in a love of display or extravagance, in parody. Self-display and theatricality are and have been among the most important means of defying the heteronormative hegemony—and this is why they have always been the objects of such virulent attacks. Shame cedes its energy to self-exhibition, to self-affirmation by way of theatricality, and thus to self-affirmation tout court.

14

Existence Precedes Essence

The coming out of any individual, whatever conditions facilitate it or hinder it, is always an intensely personal act, one that resembles what Sartre calls an "original choice," that is to say, the choice that each person can freely make of himself or herself and of his or her life. It is, of course, rather difficult today, after all we have learned from psychoanalysis, anthropology, linguistics, sociology, and so on, to ascribe fully to the Sartrian philosophy of freedom, which supposes that one's consciousness is transparent to oneself, or, at least, that that consciousness is only limited by itself. We have seen how social, historical, and sexual structures are written into the body and the mind of individuals, producing determinations that cannot be taken in by an analysis that proceeds in terms of conscious choices. For instance, it can be observed that this gesture of coming out is not evenly distributed across social groups. Michael Pollak has shown that the probability that a gay man will assume his identity is much greater the higher the educational level he has attained.[1]

Nonetheless, this Sartrian idea of a choice that you make—a choice that you can or should make—as to what you are at any and every moment of your life, a choice that becomes crucial at the particularly determining moment when someone chooses what to be, launching a "project" directed toward the future, seems to me to describe remarkably well the profound rupture that occurs in gay lives at the moment a decision is made to change one's relation to the world and to others. (Sartre presents this choice as one between "authenticity" and "inauthenticity.") The question, the stark dilemma which one day or another confronts gay people, is this: either to say what you are or not to, either to choose to be yourself or to fail to do so because it is too difficult. This is a choice between a freedom you choose and a form of conduct based on "bad faith," conduct that is the result of a refusal to face up to your freedom. Whatever class one may belong to—and even if the choice to be "free" is made easier by a high level of education or by coming from a certain background—all stigmatized individuals are inevitably confronted at some moment, be it in their daily life, at work, in their family circle, or with friends, by the question of whether to continue to hide what they are or to choose to assume that identity openly. Nietzsche famously wrote, "You shall become the person you are." We should not forget that a few aphorisms later, he wrote that the fundamental freedom consists in "no longer being ashamed in front of oneself."[2]

For a gay man there is a constant question as to whether he should accept himself as such or live out his days in pain and shame. Now even if the mental structures of shame and domination cannot be fully grasped within the terms of a philosophy of consciousness, we must nonetheless leave open a place for an individual decision at the foundation of freedom and emancipation—even if it is clear that this individual choice is only made possible (save in a few very exceptional cases) by the existence of the social and cultural context created by "gay culture" and by the possibility of a kind of countersocialization that that culture enables, even if it does so at a distance.

"To say 'instant' is to say *fatal instant*," Sartre writes. It is true that the instant in which the choice is made involves one's whole future. Sartre continues, "The instant is the reciprocal and contradictory envelopment of the before by the after. One is still what one is going to cease to be and already what one is going to become" (*stG*, 2). This is a marvelously apt description of the temporal structure of a relation to the gay world. The decision no longer to pretend and the choice to be oneself open onto a new temporality—one's entire future is changed. Here one could think of Sartre's analysis of freedom as "anxiety," for the "choice" is like a moment of madness that will change everything about the way one is. If young gay people experience a great deal of anxiety (in the ordinary sense of the word) at the age when the question of this choice presents itself (and it often worries the mind for many years), it is because the free act of affirming one's freedom is tied up in a more profound kind of anxiety (here in the Sartrian sense of the term), meaning that the act of freedom has nothing but the freedom per se on which to support itself.

Of course, this metaphor of the "instant" can lead one astray: it might encourage us to believe that a gay person participates in only one temporality. But in fact there is the temporality of the workplace, that of the family, that of one's friendships, and so on. One's coming out might happen in one space and not in another. In any case, that coming out, which is often experienced as a leap into the void by those who finally take the step, has always been preceded by various hesitant attempts, roundabout and abortive admissions, and so on. There are the letters written but never sent; there are last minute changes of heart after one had promised to tell a friend, one's mother, one's brother, one's sister, and so on. This can last for months or even years. Yet there will always be one day, one instant, when something—however partial, however limited—is said: the first time a friend is told or the first time pretense is abandoned. These kinds of statements can take many different forms. Some people make them quite explicitly: "I have to tell you something." Some people intentionally leave a book or magazine lying around. Some people simply introduce their partner.

In that way an individual—who had been the "object" of someone else's gaze, who had been made into an "object" by that stigmatizing gaze, who had been silenced and shamed by insult, and who had been devalorized by the dissymmetry in the social positioning of homosexuality—thus decides to turn around and become what it is that the gaze would see. He or she chooses to identify with that assigned identity. And it can thereby be overcome, exceeded, transformed, or reinterpreted. No longer need it be defined from outside. It can be reworked from inside. One can make of it what one will, free it from its reified state, make it the basis of one's freedom. "To wrest from this gaze its constituent power" (stG, 69), writes Sartre, and to reclaim the power to constitute oneself as part of one's own freedom: this is the meaning behind his oft-cited phrase: "What is important is not what people make of us but what we ourselves make of what they have made of us" (stG, 49).

❧ Of course, Sartre's treatment of gay people in some of his writing (philosophy, novels, plays, political essays) can sometimes be quite distasteful. He has a tendency—for obvious historical reasons as well as because of unthought homophobic attitudes that one also finds in Simone de Beauvoir—to lump homosexuals (because they keep so many "secrets" about themselves, because they pretend, because they seem so rarely capable of choosing authenticity) with those who practice "bad faith." One finds in Being and Nothingness, as in many other texts, intolerable statements on this subject. We are inevitably confronted here by the limits of a thought that remained in the grip of the prejudices of its moment.[3] It is only at the very end of his life that

Sartre will make an effort to produce a more political analysis that involves a rejection of his previous statements.[4]

It is nonetheless still the case that his analyses of an "original project" or of the "fatal instant"—analyses that purport to have a general applicability (for let us not forget that Sartre's philosophical program in Being and Nothingness was to set out a "phenomenological ontology")—can be taken as wonderful descriptions of the lives of gay people and of the moment of choice that they must face—or refuse to face—if they wish to escape from the "ventriloquism" of which Paul Monette spoke. From this point of view it would not be unreasonable, given the context, to translate what Sartre calls "authenticity"—the choice to be free—by "pride" in oneself. And then "shame," "disguise," and "pretense" can be taken to fall under the heading of "bad faith."

It requires no distortion of Sartre's texts to do this. The philosophical notions worked out in Being and Nothingness provide the foundation for his 1946 reflections in Anti-Semite and Jew (Réflexions sur la question juive), and many of the thoughts in that work can readily be transposed to the "gay question." Perhaps this is not the place to discuss at length his famous statement: "The Jew is one whom other men consider to be a Jew."[5] Hannah Arendt's criticisms of this idea are well known, even if they are not always pertinent.[6] Yet, given our concerns here, it is important to emphasize that Sartre offers the notion of a "situation" as an anchor for that which "serves to keep a semblance of unity in the Jewish community." It is not the past, not religion, nor any territory that founds "being-Jewish": "If all of them deserve the name of Jew, it is because they have in common the situation of a Jew, that is, they live in a community which takes them for Jews."[7] Consequently, there is always the "necessity imposed upon the Jew . . . of assuming a phantom personality . . . that haunts him and which is nothing but himself—himself as others see him" (78). This "assumption" can happen in two opposing ways:

> Authenticity, it is almost needless to say, consists in having a true and lucid consciousness of the situation, in assuming the responsibilities and risks that it involves, in accepting it in pride or humiliation, sometimes in horror and hate. There is no doubt that authenticity demands much courage and more than courage. Thus it is not surprising that one finds it so rarely. . . . And the Jew does not escape this rule: authenticity for him is to live to the full his condition as Jew; inauthenticity is to deny it or to attempt to escape from it. (90–91)

It is because such a "phantom personality" haunts the gay man despite himself and because this "personality" is nothing other than "himself as others see him"—or, what amounts to the same thing, himself occupying the specific derogatory place he is assigned in the sexual order—that every gay man must one day "assume" that personality, must choose to be what he is or else give up freedom and annihilate himself as a person in order to comply with the demands of the society that both insults him as a homosexual and denies him the right to declare that he is gay. "Inauthentic Jews," Sartre says, "are men whom other men take for Jews and who have decided to run away from this insupportable situation."[8] Thus is "inauthenticity" a form of submission to the social order and to oppressive structures, while "authenticity" is above all a refusal of this order. It is clear why Sartre is able to say that authenticity can only manifest itself "in revolt."[9]

Authenticity is to be found in the decision to assume the burden of being what one is: to be gay not simply as it were *en soi* (which is to say according to the gaze of others, of society), but rather *pour soi* (that is, having assumed the identity for oneself as a project of freedom). That social gaze establishes for all gay people, even ones who are not out, the *en soi* of homosexuality: the image and the "role," the "discreditable" identity, assigned to them. The gay man thus must *make* himself gay in order to escape from the violence that the society that makes him *be* gay also threatens him with. In a political text from the 1970s, for instance, Sartre will say that a Basque person must "make himself (or herself) Basque [se faire basque]" in order to fight the oppression suffered due to *being* Basque.[10] Someone could, of course, raise the objection that it is much easier to know what "being Basque" means than to know what "being gay" means. Indeed, much of the difficulty with "authenticity" for a gay person lies in the difficulty in identifying with an "identity" that is necessarily plural, necessarily multiple: it is an identity without identity, or, better, an identity without an essence—an identity to be created.[11] In effect, for a person who has decided to have no further truck with all the kinds of psychological meanings imposed by social and cultural discourses on homosexuality (be they legal, medical, psychoanalytical, and so on), there is no "me," no "ego," to *be* that would preexist that which must be brought into existence. This is why Henning Bech can say that a gay person is a "born existentialist," for existence (always) precedes essence: gay identity, as soon as it is chosen rather than merely submitted to, is never simply given.[12] In order to be constructed, it will refer to already existing, already visible models (in all their multiplicity). One can therefore say that the project of "making" oneself gay (*se faire gay*) not only means creating oneself, but creating oneself in the light of, through the inspiration of, all the examples already available in society and in history. If there is to be an "identity," it will be a personal identity made in relation to a collective one. It will invent itself in and through the "social types," the "roles" that one "plays," to whose existence one contributes in a form of collective recreation of gay subjectivity.

There is always another "phantom personage" that haunts every gay person in contemporary society. It is not the one created by the "gaze" of the other, but the one opposed to that gaze, constructed in opposition to it by gay visibility itself. Consequently "making" oneself gay takes on a meaning much less metaphysical than that of the "authenticity" of which Sartre speaks: for it is simply a matter of identifying oneself with an already existing collective—even if the identity produced by that collective is itself never stable. It has evolved endlessly over the past century. (It seems probable that even over short time spans there have been profound changes, to the extent that a gay man from the late 1990s is remarkably different from a gay man from the early 1970s.) Collective creation is forever moving beyond itself. It is profoundly unpredictable. It opens history to freedom.

15
Unrealizable Identity

Whatever "roles" gay people take up, however they might transform them, these available "identities" all share the characteristic of—now and then, here or there—being in a compromised position vis-à-vis the social world around them. A gay person is never done with the necessity of choosing to be himself or herself in the face of a stigmatizing society. What Sartre calls "authenticity" can only be understood as an unending process of self-invention and self-construction.

Coming out is a conversion experience. If it can be described as the act of a particular moment, of the instant in which a decision is made, we must add that such a decision will need to be made over and over again. Basically, coming out is a lifelong process. It will always be an open question as to where, when, and with whom it is possible not to hide what one is. The need to choose reappears in every new situation in life: when a teacher finds himself or herself in front of a new class or a different lecture hall, when a student meets a dissertation director, when any gay man or lesbian sees a new doctor or a new employer, enters a new workplace, is admitted to a hospital, enters a retirement home, or finds him or herself in front of a newspaper salesman or a taxi driver who is saying something homophobic.[1]

Becoming socialized within a gay context (made up of bars, cruising places, and so on), a process that allows one to find friends who are them-selves gay, can reinforce this strongly dichotomous structure: freedom within the confines of a carefully built up, chosen area and "discretion" within the space of the family and the workplace. Yet such a polarity exists even for the most open gay men and lesbians. Doubtless there is no gay person so "open" that he or she has not, at one moment or another, made compromises with the closet. This is why coming out is never done only once and for all. Rather it is a point of departure, a kind of "ruling ideal" that shapes one's conduct but can never be fully attained. The closet is structured in such a way that you are never simply either in or out, but always both in and out, more or less in or more or less out depending on the particular instance and your own evolution. You can never be fully in the closet to the extent that, as we have seen, the closet can always become a sort of "open secret." There is always at least one person who seems to know, whom you know knows, or whom you suspect must know. And you can never be fully out of the closet, for at any moment you can once again find yourself in the situation of having to disguise what you are or of simply not feeling like making things perfectly clear. Thus the decision no longer to pretend, to be open about what you are, can only be the beginning of a necessarily interminable process, in the sense in which Freud could speak of an "interminable analysis."

It is not just a matter of lapses in the degree of individual courage it is necessary to summon up in life's various situations—often (and quite stressfully) when you least expect it. Nor is it a question of an inevitable and provisory flagging of the psychological energy required by the will to be "out." For it is indeed a tedious experience, to desire to be or to be required to be, permanently out. Often enough it is simply easier not to say the words, not to make the gesture, that would reaffirm your coming out, once you have realized that the words will have to be said, the gesture made, again and again. Here we are dealing on a very deep level with the definition of the very structure of gay identity. As Henning Bech puts it, when you have made the choice no longer to pretend, you move "from the uneasiness of not being able to be [yourself] as a homosexual . . . to the uneasiness of having to be [yourself] as a homosexual."[2]

» Being true to oneself is doubtless easier for heterosexuals. This is not to claim that heterosexual lives have no rifts in them or that all heterosexuals are people who live with a happy sense of self-adequation. Yet, perhaps a certain stability is ensured by family life, along with the powerfully heteronormative context of professional life and, when you get right down to it, the entire sexual order that makes heterosexual behaviors seem legitimate and "normal." That stability can allow one to feel at home with oneself, to feel that one coincides with established social roles and with well-known and accepted social identities that are themselves presented as normative models by and for heterosexuality. The norm and social institutions are themselves homophobic (as the refusal to allow gay men and lesbians to marry reminds us, and as all the discourses that work to justify this prohibition often naively admit).

When I used the theory of performativity to define the power of insult, I recalled that among the examples Austin provides is the example of the words spoken to perform a marriage. The example recurs throughout his book almost like an obsession: "I do take this woman . . ." or "I now pronounce you. . . ."[3] These statements are performative in that they perform the act that they announce. But the performative power of such statements is never the expression of an individual will. The person who says them must be authorized to say them, and the situation in which they are said must fulfill certain conventions. Therefore a performative utterance must have been said before. It is always a citation. An utterance is only performative if it is empowered by the social order or the law (even if it is only the law of repetition) that institutes it.[4] Now it is worth noting that the performative utterances of a wedding ceremony (and therefore of the entire structure of iteration and citation that support them) accomplish more than what they explicitly set out to do: they do effectively unite two people "in the bonds of matrimony" (taking for granted the entire set of all preceding marriages and also the institution of matrimony that allows such a ceremony to have any meaning at all), but beyond that they also exclude all those persons to whom the right to marry is refused. Every time a justice of the peace pronounces those words, he or she not only marries two people, he or she also reenacts all the rules (and the laws) of marriage—thereby reproducing the social and juridical exclusion of gay people. In this regard, marriage has a relation to what Pierre Bourdieu has labeled "rites of institution," rites that produce two effects simultaneously: they perform the separation between those who have already been marked distinctively in a certain way and those who have not yet been marked (because they are too young); and they also separate those who have been distinguished in a certain way from those who may never be distinguished in that way. (For example, the "rites" that mark the entry of young men into adulthood by definition obviously exclude women.) Marriage performs this same double separation: most visibly between those who are married and those who are not, but also—less visibly but just as effectively—between those who have the right to marry and those who do not. Consider the argument put forth by the supporters of the various proposals for national domestic partnership legislation in France. They all stated that the goal is to offer "a legal framework to those couples who do not wish to or who are not allowed to marry."[5] Clearly, this referred both to heterosexual couples who did not wish to be married yet wished to have access to some of the advantages associated with marriage and to same-sex couples, who had no access to marriage. A phrase like that is an effort to solve a problem without even noticing that it exists. For surely each time something like that is said, a question should occur to us: who are these couples who want to marry but are not allowed to? Again we see how the institution of matrimony works to perform exclusions. By the daily act of saying "I now declare you husband and wife," the justice of the peace implicitly reminds all same-sex couples that no official will unite them in the bonds of matrimony, or, more explicitly, they are told that the bonds of matrimony are not meant for them. By uniting in marriage, the justice of the peace also performs an exclusion, recalls and perpetuates a system of inferiorization. Such an exclusion has an effect even on people who do not wish to get married. (Roland Barthes, for example, in *Roland Barthes by Roland Barthes*, describes his painful feeling of rejection at the hands of the social order upon seeing a marriage ceremony being conducted at the Église Saint-Sulpice.[6])

But marriage and the question of the legal recognition of couples are only one example of the ways institutions reject gay men and lesbians. (One would also have to speak of schools, the military, churches, the law, sports, and so on.) These institutions work to establish and to reproduce an uncrossable divide between the norm and homosexuality—and another form of self-division within a gay person.[7] Here we could have recourse to another Sartrian concept in order to say that gay identity is "unrealizable." The notion of being "unrealizable" refers both to the fact that one can never coincide with oneself and that one must nevertheless pursue this very goal of self-coincidence.[8] A gay person must forever be replaying the moment in which he or she decided to be himself or herself, decided to be what he or she is. Such constant work on the self, far from ensuring stability, is perpetually unsettling. Perhaps we should not deplore this, even as we notice the ravaging effects such constitutive instability can have on individual minds—effects that provide a livelihood for psychoanalysts. This inadequation of self to self, this division within one's own self, is most often experienced (especially by gay men and lesbians who are in the closet) as a painful and profound break within one's own personality, within one's own individual subjectivity. Such a division, when it is unchosen and unpleasant, can perpetuate all the effects of a "double life" or "double consciousness." Yet one can assert that this same inadequation, this same division within the self, provides the possibility for a kind of existential and cultural richness. American advocates of "queer politics" have pointed to the potential freedom it could enable: if you are inadequate to your own identity, then you are inadequate as well to all the shackles that accompany various ways of stabilizing an identity.[9] Doubtless it is because a gay person must always be working on his or her self that Foucault spoke of the idea of a "homosexual ascesis," which is to say, an "aesthetic of the self," a self-fashioning which is nothing more than the coming to consciousness and deliberate assumption of this structure of inadequation that is at the heart of the daily life and consciousness of gays and lesbians.

This is not a new idea. We might recall that Oscar Wilde, using words that Foucault would spontaneously rediscover a century later, was already speaking of "making of one's life a work of art." In the second part of the present study, we will see that the idea of creating oneself was basically consubstantial with gay discourse from the very moment it emerged. One can understand, then, why Foucault would say that "homosexuality is not a form of desire but something desirable." We should not be thinking of discovering some preexistent form of desire within ourselves: "We have to devote ourselves seriously to becoming homosexuals and not stubbornly limit ourselves to discovering that that is what we are."[10]

Foucault clearly means to suggest that there is no natural, transhistorical truth to homosexuality waiting to be discovered once the prohibitions on it have been overcome. "Gay identity" is a historical construction, a product of history. Consequently, it can be modified through historical action, through individual and collective reinvention. Further, this implies that, to the extent that this identity is not a given, but something made, something always being remade, we have to give up the illusion that we could someday achieve some kind of stable and definitive identity. Some people may like to think that, thanks to the victories of the gay and lesbian movement, it may become possible, simply by wanting to "be gay," to achieve some kind of existential repose, something that would be both social and psychological, and that this repose will perhaps happen within the space of freedom known as the "gay world." Or, if it does not happen there, then perhaps, to the contrary, it will happen with the achievement of full and equal rights, notably the right to marriage. No, identity will *always* be something that must be created. What we have on our hands is something that is essentially unfinished. Instead of looking for repose, instead of looking for some collective or individual "end of gay history" in the complete and full adequation to oneself, we had better accept the inevitably provisional unforeseeable character—on both the individual and collective levels—of what it means to be gay.

⊁ My intention is not to perpetuate the literary myth of the "gay outlaw," whose very existence would be synonymous with political and cultural subversion. Leo Bersani has recently given us a masterly analysis of this mythology (an analysis that was also an eloquent defense of it, though a defense perhaps too strongly marked by a clear nostalgia for a form of literary transgression that we should not forget was made possible by all sorts of class allegiances and repressive social circumstances that were all presupposed by the literary transgression itself).[11] Yet one might still think that there will always be a potential "pariah" in every gay person, even in the one who is most careful regarding his or her integration into the system of dominant values. This may only be for the simple reason that the world into which such a person would assimilate, into which he or she (sometimes) dreams of blending, is not interested and will reject, even violently, this request for integration, with the reminder that people like him or like her merely encourage the dissolution of society and its values. (Yet at the same time, that society will insist on "assimilation," that is, insist on a gay person denying what he or she is, or at least refraining from displaying it.) The gay people who care most about "integration" thus must "disassimilate" themselves in order to advocate for "assimilation." They must set themselves up as a specific group in order to ask that they be seen and treated as no different from anyone else. Such demands will unleash reactions that both insist that they are different and insist that they not ask to be treated as different. That is to say, they are inevitably forced back to their point of departure: the perpetual choice between silence and "rebellion," between returning to the closet and affirming who they are. This is how gay people remain torn between two different levels of what is commonly referred to as "assimilation." There is assimilation by way of invisibility—to be silent, not to exist as gay. And there is the assimilation a certain number aspire to, the assimilation that would come with achieving equal legal rights. Some no longer care for the first form and find the second violently refused to them by the homophobic majority. This is an insurmountable paradox.[12] Yet it is in this paradox that one finds all the political and cultural stakes of gay "resubjectification" today, whether it be individual or collective.

One should not believe that a glorious future is looming on the horizon, one in which homosexuality will be considered as "normal" as heterosexuality, one in which homophobia will have disappeared along with the stigma attached to the category of homosexuality, one in which there will be merely a continuum of practices and behaviors, each as normal as all the others. Such a utopia—one no one really believes in—is a chimera whose only function is as part of an effort to cause the gay movement to lay down its arms, to turn to a kind of self-effacement—the only form of "assimilation" allowable today, and one endlessly called for.

Homosexuality is perpetually disturbing. It causes worry and perturbation. It produces rejection and hatred. Still, that idea developed by gay movements in the 1970s, according to which there would be a strong link between homosexuality and revolution or, in the lingo of today, between homosexuality and "subversion," seems merely a pipe dream or a silly article of faith. Such ways of thinking and speaking had a considerable importance in creating the gay and lesbian movement, but they have more to do with wishful thinking than with analysis, or with a firm grasp on reality. For obviously there is neither a direct nor a unique way of linking sexuality and politics. One need not even enter into a discussion of the personal opinions of gay people past or present (opinions that certainly cover the same political spectrum as those of the general population and probably are distributed according to the same social and cultural criteria and determinants). It suffices to mention a few of the more famous gay people of the twentieth century or to recall the political attitudes of a certain number of movements and organizations from the same period to show not only that homosexuality can happily dwell hand in hand with a whole range of conservative, reactionary, elitist, and nationalist ideologies, but even that it can count as one of their primary justifications or founding principles.[13] One should doubtless confront head-on the opposite question, considered forcefully by Leo Bersani in *Homos*, according to which there might be a continuity between, on the one hand, gay male desire and the fantasies associated with a desire oriented toward the most obvious signs of masculinity and, on the other hand, the phallic structures of political and social oppression.

Still, whatever kind of fantasmatic inscription of homosexual desire there may be for this or that gay person, whatever his or her political positions may be, however socially or politically conformist he or she may be, however willing to submit to dominant values, established norms, and the institutions that reproduce them, however great his or her desire may be to dissociate himself from any other gay person who creates a "bad image" or makes social acceptance more difficult, it nonetheless remains the case that the world to which that gay man or that lesbian would assimilate is the world of insult. It is a world in which that person has been called or might potentially be called a "stinking faggot" or a "dyke" and in which he or she will consequently always be, in one way or another, marginalized or ostracized. This cannot fail to have psychological consequences. (Among them might be a reinforced desire to adhere to the social order, a redoubled effort at conformism, so that by way of this will to assimilation, one might achieve recognition from social institutions. Or, in inverse fashion, we might observe the realization being made that such assimilation is an impossible project, a trap gay people set for themselves, and that one's time is better spent turning one's back on the kinds of claims whose aim would be to integrate gay people to the social order and, instead, learning to enjoy the benefits of marginality.)

Doubtless we should be calling radically into question this whole series of oppositions between integration and subversion, between assimilation and separatism—between these and a whole similar range of notions constantly reproduced by lazy habits of thought. For, in the first place, these are notions that are never analyzed and that fail to stand up to the most cursory examination. What, for example, could "assimilation" really mean for gay people? They are not immigrants who may have to integrate into a new culture but, in large majority, people who work, pay taxes, vote, participate in cultural life, and so on. Should they be learning to integrate as gay people? But can they? Integrate by pretending not to be gay? Indeed! Further, what could something like "separatism" really mean, when the idea seems to apply only to those people who (only during certain hours of the week) spend their time in neighborhoods or locales understood to be gay, yet who also have jobs, go out to dinner, go to the movies, and do any number of other things that can hardly be thought of as separatist? Certainly there are also plenty of gays who speak in favor of assimilation and yet spend a lot of their time in gay bars, whereas there are others who speak all the time about subversion and yet would never set foot in such a place for fear of being snared by capitalism or of participating in the increasing commercialization of the gay community. All these false oppositions can be left to careless essayists or to journalists who have a hard time locating the truly important social debates of our time (such as the profoundly homophobic opposition— present in so many French discussions—between "separatism" or identity politics and "universalism," an opposition whose only purpose seems to be to deny gay people the right to speak in the first person).

Rather than trying to establish one's position vis-à-vis these oppositions, rather than choosing one term over another, it would be more worthwhile to take the oppositions themselves as objects for analysis. For it would seem that the entire history of homosexuality, at least in the twentieth century, has been divided between these two poles: there is on the one hand all the work that has been done to establish a "gay world" that belongs to a specific "minority" (although there is not an exact correspondence between that world and that minority), and there is on the other all the work that has been done to allow gay people to be considered individuals like any other, whose sexuality should not matter. Is it not the interaction between these opposing aspirations that has been the basis of what we call the gay movement or gay culture?

We could certainly think, as does Eve Kosofsky Sedgwick, that the tension between "universalizing" aspirations (that think of homosexuality as fitting into a continuum of sexual practices) and "minoritizing" aspirations (that, to the contrary, think of gay people as a distinct group) does effectively constitute the history of the gay movement, and, more generally, the history of twentieth-century homosexuality. We might also think that all the notions referred to by these currents (assimilation, integration, lack of notable differences, on the one hand; and a gay world, minority status, and fundamental differences on the other) have never shown themselves to be particularly stable, have sometimes shifted sides, and have taken on different and contradictory meanings in different cultural contexts. For the very same discourse can mean opposite things and can aim at different ends in different historical moments or in different countries.

For instance, it makes no sense to imagine that on one side of the division we will find militant activists working to establish the claim that gays form a special minority, while on the other we will find politically unengaged people who only wish to blend into society and be accepted by it. The gay movement itself has been, from the outset, divided between these two tendencies. One and the same organization can harbor them both at the same moment, or move from one position to the other. One can see this in the case of the Mattachine Society in the United States, founded in 1948 by former members of the Communist Party who wanted to foster the growth of a self-conscious homosexual minority. They would soon be replaced at the head of the organization by representatives of the opposing tendency, who were trying to advance an assimilationist agenda.[14] Yet was this not also already the case in Germany, at the very beginning of the century, when the "minoritizing" theory of a "third sex" as put forth by Magnus Hirschfeld was challenged by those who favored masculinist (and misogynist) theories whose aim was to integrate male homosexuality into the continuum of social relations between men, and which relied on the theme (one that would have a long life ahead of it) of an inborn bisexuality (inborn at least in men) rather than on the idea of a specifically homosexual minority?[15] Many of the revolutionary discourses of the 1970s spontaneously rediscovered these myths of bisexuality or poly-sexuality—but with the opposite political and ideological implications in mind. They dreamed of a new day after the revolution when gay people would no longer be oppressed because they would have disappeared into a large new—"transverse"—form of sexual communication.[16] In the early 1970s there was a large group of available discourses (often mingling and borrowing from each other with little concern for coherence) that can be summarized schematically as involving a discourse of "identity" (there was something like a homosexual "identity" that had been repressed through various prohibitions and that needed to be liberated and to speak for itself) and another discourse that claimed that the opposition between homosex-uality and heterosexuality was itself the product of nineteenth-century bour-geois society.

In order to make it even clearer that all the various ways of thinking about sexuality and all their various political connotations cannot credibly be re-duced to oversimplified schemas (such as the opposition between assimila-tionists and separatists), we could note that in the context of the 1960s and 1970s, the conservative discourse of a homophile organization such as Ar-cadie tended rather toward the minoritizing point of view, considering homosexuals as a separate "people," whereas the radical discourse that took its inspiration from Deleuze and Guattari's *Anti-Oedipus* tended toward "uni-versalism." Its aim was the abolition of the boundaries and dualisms that set up different categories for individuals according to their sexualities. Ar-cadie's discourse could therefore be described simultaneously as "separa-tist" and "assimilationist," for it considered gay people as a group apart, yet sought recognition and integration for them from social norms and institu-tions. Whereas the discourse of the far left was, to the contrary, "antisepara-tist," but also "antiassimilationist." It wanted to break down established values through the liberation of desire and through the notion of "deterritorialization" that was so important to Deleuze and that of "transversality," so important to Guattari. This is why the queer movement in the United States, which places itself in opposition to a tendency within the gay movement to be both separatist and assimilationist, has wanted to resurrect the subversive inspiration of the movements of the 1960s and 1970s, to reclaim the possibilities of being antiseparatist and antiassimilationist. That this movement would find a friendly precursor in Guy Hocquenghem is easily understandable, even if it obviously chooses to leave behind (or perhaps it does not always do this) his utopian and revolutionary inspiration.[17] One might here wonder if "queer theory" is correct when it relates the thought of Hocquenghem to that of Foucault. For if it is Foucault's intention to dissolve the notion of identity (not by saying that it does not exist, but by showing that it was forged by psychiatry), this is not in order to oppose to identity a theory of the liberation of desire and its "transversal" potentialities. Foucault's critique is pointed quite directly at the idea that "sexuality" and "desire" could be the agents of subversion, given that they also need to be thought of as part of the deployment of the disciplinary technologies Foucault is subjecting to historical analysis. Seen in this light, Foucault's La Volonté de savoir is as much a critique of the theory of desire as of the theory of identity, to the extent that theories of desire share with theories of identity the presupposition that sexuality defines the interior "truth" of an individual. Foucault, as we will see in the third part of this book, will later abandon this approach and return to something closer to what Eve Kosofsky Sedgwick has called the minoritizing tradition. He will develop the idea of a "gay culture" that needs to be created, which amounts to saying that individuals, by way of their sexuality, weave among themselves forms of collective belonging, forms to which one can give a shape, a physiognomy, a content—all of which are forever being invented, and cannot be prescribed or defined in advance. But this minoritizing conception of Foucault's, as we shall see, is neither separatist nor assimilationist. The "gay culture" that he would wish for is not assimilationist, for he conceives of it as something that will allow one to evade and thereby destabilize the institutions of the established order. Nor is it separatist, for it will produce social and cultural changes that will be as relevant to heterosexuals burdened by the yoke of normalcy as to gay people.

16

Perturbations

The idea that some kind of sexual "subversion" would necessarily be linked to politically progressive attitudes is an idea that needs to be abandoned. Just as an avant-garde painter might have quite traditional taste in music or literature or reactionary political beliefs, so one can be (more or less) "subversive" as regards sexuality and (more or less) conservative politically speaking. One has only to think of Jean Cocteau or Gertrude Stein, whose right-wing political opinions existed comfortably alongside radically subversive behavior as regards sexual codes. It is clear, then, that we have to proceed on a case-by-case basis, always inquiring into the true content of what is called "subversion," inquiring as to what is to be subverted, and why, and even if there is anything whatsoever being subverted at all.

Consider, for example, some of the "assimilationist" demands that one finds being made by gay and lesbian movements in many countries around the globe. Leo Bersani has described them quite cruelly (but justly) as revealing a "desire to demonstrate that we too can be good soldiers, good parents, good priests."[1] Are such demands not necessarily shaped from the inside by the "unrealizable" quality of gay identity? That quality of gay identity—however it is conceived—introduces a slippage into any assimilationist project, any project that has as a goal to allow one to inhabit the social order. For no gay person will ever be accepted according to the established set of values into whose sanctum he or she may sometimes entertain the silly illusion of being admitted. This is shown, as we have seen, in all of the baroque arguments adduced by all the social and cultural agents of homophobia against the manifest desire of gay men and lesbians to be granted normal rights and normal forms of institutional recognition. These agents and their agencies repetitively reproduce a violent discourse that asserts on every occasion that gay people represent a great danger to society and to civilization. They thereby at least perform the service of reminding anyone worried about the "conformism" of assimilationist programs, that even those very programs contain the capacity to induce a kind of social and cultural instability—one that homosexuality will always carry with it—in the institutions that, some day or other, are going to have to make a place for it.

The panic evinced by the guardians of the heterosexual order when confronted by this programmatic destabilization has taken on many forms in recent times. One of the more notable among them has been the argument one can hear not only from the defenders of a certain Christian order, but also from those who preach the faith of psychoanalysis as well as both people of the far right and even the socialist or Catholic left, all of whom wish to defend "the-right-of-children-to-have-both-a-father-and-a-mother." No matter how ridiculous such an assertion should seem in the world of today—a world in which so many children are being raised by a single parent or by two parents of the same sex—it gives expression to the horror felt by homophobic people of all political or philosophical persuasions when faced with the power of innovation and invention that homosexuality exhibits. Such a horror can be felt even when the gay or lesbian people involved claim—as many of them do—that what they most wish for is to fit in with everyone else as normally as possible. But for gay people, to integrate themselves into the norm is doubtless more difficult than to remain marginalized. One might think here of the half-serious, half-ironical comments Michel Foucault made in speaking about the organization Arcadie, at the moment when that organization's founder had decided to close it down: "It is in the very nature of such a movement to wish to gain acceptance for homosexuality from the arbiters of established values, to find a way to include it in existing institutional frameworks. But once you have thought about it, such a project seems infinitely more difficult, and crazier [plus folle], than the project of creating spaces of freedom that exist outside established institutions. For after all, these kinds of spaces have always existed."[2]

We should not conclude from these remarks that Foucault considered this "crazy" [folle] project to have more legitimacy than the project of creating free spaces. It seems rather that he wanted to insist that such a project was fundamentally doomed to failure and that the free spaces represented the only real possibility for gay people to be able to live out their lives and invent themselves. Throughout all the battles gay people have led for that institutional recognition so regularly refused to them, it seems true that only partial successes have been possible, successes that are also fragile and ephemeral. Still, it should go without saying that these partial successes do not only gain for many gays and lesbians rights that they need or long for. They also greatly perturb those institutions that are ever so slowly forced to recognize these "peculiar situations," situations whose concrete existence has now been brought to the attention of even the most obtusely homophobic individuals.

✣ The richness of argument in Leo Bersani's Homos lies for me not so much in the way he seeks to recover the subversive potential of certain writers but in his wonderful demonstration of how, within the history of gay culture, even in the case of an individual author, a tradition of conformism and a tradition of subversion can coexist to the point of being indissociable, even indistinguishable, from one another. The two are one. It is perhaps even the very inextricability of the two traditions that defines what we call gay culture. This would apply equally in the case of women or men.[3] It would also apply to transsexuals, as one can see by reading the interviews given by the Israeli singer Dana International. Given the scandal she created in her country, and given the way in which she has become a symbol of the revolt against the moral and religious order that certain groups wish to impose there, it might seem paradoxical to read the statements in which she describes her ideal of a life that seems to come straight out of the pages of a romance novel or to correspond to the fantasy of a little house with a white picket fence.[4] It would be a serious error to make fun of these dreams of normalcy. It is clear that what we see here is not so much the existence of transsexuality provoking the fury of the guardians of the norm as it is the unshakable will of a transsexual to affirm that she is a person like anyone else, that her tastes are more or less like anyone else's, and that she can even represent her country in international competitions. This is a particularly intense example of the mixture of a will to integration with subversive potential, in which the interaction between the two is also very clear. One easily imagines the uproar that would ensue were she to demand the right to marry.

Subversion is always partial and localized. Those who forget that run the risk of being trapped in the narcissistic pleasure of assuming poses from which to emit radical discourses that are perfectly empty of content. If subversion does not subvert something specific at a specific moment, it does nothing at all. Thus one always needs to ask what the aim of subversion is, and what it is destabilizing. In every different situation one has to consider what would be more subversive. One thereby realizes that in certain situations conformist aspirations are more destabilizing and can turn out to be more subversive than any number of revolutionary proclamations. It can be seen today that those who defend the social (or the "symbolic") order against the campaign to establish the right to gay marriage are perfectly capable of letting slip by all sorts of *soi-disant* subversive behaviors. The more liberal of those defenders might even appreciate or encourage those "subversive" behaviors for the way they help construct an exotic elsewhere in which gay men and lesbians could be locked away—and from which they would no longer clamor for access to equal rights. Gay men and lesbians are free to go on being "subversive" as long as they limit themselves to that. One might therefore tend to the idea that what would be truly subversive today would be to refuse the social role to which one is assigned. The obsessive need in France at the beginning of the 1990s to denounce identity politics (that is to say, the creation of the free spaces Foucault was speaking of) has given way to the relentless denunciation of the "universalist" struggle to claim the right to marriage. Evidently such a claim (a claim on institutional recognition, the kind Foucault referred to as "crazy") is seen as more critical to the defenders of the established order. One even sees the two forms of denunciation (of identity politics and of universalist efforts respectively) incoherently and illogically inhabiting the same discourses, as if gay people should always be denounced for something, as if they can never be right about anything.

⊁ We should add that if "subversion" is always partial, this is partly because a subject's position within relations of domination is never simple. There are always multiple hierarchizations, sometimes contradictory among themselves: a gay man may be in a dominated and vulnerable position within the hierarchy of sexualities while being well positioned to dominate in terms of his sex, his class, his ethnicity—that is, he could be a man, a well-to-do man, a white man, and so on. To take another example, a black woman will perhaps feel more oppressed because she is black than because she is a woman and may therefore feel more solidarity with black men than with white women—and thus more inclined to struggle against racial domination and racism than against masculine domination and sexism. We need to try to conceive of the ensemble of systems of domination and oppression together as a totality, to think of these systems in their multiplicity and with all of their articulations. Yet clearly, in the context of a political action or an act of cultural subversion, any given person will have a tendency to emphasize this or that aspect of the multiple forms of oppression that concern her or him. And we could go on to add that the fact of belonging to one oppressed category has never stopped anyone from contributing to a different form of oppression. (To be the victim of racism does not stop someone from being racist or homophobic; to be gay does not stop someone from being racist or politically conservative, or reactionary, or even fascist.)[5] As Goffman puts it, "In many cases he who is stigmatized in one regard nicely exhibits all the normal prejudices held toward those who are stigmatized in another regard."[6] One should not have any preconceived ideas regarding solidarity between oppressed or dominated peoples. Such solidarity must be constructed and acquired, often despite prejudices that structure the ways of thinking of the dominated themselves.

Even if he is socially dominant, the gay man is always dominated as a homosexual. Just as women, as Bourdieu puts it in *Masculine Domination*, no matter how they are positioned in the social hierarchy, are always, within the particular social space to which they belong, in an inferior relation to men—or, more precisely, to use Bourdieu's phrase, "are separated from men by a negative symbolic coefficient"—so gay men are always in an inferior symbolic situation within their specific social space.[7]

Yet perhaps this also explains why, whatever their position within the social order, individual men separated in so many ways can feel a profound affinity for each other—even if it is only for a moment—precisely because they occupy a homologous position within a sexual order that governs in a similar fashion the very different social spaces to which they each belong. It seems quite probable that this "sexual" solidarity, if we can call it that, will have a tendency to diminish progressively as the effects of a clandestine existence lessen and as gay and lesbian visibility develops.

Indeed, once the more or less "secret" group (with its meetings in bars and parks, in which barriers of class are often effaced) becomes visible as a group, an internal differentiation inevitably manifests itself. One doubts that the gay and lesbian activists who demonstrate alongside illegal immigrants feel much affinity for "A-list" gays or for women belonging to the "lesbian chic." Clearly the main difficulty for creating an enduring "gay and lesbian movement" lies in the fact that such a movement must mobilize people based on a common positioning within the sexual order independent of their position in the social order. Yet the affirmation of gay and lesbian visibility helps class affiliations and political positions to become internal principles of vision and division. Still, we might choose to think that the experience of a large number of individuals having a possible identification with the gay and lesbian scene—and with the cultural and political mobilization that is one of its forms of expression—could result in a certain social uprooting. Such an identification might help those individuals break from the set of social determinations that had been weighing upon their political choices. It might, thanks to the kind of progressive awakening it can make possible, offer them a principle around which to reorganize their position-taking, a position-taking whose focus might then become the struggle for minoritarian affirmations or against forms of discrimination and exclusion. In the huge study of "homosexualities" that they conducted in the 1970s, Bell and Weinberg reported that although the majority of those who responded claimed that their homosexuality had had no effect on their politics, nonetheless about a third of the white gay men who replied imagined that their sexuality had made them more "liberal." None of the black gay men who replied said the same. A few of them claimed their sexuality had even made them less "liberal." Largely speaking, gay men were more "liberal" or "radical" than straight ones.[8] Doubtless one should make a distinction here between closeted gay men and open or even activist ones. Barry Adam, for example, cites studies that seem to show that the most closeted gay men, those whose sexuality expresses itself in the most furtive and secretive encounters and who lead an apparently "normal" life within their small town, are often found to hold conservative or even reactionary political beliefs.[9] As a counterexample, we could cite the case of Gide, who claimed to have been led to his progressive political engagements by his homosexuality (as was also the case for Isherwood).[10] That Gide's political evolution, from right to left, should have corresponded to such an extent to his will to affirm his homosexuality publicly and to make himself into a defender of this "cause" remains quite striking.[11]

Without giving way to utopianism, without trying to be irenic, we might still affirm the probability that the gay and lesbian movement (understood in the broadest and vaguest way) can be thought of as a force that encourages profound transformations in the way previously isolated individuals come to regard society and come to take positions regarding problems that extend far beyond simply those of sexual politics.

17

The Individual and the Group

A gay man is always torn between two opposing realities that shape his very being. He is produced as an inferiorized individual, and his subjectivity is shaped by self-hatred, by a refusal to identify himself with those who experience the same kind of inferiorization. A gay individual is made for a kind of isolation or individualism, perhaps based in shame (the dislike of his own gayness) or perhaps in pride (an elitist scorn directed at other gay men). Yet, given that he has been produced by the same "subjecting-subjugating" processes as other gay people (of which the violence of insult is a condensed form, insult as the basis of a relation to a world defined by the norms of the sexual order), he necessarily belongs, whether he wishes to or not, to the "collective" he wishes to dismiss. He belongs to it all the more in that he has little choice but to frequent its meeting places (bars, parks, internet chat rooms, and so on) and to be drawn into its visible forms, or its material or social aspects. In any case, this collective is already part of his unconscious, which already contains the invisible link—one he may well wish to break—between him and other gay men.

Such a double movement has been described admirably by Proust. When he wishes to express his hostility toward the nascent gay movement (doubtless he was thinking of Germany and of the efforts of Magnus Hirschfeld), Proust denounces its uselessness and its impossibility: every potential member, he says, would prefer to flee from all the others rather than be associated with them. Yet, at the same moment, he describes gay men as already belonging to a self-constituted group, one built on the model of an ethnic community:

> I have thought it as well to utter here a provisional warning against the lamentable error of proposing (just as people have encouraged a Zion-

ist movement) to create a Sodomist movement and to rebuild Sodom. For, no sooner had they arrived there than the Sodomites would leave the town so as not to have the appearance of belonging to it. . . . They would repair to Sodom only on days of supreme necessity, when their own town was empty, at those seasons when hunger drives the wolf from the woods. In other words, everything would go on very much as it does to-day in London, Berlin, Rome, Petrograd or Paris.

Yet he had commented, only a few lines earlier: "Certainly they form in every land an oriental colony, cultured, musical, malicious, which has charming qualities and intolerable defects" (RTP, 2:655–56).

On the one hand Proust presents the subterranean and secret evidence of the existence of a collective (an "accursed race") whose members immediately recognize each other thanks to hidden clues that only they know how to recognize. They form

a freemasonry far more extensive, more effective and less suspected than that of the Lodges, for it rests upon an identity of tastes, needs, habits, dangers, apprenticeship, knowledge, traffic, vocabulary, and one in which even members who do not wish to know one another recognise one another immediately by natural or conventional, involuntary or deliberate signs which indicate one of his kind to the beggar in the person of the nobleman whose carriage door he is shutting, to the father in the person of his daughter's suitor. . . .[1]

Yet on the other hand, the will of each member of this "freemasonry" is to differentiate himself from it, to break away: "Shunning one another," they "complain of being too many rather than too few" (RTP, 2:639, 654). Such observations would seem to contradict all that Proust says in these same pages about gay men who form circles of friends that meet in cafes, and which he compares, as we have seen, to "professional organisations." Yet, rather than being contradictory, this reminds us that there are many types of gay men or, in any case, many kinds of behaviors enacted by gay men (ranging from men who try to remain entirely secret to those "extremists" who "coo" aloud in cafes to, somewhere in between, those who lead a double life, who "have formed two societies of which the second is composed exclusively of persons similar to themselves") (RTP, 2:641–42). It also reminds us that these types and these behaviors that differentiate between individuals also coexist within a given individual as contradictory impulses that fragment one's consciousness, producing the kind of internal separation we have spoken of earlier.

So it is that one discovers in Proust both that a gay man will do anything not to be associated with others like him, to hide what he is (think of Saint-Loup, who we later learn frequents Jupien's all-male brothel, having a fist-fight with a man who accosts him on the Champs-Élysées) and that such a man belongs, sometimes willingly, sometimes unwillingly, but in any case, inevitably, to the collective that he forms with those other men, to a "race."[2]

Proust may have chosen to be dismissive—given his belief that the desire not to be associated was stronger than the necessity and thus, a fortiori, the desire to assemble—of the utility or even the possibility of the gay movement ("le mouvement sodomiste"). Yet he clearly saw that that movement was the taking up on a conscious level and in a deliberate fashion of a preexisting collective which unites gay people whether they will or not, a collective that brings them together—despite their will to remain separate from those like them—in a kind of movement of "sympathy" at times of "general misfortune," which is to say, when repression strikes one of them in a particularly notable fashion: "as the Jews rallied around Dreyfus" (RTP, 3:638).

It is precisely this passage from a "collective" that only exists in dispersed fashion, to a "group" that wills itself as such and whose members share a common project, that Sartre analyzes in his Critique of Dialectical Reason. He defines the passage as one from "seriality" to a "fused group."[3] To explain what constitutes seriality, Sartre gives the example of people waiting for a bus. They are each alone together, all of them individually stuck in the "practico-inert," which is to say in the sedimented history that makes up their surrounding world and constitutes them as what they are. But that is not to say that they are totally separate from each other. They are united one to the other by a relation of exteriority which constitutes each individual as Other for all the others, given that they live in the same neighborhood, the same city, or given that they are all on their way to work, and so on. Everyone exists for an other in a unifying relation that is neither willed nor chosen, but rather produced by objectivized history in the very materiality of the city (or of professions, and so on). Consequently, these individuals are similarly situated in the world and are linked to each other, but passively so. They constitute for Sartre a "collective."

In order to make clear what a "collective" is, Sartre, as usual, uses the example of Jews:

In fact, the being-Jewish of every Jew in a hostile society which per-
secutes and insults them, and opens itself to them only to reject them
again, cannot be the only relation between the individual Jew and the
anti-semitic, racist society which surrounds him; it is the relation in so
far as it is lived by every Jew in his direct or indirect relations with all the
other Jews, and in so far as it constitutes him, through them all, as
Other and threatens him in and through the Others. . . . *The Jew, far
from being the type common to each separate instance, represents on the
contrary the perpetual being-outside-themselves-in-the-other* of the members
of this practico-inert grouping. (I call it this *because* it exists within
societies which have a non-Jewish majority and because every child—
even if he subsequently adopts it with pride and by a deliberate practice—must begin by *submitting* to his statute.) (267–68)

The "collective" is a passive unit, constructed by objectivized history out
of a group of individuals. It is not a unit to which one chooses to be assigned.
There is no point, therefore, in thinking that all gay men (no more than all
Jews) are "identical" to each other or that they are individual representatives
of a common type. Rather, they are all linked together (despite, and perhaps
even because of, their differences) through the mediation of their lived relation to the homophobic society that constitutes each of them as a "being-
outside-themselves-in-the-other." For every gay person (just as is the case
for every Jew) is that person who creates for another gay person the over-
population that threatens a homophobic or antisemitic society. The "seriality" that isolates individuals is not opposed to the sense of belonging to a
"collective" in the way it is understood by Sartre. It is a mode of belonging to
a collective: individuals atomized by their serial situation are also united by
this situation—one which causes them to exist as a group of people passively
constructed as such by the material order of things around them, the social,
cultural, racial, or sexual order. The "collective" is thus a "practical grouping" that exists despite the individuals grouped together by it. Indeed, to a
certain extent, they may not even be aware that it exists. Or they may refuse to
acknowledge the possibility that it exists. For it is not just objective "seriality" that atomizes individuals, it is also "serial thought," a spontaneous
or elaborated way of thinking that conceives of the individual as necessarily
separate from others, autonomous, without relation to them. This is a way of
thinking that perpetuates the isolation of individuals and thereby presents an
obstacle to collective action and to collective self-consciousness.[4]

"Serial thought" is thought in the service of oppression, for it insists that individuals are no more than individuals, that they have no collective interests and therefore no reason to organize as a group. It is a way of thinking that encourages and advocates resignation. Sartre says that it should be called a "thought of powerlessness" produced by or accepted by an individual to the extent that he or she is his or her "own enemy."[5] As Sartre so pertinently points out, this is not a way of thinking that can be refuted in the course of a rational discussion, for it is not a coherent set of arguments against which other arguments could be offered. It is more an ideological obstacle that one overcomes by acting. A "group" takes shape when dissatisfaction and the formation of demands cause the barriers separating individuals to fall, allowing them to "fuse" into an organized movement animated by a common project. The weakness and vulnerability of isolated individuals then gives way to a power that enables individuals to take their destiny into their own hands, even if only for a moment, even if only partially. The transformation from "seriality" to a "fused group" has the effect of a "refusal of alienation."[6] The collective organizing that establishes the group, what Sartre calls the "group in fusion," lifts individuals out of "seriality" and transforms their relation to history: instead of beings who are simply shaped and acted upon by structures, they become beings who act upon them. Implied in this transformation is a recognition of the other in a relation of "reciprocity" and interiority, a choice to accept what links me to him or her, whereas previously, in the "collective," that link was imposed upon me, was dictated to me, from outside.

Still, it seems quite clear that this distinction between a "group" and a "collective" can only really refer to theoretical constructs (extreme cases) that are usefully distinguished for analytical purposes, but do not capture concrete realities. The "practical ensembles" to which Sartre refers are rarely, except in the most exceptional historical circumstances, one of these pure forms or the other. There is something of the "group" in every serial unit (for there have already been struggles, discourses, organizations, individual acts of awareness). But it is also true that there is always something "serial" in any "group," for an organization can never mobilize all the individuals linked together in the passive "collective" of the practico-inert. More significantly, the "serial" (the preexisting "collective") is always both what the "group" must overcome and what the group is based on. Thus every "group" could be said to be haunted by seriality, just as seriality itself is haunted by the "group" that coexists with it and works to transform it.[7] This seems particularly to be the case for the ensemble that gay people make up. It existed in a serial "collective" for quite a long time, with individuals being separated while nonetheless linked by way of a common relation to homophobic society, while the "group" was often no more than a potential fulfilled by only the smallest minority of them. Every time that the possibility of the "group" became a reality there would be a subsequent fall back into the seriality of the collective—for no mobilization is ever permanent.

⊁ Sartre takes movements for cultural affirmation or for minority recognition as manifestations of a certain ethical stage of "revolt" or moment of "dignity."[8] He thereby lets it be understood that this is merely a stage that will someday be left behind. One's reappropriation of oneself will lead to a later and higher stage that Sartre calls "universalism," in which "mankind" appears in all his "nudity," which is to say, without any social, sexual, or racial determinations. He states this quite clearly in his 1948 text on Negritude, in which he describes the black poet and, more generally, any person of color, as "he who marches on a ridge between the past particularisms which he has just climbed and the future universalism that will be the twilight of his Negritude; it is he who lives particularism to the end to find thereby the dawn of the universal."[9]

Sartre's utopianism is astonishing. It can only be understood in the light of his faith in the revolution to come and in the promises of a "socialist" society. Yet clearly it makes little sense. One would have to be blinded by a rather unrealistic enthusiasm in order to think that blacks who are "offended, humiliated . . . probe to the most profound depths to find again their most secret pride, and when they have finally discovered it they find themselves inwardly torn over its possession. By supreme generosity they abandon it."[10] The dream of a better world, freed from racism, antisemitism, or homophobia, is obviously something we could shelve in the "proproom" alongside the "impossible Salvation" that Sartre speaks of in The Words.[11] There is no stage of generalized reconciliation that follows the stage of "revolt," just as there is no step beyond "dignity" or "pride." Dignity and pride will need to be ceaselessly reaffirmed. There is no "end of history," accompanied by a state of reconciliation in universalism and indetermination, at which point pride and dignity would have outlived their usefulness. Rather, the "ethical stage" will need to be continually reactivated; the revolt will have to be performed over and over again. If they inevitably run out of steam or dissipate, it is not because racism or homophobia are in retreat, but because mobilizations inevitably come to an end.

⊁ It is possible to investigate historic oscillations between moments of activism and political organizing and moments in which these activities subside. Albert Hirshman has studied the alternating cycles of involvement in "public passions" and then withdrawal into the concerns of "private happiness."[12] There is some general truth in this idea: one might think of the years just before and after May 1968 as being an exemplary period of powerful political involvement. The idea is also applicable in more localized ways, for each category, each group will have its own temporality that may only partially coincide with the general one. No group, no category, can be permanently in a state of uprising; periods of retreat seem almost inevitable. Moreover, a movement's achievement is one of the primary factors in its demobilization.

We might then agree with Barry D. Adam that one of the reasons explaining the absence of a powerful gay and lesbian political movement would be the fact of a developed "subcultural" life, which will have, in the eye of many gay people, rendered less urgent activism aimed at new political and social gains. The gains already made—ease of access to gay bars, cafes, restaurants—have been important enough.[13] Yet this historical observation needs to be qualified given that a subcultural life can, to a certain extent, work in the opposite way: to support organization. (One might think, in this regard, of the strong showing at the Lesbian and Gay Pride festivals in France these past few years, even as the lesbian and gay movement itself has remained rather undeveloped. Or we could think of the moment at the beginning of the 1980s when a new group of AIDS activists rose up out of the subculture while those who had represented militancy up until that moment were sometimes slow to realize the urgency of the situation.) Taking a historical point of view would lead one to think that collective consciousness—without which political organizing would not be possible—was able to be developed thanks in large measure to the shared experience of life in a developed subculture.[14]

The slippage from a "group in fusion" back into the "practico-inert" can obviously be the fate of any movement; indeed, it seems inevitable. It might take the form of a return to a dispersed state, or it might happen as the institutionalization of what had been a popular movement. None of this would detract from the importance a movement might have had, the liberating gesture it embodied. Consider the set of diverse phenomena that could be described as making up the "gay and lesbian movement," allowing that term all its vagueness and imprecision: the process of producing collective visibility, of gay affirmation, of the creation of autonomous discourses and autonomous sexual and cultural codes, of individual and collective "re-subjectification" (meaning one's own production of oneself as a subject, the reinvention of one's subjectivity). This movement is necessarily always threatened by a return to the "practico-inert," a return to a state in which individuals revert to isolation and forget about collective activism—perhaps returning to a serial way of thinking of themselves (with the result that organizations dissolve, a sense of community becomes vague, activists disappear, and so on). Perhaps people are content to allow what had been a dynamic process to become an institution. This is surely what transpires in those neighborhoods populated by gay businesses in which the cults of fashion, youth, beauty, and virility display themselves with such ease, and in which we see being reformed and reformulated the various modalities through which people who do not meet these norms again find themselves excluded.

It would be interesting to gain a sense of the kinds of insults that circulate within such a space. They would show that the victims of one form of oppression are not slow to enact many other forms: racism, misogyny, ageism, and so on. The hatred directed at older men, for example, would seem to be one of the structuring schemas of conversation inside the gay milieu, to the extent that the potential sexualization of relations between individuals occupying that space leads to insulting, scornful ways of speaking of those who no longer have value in what can only be called the sexual marketplace. It is, moreover, worth pondering the striking fact that participation in this gay world, in this "scene," is in the end almost always provisional. As Michael Pollak noted, most individuals more or less completely withdraw from this world after turning forty.

Still, it would be worth our while to inquire as to whether gay neighborhoods or the gay subculture do in fact belong to the "collective" side of things (in the Sartrian sense), whether they tend toward "seriality," or whether they are not rather, or at the same time, one of the modes for self-affirmation as a group. What is called the gay "movement" or the gay "community" is a reality that is difficult to grasp analytically, and even more difficult to grasp, of course, if you are making use of those reductive doxic considerations that shape certain journalistic points of view. For such clumsy "-isms" as "*commu-nautarisme*" or "*séparatisme*" (identity politics) seem more likely than not entirely to miss the complex nature of the phenomena in question.

An inventory of all the components of today's movement for gay and lesbian affirmation would necessarily include such diverse entities as militant (or cultural or sports) organizations, newspapers and magazines (ranging from political bulletins to pornography), neighborhoods in which shops and bars (but also bookstores) are concentrated, conventions and conferences, film festivals, and so on. The audiences or participants of these various entities may or may not overlap. There are those who might spend every evening in a gay bar and still claim to detest Gay and Lesbian Pride festivals. There are those who might read pornography and not care for the activist press. Or vice versa. Or some combination of all those things together. The proliferation of certain kinds of businesses (clothing stores, for instance) is seen by some more activist gay people as a regressive return to commercialism or as a crushingly inevitable part of the attitude of futility that confronts any effort at organization or political consciousness raising. Accusations fly against gay capitalism and gay commercialism and against the "fashion victims" who sustain it. This same commercial proliferation can be simultaneously denounced by the opponents of the gay movement, who see in it the incarnation of a dire "identity politics." These people see in such a notion a voluntary form of action, consciously chosen, politically and ideologically motivated. One group complains of a stubborn refusal to budge from the "practico-inert." The other would frighten us with the bogeyman of a militant minority. Of course it is probably the case that both positions have something right (and both have something wrong). Surely the fact that a "group" and a "collective" are always mutually implicated, that there is always something of a "group" in a "collective" and something of a "collective" in a "group," should suggest to us that we need to rethink the way we use these categories in order to grasp this reality. Perhaps we could come to think of the "group" as more than a specifically political or cultural action; perhaps it could also be a locus of creation of "ways of life."

So even if one judges the effects of "commercialization" to be alienating ones, it should still be remembered that the very establishment of a gay milieu, of a "gay world," was at the outset—and remains fundamentally—productive of freedom. This is all the more the case when one considers—as George Chauncey's book on New York has shown—that commercial venues (bars, saloons, restaurants, dance halls, and so on) have throughout gay history been vectors for sociability, for culture, for ways of life that could not have been developed without this framework. Spaces of freedom have often, if not always, been commercial spaces. Such spaces are certainly proliferating today, and thus the effects of uniformity that they inevitably produce (uniformity of dress, of speech, of hairstyle) are also spreading on a wider scale. But how different in their cultural and sexual meanings are the short hair, faded jeans, and work boots worn today by gay men in Paris, London, or Berlin from the suede shoes worn in England in the 1920s or the red ties worn in the United States in the same era?[15]

We might note in passing that no one among the critics of the mechanisms of "uniformity" and group identification is obliged to submit to them. Moreover, group identification is hardly synonymous with uniformity. Indeed, it is hard to comprehend why it is that we hear so much about uniformity when there are so many different gay "types" perfectly available to public view. Such diatribes against "uniformity" become all the more tedious when they are heard from individuals who spend so much of their time in places they claim to detest. Certainly the "alienation" symbolized by what is denounced today as "uniformity" or "communitarianism" or "ghettoization" is preferable (because it is *chosen* and therefore to some extent controlled) to the alienation that is forced on you by shame and the obligation to remain in the closet. One cannot help asking if this perfectly conformist and ritualistic practice of denunciation is not the persistent effect of the never-ending double consciousness by way of which gay people are always—in every circumstance—brought back to the point of reproducing the hatred of one's own and others' homosexuality. How far, then, can we be from Proust, who was already writing that there is an "anti-homosexual hiding inside every homosexual," and who described "inverts" who are "full of scorn and outrage" for the most visible representatives of the "race" to which they belong? The endurance of these psychological traits, the fact that they are as vigorous today as ever, show that interiorized homophobia is capable of reproducing itself, of proliferating, forever. Whatever transformations the past century might have seen, self-hatred still manages to take the form of hatred of other gay people, people with whom one is apparently still ashamed to identify.

↠ There will always exist a tension between the act of falling back into the "en soi" and the act of renewing the sense of the "group" that is conscious of itself as such and conscious of the historical achievements that have enabled the process by means of which "resubjectification" can take place, the process in which individuals can invent themselves as free and autonomous. To choose to refuse identification with the group in the name of the individual is pointless. The point is to choose identification with the group insofar as that produces freedom and individual autonomy and to refuse that identification once it begins to produce alienation and conformism. Yet we need not imagine these to be two distinct moments: identification and dis-identification can be simultaneous. The one can exist by means of the other. It is a matter of taking up the act of claiming freedom at the point to which others have brought it—but also at the point at which some may have left it behind. The process of self-creation and self-recreation must always be revivified. New struggles will have to be invented when we are surrounded by past achievements that have over time become what Sartre has called "old victories that have rotted."[16]

PART 2

Specters of Wilde

Specters are always there, even if they do
not exist, even if they no longer exist,
even if they do not yet exist.

JACQUES DERRIDA

1

How "Arrogant Pederasts" Come into Being

This scene takes place in 1895. At the end of the trial, stunned by the sentence he has received, Oscar Wilde mumbles a few words to the judge who has just condemned him to two years of hard labor: "And I, may I say nothing, my Lord?" The judge does not even deign to reply. A few moments earlier he had expressed regret that the maximum sentence permitted by law to punish the crime of "gross indecency" was not more severe. He merely makes a gesture to the guards indicating that they may take the prisoner away.

This scene, as recounted by Montgomery Hyde, who based his account on newspaper and other accounts from the time, may or may not be completely authentic. In his classic biography of Wilde, Richard Ellmann describes it, but with some reservations. He indicates that sources do not agree as to Wilde's final words.[1]

Whether or not Wilde actually spoke those exact words seems unimportant, for the general meaning of the condemnation he received was perfectly clear: it was meant to silence him, to take away his right to speak. The point was to reduce to silence a voice that society would otherwise have been required to perceive as homosexual, a voice that it did not wish to have appear in public view as homosexual. Wilde's career, like his life, would be broken by those two years of extremely harsh prison treatment. He would, in fact, write nothing more, with the exception of the *Ballad of Reading Gaol* and *De Profundis*, the long prison letter to Alfred Douglas. He died three years after his release from prison at the age of forty-six.

At the origin of the series of events that would lead Wilde to his downfall was an insult. The father of his lover, Alfred Douglas, had left at Wilde's club a card on which he had written: "To Oscar Wilde posing as a Somdomite [sic]." Wilde was foolhardy enough to sue him for libel. How could he have forgotten that insults against those who do not conform to the norm are upheld by the social order—an order he had been defying and that would now call him to account? He would say as much in *De Profundis*:

> Of course once I had put into motion the forces of Society, Society turned on me and said, "Have you been living all this time in defiance of my laws, and do you now appeal to those laws for protection? You shall have those laws exercised to the full. You shall abide by what you have appealed to."[2]

Yet would there have been any other choice for Wilde faced with a man pursuing him with insults all across London? As he says in that same text, he "would be ruined" if he did not react to the insults, just as he "would be ruined" if he did.[3]

❧ And what do we know of the others? Other gay people, I mean. Here is Wilde insulted in every newspaper, condemned, thrown into jail. It is easy enough to imagine what those who followed the reports of his trial from day to day must have been feeling. They would have watched the justice system and the agents of social order trampling on their very being: their loves, their hopes, their sexuality, sometimes their ways of life, and for some among them, their culture. Insult operates collectively. All the invective, the caricatures, the dirty jokes, the laughter, the scorn, all the muckraking the press performed—it was directed at them as well. What fear it must have produced, what a sentiment of shared guilt with the victim, what a sense of relief at escaping punishment, having slipped through the net, having survived. Think of it: two years of hard labor! How strong the effort at discretion, the effort not to be noticed, must have been right at that moment. And yet . . .

And yet perhaps, as Neil Bartlett has pointed out, Wilde's trial allowed them to become conscious of the fact that they were not alone in the world. Perhaps Wilde's trial somehow offered them what we might call cultural reference points or models.[4] In any case, the trial brought the subject of homosexuality into public view, made it visible, a subject of discourse, even if it was the discourse of the powers that be. It is possible that for many of those who also felt victimized by the verdict, the effect of it was not (or not only) the one intended by the forces of repression. For the notable trials that occurred at the end of the nineteenth and the beginning of the twentieth centuries proved to be key moments in the creation both of a gay *self-*

consciousness and of a *collective* one. As we saw in the first part of this book, both the insults of daily life and the structure of the sexual order of which they are the symptoms are determining factors in gay "subjugation" (subjectivity produced as a subjection). Yet they are also, simultaneously, determining factors of a possible—a necessary—resubjectification (the reinvention of a subjectivity as an autonomous consciousness). Moreover, the historical form of insult represented by homophobic discourse and the inscription of it in the social, legal, and cultural order have been important forces in the creation of a counterdiscourse, an autonomous way of speaking, that has across the centuries allowed for the emergence and the existence of a self-consciousness and a collective memory.

Oscar Wilde's condemnation shook up people's minds. For many gay people, especially men, his name quickly became the symbol both of gay culture and of the repression it inevitably calls down on itself whenever it goes too far in the direction of making itself public. "Oscar" became a word that could be used as an accusation of homosexuality ("he's an Oscar"), but "Wilde" also became a way for gay people to talk of themselves and think of themselves. The hero of Forster's novel *Maurice* does not know how to designate himself to a doctor, so he says, "I'm an unspeakable of the Oscar Wilde sort."[5] Thanks to the reference provided by Wilde, Maurice can name what he is while insisting that it is unnamable. Thus Wilde's name and his figure have played a considerable role in the establishment of gay culture—and also of lesbian culture—in the twentieth century. His example, his books, his life, his sufferings inspired people as various as the founder of the German gay movement, Magnus Hirschfeld, or writers such as Virginia Woolf—and many others.[6]

Wilde's personality and his tragic end obsessed authors such as André Gide and Marcel Proust. In many ways they were determinant in the definition of Gide's and Proust's literary projects. There is no doubt that Gide's tenacious desire to write a "defense" of his sexual tastes is closely linked to his meetings with Wilde and to Wilde's fate. We know that at the beginning of 1895, at the moment of Wilde's trial and his condemnation, Gide began to assemble a file he labeled "Pederasty" in which he kept notes on his ideas as well as press clippings.[7] He had gotten to know Wilde rather well in Paris in 1891 and had seen him again at the very beginning of 1895, during the famous trip to Algeria that he would recount thirty years later in *If It Die . . .*, a text that still trembles with the emotion Gide experienced during the intimate night he spent together with the "little musician" Mohammed, whom

Wilde practically placed in his arms. This would have taken place only weeks before Wilde was sentenced to prison.[8] When Wilde was released from prison in 1897 and went to stay at a seaside resort in Normandy, Gide wanted to be the first to see him again and hurried there as soon as he managed to obtain the address.[9] Upon Wilde's death in 1901, Gide wrote his moving "In Memoriam," in which he spoke of the profoundly destabilizing effect on him of his encounters with Wilde.[10] Homophobic critics have seldom failed to blame Gide's assumption of his homosexuality and his homosexual advocacy on the bad influence of Wilde. In the book that he devoted to The Youth of André Gide, the psychiatrist Jean Delay cites letters from Gide to his mother in which Gide tells her to what an extent he is drawn to Wilde and Douglas. Delay hammers home his diagnosis: "We are certainly not claiming that if he had never met Wilde, Gide would not have become homosexual, but it is likely that he would not have so quickly adopted and interiorized the attitude of an arrogant pederast, insistent on claiming his anomaly as his norm. The moment at which he began to think that that which he had previously held as a kind of inferiority could represent or be represented as a superiority can be quite precisely situated after the meeting with Wilde in Algeria."[11]

In point of fact, the meeting with Wilde liberated Gide from the feelings of guilt and inferiority that had hitherto held him in their grip. Wilde's trial and sentence led Gide to understand that it was no easy matter to free oneself from social pressures. He set himself to think about this, about the problem of how to speak of homosexuality. Shortly thereafter, in 1902, he would write The Immoralist. It is thus clear that Gide's "apologetic" project is at least partly rooted (for we should not forget his own drive toward "confession") in the pain he experienced due to Wilde's rapid decline and the sad ending of his life. It would be shortly after another trial, another homosexual scandal—the Eulenburg affair that was unleashed in Germany in 1908—that Gide would undertake to write Corydon.[12]

From the very first page of Gide's book we are plunged into the history of homosexuality: Oscar Wilde's trial in England, the Eulenburg affair, Krupp's suicide in Germany, and so on. There is every indication that Gide followed the Eulenburg trials attentively and that this "affair" was one of the factors producing his feeling that it was necessary for him to write this defense. In 1908 he drafted a good portion of it. A first edition of twelve copies was published in 1911. On the very first page, the narrator of the book, who speaks with the voice of "common sense," alludes to these trials without giving a precise date: "In the year 190—, a scandalous trial raised once again the irritating question of uranism. For eight days, in the salons as in the cafés, nothing else was mentioned."[13] In an earlier, unpublished version, Gide had written: "In the year 189—, a scandalous trial raised once again the irritating question of uranism."[14] The date he had been thinking using was thus that of the Wilde trial rather than the Eulenburg trial.

The Eulenburg affair, and the enormous press coverage it received along with its general impact on European culture, would help crystallize in Proust's imagination the idea of a vast novelistic project that would have at its center the accursed race of inverts.[15] In his "1908 Notebook," Proust mentions among the guiding threads of the book he is contemplating, "Balzac in A Harlot High and Low [Splendeurs et misères des courtisanes]" and "Eulenbourg."[16] These are the two capital references around which the project of his book will be elaborated, the book he will claim in a 1909 letter to Alfred Valette, director of the publishing house Mercure de France, is nearly finished and whose provisional title is Against Sainte-Beuve: Reminiscence of a Morning. Yet that title, he insists, should not be allowed to conceal the fact that this is a "real novel," indeed "an extremely shameless novel in certain parts," for "one of the major characters is homosexual."[17]

At the starting point of the Proustian enterprise we thus find a literary theme—the character Vautrin from Balzac, of whom Charlus will in some way be a reincarnation—and a scandal that had inscribed itself deeply into the minds of Proust's contemporaries. It is therefore hardly surprising to find in a draft of part of the novel that dates from 1912 remarks that link Balzac and the Eulenburg affair. In that draft, Proust holds the Eulenburg affair responsible for the spread of the word "homosexuality" in France, a word he finds "too Germanic and pedantic." He would prefer the word "invert," not feeling himself authorized, as we saw earlier, to take up the word used by Balzac: "tante," auntie. Moreover, the draft of the theoretical essay that will open Cities of the Plain (Sodome et Gomorrhe) is at that point titled "The Race of Aunties."[18]

All this will disappear before the final version. Yet references to Balzac and Eulenburg can certainly be found in Cities of the Plain. Balzac first: Baron Charlus says to the narrator: "What! you've never read Les Illusions perdues? . . . And the death of Lucien! I forget who the man of taste was who, when he was asked what event in his life had grieved him most, replied: 'The death of Lucien de Rubempré in Splendeurs et Misères'" (RTP 2:1084). It is probably worth pointing out in passing that the "man of taste" in question here was Oscar Wilde.

As for the Eulenburg affair, Charlus cannot prevent himself from speaking of it—just as, more generally, he is unable to help speaking of his "secret," of anything that would allow him to refer to it without really seeming to. At a certain point, Charlus launches into a tirade about the German emperor: " 'As a man, he is vile; he abandoned, betrayed, repudiated his best friends, in circumstances in which his silence was as deplorable as theirs was noble,' continued M. de Charlus, who was irresistibly drawn by his own tendencies to the Eulenburg affair, and remembered what one of the most highly placed of the accused had said to him: 'How the Emperor must have relied upon our delicacy to have dared to allow such a trial! But he was not mistaken in trusting to our discretion.' "[19] Proust thus takes up, or attributes to Charlus, the idea, prevalent at the time, that the Emperor was himself homosexual and had allowed his friends to be tried in order to avoid being personally implicated or revealed.

If Proust's writing finds inspiration in the scandal that tainted the German aristocracy, this nonetheless does not imply that he himself chooses to retell Eulenburg's story. For him it is a question of transforming life into art, and he has other models as well to help him in this work of elaboration and of literary creation. He has, among others, for example, Count Robert de Montesquiou (about whom one might also note that he had already been a model for the 1884 book *Against Nature* by Huysmans, a book that had a great influence on Oscar Wilde, as we shall see in the pages ahead).[20] But many of the themes that will be woven together in *Remembrance of Things Past*—the secret, underground life of the "sect" of "*tantes*," the ties between a man who belongs to high society and more popular types, the inexorable downfall of someone who had thought himself invincible, and so on—had all been more or less directly suggested to Proust by the Eulenburg affair and by all that was written about it in subsequent years, as by his fascination for Balzac, in whose work one already finds the project of describing the real life that lurks hidden beneath the surface of things.

A number of books had in fact appeared about the series of trials that took place in Germany.[21] Proust first had the idea of writing an article, an "essay on pederasty," in order to enter the debate around the Eulenburg affair.[22] Yet he realized quite quickly that "art" would allow him access to a higher level of reality than would the simple description of facts from real life. What was to have been an article quickly became a "story."[23] There is thus no exaggeration involved in asserting that Proust's work is grounded in part in his will to intervene in the debate about homosexuality that had been

produced in this moment of noisy repression, one accompanied by a proliferation of homophobic discourses. The theme of the "curse" of homosexuality can perhaps be better understood when it has been resituated in its
historical context. The transfiguration of this theory through novelistic genius was to produce not only one of the monuments of twentieth-century
literature, but also one of the crucial books of gay culture—or in any case,
one of the books that played a decisive role in the collective self-perception of
gay people. Surely this is not what those who had condemned Wilde and
screamed about Eulenburg had been hoping for.

➤ Gide was perfectly aware of these kinds of paradoxes. It is doubtless with
a certain amount of malice that he has the homophobic narrator of *Corydon*
say: "I've always thought it was best to speak of such things as little as
possible—often they exist at all only because some blunderer runs on about
them. Aside from the fact that they are anything but elegant in expression,
there will always be some imbecile to model himself on just what one was
claiming to condemn."[24] Gide knows perfectly well that it is not by reading
books or magazines that one becomes gay. But he also knows that any
speech *against* homosexuality is also speech *about* homosexuality: it can thus
be consumed with a certain avidness, an uneasy fervor, by those who thereby
hear themselves and their "vice" spoken of. Any public statement about
homosexuality immediately finds a profound echo in gay people, simply
because they are there being spoken of in a world where the reality of their
feelings, of their sexuality, of their personalities, usually remains unspoken,
impossible to speak about. It is thus easy to understand why gay men and
lesbians have always eagerly consumed works in which they knew they
would find images of themselves, even when they were sinister and deformed ones (as was almost inevitably the case until recently). Certain characters from the movies would become fetish objects for gay men and lesbians even when they were marked out for tragic fates and for violent deaths,
or even when they were simply portrayed as monsters. (Vito Russo has
provided many telling examples of this in *The Celluloid Closet*—think of Man-
kiewicz's *Suddenly Last Summer*.) Even if the reason behind their monstrous-
ness was not clearly in evidence, for gay and lesbian eyes there were clues
that allowed the enigma to be deciphered or the mask seen through. To
caricature, to ridicule, to insult homosexuals—for a long time there were few
other publicly accessible forms of discourse about them—was at least to

speak about them. And to speak about them was in some way to allow them to recognize themselves. It allowed them to move beyond the feeling they all must have had of being alone in the world.

The censors also understood this, and not only those in the Hollywood studios who worked diligently for years in order to eliminate any trace of homosexuality from the movies, even including mentions that condemned it. Lucidity on this point has a long history. In the late eighteenth and early nineteenth centuries certain legal experts had made the point that it was better not to bring homosexuals into court, because the publicity that would be produced by the scandal could well have the opposite effect to the one they were counting on. Moreover, it seems quite likely that this was the reasoning behind the decision not to criminalize sexual relations between persons of the same sex in the French penal code. Surely it was not (or not only) because Cambacérès was homosexual, even less because Napoleon was inclined to tolerance on the issue of homosexuality, that the decision was made to favor certain policing measures (such as banishment) and to avoid court cases. Rather it was because Napoleon worried about the uncontrollable effects of publicity.[25]

∗ If gay speech has often risen up in reaction to repression, it has, especially in literature, in return often subsequently encountered a profound, hate-filled hostility. Gide, who published The Immoralist and then If It Die . . ., Corydon, and The Counterfeiters, was not spared these attempts to impose silence upon him, attempts he resisted with an obstinacy that grew all the stronger as his growing fame permitted it to do so. A large part of his work can be interpreted as the slow maturing of his desire to speak of himself, of his sexuality, of the forms of his emotions. He wanted to say who he was—to say it for himself, and to say it in order to help those who did not enjoy, as he did, the protections that went along with being a famous writer.[26] But at every step the attacks against him became more violent.

Given all of this, how could gay speech ever avoid being marked, even from the interior, by the hostility that it provoked? Would its content not be necessarily constrained and restrained by such reactions, given that it could easily anticipate them and therefore somehow conform to the exigencies of a certain kind of prudence? More fundamentally, would this content not have been defined and shaped by the preexisting hatred, the hatred that was there waiting to burst forth? Gay speech, in all of its various forms, constructed itself in an essential relation to the violence it was going without fail to provoke. Eve Kosofsky Sedgwick is certainly not wrong to point out that homophobia preceded the construction of modern homosexual identity, historically and structurally speaking. In effect, as she writes, "however radically . . . the meanings of homosexual identity were changing during the two centuries after the Restoration," its evolutions made an astonishing contrast to the "most stable and temporally backward-looking elements" that constituted the "thematics and the ideological bases of homophobia."[27] In any case, it was in the face of this always already present homophobia, in the face of this hatred that always preceded it, that any form of gay speech had to make its way forward. Given that all these ways of speaking were, for the most part, discourses of legitimation or of justification as much as they were discourses of affirmation, they could only make their case in most instances by accepting the terms of the discussion that were imposed upon them and by making an effort to reappropriate them and transform their meaning. This is why homophobia and gay speech are so intimately linked together, so tightly imbricated. Gay speech was only able to invent itself, to come into the light of day, in large measure as a "reverse discourse," to use Michel Foucault's expression, by taking up in its own way the categories of thought that it needed to fight against and that were opposed to it. Gay speech has thus often helped spread those categories, images, and representations and has contributed to their perpetuation.

A veritable war took place in the area of culture and of literature. What was to work itself out in books was not only determinant for the construction of contemporary gay discourse. That very discourse played a crucial role in the constitution of twentieth-century "gay identity" as it has been constructed and lived by gay people themselves (in all their diversity), but also as it has been perceived and fought against by the guardians of the social and sexual order. Here too, we can follow Eve Kosofsky Sedgwick when she writes that a certain number of important literary texts have "set the terms for a modern homosexual identity." She mentions *The Picture of Dorian Gray*, Melville's *Billy Budd*, and also, of course, Proust and *Remembrance of Things Past* as well as Mann's *Death in Venice*.[28] To say that in itself is not so new, but we must also follow her when she adds that these "foundational texts of modern gay culture" have also contributed to shaping the themes, images, and categories of homophobic discourse. The literary texts that guaranteed what we would call today gay "visibility" or "legibility" also mobilized and therefore nourished the most homophobic ways of thinking and perceiving. They helped enormously in the diffusion of the negative schemas through which the twentieth century would imagine the homosexual character and would reaffirm its hostility toward homosexuality.

This is why, rather than writing history in terms of a slow progress toward the right to freedom and to speech, it makes more sense to speak of the slow construction of ways of living and thinking about homosexuality. For in effect, the notion of emancipation implies the idea of a preexisting identity that needs to be liberated. But this identity is produced by the very gestures that work for its liberation. And these multiple gestures, heterogeneous and differentiated, can only take place within social, cultural, and discursive configurations on which they depend and which give them shape. Just as in the case of insult, personal identity is constructed in a relation to oneself that cannot entirely escape from stigmatizing determinations. Just as "resubjectification" must necessarily rely on a subjectivity shaped by this inferiorization, so those processes of collective and individual "subjectivation" produced by literature also take on the categories of dominant discourse. They can only be accomplished and perpetuated while being shaped by those cultural "sites" from which they borrow certain fundamental schemas, even if they mean at the same time to contest their oppressive force. It is these "experiences," all historically, culturally, and socially situated, it is these open conflicts, these struggles between power and the resistance it inevitably gives rise to, that have produced gay "subjects" and subjectivities. And these are the "subjects" and subjectivities that opened up for us the history that we have inherited.

2

An Unspeakable Vice

In a text published in 1984, shortly before his death, George Dumézil recalled a scene from his youth: "It was again in 1916, at the Sorbonne, that one of the sharpest connoisseurs of both ancient and modern Greece, the famous Delphist named Emile Bourguet, was explaining *The Symposium* to some undergraduates. When he came to the scene to which Victor Cousin had given the noble title of 'Socrates Refusing the Offerings of Alcibiades,' he warned us: 'Above all, do not go off imagining there are things going on here.' "[1] Dumézil scoffs: "Imagine? All one had to do was read!" He does not go on to tell us what the students might have said among themselves as they left the class or if they said anything at all. After all, if the professor himself emphasized that these things should not be spoken of, it is possible that these young men (Dumézil was 18 at the time) would have chosen to avoid discussing them among themselves, even if perhaps they thought about them quite frequently. But then, what would they have been thinking? Such things are difficult to know. Especially given that the relation to homosexuality of many young people was about to be entirely transformed by an experience with little bearing on the reading of classical texts: Dumézil was to be called up and sent to the front a few months after this class at the Sorbonne. It is more than likely that the masculine fraternity in the trenches (and the affective relations or relations of love that could occur there even during the bombardments, which Dumézil would recall one day in speaking of the "noisy parties we had in our twenties") was going to provide an entirely new basis for the need to legitimate homosexuality. Doubtless it would also cause deep transformations in the ways in which individuals who had lived through such situations would think about their own homosexuality.[2] The war wrought deep changes in the gay culture of Europe, and notably in France.[3]

In his text from 1984, Dumézil continues: "At about the same moment [1916], in a note to his *Démocratie athénienne*, one of the two no less well-known Croiset brothers warned his readers that what happened in the area of the Parthenon in the fifth century had nothing to do with the odious counterfeit practices one finds going on today." Yet, given that Dumézil's text is intended to preface Bernard Sergent's book on homosexual practices as rites of initiation in the Indo-European world (and in ancient Greece, which inherited these traditions), he adds: "If one sets aside the moral judgment, Croiset was not entirely wrong—at least if one goes along with Bethe, leaving behind an Athens that is already modern, and comes to the Dorians of Crete and Lacedemonia. There, love, or at least the sexual customs involving adolescent boys, can be found to be institutionalized as an essential mechanism provided with a justificatory ideology."[4] Who is Bethe? Dumézil is here speaking of a German Hellenist who, as he notes, had at the very beginning of the century already had the audacity to violate that "unspoken but quite constraining prohibition in classical philology by publishing a justly famous article in the *Rheinisches Museum*, 'Die dorische Knabenliebe, ihre Ethic, ihre Idee.' "[5]

If Croiset felt obliged to assert that what went on in Athens had nothing to do with what goes on today under the same name, we might assume that this was not only because academics who talked or wrote about these texts were obliged to say something about the passages that referred to relations between people of the same sex. It might also have been because he was perfectly aware that the reference to ancient Greece might serve as (and was serving as) a way of legitimizing discussions of homosexuality. He could hardly ignore that a certain homosexual discourse and culture had been emerging since the mid-nineteenth century, one that was working to dignify homosexuality by inscribing it in a tradition deriving from this ancient and glorious past.[6]

The story told by Dumézil about a class at the Sorbonne in 1916 is astonishingly similar to a famous passage from E. M. Forster's novel *Maurice*, written in 1913 and 1914, but only published in 1971, after Forster's death. The scene takes place in Cambridge in 1912. A professor interrupts a student who is in the process of translating a Greek text, and says, "in a flat and toneless voice: 'Omit: a reference to the unspeakable vice of the Greeks.' " Upon leaving the class, the novel's two main characters discuss this remark, and Durham, after expressing his indignation at the hypocrisy of the professor (whom he suspects is inclined to this "unspeakable vice"), declares that "the Greeks, or most of them, were that way inclined, and to omit it is to omit the mainstay of Athenian society." Maurice asks him, "Is that so?" To which Durham replies: "You've read the *Symposium*?" This provides Forster with the occasion for a lyrical description of the feeling of freedom given to Maurice by the simple fact of being able to speak with someone about a subject that he had never before been able to speak about and that he had never imagined it possible to speak about.[7]

The ways in which the professors described by Forster and Dumézil— whatever their own sexualities may have been—strive to cover over any reference to this "unspeakable vice" clearly reveals how scholarly and university traditions (even up to the 1970s) worked to censure an entire aspect of a culture whose greatness and importance for contemporary civilization they never ceased celebrating. When certain passages were not merely suppressed from published versions of Greek texts, they would be printed in Latin! Or, if the texts were in Latin, they would be printed in Italian![8]

This battle over the interpretation of Greece, and thus over the reference to Greece as a locus of legitimation for loves between members of the same sex (or, more exactly, of the male sex), had begun long before the end of the nineteenth century. Voltaire had already, in the article on "Socratic Love" in his *Philosophical Dictionary*, waxed indignant over the idea that what in his eyes had to do simply with friendship could be taken as love. And Jeremy Bentham, in an unpublished essay from 1785, had set out to refute him: "But the Greeks knew the difference between love and friendship as well as we— they had distinct terms to signify them by: it seems reasonable therefore to suppose that when they say love they mean love, and that when they say friendship only they mean friendship only." Bentham is able to poke fun at the "spectacle amusing enough . . . to observe [of] the distress men are under to keep the peace between 2 favourite prejudices that are apt cruelly to jar: the one in disfavour of this vice, the other in favour of antiquity, especially antient Greece."[9] Bentham takes up the defense of love between men in the name of tolerance and sets out methodically to refute homophobic arguments (notably those of Voltaire, who worried over the destruction of humanity in the case where homosexuality would become generalized, and Montesquieu, who deplored the idea of one sex taking on the "weaknesses of the other," that is, men becoming effeminate).[10] Bentham even puts forward an argument that will become common in one form or another: he points out that a certain number of famous historical personages would be condemned by "our laws." He gives a list of famous Greek and Roman men, "idols of their Country and ornaments of human Nature," and asks what would have become of them: "They would have *perished on your Gibbets.*"[11] Yet his writings on the subject were probably too far in advance of their time: they were never published, remaining in the state of notes, manuscripts, fragments, or else private correspondence.

This dispute over the "customs" of ancient Greece was not simply an intellectual squabble over the interpretation of the past. As can be seen both in Voltaire's text and in the critique of it that Bentham wrote, the stakes in question are contemporary ones. One person wants to delegitimate an "unnatural" vice, the other to legitimate it, and both wish to offer an interpretation of ancient Greece in order to do so. In 1836, a Swiss writer, Heinrich Hössli, made such stakes clear by publishing a short work that affirmed that Plato certainly had a much better understanding than many of our contemporaries as to what was or was not "natural" as far as love was concerned.[12] Forster's novel and Dumézil's story also give us some insight into the ways in which the reference to Greece served as a form of cultural legitimation that enabled homosexuality to be brought into discourse. By way of that legitimation, and the ability to be "proud" of oneself, isolated individuals could begin to think of themselves as other than monstrous; they could begin to forge a positive personal identity despite the considerable weight of taboos and prohibitions. A cultural and historical gaze turned toward Greece served for a long period (up until quite recently) as a way for gay people (mostly from privileged backgrounds, of course) to provide themselves with a set of references that justified what Christian culture, social prejudices, and even the law condemned to silence. That vice which is "unnamable among Christians," according to the well-worn expression, could, for a long time, only be named in this roundabout way. The reading of Plato and other classical authors was the starting point for a gay "resubjectification," just as gay literature can be today.

⊁ It was in large measure in the field of studies of classical Greece or, to a lesser extent, in the field of Renaissance studies and, more generally, by way of references to ancient Greece or the Renaissance, to Platonism or Neo-Platonism, that the battle between the prohibition on speech and the right to speak played itself out. The mechanism by which it proceeded is hardly surprising. It is a well-recognized process in the case of many stigmatized minorities and consists of showing that a particularity that has been denounced as shameful can in fact be shown to be associated with the prestige of certain great names in the history of the arts, literature, or thought. At the beginning of *Cities of the Plain*, Proust will make fun of homosexuals who "[seek] out (as a doctor seeks out cases of appendicitis) cases of inversion in history, taking pleasure in recalling that Socrates was one of themselves, as the Jews claim that Jesus was one of them" (*RTP* 2:639). Proust's irony is directed at what could appropriately be called the creation of a mythology. Such a mythology is necessary for founding a discourse or even for political action. It is by reference to the speech of Pausanias in Plato's *Symposium* that the jurist Karl Heinrich Ulrichs (whom we might take to be the first activist for the rights of sexual minorities and whose earliest writings are from 1862) came up with the word "Uranian" to refer to those who, a few years later, in psychiatric writings, would begin to be called "inverts" or "homosexuals."[13] In 1870 Ulrichs would create in Germany the first gay journal, to which he would give the title *Uranus*.[14] The label given by the activist (Uranian) thus preceded the label given by psychiatrists (invert, and then homosexual). It is worth noting, moreover, that Freud himself, when he set out to overturn the psychiatric theory according to which sexual inversion would be the sign of "degeneracy," would invoke those great minds about whom it would be difficult to say that they showed signs of degeneration. Inversion can be found, he wrote, "among persons . . . who . . . are distinguished by especially high intellectual development and ethical culture." He adds in a note, "We must agree with the spokesman of 'Uranism' (I. Bloch) that some of the most prominent men known have been inverts and perhaps absolute inverts." Another argument put forth by Freud—and which shows how well he knew the writings of the apologists for sexual inversion, notably those of Ulrichs—is that inversion is "a frequent manifestation among the ancient nations at the height of their culture. It was an institution endowed with important functions."[15]

This literary combat took a spectacular turn in 1895, when the scene shifted to the courtroom, giving the combat a considerable level of public visibility. But however mythical Wilde's name has become, we should not forget that he was simply one figure among many in a large movement to gain access to speech, a movement that involved poets, writers, scholars, and artists. No one author invented "gay culture" ex nihilo, and the role of any one person in its creation can only be understood if it is reinserted into his or her history, only if one returns to the mid-nineteenth century, and to the efforts of intellectuals, artists, and poets to give expression to a type of desire that had barely any claims on public recognition.[16] One could even go further back in time; there are always precursors.

❧ When he writes the poem called "Two Loves," one year before the Wilde trials, Alfred Douglas expresses well the feeling of novelty that he experiences in being able to name the unnamable, for he has heterosexual love say that it was "wont to be alone. . . ." The poet, in a dream, in fact meets two persons: one is sad, somber, and tearful—melancholic, we might say. The poet asks him his name, and he replies: "My name is Love." But then the other person speaks up and cries to the poet:

> He lieth, for his name is Shame,
> But, I'm Love and I was wont to be
> Alone in this fair garden, till he came
> Unasked by night. I'm true Love, I fill
> The hearts of boy and girl with mutual flame."
> Then sighing, the other said: "Have thy will,
> I am the love that dare not speak its name."[17]

Legitimate love says of shameful love that he came "unasked." The poet indicates his own gesture here: he would allow the love that dares not speak its name, the love rejected as "shameful" by "authentic" love, to speak. (This seems to suppose that the love that dares not speak its name has a name and knows it, a name it gives to itself and not only when others are looking on.) The poem was printed in The Chameleon, an Oxford journal published by friends of Douglas. The goal of the journal was to give visibility to homosexual literary expression. This resulted in its being obliged to stop with its very first issue, having been denounced by the writer Jerome K. Jerome. Along with Douglas's poem, this first and only issue also included Wilde's "Phrases and Philosophies for the Use of the Young." Previously, in 1892 and 1893, Alfred Douglas had become editor of an Oxford journal called the Spirit Lamp, with the goal of turning it into a forum for homosexual expression. He published texts by Ross, Symonds, Wilde, and others. Douglas wrote to his friend Kains Jackson that Wilde was doing a good deal for the "new culture" and for the "cause."[18]

It was George Ives, a friend of Wilde's, who suggested using the chameleon as the name for the journal—an animal that, one might say, symbolizes the closet and the games involved in a double identity. Ives noted in his diary:

"If Bosie [Douglas] has really made Oxford homosexual, he has done something good and glorious." Ives was the founder of the Order of Chaeronaea,
a homosexual secret society that Wilde apparently did not join.[19]

❧ Many people, well before Douglas and well before Wilde, had worked
toward the existence of a discourse on homosexuality. Wilde and Douglas
drew their inspiration and their energy from these figures. We can situate
one of the birthplaces of modern gay culture in the milieu of the Oxford
Hellenists that included Walter Pater and John Addington Symonds. The
discourse of this milieu would blossom in Wilde and again in Gide. As
Robert Merle saw in a book from a few decades ago (one that now may seem
dated, but was quite remarkable for the moment in which it was published),
there is an evident line of descent from Oxford Hellenism to Wilde and from
Wilde to Gide: "Wilde is a descendent of Pater's. Gide is a descendent of
Wilde's," he wrote.[20]

Pater and Symonds were two of the most famous intellectuals of their
time. Both liberals in the tradition of John Stuart Mill, deeply influenced by
his *On Liberty*, their goal was to give England a push in a new direction, a new
start. The regeneration they longed and worked for was to be grounded in
the rediscovery of Greek thought that had been encouraged by the reorganization of the program of study at Oxford and by its declericalization.[21]

This new opening onto Greek studies, accompanied by translations of
Plato (Benjamin Jowett's translation of the *Symposium*, for example), had
remarkable consequences. With it came the possibility to create a space for a
new discourse. If, for certain intellectuals of the time, the Greek ideal provided a model for the spiritual regeneration of modern England, for Pater
and Symonds, this ideal, together with the idea of a "spiritual procreation"—
found in the *Symposium*—could not be separated from the conditions described by Plato. "Spiritual procreation" was not something that happened
simply by way of teaching, it also happened by way of "pederastic" love, a
relation between an older and a younger man. Thus, as Linda Dowling notes,
these two authors came quite seriously to consider that Socratic love would
be a means to gain for England a new strength, a new vibrancy. This love
could be the avenue for a new intellectual fertilization, giving rise both to
creative arts and to philosophy, mother of all forms of wisdom.[22]

3

A Nation of Artists

If references to Plato and to "Greek Love" were able to become part of a discourse of legitimation, this was largely due to the fact that such references could be linked to the idea of a kind of spiritual procreation and thereby to the constitution of an intellectual and cultural elite that would reinvigorate the land. That such references were linked to an exaltation of "masculinity" was also important. In effect this praise of Greek philosophy was able to become a counterdiscourse only because it allowed those who took it up to dismiss the accusations of "effeminacy" or of decadence (those very accusatory schemas psychiatry would shortly take on as its own) that were traditionally directed at anything that had to do with love between men. Linda Dowling clearly demonstrates how the category of effeminacy, along with those of corruption and luxury, was linked in many seventeenth- and eighteenth-century English political and philosophical texts to the idea of the progressive downfall of the country. An author like John Brown, who, in his *Estimate of the Manners and Principles of the Time* (1715), sets out to renew the ideal of a nation made up of warrior citizens, posits the notion of effeminacy as the epitome of that which leads to the downfall of a society, where "private interest has begun to prevail against those things that concern the public welfare."[1] This particular thematic can obviously be traced throughout the nineteenth and twentieth centuries, right up to our own moment.

Yet its predominance in the nineteenth century was such that the invention of a homosexual discourse was enduringly marked by the question of masculinity and by the opposition between the masculine and the feminine. It was by accepting this point of departure, by creating a response to it, that a means to speak about love between men came into being. This discourse was born and laid claim to legitimacy either by showing that love between men was authentically masculine, that is, that it corresponded to a collective ideal worthy of a community of warriors, or by showing that rather than leading to decadence, such a love contributed to the intellectual and artistic creativity of elite groups. One book was particularly important here: *Die Dorier* (*The Dorians*), a study by the German Hellenist, K. O. Müller. This book placed Athenian pederasty in a lineage that included Cretan and Spartan initiation rites; that is to say, it linked pederasty to the prehistoric military heritage of the "Dorian race."[2] Müller's book enabled certain subsequent writers to reverse the discourse concerning the decadence and effeminacy of love between men. By tracing the military origins of pederasty, a claim could be made that it was socially "healthy." The accusations of effeminacy, vice, sin, and so on that were usually attached to relations between men could be set aside. By establishing the virility and martial qualities of masculine loves, Müller enabled (once his book was translated into English in 1830) a positive and even militant way of speaking about what was not yet called homosexuality (a word that would be made up later). To give just a single indication of the importance of Müller's book in the emergence of a homosexual culture, we might simply recall that it is the source of the non-Christian first name that Wilde would give to the protagonist of his only novel: *The Picture of Dorian Gray*.

I will not here enter into the debate as to whether or not the circumscription of Greek homosexuality to "pederasty"—to the relation of an older man with a younger one—is historically exact. Specialists disagree about the matter, and it seems quite possible that the representation we receive from the texts left to us does not correspond to real practices—or to the whole extent of real practices. It seems more likely that the image we have, rather than being a true picture of daily life in a given society, is the product of acts of literary adjustments, ideological justification, or philosophical representation. John Boswell argues this.[3] He goes so far as to speak of a "cultural myth" that was dominant during antiquity and that has been taken for practical reality by the historians and commentators of today.[4]

Unlike Boswell, Bernard Sergent, following in the path of K. O. Müller, attempted to show how pederasty as an initiation rite was one of the characteristic traits of the Indo-European as well as of the Greek world. He wanted to show how the Greek world could have inherited a more archaic initiatory tradition, one Indo-European in origin. We might note, however, that in his preface to Sergent's volume on the Greek world, Georges Dumézil, while insisting, as we have already noted, on the differences between ancient pederasty and contemporary homosexuality, was unable to avoid a discreet expression of reticence in the face of an attempt to mark too clearly the specificity, and therefore the difference, of practices from one cultural era or one historical period: "Are the relations between men, is the love of young men best grasped in a comparative Indo-European context? In the ancient Indo-European world, such relations existed elsewhere than in Greece, but are the *forms* sufficiently typical or sufficiently 'improbable' to justify speaking of a common heritage? As André Gide once said, about more elementary kinds of play: 'These things reinvent themselves.' "[5]

‣ Many coded references to Greek love can be found in the book that John Addington Symonds published in 1873, *Studies of the Greek Poets*. A pertinent example can be found in a note, when he describes the gap that exists between ourselves and the Greeks as "due to something outside us rather than within," that is, due principally to the influence of the Judeo-Christian culture to which we are subjected in our childhood, and that represses individual aspirations.[6] Symonds also mentions in that note people for whom Greece is "a lost fatherland," people who "[spend] the nights in golden dreams and the days in common duties." In order that the best of what ancient Greece has to teach us not be forgotten, Symonds asks if it might not be possible to resurrect this tradition by struggling to approach its free-spirited state, by endeavoring to be "natural." He also praises the poet Walt Whitman, whose *Leaves of Grass*, published in the United States in 1855, was (as we shall see) fated to have a considerable influence on the formation of a gay literary tradition. Whitman, Symonds writes, is "more truly Greek than any other man of modern times" because he is "hopeful and fearless, accepting the world as he finds it, recognizing the value of each human impulse."

These remarks are certainly somewhat veiled, but clear enough for any attentive reader. One result of them was that Symonds would be obliged to give up any hope of being named to the chair of poetry for which he had applied at Oxford. Walter Pater, we might add, was also a candidate and would also be obliged to withdraw his name.

In the same year that Symonds expresses himself in this coded way in his study of the Greek poets, he evokes "Greek Love" directly in another work: *A Problem in Greek Ethics*. This small volume he did not, of course, attempt to publish. It would be ten years before he would have it printed, and then only in ten copies, destined for a small circle of confidants. From the beginning of this book, Symonds insists on the necessary distinction between two types of love, one noble and one vulgar, or one spiritual and one carnal. The Greeks valorized the former as the source of courage and greatness of soul, whereas "they never publicly approved the other." This distinction existed throughout their history, says Symonds, hastening to add that in reality "boy-love in its grossest form was tolerated in historic Hellas with an indulgence which it never found in any Christian country, while heroic comradeship remained an ideal hard to realise." Still he insists on the fact that such a distinction is omnipresent in "the language of philosophers, historians, poets and orators." With the Dorians themselves, things were a bit different, Symonds explains; for them masculine friendship and carnal love could be perfectly integrated because that friendship was cemented in wartime situations. After the warlike conditions that gave it nobility and meaning had disappeared, carnal love turned into pure "luxury." At that moment a clear dissociation occurred between pure, noble love and the "base" practices of "vice" (5–6).

Pederasty, as the reference to the Dorians is intended to remind us, has a martial origin for Symonds, and it has never fully lost the "virile character" that was part of its earliest history. The Greek world simply idealized—and also codified—this noble institution that it inherited from its ancestors. Further, Symonds comments that "it was just this effort to elevate paiderastia according to the aesthetic standard of Greek ethics which constituted its distinctive quality in Hellas." Therefore, "we are obliged . . . to separate this, the true Hellenic manifestation of the paiderastic passion, from the effeminacies, brutalities and gross sensualities which can be noticed alike in imperfectly civilized and in luxuriously corrupt communities" (18–19). Here we see to what an extent the legitimation of homosexuality by way of the rediscovery of the "virility" of antiquity was complicit both with a vehement reaffirmation of all the values of that homophobic discourse that criticized passivity, corruption, and effeminacy and also with the idea that sexuality degraded the purity of some ideal.

Symonds indicates that his topic in his text is to be this noble love. The vulgar love is a sort of "vice" that "does not vary to any great extent, whether we observe it in Athens or in Rome, in Florence of the sixteenth or in Paris of the nineteenth century" (7); whereas he insists that the noble form of masculine love developed by the Greeks has almost no equivalent in history. Before launching fully into his study, he intends to define the "nature of this love." The definition must be linked to "its origin and essence," which are "military": "Fire and valour, rather than tenderness or tears, were the external outcome of this passion; nor had *Malachia*, effeminacy, a place in its vocabulary" (8). While it may have been purely virile, this passion was nonetheless intense and absorbing, and Symonds cites as an example a passage from Plato's *Phaedrus* to show that "it would be difficult to find more intense expressions of affection in modern literature."

Symonds's entire analysis, based on his erudite and sharp reading of the texts in question, is a moving effort not only to celebrate what he considers to be the nobility and the purity of the culture of "masculine friendship" found in Greek antiquity, but also to reflect some light from that earlier moment onto himself and his own epoch. In the chapter that he devotes to the Dorian origins of pederasty (for Symonds only ever considers "Greek love" as a relation in which a difference in age is a determining feature), he of course cites the work of K. O. Müller, and writes:

> The Dorians gave the earliest and most marked encouragement to Greek love. Nowhere else, indeed, except among the Dorians, who were an essentially military race, living like an army of occupation in the countries they had seized, herding together in barracks and at public messes, and submitting to martial drill and discipline, do we meet with paiderastia developed as an institution. In Crete and Lacedaemon it became a potent instrument of education. . . . It would appear that the lover was called Inspirer, at Sparta, while the youth he loved was named Hearer. These local phrases sufficiently indicate the relation which subsisted between the pair. The lover taught, the hearer learned; and so from man to man was handed down the tradition of heroism. (13)

Symonds then turns to pederasty in Athens and shows how it was governed by strict rules and by an at least equally severe code of honor. He admits that it may well have split itself into two distinct currents: one noble, the other vulgar. But he insists throughout his study that in Athens it remained "closely associated with liberty, manly sports, severe studies, enthusiasm, self-sacrifice, self-control, and deeds of daring" (44). Symonds devotes much space to the gymnasiums, to the "*palaestra*": spaces in which the relations between lover and beloved were developed. "The Greeks were conscious that gymnastic exercises tended to encourage and confirm the habit of paiderastia," he writes (40). In this regard, he cites a phrase from Plato's *Laws* which indicates "the cities which have most to do with gymnastics" as the places with a predilection for pederasty (40). He makes no attempt to hide his happiness about the fact that he is able to link this form of love to youth, virility, and physical health.[7]

It would only be in 1891, twenty years after his text in praise of Greek love, that Symonds would publish his second monograph, A Problem in Modern Ethics, in which he offers an overview and a radical critique of the medical and psychiatric literature on homosexuality. In the later work the reference to Greek antiquity that had previously served to legitimate "masculine friendships" would become a veritable instrument of war against the medicalization of discourse on homosexuality.

In the years between these two volumes, from 1875 to 1886, Symonds would publish a total of seven books dealing with the Italian Renaissance, including notably a biography of Michelangelo. He made no secret of the fact that he found the energy for this mammoth project in the passion he felt for this historical period. It was "one of the most lawless periods of modern history," one in which people praised the beauty of men and of nature. Yet while this immersion in the past "stimulated" his imagination, it also "irritated" it, for it awoke in him "cravings which cannot be satisfied by simple pleasures." His nervous exhaustion was not alleviated simply by the completion of the books he wrote.[8] This work, which was part of an effort to forget the difficulties—the distress—Symonds experienced in living out his homosexuality, in fact reminded him of those difficulties: the gap was so great between the reality of his own existence and the lives of the men from the past of whom he dreamed; the difference was so marked between the splendor of that bygone era and the only too real torments of his own soul and his own body.

Symonds was quite literally fascinated by the Renaissance and by what he imagined to be the sexual freedom of that time. During a trip to Florence, he discovered and translated the letters between Michelangelo and his greatest love, Tommaso Cavallieri. In a letter to one of his friends, Symonds expresses the deep emotion he felt upon reading, four and a half centuries after they were written, these "passionate letters and verses, indited by aged genius and youthful beauty."[9] In 1878 he published a translation of Michelangelo's sonnets and sent a copy to Oscar Wilde.

Wilde, in writing The Portrait of Mr. W. H., which is devoted to the young man who some claimed to be "the very source of Shakespeare's inspiration," will often make reference to all that he learned from Symonds about the Renaissance and about Platonism and Neo-Platonism. "It is only when we realise the influence of neo-Platonism on the Renaissance that we can understand the true meaning of the amatory phrases and words with which friends were wont, at this time, to address each other," writes Wilde. "There was a kind of mystic transference of the expressions of the physical world to a sphere that was spiritual, that was removed from gross bodily appetite." Wilde then mentions the sonnets that Michelangelo addressed to the young Tommaso Cavallieri and emphasizes "with what intense and religious fervour Michael Angelo addressed himself to the worship of intellectual beauty, and how, to borrow a fine phrase from Mr. Symonds, he pierced through the veil of flesh and sought the divine idea it imprisoned." He also recalls another of Michelangelo's sonnets, written for Luigi del Riccio upon the death of his young friend Cecchino Bracchi, and adds that there too one can find, "as Mr. Symonds points out, the Platonic conception of love as nothing if not spiritual, and of beauty as a form that finds its immortality within the lover's soul."[10]

Wilde had begun reading Symonds at university. In 1876 he drafted an article that was never published in the second volume of The Greek Poets. In that article he commented that one could find in Symonds the same picturesque qualities, the same beauty that is so admired in the writings of "Ruskin and Pater."[11] The aesthetic idea developed by Symonds was one Wilde found striking. Symonds wrote, after all, that even if Greek morality "was aesthetic and not theocratic, it is none the less on that account humane and real." And, finally, Symonds concluded that "the Greeks were essentially a nation of artists. . . . Guided by no supernatural revelation, with no Mosaic law for conduct, they trusted their aesthesis, delicately trained and preserved in a condition of the utmost purity."[12] This is, of course, a clear allusion to the noble purity of "pederasty."

Wilde liked Symonds's book so much that he entered into a correspondence with him, one which has unfortunately been almost entirely lost. Yet Wilde clearly kept an enthusiastic eye on Symonds's later publications, especially those devoted to the Renaissance.

⊁ From all these apologetic efforts, what must first and foremost be kept in mind is the need these authors experienced to justify themselves to themselves. Symonds, like Pater, Wilde and so many others, was struggling, as Neil Bartlett puts it, "to find an identity through reworking the biographies of the past." He continues: "They could not believe that theirs was a unique experience. Instead they subscribed to the opposite theory: the idea that one man's experience may be a repetition of another's. They found their peers not in other men, but in other texts."[13] These nineteenth-century intellectuals, he adds, were looking for "proofs of their own existence, ransacking their libraries with a scholarly enthusiasm for Classical or Renaissance culture" (226–27). It is no surprise, then, that it was Wilde who would write, in *Dorian Gray*, that "one had ancestors in literature, as well as in one's own race, nearer perhaps in type and temperament, many of them, and certainly with an influence of which one was more absolutely conscious." To make Wilde's point perfectly clear, and to make inescapable the link to the portraits Symonds traced in his studies of the Renaissance, it suffices to add the following: "Dorian Gray . . . felt that he had known them all, those strange terrible figures that had passed across the stage of the world and made sin so marvellous, and evil so full of subtlety."[14]

4

Philosopher and Lover

In not all positive evocations of pederasty was it felt necessary to reaffirm the virile character of this kind of relationship. Some authors proved able to resist the social pressure in that direction. But their evocations of pederasty often then became so coded that only the initiated were able to understand them. Already in 1864, the twenty-five-year-old Walter Pater had read his essay "Diaphaneitè" to the Old Morality club (an all-male, politically liberal group that met to hear texts read out, and to which John Addington Symonds also belonged). In that essay, Pater describes the kind of human character that would be able to induce the "regeneration" of society. The figure of the diaphane, "this clear crystal nature," is a person so perfect that his simple presence would do more for the world than others manage to do through their actions. Pater insists on the physical beauty of this figure, a physical beauty that is matched by a correspondingly great inner beauty. Pater anoints this man—more exactly, this *young* man—with a great "pride of life."[1]

The presentation Pater made to this all-male club (and in the presence of the young man in question) contained a good many references to Platonic philosophy. Indeed, what we find in Pater's text is more than a literary or philosophical evocation of the *Symposium;* the scene of the reading of this text is a recreation of the practice of meetings that were a combination of all-male sociability and philosophical discussion. Pater here enacts one part of the distinction made by K. O. Müller between "he who teaches" and "he who listens." What in fact comes to life again here is the Platonic theory of "*philosophesas poté met' erotos,*" an expression Pater would translate as "lover and philosopher at once." The homage he pays to the person to whom his discourse is addressed is, as Linda Dowling puts it, "an almost classical paean to beautiful youth by an older admirer."[2] Oxford, it would seem, offered at this point in time a nearly perfect location for the expression of this kind of love—which was, in theory, totally desexualized: the professor "loves" the student and nourishes him intellectually, but has no intention of touching him. (All the texts insist on this "purity.") Of course, touching doubtless happened, as is attested to by the repeated scandals that cropped up in Oxford, at least one of which shows that Pater himself was not always as distant from physical passion as his "Platonism" might have required.[3]

Pater's essay would only be published after his death, by the person to whom it was addressed, but Pater would return in ever more noticeable ways to the question of masculine loves, notably in 1873, in the volume of essays called *Studies in the History of the Renaissance* (a volume dedicated to the same young man). The volume of course contains chapters on Michelangelo and Leonardo da Vinci. Yet it is in the final chapter of the volume—one devoted to the eighteenth-century German art historian, Winckelmann, already made famous by Hegel and Goethe—that Pater most explicitly invokes homosexuality. For in Pater's eyes, the spirit of the Renaissance lived on in Winckelmann's work and in his passion for Hellenism. In this text from 1867, Pater establishes a direct relation between Winckelmann's sexual tastes and his deep understanding of Greek art, notably of sculpture. He writes: "That his affinity with Hellenism was not merely intellectual, that the subtler threads of temperament were inwoven in it, is proved by his romantic, fervent friendships with young men. . . . These friendships, bringing him into contact with the pride of human form, and staining the thoughts with its bloom, perfected his reconciliation to the spirit of Greek sculpture."[4] Pater gives a long citation from a letter written by Winckelmann to one of his young friends, a letter in which the historian praises the tendency to be attracted to young men, claiming it as a guarantee of an authentic taste for art, an authentic aesthetic sensibility:

> I have noticed that those who are observant of beauty only in women, and are moved little or not at all by the beauty of men, seldom have an impartial, vital, inborn instinct for beauty in art. To such persons the beauty of Greek art will ever seem wanting, because its supreme beauty is rather male than female. But the beauty of art demands a higher sensibility than the beauty of nature, because the beauty of art, like tears shed at a play, gives no pain, is without life, and must be awakened and repaired by culture. Now, as the spirit of culture is much more ardent in youth than in manhood, the instinct of which I am speaking must be exercised and directed to what is beautiful, before that age is reached,

at which one would be afraid to confess that one had no taste for it.
(123–24)

Thus heterosexuality is on the side of nature, homosexuality on the side of culture. Moreover, "the spirit of culture" is closely allied to youth, and this belief is what makes possible Pater's claim that Winckelmann's personal letters shed important light on his writings about art.

It is Winckelmann's lively, tactile relation to beauty that inspires his deep and instinctive understanding of the Greek spirit. "He is in touch with it," says Pater, "it penetrates him, and becomes part of his temperament. . . . He catches the thread of a whole sequence of laws in some hollowing of the hand, or dividing of the hair." Then, taking up his translation of his favorite expression from Plato, Pater writes that Winckelmann "seems to realise that fancy of the reminiscence of a forgotten knowledge hidden for a time in the mind itself, as if the mind of one, lover and philosopher at once in some phase of pre-existence . . . fallen into a new cycle, were beginning its intellectual career over again, yet with a certain power of anticipating its results" (125).

To put things bluntly, for Pater it is the spirit of pederastic love that is reborn in Winckelmann. When Pater cites Goethe's judgment, in which Goethe enthusiastically describes Winckelmann's work as "a living thing, designed for those who are alive," it is easy enough to understand what this Oxford scholar is choosing to mean by "alive" (125). Pater follows in Winckelmann's footsteps. As he pursues his line of reasoning to the end, recalling the religious origins of gymnastics, by means of which the devotee of the gods strives to be worthy of them by striving to be beautiful, Pater writes that Greek art had a direct link to physical beauty. So "the beauty of the palaestra, and the beauty of the artist's workshop, reacted on one another," for "the youth tried to rival his gods; and his increased beauty passed back into them" (134).

In Pater's text we see how important the ardent descriptions Winckelmann gave of Greek sculpture were to those men seeking to legitimate their own desire. After all, the statues were of young men—indeed, of extremely handsome young men.[5] It is not here a question of virility in the military sense, but of the youthful virility of the gymnasium, the palaestra; we are dealing with idealized representations. At this point, Pater sets down a radical argument regarding those who are resistant to the notion of the greatness of Greek art. For him, as for Winckelmann, there is a simple explanation for their reticence. Greek art seems imperfect to them because they are heterosexual. We can also see that Pater is implicitly calling for the creation of a specifically homosexual culture whose goal would be to revivify the ideals of ancient Greece and of the Renaissance. This helps to explain the considerable extent of his influence, for the link that he, following Winckelmann, established between artistic creation, masculine beauty, and love between men would open the way for new discourses and for a new feeling of self-esteem for many young men.

Pater's book gained quite a following for itself. To understand why, it helps to understand its context: the Victorian atmosphere and the suffocating effect of religious and moral traditions on Oxford colleges. In Pater's apologia for ancient Greece and the Renaissance, people found a breath of fresh air, a taste of freedom. Students found its paganism, its celebration of the body, of beauty, and of nature seductive. But there was another theme in the book that would also be influential—the idea, expressed in the book's conclusion, that one had to seize passions in the moment. "Not the fruit of experience, but experience itself, is the end," he writes. One must strive "to burn always with this hard, gem-like flame, to maintain this ecstasy." That constitutes "success in life." Pater therefore exhorts us to reject all philosophical systems:

> With this sense of the splendour of our experience and of its awful brevity, gathering all we are into one desperate effort to see and touch, we shall hardly have time to make theories about the things we see and touch. What we have to do is to be for ever curiously testing new opinions and courting new impressions, never acquiescing in a facile orthodoxy. . . . Philosophical theories or ideas, as points of view, instruments of criticism, may help us to gather up what might otherwise pass unregarded by us. . . . The theory or idea or system which requires of us the sacrifice of any part of this experience, in consideration of some interest into which we cannot enter, or some abstract theory we have not identified with ourselves, or of what is only conventional, has no real claim upon us.[6]

The sense of the brevity of life leads to an exalted aesthetic sensitivity. "Nous sommes tous condamnés," he says in French, citing Victor Hugo. "We are all under a death sentence." We are only granted a brief "interval," and our one chance lies in somehow dilating it, in "expanding that interval . . . getting as many pulsations as possible into the given time." Such wisdom, he tells us, is best found in, "the poetic passion, the desire of beauty, the love of art for its own sake. . . . For art comes to you proposing frankly to give nothing but the highest quality to your moments as they pass, and simply for those moments' sake" (153).

» It is worth adding that other currents were helping create the sense that the Renaissance belonged at the front and center of the cultural scene. Artists from the Pre-Raphaelite movement, such as the poets Swinburne and Dante Gabriel Rossetti or the painter Simeon Solomon, were active in this project. The idea was beginning to spread that the periods of greatest artistic attainment were also those in which love between men had been the most developed, the most visible, and the least repressed. Yet the aestheticism and dandyism that could be found in certain apologists for the thought of Plato or for the Renaissance seemed often to coincide with ways of being that could only be perceived as "effeminate" by other contemporaries. This placed such figures at the antipodes of the dominant theme of masculinity that one finds in this cultural universe. Certainly the great theme of "androgyny" cohabited with discourses on masculinity toward the end of the nineteenth century. One has only to glance at Solomon's paintings from the 1860s and 1870s to understand that sexual ambiguity was one of the most forthright and marked ways of destabilizing normative representations of virility. (It is worth noting that this topic of androgyny was an obsession of late-nineteenth-century French culture as well.) While certain people (such as Symonds) were working to reappropriate discourses of virility, others were working to find ways around them or to reject them outright.[7] Wilde owned paintings by Solomon. When, after his trial, he was declared bankrupt, the paintings would be sold at auction to cover legal expenses. Wilde was clearly an heir to the Solomon tradition as well as to the tradition of Symonds and Pater.

In fact, it is often hard to hold the two traditions of this moment—the affirmation of conventional masculinity and the play with sexual ambiguity—in clear distinction the one from the other. Those who spoke ecstatically of the beauty of gymnasts did not always exhibit behavior in keeping with their discourse. On May 5, 1878, Mark Pattison, dean of Lincoln College, makes a journal entry after a tea at Walter Pater's:

> To Pater's to tea, where Oscar Browning who [was] more like Socrates than ever. He conversed in one corner with 4 feminine looking youths

'part dawdling' there in our presence, while the Miss Paters and I sat looking on in another corner. Presently Walter Pater, who, I had been told was "upstairs" appeared, attended by 2 more youths of similar appearance. . . ."[8]

Richard Ellmann, who cites this passage, adds that the description might tend to create a false impression. One might be led to think that members of this circle displayed their homosexuality fearlessly. But in fact, as Ellmann points out, Pater was extremely prudent and became even more so after the publication in 1873 of his *Studies in the History of the Renaissance*. As Oscar Wilde would say to Charles Ricketts, "Poor dear Pater has lived to disprove everything he has written." Or to Robert Ross, "Dear Pater was always frightened of my propaganda."[9] Whatever can be said about his personal comportment, trapped between audacity and prudence, between the defiance of instituted norms and fearful compliance in the face of established power, it can certainly be said of Pater that he contributed to the creation of a visibility for this love, a visibility which, even if coded in many ways, nonetheless seemed able to catch the attention of certain uninitiated people—both Pater's enemies and his young adepts. Pater's prudence doubtless grew out of the fact that he had been the object of some attacks of considerable violence. The conclusion to his *Studies* did not go unnoticed. He was denounced in 1877 in a pamphlet entitled *The New Republic*, authored by W. H. Mallock. In that satire, Pater was portrayed under the name of Mr. Rose, a ridiculous and effeminate esthete, pale, with a high voice, who hides his sexual tastes behind a screen of classical references. Mallock wanted to demonstrate that Pater's Hellenism, far from belonging to the tradition of "spiritual regeneration" that John Stuart Mill had called for, could only lead to "dissolution," to the collapse of a culture and a society. But, because of the way he insisted on the links between Hellenism, aestheticism, and homosexuality, Mallock in the end achieved the paradoxical result of giving greater visibility to this movement of self-affirmation, in a certain way providing it with avant-garde credentials, calling it to the attention of young men with literary and intellectual ambitions. Mallock publicly exposed the subtext of Victorian Hellenism and thereby helped it move from being the abstruse province of an Oxford elite to becoming something with much wider visibility. Once again we notice that homophobic discourse is always productive in this paradoxical way. It helps to crystallize previously disparate aspects of a gay consciousness. Without a doubt, Oscar Wilde was heavily marked by this polemical atmosphere, one in which he realized that it was possible to make a name for oneself by transgressing rules and taboos and that it was possible to ground his own personal quest by reference to Greek antiquity.[10]

✥ Oscar Wilde himself had manners that were quite effeminate, and he seems to have cultivated this stance as part and parcel of the aestheticism he wanted to incarnate. When, for example, he traveled to the United States in 1882 to give a series of lectures, many members of one of the clubs that invited him, the Century Association, refused to be introduced to him. One of the older members of the club went around saying, "Where is she? Have you seen her? Well, why not say 'she'? I understand she's a Charlotte-Ann."[11] Ellmann's biography provides a whole series of testimonies to his sashaying walk, his provocative demeanor, his audacious play with the codes of sexual appearance. It comes as no surprise, then, to find the *New York Times* printing (in January 1882) the malicious observations of a former classmate of Wilde's, claiming that Wilde lost any chance of ever obtaining a teaching post at Oxford because "he assumed a guise that sturdier minds thought of as *epicene*."[12]

In fact, Oxford students seem to have had little doubt as to Wilde's personality. Ironic comments on his effeminate manners were to be heard even during his student years, before he arrived at Oxford, when he was still at Trinity College, Dublin. The plays on words to be found in the Suggestion Book of the Philosophical Society, where students were free to write their commentaries, are unambiguous and make persistent fun of Wilde's mannered aestheticism. On one page of this book, there is a caricature of a policeman, reprimanding Wilde for a nocturnal adventure that was perhaps not purely aesthetic in character.[13] It is also quite clear that at the time aestheticism, or aesthetic leanings, or simply the choice of artistic pursuits were tantamount to a renunciation of virility, and further, that they laid someone open to suspicion of homosexuality. Equally clearly, for many homosexuals, the aesthetic pose was one way of affirming and expressing their homosexuality. An artistic air, a fervor for the arts, or an aesthetic temperament—all of which were ways of expressing a revolt against the normative masculinity of the dominant class in England—also allowed many homosexuals to adopt publicly a recognizable set of gestures, of mannerisms, of tastes, of cultural references. They created a "role" in which one's sexuality and one's personality could find expression. This was true to such an extent that toward the end of the nineteenth century and well into the twentieth "artist" was closely associated with "homosexual." In any case, Wilde's classmates perceived things in this way. Wilde detested the athletically inclined among the students at university, and they were happy to return the favor. Many stories, true or false, circulated regarding the cruelties they inflicted on him. One evening a group of them went to visit him, four of them having been charged to beat him up and destroy his furniture—the symbols of his aesthetic taste (which is to say, of his rejection of the values they held dear), symbols of his supposed homosexuality. Much to everyone's surprise, Wilde defended himself so successfully that he was able to throw his assailants out the door.[14]

The humiliation of the homosexual or of the effeminate man by means of a violent manifestation of "virile" force is a strikingly constant occurrence, one attested to in many historical periods. It hardly needs to be said that things have not changed greatly from Wilde's moment to our own.[15]

5

Moral Contamination

Symonds's and Pater's books were clearly of immense importance to Oscar Wilde. He was passionately interested in ancient Greece from his school days onward. As we have seen, if he chose to name the hero of his only novel Dorian, it was a reference to the milieu of Oxford Hellenism in which he had immersed himself. At the time of his trial, he would recall in his defense all the cultural references that went into his formation. The circumstances are well known: the Marquess of Queensberry, the father of Alfred Douglas, left a calling card for Wilde at Wilde's club. On that famous card he wrote: "Oscar Wilde, posing as a Somdomite [sic]." Queensberry, who had left school at a young age to join the navy, only barely knew how to read and write, so his spelling mistake in writing the word "sodomite" is hardly surprising. For him the word probably had little meaning other than as an insult. Wilde takes him to court for defamation—even though the porter at the club had been careful to put the card in an envelope, ensuring that the insult was in no way a public one. How could Wilde have been so foolish? In De Profundis, he would accuse Alfred Douglas at some length of having urged him on to this fatal error. Douglas, Wilde claims, motivated by a vengefulness for a father he despised, pushed Wilde to take legal action against that father, thereby setting in motion a disastrous chain of events. Wilde's friends, on the other hand, did all they could to prevent him from taking the matter to the courts. But Wilde, unable to resist "Bosie," went ahead with his suit against Queensberry. Unfortunately for Wilde, the law authorized the defendant in a trial for defamation to introduce evidence to prove the accuracy of the statements that had been made. Queensberry hired private detectives to undertake a secret investigation that would furnish all the evidence he needed.[1]

During the first trial, Wilde was interrogated first by his own attorney and then cross-examined by Queensberry's attorney, Edward Carson. When asked a question by his own attorney regarding a love letter he had written to Douglas and which had been stolen by a male prostitute hoping to use it for blackmail, Wilde replied that he told the young swindler the letter was a prose poem. He then recounted a threatening surprise visit he had received from Lord Queensberry, whom he asked, before showing him the door, "Do you seriously accuse your son and me of improper conduct?" Then he gave Queensberry's reply: "I do not say that you are it, but you look it . . . and you pose at it, which is just as bad." During cross-examination, Carson asked Wilde about The Picture of Dorian Gray: "The affection and love of the artist of Dorian Gray might lead an ordinary individual to believe that it might have a certain tendency?" Wilde replied, with all the characteristic scorn of the aesthete he was: "I have no knowledge of the views of ordinary individuals."[2]

As is well known, Wilde lost his case against Queensberry, and this inevitably set in motion further judicial procedures. If Wilde had not been defamed, the legal authorities could assume that Queensberry's accusation had been proved and that Wilde should himself be tried for "indecent acts." It was during the second trial that the prosecutor asked Wilde about the poems Alfred Douglas had written, notably about the verse that mentions the "love that dare not speak its name." Wilde, whose wit had up to this point provided him with ample means for denials, lies, and pirouettes, launched into an eloquent extended statement in defense of homosexuality:

> The 'Love that dare not speak its name' in this century is such a great affection of an elder for a younger man as there was between David and Jonathan, such as Plato made the very basis of his philosophy, and such as you find in the sonnets of Michaelangelo and Shakespeare. It is that deep, spiritual affection that is as pure as it is perfect. It dictates and pervades great works of art like those of Shakespeare and Michaelangelo, and those two letters of mine, such as they are. It is in this century misunderstood, so much misunderstood that it may be described as the 'Love that dare not speak its name' and on account of it I am placed where I am now. It is beautiful, it is fine, it is the noblest form of affection. There is nothing unnatural about it. It is intellectual, and it repeatedly exists between an elder and a younger man, when the elder man has intellect, and the younger man has all the joy, hope and glamour of life before him. That it should be so the world does not understand. The world mocks at it and sometimes puts one in the pillory for it.[3]

Wilde's eloquence provoked spontaneous applause from the audience in the Old Bailey, but the prosecutor, feet firmly planted on the ground, remarked that this fine definition, which refers to the purity—the absence of sexuality—of a pedagogical relation, seemed hardly applicable to Wilde's relations with the male prostitutes who were implicated in the affair. Wilde was forced to admit that such a love as he described is unlikely to be met with more than once in a lifetime. Still, his eloquent and spirited outburst saved him from losing this first prosecution against him. The jury was unable to come to unanimous agreement to convict him. (It seems that one juror favored acquittal whereas eleven others were willing to condemn him.) The case therefore had to be retried. Wilde's sentence came at the end of the second trial against him. Before announcing the sentence, the judge turned to Wilde and his co-defendant, Alfred Taylor, and said: "It is no use for me to address you. People who can do these things must be dead to all sense of shame, and one cannot hope to produce any effect upon them. It is the worst case I have ever tried. That you, Taylor, kept a kind of male brothel it is impossible to doubt. And that you, Wilde, have been the centre of a circle of extensive corruption of the most hideous kind among young men, it is equally impossible to doubt."[4] Earlier, the Crown's prosecutor had laid out the terrible charges to the jury in the following terms: "You owe a duty to society, however sorry you may feel yourselves at the moral downfall of an eminent man, to protect society from such scandals by removing from its heart a sore which cannot fail in time to corrupt and taint it all."[5] Wilde had doubtless intended to head off a charge like this when, during the second of the three trials, he invoked the pure and intellectual character of the love that is the basis of Plato's philosophy and Michelangelo's sonnets. We see here then the functioning of this pair of notions—we might better say of mental schemas: for some homosexuality is a form of social corruption, while for others, those trying to legitimate it, it is related to purity, nobility, and art, to what is most elevated in society. In Wilde's trials we witness the brutal confrontation of these two conceptions, and that confrontation sheds light on the pages written by Symonds twenty years earlier, in which he insisted on contrasting the noble and the vulgar, the high and the low, the pure and the impure. Or on the pages written by Pater in which he invokes the grandeur of art and the possibility of another renaissance produced by the spiritual fecundation of a younger man by a philosopher-lover. Symonds and Pater had tried to establish a counterdiscourse. They had undertaken to provide a historical and philosophical rejoinder to the dominant ideology (the one found in the mouths of Wilde's prosecutors) that claimed that homosexuality meant the ruin of civilization. Wilde gave voice to the discourse of Pater and Symonds in the courtroom. But the encounter did not take place on level ground. Those who favored eradicating or silencing homosexuality held the positions of power. They were the ones deciding the men's fate. So, after expressing his personal indignation at the "horrible charges" leveled at the two accused men (Wilde and Taylor), the judge sentenced them to two years of hard labor.

Richard Ellmann's description of that labor and of the prison conditions under which those sentenced to such labor were required to live is quite simply terrifying. Such a sentence often meant a quick death shortly after release from prison. This fate was all the more likely for someone previously unaccustomed to manual labor—which was evidently the case for Wilde. Wilde would in fact die three years after his release from prison. In his 1901 article, Gide describes the "weakened and broken" Wilde "whom the prison returned to us," a man so different from "the prodigious being he was at first."[6]

⊁ If I have given so much space to the trial of Oscar Wilde, it is because we see in it the intersection of a certain number of themes that must be taken into account in any approach to gay culture. Even if we decide to think that Wilde was highly imprudent in taking Queensberry to court for defamation, we should probably accept, as Ellmann does, that he was headed for a fall. This is not to countenance some stereotypical idea of inevitable downfall— an idea that haunts both gay and homophobic literature throughout the first half of the twentieth century (and films until the 1960s). But it remains true that because he played with the limits imposed by English society in the nineteenth century, because he (consciously or unconsciously) politicized his way of life, Wilde could not help but provoke a strong reaction against him. His way of displaying his homosexuality, of surrounding himself with young men who were for the most part lovers or former lovers of Alfred Douglas, obliged him to find his way between, as Ellmann puts it, "blackmailing boys and furious fathers," the former being all too ready to sell themselves or him.[7] So sooner or later, given a society in which homosexuality could only be lived out discreetly or secretly, an artist who exhibited scandalous behavior was bound to find himself convicted and broken by "justice" and by prison.

As Neil Bartlett puts it, Wilde was not convicted simply for being homosexual, but for being a public figure who was also homosexual, and further, who refused to remain silent and hide what he was. Perhaps this was, in Henri de Régnier's words, a "chronological error": "Mr. Wilde imagined himself to be living in Italy during the Renaissance or in Greece in the age of Socrates. He was punished—severely—for this chronological error, given that he lived in London, where this anachronism is apparently quite common."[8] Even if the tail end of de Régnier's sentence does qualify the idea of the anachronism (suggesting rather that the reality being described was both widespread and well-known), still his notion might help us to see that Wilde's fate was sealed as soon as the scandal became public knowledge. Wilde would at that point have to be silenced. Gide, in his "In Memoriam," recounts something Wilde had said to him a few years before his downfall: "Prudence! But can I have any? That would be going backwards. I must go as far as possible . . . I can not go further . . . Something must happen . . . something else . . ."[9] Indeed, Gide seems deeply convinced that Wilde was destined for a terrible end. Proust too describes Wilde's conviction as the fulfillment of a destiny. In fact, this is one of the examples he uses at the outset of *Cities of the Plain* (*Sodome et Gomorrhe*), when he speaks of the curse laid on the race of inverts, "their honour precarious, their liberty provisional, lasting only until the discovery of their crime; their position unstable, like that of the poet one day fêted in every drawing-room and applauded in every theatre in London, and the next driven from every lodging, unable to find a pillow upon which to lay his head."[10] Wilde himself, in *De Profundis*, his long prison letter to Alfred Douglas, repeatedly invokes "Destiny," and even "Doom," to describe what has happened to him. And was not the idea of an unavoidable fate already the very subject of *The Picture of Dorian Gray?*

⋈ By studying Wilde's trials, one can also learn to what an extent the question of blackmail has been central to the history of homosexuality—throughout the world. Ulrichs, in his struggle to decriminalize homosexuality, had already put forward this argument (and Hirschfeld would repeat it): blackmail places honest men under the influence of scoundrels who have them at their mercy, and a single unfortunate encounter can thus destroy a man's whole life. How many broken lives, tragedies, and suicides have been caused by blackmail? In light of the Wilde trials, it becomes apparent how great the solitude of a gay man could be once justice had dealt with him publicly. If, among all those in high society who had only a few months previously delighted in Wilde's company, no one was willing to take it upon themselves to intervene to prevent the legal proceedings from getting underway, this is because everyone realized that any intervention in Wilde's favor would rebound on whoever tried it. Any such persons would be suspected of sharing Wilde's tastes and of wishing to protect themselves.

Surely this was the case with the Prime Minister, Lord Rosebery, who had privately been accused by Alfred Douglas's father of having led Drumlanrig, Queensberry's oldest son, who was also Rosebery's personal secretary, into the accursed practice of homosexuality. Drumlanrig's suicide, in October 1894, was perhaps the result of his fear of becoming the victim of a blackmailer and ruining the minister's career. This would easily explain both Queensberry's fierce anger at Wilde and Rosebery's hesitancy about intervening on Wilde's behalf, even though he knew him and had dined with him on a number of occasions.[11]

Indeed, it may well be *because* of the rumors that were circulating about Rosebery, in order to chase suspicion away, that the solicitor general was so intent on continuing to prosecute Wilde even after the first jury had failed to arrive at a unanimous verdict. For the prime minister had been named in one of Queensberry's letters that had been read aloud in court. Even then, it seems Rosebery was on the point of intervening—until, that is, Lord Balfour said to him: "If you do, you will lose the election." So he did not intervene. And he still lost the election.[12]

6

The Truth of Masks

The conception of the "love that dare not speak its name" that Wilde put forth during his trial bears the imprint of the reference to ancient Greece and to the Platonism and neo-Platonism of the Renaissance. The ghosts of John Addington Symonds and of Walter Pater loom large, as we have already said, in this discourse. In point of fact, all of Wilde's writing is steeped in Oxford Hellenism.

We have already seen this to be the case for *The Portrait of Mr. W. H.* But in *The Picture of Dorian Gray*, published in 1891, one also finds this mixture of a scarcely veiled affirmation of homosexuality and of a dissimulation in codes that are nonetheless nearly transparent and wouldn't fool anyone. Some sentences thought to be overly explicit were cut when he revised the earlier version of the novel, published in 1890 in *Lippincott's Monthly Magazine*, for its publication as a book. An example would be the passage in which Hallward said to Dorian: "It is quite true that I have worshipped you with far more romance of feeling than a man usually gives to a friend. Somehow, I had never loved a woman."[1] This declaration of love was replaced by a different sentence which makes of Dorian the incarnation of an ideal that the artist had dreamed of: "You became to me the visible incarnation of that unseen ideal whose memory haunts us artists like an exquisite dream."[2] Yet this latter sentence, which "encodes" a homosexual enunciation, is obviously a paraphrase of an idea developed by Pater in speaking about Winckelmann, that of homoerotic friendship appearing to us as the "reminiscence of a forgotten knowledge," as the new "intellectual career" of someone who is reliving the past life of a Greek philosophical lover. It was in fact at the request of Walter Pater that Oscar Wilde removed the audacious sentence he had written for the first version of the novel.[3]

There are many other sentences in *Dorian Gray* that seem to come out of

Pater. A good example would be the moment in the second chapter of the novel when Lord Henry declares to Dorian, "I believe that if one man were to live out his life fully and completely, were to give form to every feeling, expression to every thought, reality to every dream—I believe that the world would gain such a fresh impulse of joy that we would forget all the maladies of medievalism, and return to the Hellenic ideal." The aristocrat's disquisition ends with an exhortation to "yield" to temptations and never to deny oneself forbidden pleasures: "Every impulse that we strive to strangle broods in the mind, and poisons us." A bit further along, Lord Henry continues to explain his program of practical philosophy by speaking of a "new Hedonism": "Let nothing be lost upon you. Be always searching for new sensations."[4]

In chapter 11, a long interior monologue of Dorian's presented in indirect discourse, certain sentences are simply borrowed from Pater: "Yes: there was to be, as Lord Henry had prophesied, a new Hedonism that was to re-create life. . . . It was never to accept any theory or system that would involve the sacrifice of any mode of passionate experience. Its aim, indeed, was to be experience itself, and not the fruits of experience. . . . It was to teach man to concentrate himself upon the moments of a life that is itself but a moment."[5]

Wilde's relation to Walter Pater was not a purely literary affair; they were quite close. Wilde didn't meet Pater until his third year at Oxford, but in his first term there he fell under the spell of Pater's *Studies in the History of the Renaissance*, which had been published the previous year. He spoke of it as "my golden book" and referred to Pater's essays as "the golden book of spirit and sense, the holy writ of beauty."[6] If Ruskin had been Wilde's great passion during his first year at Oxford, Pater would be the great passion of the fourth year, and the years after.[7] Many years later, while in prison, he would once again speak of *The Renaissance* as "that book which has had such a strange influence over my life."[8]

Wilde and Pater quickly became friends. Pater wrote him letters signed "affectionately yours," and soon they were deeply intimate (without that implying any sexual relations). In 1878, Pater thanked Wilde for the gift of a photographic portrait of Wilde. They often took walks together or met for tea.[9] Clearly there existed a circle made up of young men and a few professors who moved within an ambit that was unquestionably homosexual. The situation was, in fact, perhaps too clear, given that scandals broke out and students were expelled. William Money Hardinge was one, a student to whom Pater wrote letters that he signed "Yours lovingly," a fact that soon became well known. This student was also penning homosexual sonnets, which led to him being called in by the dean and given the choice either to leave Oxford or to be brought before a disciplinary board.[10] Hardinge chose to leave Oxford. Wilde thus knew what risks he was running. This did not prevent him from taking up with Pater only three years after the Hardinge affair and without taking many precautions. Marc-André Raffalovich would later, in his book Uranisme et unisexualité, tell of Wilde boasting that he took as much pleasure in speaking of homosexuality as others took in practicing it. In 1877, for instance, Wilde published in a review called Kottabos a poem celebrating the beauty of a young man, inspired by a painting by his friend Violet Troubridge:

> A fair slim boy not made for this world's pain,
> With hair of gold thick clustering round his ears . . .[11]

Four years later, when he reprinted these lines in his collection of verse, he would change the sex of the person referred to. At that point, the poem, entitled Madonna Mia, read as follows:

> A lily-girl, not made for this world's pain,
> With brown, soft hair close braided by her ears . . .[12]

Of course, one could say that this is simply a question of a later version of a poem that has undergone revision, but perhaps we should also see here the necessary imposition of a kind of "recoding," one that is the inverse of what Linda Dowling has called the "homosexual code." The recoding would indicate a need to dissimulate something that had been too visible. It was no longer a question of trying to make something visible and at the same time dissimulating.

Doubtless this obligation to transpose the sex of one's characters was for a long time one of the characteristic traits of literature written by gay people. Any gay writer would have had to ask the question: can the narrator be explicitly homosexual? If not, how can things be arranged so that the reader will not see in a physical description the expression of sexual desire? Christopher Isherwood's 1976 autobiography has many interesting things to say about such questions. For example, he tells how, in his first novels in the 1930s, as a way of covering his tracks he gave legs that were "spindly" to a young character whose beautiful torso he had just praised.[13] Isherwood also mentions the problem of the sexual identity of the narrators of his novels. He did not dare let them be homosexual, but he could not bring himself to have them be heterosexual, so he preferred to deprive them of all desire. This meant he could not then place them in any situation in which they might need to manifest some desire.[14] Speaking of his mostly autobiographical novel, *Mr. Norris Changes Trains*, Isherwood emphasizes that the book "fails to reveal what was the most enduring bond between Gerald and Christopher, their homosexuality."[15] Even the first volume of his autobiography, *Lions and Shadows*, which deals with his early years, leaves his homosexuality obscured, despite the fact that certain of the events he recounts make little sense otherwise.[16]

It is, alas, rather rare that an author, fifty years after the fact, takes the occasion to shed this kind of retrospective light on his previous writings. By publishing an autobiography in the 1970s that deals with the 1920s and 1930s, Isherwood is, temporally speaking, almost ideally situated to help us understand these kinds of disjunctures. Take the example of Forster. How would we be able to read or understand how to decode all his veiled allusions if the manuscript to *Maurice* had been lost? The question is of major importance. After all, Forster stopped writing novels once he finished *Maurice* (which he considered impossible to publish once it was written) because he no longer felt capable—once having decided to tell the truth—of continuing to lie. He no longer felt like writing about love between men and women or about marriage; he no longer wished to force himself to keep silent about the nature of his own feelings.[17] It's also difficult to avoid mentioning in this context a poem by Auden, "The Truest Poem Is the Most Feigning." There is no doubt that Proust was only able to talk so freely of what he called, in his draft from 1909, the "Race of the Aunties" (*la race des tantes*) because he was always at pains to pretend he was describing it from the outside. Much ink has been spilt over the fact that his character Albertine is a literary transposition of his chauffeur, who was named Alfred Agostinelli. Even if we try to take into account merely the twists and turns of the plot of Proust's novel, the idea of this transposition doesn't make a whole lot of sense. For if that is our hypothesis, what are we to do with the exploration of lesbianism in the novel, whose mysteries (in the narrator's eyes) produce the material for many passages? It might nonetheless be possible to say that this whole question of transpositions was initially produced out of the necessity that the narrator be heterosexual. As evidence for this, we could mention the moment at which the storyline of *The Captive* is interrupted so that the "author" can intervene in order to offer a justification for the important place homosexuality is given in his book, but also in order strenuously to distance himself from it: "The author would like to say how grieved he would be if the reader were to be offended by his portrayal of such weird characters. . . . But it is none the less true that considerable interest, not to say beauty, may be found in actions inspired by a cast of mind so remote from anything we feel, from anything we believe, that they remain incomprehensible to us, displaying themselves before our eyes like a spectacle without rhyme or reason" (RTP, 3:40). The "author" is here attempting to reveal to the "reader" (presumed to be heterosexual) the "cause" of all these behaviors, of these deeds and gestures, of these psychological formations that are present and visible on a daily basis, but that cannot really be understood in the absence of the right key—the key that opens the door to all the mysterious secrets of these strange people, whose "actions" will become crystal clear as soon as one understands their true "nature."

Proust is insistent on this point: all the gestures, all the stances a person takes, however contradictory or bizarre they may seem, take on a clear meaning, become coherent, as soon as one knows that said person belongs to the "accursed race." The individual's entire personality falls into a new pattern once the "secret" is revealed. Yet who is it who reveals the secret, who provides the key? Proust always holds himself at a distance from the object under description. The terms in which he describes these "weird" personages often function to create the impression that he has no part in the life that his novel sets out to reconstitute. His first readers and critics certainly had this impression. If it is possible to describe the pages of Proust's novel that deal with the Baron de Charlus as, in the words of Eve Kosofsky Sedgwick, a staging of the "spectacle of the closet"—and, as we have seen, this may well be the paradigm for the predicament in which a gay person is always located—we should add that this "closet," closely scrutinized by the novel's own heterosexual characters, is also being scrutinized by the narrator and, even more so, by the author. Indeed, the spectacle of this "spectacle" is called to our attention, is revealed to us by someone who is working hard, by means of this very revelation, to shield his own "closet" from any unwanted attention, to prevent its own spectacularization.[18] Yet, due to a rather unsurprising boomerang effect, this person is in fact thereby precisely exposing himself to the danger of becoming the object of this same "spectacle of the closet." He finds himself in danger of becoming the object of rumors and insinuations—a situation he described so marvelously in the case of Charlus, and yet of which he was so afraid that he asked his friends to counter those rumors and insinuations. Yet who, if not a homosexual, would have been able to describe so perspicaciously and with such a sharp and intimate sense of it, that situation he claimed was hidden from general view? Such an impression of the narrator is only reinforced by the fact that when it is a question of *male* homosexuality, the narrator is forever demonstrating that what remains hidden to the eyes of others is all too obvious to him; yet he frequently insists that lesbian life and the world of lesbians remain mysterious and impenetrable to him.

What we can learn from Isherwood is that literary texts do not necessarily reveal to us the "truth" about the sexuality of a given moment in time. One must always take into account the work of encoding, of feigning, of dissimulation in order to ascertain whether or not the discursive categories in question, the descriptions, the judgments, and so on, correspond to real practices. It is probably wiser, when dealing with the subject matter at hand, to begin with actual historical studies before moving on to the study of literary texts rather than, as is the case with too many scholarly works, moving from the study of literary texts to an interpretation of history.

Here again, André Gide (whose lucidity in these matters is quite modern) has some helpful things to say. In his *Journal*, Gide protested against the idea put forward by André Maurois, to the effect that Oscar Wilde's sexual morals were nothing more than a kind of accessory to his aestheticism:

> I believe quite on the contrary that this affected aestheticism was for him merely an ingenious cloak to hide, while half revealing, what he could not let be seen openly; to excuse, provide a pretext, and even apparently motivate; but that very motivation is but a pretense. Here, as almost always, and often even without the artist's knowing it, it is the secret of the depths of his flesh that prompts, inspires, and decides.
>
> Lighted in this way and, as it were, from beneath, Wilde's plays reveal, beside the surface witticisms, sparkling like false jewels, many oddly revelatory sentences of great psychological interest. And it is for them that Wilde wrote the whole of the play—let there be no doubt about it.
>
> Try to let some understand what one has an interest in hiding from all. As for me, I have always preferred frankness. But Wilde made up his mind to make of falsehood a work of art. . . . That is what made him say: "Never use I." The I belongs to the very face, and Wilde's art had something of the mask about it, insisted on the mask. . . . Always he managed in such a way that the informed reader could raise the mask and glimpse, under it, the true visage (which Wilde had such good

reason to hide). This artistic hypocrisy was imposed on him by respect, which was very keen in him, for the proprieties; and by the need of self-protection. Likewise, moreover, for Proust, that great master of dissimulation.[19]

Already in 1921, Gide had recounted a conversation with Proust who had said more or less the same thing to him. During a conversation in which Gide was telling him about his project of writing his memoirs, Proust replied: "You can tell anything . . . but on condition that you never say: *I.*" To which Gide's reaction was: "But that won't suit me" (2:265).

Gide wrote these journal entries in 1921 and 1927. Yet had he not himself practiced various forms of "dissimulation" at earlier moments? After all, in 1911 he only published a few copies of *Corydon*, with no author's name provided. And what might we say of *The Immoralist* or of *Fruits of the Earth?* Even if they do mention homosexuality explicitly, still the play between revelation and dissimulation that one finds in them is closer to Wilde than the author seems to remember. Moreover, contrary to what Gide might think, it was perhaps not only a sense of social niceties that encouraged Wilde to dissimulate. There were social constraints involved, and there was the matter of prudence, to which many of his friends were constantly exhorting him— just as Gide's friends would do in attempting to convince him not to publish *Corydon*.

⊁ When *The Picture of Dorian Gray* appeared, it was without a doubt perceived as a homosexual manifesto—both by homosexuals and by others. That is why, when Wilde applied for admission to the Crabbdt Club, one of his former classmates at Oxford, George Curzon, used his reputation as a sodomite and his manner of treating the subject in *Dorian Gray* as grounds for opposing his admission. Wilde defended himself with a certain ease and malicious wit, but he never returned to the club.[20] *Dorian Gray* quickly became a reference and a rallying point for English homosexuals: Wilde's young friends were amazed at his audacity. In order to celebrate the book, Max Beerbohm wrote his "Ballade de la vie joyeuse" and Lionel Johnson wrote a poem in Latin which described Dorian as someone who "avidly loves strange loves . . . and plucks strange flowers." The poem addressed Wilde with these words: "Here are the apples of Sodom, here are the very hearts of vices, and tender sins. In heaven and hell be glory of glories to you who perceive so much."[21] It therefore hardly seems surprising that Lionel Johnson would have lent his copy of the novel to one of his young cousins, who read it passionately—fourteen times, he claimed—and seized upon the first occasion that presented itself to accompany Johnson on a visit to Wilde. The cousin's name was Alfred Douglas.

7

The Greeks against the Psychiatrists

Michel Foucault's assertion that homosexual literature came into being as a reaction to psychiatric discourse and to the invention by nineteenth-century medical science of the personage of the homosexual is not an assertion that we can accept. In support of his thesis, Foucault provides the examples of Oscar Wilde and André Gide. He suggests such a historical chain of events in an interview that appeared shortly after the publication of *La Volonté de savoir*:

> In the 1870s psychiatrists began to make it into a medical analysis. . . . They began either to incarcerate homosexuals in asylums or attempted to cure them. They were formerly perceived as libertines and sometimes as delinquents. . . . In the future we'll all see them in a global kinship with the insane, suffering from sickness of the sexual instinct. But taking such discourses literally, and thereby even turning them around, we see responses appearing in the form of defiance: "All right, we are what you say we are, whether by nature or sickness or perversion, as you wish. And so if we are, let it be, and if you want to know what we are, we can tell you better than you can." An entire literature of homosexuality, very different from libertine narratives, appeared at the end of the 19th century: think of Oscar Wilde and Gide. It is the strategic return of a "same" will to truth.[1]

This particular version of history seems cavalier, to say the least. Foucault seems unaware that Wilde's writings were not conceived as a reaction to psychiatric theories. Nor were those of Pater or of Symonds. One might in fact wonder if precisely the opposite is not the case. Perhaps the invention of a culture by homosexuals themselves was prior to any attention that psychiatry was beginning to pay to them. It is, in any case, probably impossible to establish any clear and direct causality in one direction or the other. The two discourses are probably best thought of as developing separately and simultaneously. Thereafter, a kind of disciplinary battle arises, in which the domains of literature and philosophy struggle with medicine, psychology, and psychiatry over who has the right to speak, and who is saying what on the subject. Homosexuals themselves spoke from the literary and philosophical domains and found themselves in opposition to psychiatrists—for the most part heterosexual—who set out to give a medical and scientific account of homosexuality. To affirm that homosexual literature was nothing but some kind of reaction produced by psychiatry makes little sense; it is surprising to find Foucault offering such inaccurate approximations. It is certainly undeniable that the literary discourses were "reverse" discourses: they fought against a prohibition on speech, responded to homophobic discourse, and, in order to do so they often integrated that discourse into their own. But the discourses in question were in no way shaped by psychiatry, which came on the scene only later. Rather than the categories of medical discourse, it was the moral and religious order of Victorian England that was being called into question. Indeed medical discourse was almost entirely unknown to these writers when they elaborated their projects in their Oxford colleges. Their adversary was Christian morality, the idea of the "vice which cannot be named among Christians," of the "sin against nature." In opposition to this, they offered the pagan freedom of the Greeks, the Greek cult of beauty, and the greatness of Greek artistic accomplishments: "A nation of artists," Symonds would say of the Greeks.

If we consider the case of Symonds, we can see that the first literary texts (poems) in which he struggled to express his homosexuality date from much earlier than his acquaintance with the medical literature. Those poems are from the 1860s and one finds nothing that has to do with psychiatry in his attempt there to justify and legitimate his homosexuality. Symonds rebels against stifling traditional values and invokes the glorious Greek past in order to do so. When he did begin to take an interest in psychiatric discourse, it would not be in order to appropriate its categories while reversing their significance, but to oppose the discourse by referring once again to that mythic Greece whose greatness he had first lauded twenty years earlier.

A whole set of medical works dealing with "sexual inversion" and what would later be called "homosexuality" would appear in the years between 1870 and 1890, notably in France and Germany. For Symonds the psychiatric writings were just as contestable as were the religious or moral discourses that this science imagined it was going to replace. This is why, in the 1890s,

Symonds undertakes to confront the psychiatrists directly. "The theory of morbidity," he writes, "is more humane, but it is not less false, than that of sin or vice."[2] In A Problem in Modern Ethics, published in 1891 in a privately distributed edition of fifty copies, he specifically attacks a number of the most prominent psychopathologists of the time: Tardieu, Carlier, Moreau, Krafft-Ebing, and so on. In the chapter he devotes to Dr. Paul Moreau, the author of an 1877 treatise entitled Des aberrations du sens génésique (On aberrations in the reproductive faculty), Symonds takes some pleasure in pointing out the astonishing contradiction between, on the one hand, the description of sexual inversion as a state with hereditary causes that lies halfway between sanity and madness, and, on the other, the assertion that such is the case only for modern Europe—not for the lands that accepted pederasty in the ancient world. "In other words, an Englishman or a Frenchman who loves the male sex must be diagnosed as tainted with disease; while Sophocles, Pindar, Pheidias, Epaminondas, Plato are credited with yielding to an instinct which was healthy in their times because society accepted it." Symonds concludes his argument by stating:

> The bare fact that ancient Greece tolerated, and that modern Europe refuses to tolerate sexual inversion, can have nothing to do with the etiology, the pathology, the psychological definition of the phenomenon in its essence. What has to be faced is that a certain type of passion flourished under the light of day and bore good fruits for society in Hellas; that the same type of passion flourishes in the shade and is the source of misery and shame in Europe. The passion has not altered; but the way of regarding it morally and legally is changed. A scientific investigator ought not to take changes of public opinion into account when he is analysing a psychological peculiarity.[3]

In passing, Symonds reveals his astonishment that doctors forget in their analyses "savage races" and "classical antiquity." Such doctors, he says, "strive to isolate [the phenomenon] as an abnormal and specifically morbid exception in our civilisation. But facts tend to show that it is a recurring impulse of humanity, natural to some people, adopted by others, and in the majority of cases compatible with an otherwise normal and healthy temperament" (52).

Here one sees how Greece and historical references are used to support an argument against the position of contemporary psychopathology. One also sees how, by recalling certain famous Greek figures, Symonds is able to speak of a "psychological particularity" and thus not to limit his analysis simply to behaviors or practices that would not be tied to the psychology of the individuals involved. Symonds almost seems to be writing about an invariant sexual identity that traverses the centuries—to such an extent that he seems to forget all he had written earlier about the distinction between a "pure" love and a "vulgar" vice. Everything now fits under the rubric of "sexual inversion" (this certainly shows the influence of psychiatric discourse on his own ways of thinking), and it makes no sense to describe inversion in modern societies as pathological precisely because we know it to have been associated with health during antiquity. It is a question of tolerance or intolerance, and has nothing to do with the phenomenon itself. Now one might point out that, contrary to Symonds's assertion, "sexual inversion" was never favored in Greek antiquity, in which the "passive" role and "effeminacy" were roundly condemned.[4] But what Symonds refers to as "sexual inversion" or as the "inverted sexual instinct" is simply the attraction of one man for another and thus includes the institutionalized "pederasty" about which he had written twenty years earlier within a much larger set of practices and feelings. This makes it difficult to agree with John Lauritsen when he writes, in his preface to an edition of some of Symonds's writings, that in the transition from the 1873 A Problem in Greek Ethics to the 1891 A Problem in Modern Ethics we see—whatever the author's intentions may have been—a shift from a historical approach to a medical approach, and from a study of "a form of behavior, love between males, to a condition, 'inverted sexuality.' "[5] Lauritsen's analysis is clearly heavily indebted to Foucault and to the distinction Foucault makes in La Volonté de savior between homosexual "acts" and homosexual "personages." In order to keep the Foucauldian dogma intact, it seems necessary to assert that the idea of a homosexual "identity" could only have appeared along with or in reaction to psychiatric discourse. Yet it is impossible to interpret the evolution of Symonds's texts in this way. If some reference to Foucault must absolutely be made, it would probably be a better idea to refer to the Foucault who teaches us to think in terms of "strategies" and to consider, when trying to explain Symonds's evolution, the ways in which the discursive configuration in which he was writing in 1891 was no longer the same as the one in which he had been writing in 1873.

Yet Symonds's thought also reveals profound continuities. For one, he never ceases to invoke history in opposition to medicine. Even when he uses the term "sexual inversion" it is always, with the support of historical evi-

dence, to give a positive value to the term in the face of negative and derogatory psychiatric approaches. Further, and above all, it is extremely unlikely
that he was not already thinking of the psychology of men who love the
masculine sex in terms of identity at the time he was writing *A Problem in Greek
Ethics*. Indeed, if he is able to move so easily from one way of conceiving
things to another, it is surely because this is all the same cause for him, the
cause of men who live in the shadows because of their difference from other
men, whereas in ancient Greece they could live in the light of day. If, in 1891,
he feels the need to emphasize not the purity and the nobility on which he
focused in 1873, but health and normalcy, it is because his adversaries have
changed. Clearly his 1873 apologia for Greece was also a way of justifying
himself to himself. He assimilated himself to that Greek culture, claimed to
be its heir, and imagined himself along the same lines as the men he was
describing (just as would Pater with his remembered dream and his philosopher lover). His poems from the 1860s provide further evidence of this, as
does his autobiography and his frequent references to the poems of Walt
Whitman as ways of justifying his own views. Symonds unquestionably held
to the idea of a sexual "identity" long before he entered into his polemics
with the psychiatrists. It is not possible that he got the idea from the psychiatrists against whom he was arguing.

Quite the contrary: he would build his contestation of the notion of
identity being constructed by the psychiatrists on his own idea of homosexual identity, developed in his study of ancient Greece. He insists on this in his
letters to Havelock Ellis and Edward Carpenter and others in the 1890s: "The
historical study of Greece is absolutely essential to the psychological treatment of the subject now."[6] The psychiatrists are making a colossal error, he
writes to Ellis in 1892, "by diagnosing as necessarily morbid what was the
leading emotion of the best and noblest men in Hellas." He goes even
further in his denunciation of the ignorance of the psychiatrists: "The ignorance of men like Casper-Liman, Tardieu, Carlier, Taxil, Moreau, Tarnowsky,
Krafft-Ebing, Richard Burton is incalculable, and is only equalled to their
presumption. They not only do not know Ancient Greece, but they do not
know their own cousins and club-mates" (3:693–94). In short, some of their
cousins and fellow club members are the direct heirs of a psychological
character that flourished openly in Greek antiquity yet in the contemporary
world is forced to hide itself.

As Symonds takes on the psychiatrists, shifting from the register of the
noble purity of homosexual desire to that of the healthy normality of the

homosexual person, there is one theme that remains constant: the question of masculinity. In the chapter he devotes to Krafft-Ebing, Symonds emphasizes that in the case studies Krafft-Ebing presents one finds many "Urnings," men whose only distinguishing feature from other men is the direction of their sexual leanings. "The class includes powerfully developed masculine beings, who are unsexed in no particular except that they possess an inordinate appetite for males, and will not look at females."[7]

In 1892, Symonds entered into a collaboration with the doctor and sexologist Havelock Ellis. The collaboration was intended to produce a collectively authored work titled *Sexual Inversion*, although Symonds's death would necessitate changes in the form of the project. He explains his conception of this work in a letter to Edward Carpenter:

> I am so glad that H. Ellis has told you about our project. I never saw him. But I like his way of corresponding on this subject. And I need somebody of medical importance to collaborate with. Alone, I could make but little effect—the effect of an eccentric.
>
> We are agreed enough upon fundamental points. The only difference is that he is too much inclined to stick to the neuropathical theory of explanation. But I am whittling that away to a minimum. . . . I mean to introduce a new feature into the discussion, by giving a complete account of homosexual love in ancient Greece. I wrote this some time ago, & had 10 copies of it privately printed. If you like to see it, I will lend you one of my two remaining copies. . . .
>
> All the foreign investigators from Moreau & Caspar to Moll, are totally ignorant of Greek Customs. Yet it is here that the phenomenon has to be studied from a different point of view from that of psychopathology. Here we are forced to recognize that one of the foremost races in civilization not only tolerated passionate comradeship, but also utilized it for high social and military purposes.[8]

Symonds specifies in this letter that his "hope" is, and has always been, to see the emergence of "a new chivalry, i.e., a second elevated form of human love," that would take its place alongside the earlier form dating from the Middle Ages, that is, the chivalry based on heterosexual love. Love in this new order of chivalry, Symonds adds, will be "complementary, by no means prejudicial to the elder & more commonly acceptable" form. Symonds then goes on to speak of "a different type of individual" who would be able to put energy into new forms of activity, in which "aims answering to those of monastic labour in common or of military self-devotion to duty [take] the place of domestic cares & procreative utility." Within this implicit suggestion that the partisans of love between men will be more devoted to the collective than heterosexuals involved in family life are able to be, we can see once again Symonds's old argument that this "new chivalry" would be able to offer a different kind of contribution, perhaps one more noble than heterosexuals are able to contribute, to the regeneration of the nation. In any case, this argument suggests, no harm will be done to heterosexual relations. Yet Symonds remains acutely aware of the fantastical character of his remarks, and even exclaims: "How far away the dream seems! And yet I see in human nature stuff neglected, ever-present—pariah and outcast now— from which I am as certain as that I live, such a chivalry could arise." He refers once again to Whitman, whose work "will remain infinitely helpful" even if Whitman may repudiate "the deductions which have logically to be drawn from Calamus."[9]

8

The Democracy of Comrades

In Wilde, too, one finds a rejection of the categories of thought of psychiatric medicine. In 1897, for example, Wilde writes, "The fact that I am also a pathological problem in the eyes of German scientists is only interesting to German scientists."[1] Wilde is here alluding to Max Nordau's book, *Degeneration*, published in 1893, in which several pages are devoted to him: "Oscar Wilde apparently admires immorality, sin, and crime," writes the German psychiatrist.[2] The two volumes of this work are devoted to a description of the artistic and literary currents of a "fin de siècle" in which society is heading toward "ruin." Nordau takes aim at symbolists, mystics, and Pre-Raphaelites, at Wagnerism, at Aestheticism, at the Decadents, and so on. He attacks Huysmans, of course, but also Zola. All these "pathological" geniuses are "enemies to society of the direst kind," and society should "unconditionally defend itself against them." We are, he writes, "in the midst of a severe mental epidemic; of a sort of black death of degeneration and hysteria, and it is natural that we should ask anxiously on all sides: 'What is to come next?' " He encourages all those who would protect civilization—judges, professors, elected officials, and so on—to organize effective censorship and repression. Psychiatrists will also have a major role to play in this academy of right-thinking people whose job it will be to condemn "works trading on unchastity." No quarter will be offered to the artist who makes the mistake of displeasing the small circle made up of those "men from the people who are the best fitted for this task." Nordau gives fair warning: in such a case, "work and man would be annihilated."[3]

Wilde referred to the analysis of his case by Nordau in 1895 when he made an appeal to be released from prison, pleading that his mental health was deteriorating.[4] But here it was simply a kind of tactical usage, at a moment when he was not being choosy about the source of his arguments. Fundamentally, Wilde had only scorn for Dr. Nordau and for pseudo-science. Of course, what shocked him most in being studied as a pathological case was to see his genius reduced to this level of banality. He chafed at the very idea of being studied as part of a group of people, as a simple example of a general phenomenon. In the works of "German psychiatrists," he comments, "I am tabulated, and come under the law of *averages!*"[5] Such comments belong of course to the longstanding tradition in which those who lay a claim to literary genius refuse any scientific analysis, any reduction of their "singularity" to an "average," any reduction of an individual to "statistics." But the different phrases in which Wilde sometimes ironizes and sometimes waxes indignant about being considered a psychopathological problem make it clear that he refused to grant doctors any right to evaluate his homosexuality. When the journalist Chris Healey asked him what he thought of Nordau's book, Wilde replied, "I quite agree with Dr. Nordau's assertion that all men of genius are insane, but Dr Nordau forgets that all sane people are idiots."[6] In *De Profundis*, he writes bitterly to Alfred Douglas, who had planned to publish a defense of Wilde in the *Mercure de France* that would claim that "along with genius goes often a curious perversity of passion and desire." Such a subject, Wilde objected, "belongs to Lombroso rather than to you." (Lombroso was an Italian psychiatrist who had published a book called *The Man of Genius*.) Moreover, Wilde pointed out, "the pathological phenomenon in question is found also amongst those who have not genius."[7]

⋈ Clearly then, homosexual literature is not born out of psychiatry. Rather psychiatry takes on that literature, and attempts, with its clinical gaze, to reduce it to the simple expression of perverted or sick minds. It worries about the "immorality" that spreads by means of literary and artistic works. Psychiatric categories are not at the origin of Wilde's writing. His sources are literary: Walter Pater, John Addington Symonds, Huysmans, even Baudelaire, and, of course, Verlaine. For Wilde, as for Pater or for Symonds, the invention of a "homosexual literature," or, more exactly, the effort to express homosexuality in literature, is born of an inner drive. It arises from an irrepressible need to divulge what one is under circumstances that make it scarcely possible to do so, however much one suffers in one's enforced silence. For Symonds, or for Wilde, or for Pater, taking the floor to speak of masculine loves, to put them into discourse, is something that happens by way of literature and philosophy. Ancient Greece and the Renaissance present themselves as ideals from the past that seem worth recovering. But such speech acts are also enabled by an inner necessity to be able to express what is felt at the deepest levels of one's personality. Once they discover that psychiatric discourse has no other ambition than to establish a way of controlling same-sex loves, Symonds and Wilde denounce as both incompetent and ignorant (of both the past and the present) the doctors that advance theories in this direction. Wilde insists that he is not what the doctors claim he is. Symonds insists on the need to study ancient Greece—that is, to follow the path that he had set out upon in earlier years.

In their ways of taking up these positions, Wilde and Symonds also demonstrate that there is indeed a literary body of work that has had a decisive influence on them: that of Whitman.

» At the end of *A Problem in Modern Ethics*, Symonds devotes a chapter to Whitman. Here too one finds an exemplary instance of the battle between the disciplines that I referred to earlier. Symonds once again rejects psychiatric reasoning regarding sexual difference, supporting his position by reference to Whitman's writings.

If Symonds chooses to support his efforts by reference to Whitman, it is because he finds in the poet the expression of that particular masculine camaraderie that is for him the richest aspect of ancient Greek culture. Indeed, Whitman would provide more than one English author with confirmation of their belief that it should be possible to give literary expression to relations between men. The first edition of *Leaves of Grass*, published in 1855, produced a notable emotional shock, one that was simultaneously literary, philosophical, and political. It also captured the avid attention of those men in England (and elsewhere) who were in urgent need of sources of legitimation for their effort to express what they were feeling. Whitman would prove to be an important reference not only for Symonds, but also, a bit later, for Wilde and then for Carpenter and many others, including André Gide.

In his *Memoirs*, Symonds returns several times to the subject of his discovery of *Leaves of Grass*, in particular of "Calamus," the homoerotic section of the collection of poems. "I find it difficult to speak about *Leaves of Grass* without exaggeration," he writes, recalling his excitement upon reading the poems that sang of the beauty of nature and the love between comrades. Very quickly, the book became for him "a sort of Bible."[8] In an 1892 letter to Horace Traubel, Whitman's friend and confidant, Symonds wrote that *Leaves of Grass* revolutionized his ways of thinking and transformed him into "another man," "a free man."[9] This was the moment at which Symonds began to try to write poems in a Whitmanesque vein. And there is more. He writes in his *Memoirs* in 1889 that "the immediate result of this study of Walt Whitman was the determination to write the history of paiderastia in Greece and to attempt a theoretical demonstration of the chivalrous enthusiasm which seemed to me implicit in comradeship."[10] Whitman thus seems to have provided the initial impetus for *A Problem in Greek Ethics*, written in 1873, and also for another never-published work, but one which most probably helped when it came to writing *A Problem in Modern Ethics* in 1891. The *Memoirs* also inform us that Symonds had not yet read the psychiatrists when he began (for what must have been therapeutic reasons) to draft an account of his own "singular" life, one that caused him so much suffering. In a note he added several years after having finished this autobiography—an autobiography impossible to publish at the time it was written—he specifies clearly that at the time he was writing it, he had not read the works of Casper, Liman, Ulrichs, Krafft-Ebing, the people who would later show him that his story, far from being "singular," was "one out of a thousand" (281). Even if the psychiatrists did not explain to him who he was, it would seem that they did at least teach him he was not alone in being that way.

Symonds would never stop writing to Whitman, asking whether it was legitimate to read "Calamus" as a set of homosexual poems. In the end, in 1890, Whitman would finally write to him categorically refusing any such interpretation. Symonds would reply in exasperation that he found it surprising that the American poet was not up-to-date on the fact that there existed a group of people "whose sexual instincts are what the Germans call 'inverted.'" Symonds goes on to explain, "During the last 25 years much attention, in France, Germany, Austria, & Italy, has been directed to the psychology & pathology of these abnormal persons."[11]

This is not the place to wonder what caused Whitman to refuse Symonds's "interpretations." We might just remark that when Oscar Wilde, in the course of his tour of the United States, went to the small house in Camden and visited Whitman, whom he had venerated since his school days, Whitman did not attempt to hide his homosexuality. "The kiss of Walt Whitman is still on my lips," Wilde would say later to his friend George Ives.[12] Yet we also know that Whitman ceaselessly reworked his poems, across a series of editions, slowly eliminating all the audacities concerning homosexuality that had been present in the earlier versions. So there is perfect justification for questioning the response he sent to Symonds, sent only after Symonds had insisted for twenty years on obtaining one. In any case, his work was undeniably read by his gay readers as, in Gary Schmidgall's words, "a 'coming out' work and a manifesto for sane self-acceptance."[13] Moreover, it was not only Europeans who were writing to him to tell him the story of their lives, their problems, the liberation they experienced upon reading "Calamus." Plenty of Americans wrote him as well.

Whitman's reply did not stop Symonds from devoting a chapter to him in his *A Problem in Modern Ethics* in 1891. The chapter in question is the final one in the book. After having harshly criticized the psychiatric approach to sexual inversion, Symonds offers in opposition to it the healthy exaltation of friendship between men as it can be found in the works of the American poet.[14] In the epilogue, Symonds returns to Whitman and writes, "Walt Whitman, in America, regards what he calls 'manly love' as destined to be a leading virtue of democratic nations, and the source of a new chivalry." Yet, adds Symonds with some regret, "he does not define what he means by 'manly love.' And he emphatically disavows any 'morbid inferences' from his doctrine as 'damnable' " (130).

⇥ Despite the restraining order placed on the development of gay culture by the condemnation of Oscar Wilde in 1895, its flourishing in the 1880s and early 1890s would not entirely fade away, and a new vigor would shortly appear. Symonds's correspondent Edward Carpenter, mentioned earlier, would himself soon become a guiding light for all those who were trying to affirm and to write about their homosexuality. A visit to Carpenter would become a sort of ritual pilgrimage for any cultivated gay man (just as a visit to Gide would be in France from the 1920s until his death in 1951).[15] It was after a visit to Carpenter that Forster would come up with the idea and the desire to write *Maurice*, a fact he recounts in a note added to the end of the novel in 1960: "In its original form, which it still almost retains, *Maurice* dates from 1913. It was the direct result of a visit to Edward Carpenter at Milthorpe. Carpenter had a prestige which cannot be understood today." After having described Carpenter from a number of angles—as a rebel, a socialist, an advocate for simple living, and a poet in the vein of Whitman—Forster adds, "He was a believer in the Love of Comrades, whom he sometimes called Uranians. It was this last aspect of him that attracted me in my loneliness."[16]

In the case of Carpenter, being a Whitmanian poet and a preacher of love between men seems intimately related to being a committed social democrat. Indeed, it is this Whitmanian tradition that finds itself perpetuated through Carpenter, one which affirmed the possibility of a cultural tradition in which the love of men was linked to the ideas of democracy and of socialism. In 1874, Carpenter had in fact written a long letter to Whitman telling him how important the reading of "Calamus" had been to him, for it permitted men "to be not ashamed of the noblest instinct of their nature." He added, linking his personal liberation to his political aspirations, "Between the splendid dawn of Greek civilisation and the high universal noon of Democracy there is a strange horror of darkness on us (but) slowly I think the fetters are falling from men's feet, the cramps and crazes of the old superstitions are relaxing, the idiotic ignorance of class contempt is dissipating."[17]

Personal liberation, an exaltation of the body and of nature, male homoeroticism, the greatness of the common man: *Leaves of Grass* sent a new wind blowing over an entire generation of intellectuals. Whitman declares:

> One's-Self I sing, a simple separate person,
> Yet utter the word Democratic, the word En-Masse.[18]

A bit further on, he announces that he will "sing the song of companionship" and then goes on to explain what that means:

> I will therefore let flame from me the burning fires that were
>   threatening to consume me,
> I will lift what has too long kept down those smouldering fires,
> I will give them complete abandonment,
> I will write the evangel-poem of comrades and love.[19]

Soon, the "love of comrades" and democratic passion will unite, and the poem "For You O Democracy," from the "Calamus" section, will declare:

> Come, I will make the continent indissoluble,
> I will make the most splendid race the sun ever shone upon,
> I will make the divine magnetic lands,
>   With the love of comrades,
>   With the life-long love of comrades,
> I will plant companionship thick as trees along the rivers of America,
>   and along the shores of the great lakes, and all over the prairies,

I will make inseparable cities with their arms about each other's
   necks,
      By the love of comrades,
         By the manly love of comrades.

For you these from me, O Democracy, to serve you ma femme!
For you, for you I am trilling these songs.[20]

We should not forget, after all, that Whitman is not only the poet of *Leaves
of Grass;* he is also the author of the inflammatory proclamations of *Democratic
Vistas.*[21] The love of comrades, for Whitman, is simply one aspect—clearly a
fundamental one—of his song of praise to the nation, to American democracy, just as, for Carpenter, the Love of Comrades (it is Forster who supplies
the capital letters) is of a piece with a commitment to social democracy. We
might also note that if the only role "*ma femme*" seems to have in Whitman's
poem is as a personification of democracy, Carpenter (as close as you can
come to a disciple of Whitman) would be one of the main political and
theoretical supporters of the women's emancipation movement at the end of
the nineteenth and in the early twentieth centuries.

One does, of course, still need to call into question the deeply misogynis-
tic aspect of this mythology of virility, of masculinity, of the accompanying
cult of the young and beautiful athletic male body. Also, as I have already
pointed out, it is impossible to ignore the way certain nationalist ideologies
are woven into some of the discourses intended to legitimate homosexuality.
Yet the link that is often drawn between the exaltation of masculine friendship and an attraction to fascism is far from being present in every historical
situation. Whitman, Carpenter, and even Symonds stand as examples of a
homo-democratic tradition (a tradition that is simultaneously homosocial, if
not homosexual, and democratic) that was able to coincide with a cult of
virile friendship.

Clearly it is a somewhat odd and singular path that runs from Walter Pater
and the elitist circles of Oxford to Edward Carpenter and his socialist and
democratic engagements. The set of discourses one finds as one follows this
twelve-year-long development shows extreme diversity—diversity both as
regards representations of homosexuality and as regards political commitments. Yet if these attempts to make room for gay identity and gay speech
reveal multiple and contradictory interrelations, this is of course in large
measure due to the obvious differences between the people involved. But the

multiplicity also comes about because these attempts began as attempts to justify and defend, attempts to provide a "good image" to counteract the insulting and defamatory images being consistently offered up by the social order. It is noteworthy that contradictions are to be found not only between the works of various authors, but even within the work of a single person. So Wilde could, in The Portrait of Mr. W. H., pen an apologia of the purely spiritual Platonic love of an older for a younger man, and then, in The Picture of Dorian Gray, exalt a new hedonism whose carnal and sexual meanings were scarcely hidden. And, of course, discourses would often find themselves in blatant contradiction with the behaviors of their authors. All this apparatus of legitimation—philosophical, literary, cultural, artistic—existed alongside a wide range of behaviors or ways of life, from the most provocative (the worship of androgyny, effeminate manners, flowers in the button-hole) to the most discreet (Symonds publishing his works in ten copies). There were attempts to assert a sexual "difference" that ran against established norms, and there were attempts to claim that homosexuality in fact represented the most perfect realization of masculinity or of moral duty.

Individuated strategies as well as individuated ways of imagining oneself, one's aspirations, and individuated ways of life led people to take up discourses and behaviors that were mutually contradictory. There has never been a single way to live as a homosexual. Divergent legitimating discourses could even arise from the same intellectual tradition. When Symonds, for instance, invokes Plato and Greece it is to exalt masculinity and spiritual procreation; when Ulrichs does so, it is to establish a basis for the idea of "uranism," of an "intermediate sex," one between men and women, one that would soon be called the "third sex." And these two species of discourse would even come to cohabit within a single work, as when Edward Carpenter takes up the theory of the intermediate sex at the same time as he sings of the viril love of comrades in Whitmanian terms.[22]

All these traditions, in their complexity and contradictions, can also be found at the birth of the German homosexual movement at the end of the nineteenth century. The tensions caused by the contradictions will grow stronger through the years leading up to the 1930s. An increasingly marked opposition will be found between the proponents of a biological theory of a "third sex" (Magnus Hirschfeld is central here) and the proponents of the "virility" of male homosexuality, who made regular reference to ancient Greece. Proust will take up the biological theory of the third sex in Cities of the Plain (Sodome et Gomorrhe), while Gide, in Corydon, will align himself with

Greek love, pederasty, and masculinity, specifically setting out to struggle against the image of homosexuality being put forward by Proust.

❱❱ In all of this one sees again that literature is playing a central role. Whitman himself said, "I think Literature—a new, superb, democratic literature— is to be the medicine and lever and (with Art) the chief influence in modern civilization."[23] Symonds, Wilde, and also Gide learned this lesson, and Whitman would give them leverage, would provide a reference point for their attempts to reform society, to educate it, to cure it of its prejudices.

9

Margot-la-boulangère and
the Baronne-aux-épingles

In his autobiography, John Addington Symonds makes no secret of the fact that his debt to Whitman was not merely an intellectual one, but had to do with sexuality as well. Thanks to Whitman he was able to stop repressing his desire to meet men of the working classes, men he described (revealing his consistent obsession with his ideals of purity) as the uncorrupted sons of nature. It bears keeping in mind that the entire intellectual culture I have just described was not at all far removed from the gay subculture that also existed throughout the cities of Europe.

Unfortunately, we know little about these popular gay cultures. Of them we have only fragmentary glimpses by way of literary or medical texts or the dusty files of legal and police archives. One of the reasons we tend to grant so much importance to literary and intellectual culture when searching for the origins of modern gay identity is simply that that culture has passed on to us the largest number of documents, of identifiable and interpretable traces. What do we know about all those people who never wrote anything, about what they were thinking? To put it bluntly, what was going on in the minds of the soldiers or workers who were drinking with the intellectuals, spending evenings with them in taverns, and sleeping with them? What was Dorian Gray doing on those days when he disappeared? Who did he spend that time with, time about which Wilde's novel tells us almost nothing if not, in few words, that "it was rumoured that he had been seen brawling with foreign sailors . . . and that he consorted with thieves and coiners"?[1]

What can be known of these homosexual ways of life, ones constantly being invented and reinvented within popular culture? What can be known of the life of bars and cabarets, of meeting places, the linguistic codes, ways of dressing, ways of being, ways of carrying oneself, and so on? According to Jeffrey Weeks, judicial archives demonstrate the wide extent of "homosexual life" in large cities (London, Dublin) and in garrison towns and ports. The rich slang specific to this way of life gives some indication of the widespread nature and the durability of its subculture.[2] A London correspondent of Karl Heinrich Ulrichs's writes to him in 1868 that he has just attended a party to which "uranists" came dressed as women. These men called each other by women's names ("Viola," for instance). In other letters, the same writer describes costume balls to which men came dressed in drag. Yet he notes that on an occasion in which a man in drag arrived at a cafe that was mostly frequented by respectable uranists, he was very poorly received. Dances also took place that were reserved for uranists who did not dress in women's clothes.[3] In Frankfurt, Ulrichs socialized with a small circle of uranists who called themselves Laura, Mathilda, Georgina, Madonna, Queen of the Night, and so on, and who referred to each other as "sister dear."[4]

One hundred and fifty years earlier, London "sodomites" had already developed the practice of meeting in private homes or in a reserved room in a tavern. These *molly houses* (*molly* being the word of the moment for sodomite) were numerous and, along with meeting areas such as St. James Park, helped make up a specifically homosexual universe, a city within a city. If we accept the evidence of police reports and newspaper articles published when various scandals broke out, this gay culture contained a whole set of complex customs, conventions, and rituals. Yet what most struck observers of the time was the transvestism and the extravagant effeminacy they often came across. A theatricalized femininity—apparent in clothing, mannerisms, poses, language, witticisms, and the like—was more often than not a characteristic element of their evening parties. Of course this gay life struggled under the threat of repression: police raids, trials, and even, in 1726, hangings following a series of investigations led by the Societies for the Reformation of Manners, a religious organization dedicated to struggling against debauchery.[5] It is important to note that class distinctions were not salient in the molly houses—in them all social levels mixed together. Among the visitors were, of course, many married men leading a double life. Should they have the misfortune to be arrested during a raid, even if they escaped punishment (which might have included being pilloried), their lives would be shattered.[6] During those periods in which repression was most severe, there would be fewer molly houses or they would be more discreet, at least until things returned to what we might call normal and life could return to its usual course—until the next round of police raids and arrests.

Cruising and meeting places were also placed under surveillance, of course, and numerous arrests took place there as well, helped along by the traps that were set for "potential" sodomites: a young man would wait to be approached or would approach someone, and then the police would arrest the "sodomite" who hadn't exercised sufficient caution. Arrests at cruising grounds (urinals, parks, and so on) are one of the constants of gay history. Descriptions of them can be found in judicial archives from the seventeenth and eighteenth centuries. A scene of this nature lies at the heart of Alan Hollinghurst's novel, The Swimming-Pool Library, in which an aristocrat is sent to prison in the 1950s after having been arrested in a public restroom.

⊁ In the nineteenth century, urban gay culture was often quite audacious. Young men would go so far as to walk openly in London or to go to the theater wearing dresses. This can be seen in the case of the arrest and trial of "Stella" Boulton and "Fanny" Park in 1870. The case against them was based on the assumption that given the way they dressed (as women) and carried themselves they must be sodomites. Their private letters were read aloud during the trial, and their clothes and even their underwear were produced as evidence. They were subjected to medical examination, and much time was spent discussing the question as to whether or not the dilation of the anus was proof of "sodomy." The most extraordinary thing about this story is that the two men were acquitted! Their attorney pointed out that the crime of which they were accused was so frightful that it was unimaginable that anyone would display evidence of it in public, and therefore their comportment should be taken as evidence of their innocence. As Neil Bartlett puts it, the "evidence of Fanny and Stella's visibility was converted into proof that they didn't exist."[7] Doubtless, this was the preferred outcome for the two accused. Others were surely less lucky.

There were many scandals with which the press had field days. The Cleveland Street scandal of 1886 was typical. A male brothel had been offering the services of young men employed at the post office or telegraph boys to economically more privileged clients—among them Lord Somerset, who was close to the Prince of Wales. It was in fact because this scandal lingered in people's memories that the Scots Observer could write, upon the publication of The Picture of Dorian Gray, that it was a work aimed at "outlawed noblemen and perverted telegraph boys."[8] The allusion would have been perfectly clear to any informed reader of the time. It makes clear that Wilde's novel was perceived in a similar manner both by his admirers and his detractors. It also makes clear the novel was a kind of intervention into a specific cultural world, one that extended well beyond the literary one.

Many other illustrations of this subcultural life of London could be offered, such as the fake marriage ceremonies celebrated between two men—the one, for instance, that involved Alfred Taylor, known to us as the organizer of the brothel that supplied certain sexual partners to Oscar Wilde and who would contribute to his downfall.[9] It is this entire subcultural life that would be brought to trial, judged, and condemned in 1895. After all, Wilde had a co-defendant who shared his sentence: Alfred Taylor.

❧ Such a culture existed in Paris as well and had existed for quite a while. Historians, for instance, speak of a gay way of life in the period 1700–1750.[10] Police records describe "congregations" that met in certain taverns, where greetings such as "Good evening Miladies" were used, along with feminine surnames that referred jokingly to various professions (Baronness-Hatpin or Margot-the-Baker-Girl) or that parodied aristocratic titles (Madame de Nemours). The feminine reference is characteristic of this form of sociability, one that also understood itself to be a kind of free-masonry. According to one contemporary account, "Some members with napkins on their heads imitate women and mince about like them."[11]

Police records reveal that most of these taverns were little more than places to meet, eat, and drink. Yet some such businesses had two distinct kinds of spaces, one in which to drink and chat, and another that was reserved for sexual interactions—just as today one sometimes finds in bars a separation between the bar as such and a backroom.

Most important for our purposes is that the police files also describe certain locales for cruising (public urinals, the quais of the Seine, certain parks) in which sexual acts happened on the spot. The cramped living quarters of the time with their thin walls were not well suited to what we know as "private life." Here an article by William Peniston concerning a murder that took place in 1877 on the quais of the Seine is relevant. The police file on the murder reveals that because of it a serious investigation of the gay milieu was undertaken, leading to the conviction of the killer. He had murdered his partner because his partner planned to leave him. The murderer had first claimed not even to have known the young man who had just drowned, but it turned out that they lived together. The archives reveal an entire gay universe, with festive meetings, dances (referred to as a "reunion of pederasts" in the police files, which also recount raids of such events and arrests of "suspects"), meeting places (restaurants and cafes) which, if not exclusively gay, were nonetheless known to be what would today be called "gay friendly." There were also more specifically sexual meeting places, baths and parks (notably the Tuilerie Gardens, where soldiers stationed nearby would often indulge in attacks against homosexuals), and places to find prostitutes (such as the arcades of the Palais-Royal).[12]

One police file lists the surnames of a group of young male prostitutes: La Pompadour, La Brunette, L'Africaine, La Baronne.[13] Police raids and arrests were frequent, and a good number of aristocratic and bourgeois men were among those the police interrogated. They were perhaps picked up during a raid on the "pederasts," arrested in a urinal, or denounced by one of the young prostitutes who was a police informer or else trying to weasel out of a difficult legal situation. Clearly they were participants in a gay world that included people from all levels of society. Upon reading the work of historians and the documents from the police archives, it is difficult not to think of the declamation of Proust's Baron de Charlus, in *Cities of the Plain* (*Sodome et Gomorrhe*) in which, precisely because he describes his predilection for crossing class barriers, he unwittingly reveals to his listeners the penchant he is trying to hide: "I, who have had so many ups and downs in my life, who have known all manner of people, thieves as well as kings, and indeed, I must confess, with a slight preference for the thieves . . ." (*RTP*, 2:741). Oscar Wilde, who dined both with government ministers and with prostitutes who would subsequently blackmail him, could have said something similar. (Wilde would in *De Profundis* refer to his dinners with male prostitutes as "feasting with panthers," indicating the sense of excitement he experienced because of the dangerous nature of this kind of socializing, something he also claimed not to regret.)[14]

This class "confusion" is often remarked upon in police documents or in medical texts of the nineteenth century. In the 1860s, Ambroise Tardieu expresses astonishment that men "apparently distinguished by education and fortune" could engage in sexual relations with other men characterized by moral "degradation" and by a "revolting filth." Tardieu claims that it is more this violation of the boundary between the classes that threatens public order than homosexuality itself. In the homosexual universe, he explains, aristocratic and bourgeois men socialize with the dregs of society. Being thereby exposed to theft and blackmail, they are brought too close to the world of crime.[15] This idea of the proximity between homosexuality and crime becomes one of the central themes not only of police literature and medical and psychological literature, but of literature itself.

⊁ Clearly, then, it is not possible to describe the "elite" gay culture without situating it in a much larger cultural context involving large numbers of people, a context in which male prostitutes (soldiers and workers) from the popular classes rub elbows with transvestites from the middle classes, tavern owners or brothel owners, and all their clients from quite diverse social backgrounds. For doubtless it was to these kinds of places that the honorable academics, artists, or writers repaired when in search of sexual partners. Symonds, for instance, describes how in 1877 a friend took him to a male brothel. Some time later, he tells us, he had what seems to have been his first sexual experience with a soldier who sold his services and whom Symonds met in a place to which he went looking precisely for what he then found. These kinds of meetings with the type of man that he desired, along with his own intellectual development of course, probably explain a great deal about the fact that by the 1890s he had moved on from a simple defense of "pederasty" to an apologia for "camaraderie" and for a "new chivalry" based on friendship between men. Indeed, he was so moved by his meeting with the soldier just mentioned that he decided to see him again, for the simple pleasure of speaking with him ("without a thought of vice," he says). He then reflects, "This experience exercised a powerful effect upon my life. I learned from it—or I deluded myself into thinking I had learned—that the physical appetite of one male for another may be made the foundation of a solid friendship."[16] Symonds would finally leave England to reside in Davos, in order to take care of his weak lungs—but doubtless also in order to escape from the repressive atmosphere of his social milieu and of Victorian England. In Davos, Symonds would finally permit himself to indulge in the "vice" that so appealed to him. He would enjoy dividing his time between Swiss peasants and Venetian gondoliers.

This imbrication of elite and popular culture can be found in the life—and often in the work—of a good number of the authors who could be thought of as crucial in the emergence in the twentieth century of a discourse in which to speak about one's homosexuality. It would seem that the ideal sexual type of these homosexual men from the privileged classes was a young man from the popular classes and, for many of them, a "virile" young man. Such a figure would become a kind of model at the beginning of the century. E. M.

Forster would state, for instance, that he simply wanted "to love a strong young man of the lower classes and be loved by him and even hurt by him."[17] It is hardly going too far to state that one of the principal themes of *Maurice* is precisely the encounter and interaction between, the confrontation of, these two male homosexual cultures: that of the elite and that of the popular classes. Such transgressions of class boundaries in a society in which they are so rigidly respected can often take on a utopian cast, as when Symonds declares: "The blending of Social Strata in masculine love seems to me one of its most pronounced, and socially hopeful features. Where it appears, it abolishes class distinctions."[18] Isherwood and Auden could also be mentioned in this context. After all, the novels Isherwood published in the 1930s, as he tells us directly in his 1976 autobiography, describe his meetings with young working class men in Germany, even if this reality is disguised within the novels themselves.[19] One might also imagine, as has been suggested by people such as Isherwood and Auden, that this contact with members of the working class, and the awareness it provided about the realities of life in the working class, was one of the determining factors in the leftist engagements of many such writers.

⇥ We have been emphasizing the ways in which these intellectuals are firmly situated within the homosexual subculture of their times, but there is another question, hardly a secondary one, that we should also ask: what did Symonds's wife think of all this? And Wilde's? And Gide's? For all three were married, as were many other gay men.

Symonds's *Memoirs* tell us a great deal about the difficulties he had coming to terms with his homosexuality, but very little about the suffering his wife must have undergone. Of course he loved her in his own way. He speaks constantly about his affection for her and his respect. But what could she have been thinking? We only know the little he tells us and might wonder how much he himself knew of her thoughts. We know that Gide's relations with his wife Madeleine went through moments of great difficulty. Yet most of what we know, we know through him. Jean Schlumberger, disgusted by what he saw as the hypocritical manner in which Gide spoke of Madeleine in his book *Et Nunc Manet in Te*, made an effort to allow her voice and her feelings to be heard, to understand what her experience might have been. The book he wrote is deeply moving and creates the impression of an unending sadness.[20]

10

From Momentary Pleasures
to Social Reform

When Gide publishes The Fruits of the Earth in 1897, he is still working through the effect on him of his meetings with Wilde in Paris and in Biskra in 1891 and 1895. He had also crossed paths with Wilde in Florence in 1894.

Gide's book is well known: a narrator addresses himself to a future reader by the name of Nathanaël, someone he doesn't know, yet to whom he wishes to convey his "fervor." He exhorts Nathanaël to abandon traditional morality and to give in to worldly pleasure: "Nathanaël, I must speak to you of instants. Do you realize the power of their presence? A not sufficiently constant thought of death has given an insufficient value to the tiniest instants of your life."[1] Or, a few pages earlier:

> Food!
> I await you, food!
> My hunger will stay at no half-way house;
> Nothing but satisfaction will silence it;
> No moralities can put an end to it . . . (31)

It is impossible, stumbling upon these outbursts by Gide's narrator, not to think of Walter Pater's writings, writings that electrified an entire generation of young British intellectuals and that became Wilde's personal breviary. Indeed, Gide's narrator has learned this philosophy of pleasure and of the vanishing instant from someone else, the character named Ménalque (Menalcas), who, during an evening passed in a garden at the foot of a hill in Florence facing the Fiesole, told his friends the story of his youth and adult life, singing the praises of an Epicurean hedonism. Having learned Ménalque's morality, or antimorality, the narrator wishes to pass it on to Nathanaël. There can be little doubt that Ménalque is an incarnation of Wilde. His way of opposing, on one hand, the ecstasy of "pleasure" (volupté) and physical sensations and, on the other, "argument" (*raisonnement*) and philosophical affiliations not only echoes Wilde's own writings, it also recalls Wilde's own behavior and the extraordinary example of personal freedom that he provided to Gide when they met in Biskra.[2] When Ménalque tells his guests about the nights he spent in the company of sailors ("in other ports, I forgathered with the sailors of the big ships; I went down with them to the ill-lit alleys of the town" [72]), one immediately thinks of *The Picture of Dorian Gray*.

Endless sentences, even whole paragraphs, in Gide's book seem to be copied from Wilde's novel. Pierre Louÿs, to whom Gide was close in his earlier years and who was distancing himself from him at precisely this moment, had no doubt about what was going on. After reading *The Fruits of the Earth*, he penned a malicious satirical poem on the book, in which he describes Wilde and Robert de Montesquiou (who would be a model for Proust's Charlus and had already been a model for Huysmans's Des Esseintes) as they watch:

> The entrance of a man whose soul was vile
> Gide, lord of La Roque and Cuckooverville.[3]

Ménalque would appear again under Gide's pen a few years later as a character in *The Immoralist* (1902). In the later book, Ménalque's former friends have abandoned him because he has been implicated in "an absurd, a shameful, lawsuit with scandalous repercussions."[4] The moment in which Gide writes this book is more or less the same one in which, as he tells us in his piece on Wilde, he was tempted to sit with his back to any passers-by when he joined Wilde on the terrace of a cafe on the Parisian boulevards. This was shortly after Wilde's release from prison.

In any case, it is difficult, when one reads Ménalque's famous cry in *The Fruits of the Earth*—"Families, I hate you!"—a cry transmitted by the narrator to the youth of the future, not to see it as a founding act of gay self-affirmation. The cry echoes some Paterian words spoken by Ménalque only a few pages earlier: "I hated homes and families and all the places where a man thinks to find rest; and lasting affection, and the fidelities of love, and attachment to ideas."[5] It is also difficult not to imagine that the posterity to which Gide was directing his message was made up of young gay men. This seems perfectly clear on the first page of Gide's *New Fruits*, a book which, thirty years later, takes up again, with more explicitness, the proclamations addressed to Nathanaël: "You who will come when I shall have ceased to hear the noises of this earth and to taste its dews upon my lips—you who will perhaps some day read me—it is for you I write these pages; for perhaps you are not sufficiently amazed at being alive; you do not wonder as you should at this astounding miracle of your life. I sometimes feel that it is with my thirst that you will drink, and that *what inclines you over* that other creature you caress is *already my own desire.*"[6] A few pages later, New Fruits describes in nearly explicit fashion Gide's love affair with Marc Allégret in terms that recall both the lyrical exaltation of The Fruits of the Earth and Whitman's poetry: "We amused ourselves all day long by executing the various actions of our lives like a dance, in the manner of a perfect gymnast, whose ideal would be to do nothing that was not harmonious and rhythmical."[7]

In the later text, Gide once again writes that he knows how to "enjoy the quiet of eternity in the fleeting moment." Yet when he publishes the book in 1935, he will have long since taken his distance from the philosophy that is developed in the volume from 1897. Just as Pater in Wilde's eyes spent his life giving the lie to what he wrote, Gide did all he could to disassociate himself from the song to pleasure and to the glories of the present moment found in this "book of my youth." He took the occasion of the publication of a new edition of The Fruits of the Earth in 1927 to add a preface in which he reminds the reader that the book was written shortly after his near escape from death from tuberculosis. That circumstance would explain the exalted tone, the "flights of its poetry" and even the "excess" of the book. He specifies that he has himself followed the admonition to Nathanaël on the final page to "throw away my book and leave me." "Yes, I immediately left the man I was when I wrote The Fruits of the Earth." And to those who insist on seeing in this book only a "glorification of desire and instinct," he responds that he prefers to see, in retrospect, "an apology for a life *stripped to bareness* [une apologie du *dénuement*]" (3–5).

In New Fruits, Gide calls on Nathanaël, to whom he now refers as "comrade," to attain his own happiness by working for the happiness of others (293). The idea of earthly joys has changed. The individualist fever of 1897 has been renounced in favor of a quest for collective happiness.

Still, despite these various evolutions, a part of Gide and his work will always remain attached to the hedonism of his youth. Neither success nor age will quell this tendency.

❧ In 1897, the year in which Fruits of the Earth is published, Gide writes in his journal that he does not remember the moment when he first read Whitman.[8] There is no doubt, however, that *Leaves of Grass* became a major reference for him. This can be seen clearly in *Corydon*, which was published in 1924, for it is a book that both begins and ends with Whitman. In its final version, the book is made up of four dialogues between a narrator, the "I" of the text, who represents "common sense" (homophobic, of course), and a doctor named Corydon who speaks in defense of homosexuality, or, more exactly, of "pederasty."[9] When, at the outset of the book, the narrator arrives at Corydon's office, Corydon is seated in front of a portrait of Whitman and has nearby a reproduction of Michelangelo's "Creation of Man." The presence of the reproduction and the portrait are, in Gide's eyes, given the absence of any signs of "effeminacy," which "experts manage to discover in everything connected with inverts," discreet signals as to Corydon's habits. Here, at some length, is the passage describing the narrator's arrival at Corydon's office:

> On entering his apartment, I admit I received none of the unfortunate impressions I had feared. Nor did Corydon afford any such impression by the way he dressed, which was quite conventional, even a touch austere perhaps. I glanced around the room in vain for signs of that effeminacy which experts manage to discover in everything connected with inverts and by which they claim they are never deceived. *However* I did notice, over his mahogany desk, a huge photographic reproduction of Michelangelo's "Creation of Man," showing Adam naked on the primeval slime, reaching up to the divine Hand and turning toward God a dazzled look of gratitude. Corydon's vaunted love of art would have accounted for any surprise I might have shown at the choice of this particular subject. On the desk, the portrait of an old man with a long white beard whom I immediately recognized as the American poet Walt Whitman, since it appears as the frontispiece of Léon Bazalgette's recent translation of his works. Bazalgette had also just published a voluminous biography of the poet which I had recently come across and which now served as a pretext for opening the conversation.[10]

Let us pause for a moment over the "however," which might seem somewhat odd. The narrator has already mentioned "the deplorable reputation his [Corydon's] behavior was acquiring" (3–4) and is therefore surprised to find no signs of effeminacy in the apartment. "*However*," the "behavior" in question seems nonetheless to be revealed by a photograph that brings to mind Michelangelo and the Renaissance, and which therefore functions—in the terms provided by Gide's presentation—as a homosexual "code" available to be read by those in the know. Yet were it to be necessary to give the lie to such an interpretation, the presence of the reproduction could be justified by artistic interests. It is, however, Whitman who will provide the opening for the conversation that makes up the bulk of the book. Bazalgette's biography, Corydon tells us, is based on the following syllogism: pederasty is unnatural; Whitman was "in perfect health," indeed a fine representative of "the natural man"; therefore Whitman could not have been a pederast. This is why the narrator can say to Corydon, in the first spoken sentence of the first dialogue, "After reading Bazalgette's book . . . I don't see much reason for this portrait to be on display here." To which Corydon replies, with a certain amount of common sense, "Whitman's work remains just as admirable as it ever was, regardless of the interpretation each reader chooses to give his behavior" (4–5). Clearly what is at stake is not to decide whether or not Whitman's work is admirable. Gide places us immediately within the struggle to decide whether certain discourses should be able to be appropriated by homosexuals. Corydon insists on the fact that Bazalgette "has proved nothing whatever," for "the work is there, and no matter how often Bazalgette translates the word 'love' as 'affection' or 'friendship,' and the word 'sweet' as 'pure,' whenever Whitman addresses his 'comrade,' the fact remains that all the fervent, tender, sensual, impassioned poems in the book are of the same order—that order you call *contra naturam*."[11] Corydon goes on to state that he is preparing an article on Whitman in which he intends to provide "an answer to Bazalgette's argument" (6). A few lines later, he adds that he also intends to compose "a long study" dealing with "pederasty" and arguing against prevailing psychiatric ideas about homosexuality. Corydon, who is himself a doctor, sets himself the project of demonstrating that there is nothing either abnormal or pathological about pederasty. He says, "I think you understand now why I want to write this book. The only serious books I know on this subject are certain medical works which reek of the clinic from the very first pages" (17). Corydon himself has no desire to "speak about my subject as a specialist—only as a man," because "the doctors who usually write about the subject treat only uranists who are ashamed of themselves— pathetic inverts, sick men. They're the only ones who consult doctors. As a doctor myself, those are the ones who come to me for treatment too; but as a man, I come across others, who are neither pathetic nor sickly—those are the ones I want to deal with" (18).

If Gide wants to fight against psychiatric discourse, it is clearly not to

refuse it in its entirety, not to denounce its homophobia and cultural violence. Instead, Gide's project in this book consists in distinguishing between "pathological" homosexuality, which is the homosexuality of those
who are "sick" and who are of concern to doctors and psychiatrists, and
noble homosexuality, which belongs to the tradition of Greek homosexuality, "pederasty" as it was lauded in Plato's *Symposium*. We are not far from
John Addington Symonds here. Gide in fact cites a passage from Symonds's
Greek Poets, in which Symonds gives a commentary on the passages in Homer
that speak of Achilles's love for Patroclus (108). The presence of the references to Whitman and Michelangelo reinforces the sense of similarity to
Symonds that one might feel while reading Gide's book.

In fact, Gide probably hadn't read Symonds, but rather a book by Edward
Carpenter, *Iolaüs*, an anthology of citations dealing with male friendship in
which the passage from Symonds is cited.[12] Whatever the case may be, the
fourth and final dialogue in *Corydon* is almost entirely devoted to the Greek
model, including, of course, the inevitable example of the "sacred battalion
of Thebes," whose courage and military worth—described by Plutarch—
derived from the fact that it was made up of pairs of lovers (113–14). After all,
one of the main objectives of *Corydon* is, just as it was for Symonds, to
reaffirm the link between homosexuality and masculinity and to reject any
association with effeminacy: "I can think of no opinion more false, and yet
more widely held, than that which considers homosexual conduct and pederasty as the pathetic lot of effeminate races, of decadent peoples, and even
sees it as an importation from Asia. On the contrary, it was from Asia that the
slack Ionic order came to supplant the masculine Doric architecture; the
decadence of Athens began when the Greeks stopped frequenting the gymnasiums; and we now know what should be understood by that. Uranism
yields to heterosexuality" (115–16). This is why Corydon insists on a number
of occasions on the martial, military, warrior-like value of homosexuality.
Consider this exchange with the narrator:

> "Have you never wondered why the Napoleonic Code contains no law
> aimed at repressing pederasty?"
>
> "Perhaps," I replied, disconcerted, "it's because Napoleon attached
> no importance to it, or because he reckoned that our instinctive repug-
> nance would be sufficient."
>
> "Perhaps it was also because such laws would have embarrassed
> some of his best generals. Reprehensible or not, such habits are so far

from being enervating, are so close to being military, that I must admit
to you I've trembled for us during those sensational trials in Germany,
which even the Kaiser's vigilance could not succeed in suppressing. . . .
Some people in France were naïve enough to see such episodes as signs
of decadence! while I was thinking to myself: Beware of a people whose
very debauchery is warlike and who keep their women for the exclusive
purpose of providing fine children.[13]

One might note in passing that Gide is making a concerted effort to establish not only that homosexuality is no sign of weakness or decadence (given
its links to military force), but also that the homosexual—Corydon in this
particular case—is deeply patriotic. Corydon "trembled" for his nation and
says "us" when he speaks of his endangered land. This idea is discreetly
added on to the major thread of the argument, and for once Gide does not
insist on it with a heavy hand, but instead lets it be suggested in the words he
chooses. Yet this is still clearly a way of responding to one of the loudest
themes of homophobic discourse—that the gay man is a traitor to his nation.
This was a frequent accusation during the German scandals Gide alludes to
at the beginning of his book: all the military men implicated in the Eulenburg trials in and after 1908 were accused in this way. The diplomat himself
was known for his pacifist and pro-French views.[14] This theme of treason
will culminate in the fantasy of the "Homintern" (a play of words on "Ko-
mintern," the Communist International) that would develop in England in
the 1920s and 1930s.[15] Gide himself, despite everything he says in *Corydon*,
would not be spared the accusation. He would rapidly be accused of sapping
the strength of the nation ("How the Germans must be laughing at us!")
and, in 1940, of being responsible for the defeat of the French Army because
of his corrupting influence on French youth and his contribution to the ruin
of morality, social values, and so on.[16]

» *Corydon* thus contains nearly all the themes that characterized the texts
John Addington Symonds wrote. It isn't possible to give a complete cata-
logue, but the third and fourth dialogues of *Corydon* present one after the
other all the arguments Symonds had offered. One might differentiate the
two by saying that the misogyny of Gide's text is more salient than in the
works of his predecessors. For instance, in praising the artistic flourishing
characteristic of ancient Greece and the Renaissance, Gide writes: "And

when someone decides to write a history of uranism in its relation to the plastic arts, it is not during the decadent periods that it will be observed to flourish, but quite the contrary, in the glorious and healthy epochs. . . . Conversely, it seems to me that not invariably but frequently the exaltation of women in the plastic arts is the index of decadence" (87–88).[17]

But the guiding thread of Gide's argument, like that of his predecessors, consists in emphasizing the contradiction between the admiration for Greek culture and the refusal to see the essential link between its artistic greatness and the sexual customs that enabled that greatness:

> Do you refuse to understand that there exists a direct relation between the flower and the plant which bears it, between the essential quality of its sap and its behavior and its economy? . . . As soon as Greek morals are mentioned, they are deplored, and since they cannot be ignored, they are turned from in horror; we do not understand, or we pretend not to understand; we refuse to admit that they form an integral part of the whole, that they are indispensable to the functioning of the social organism, and that without them the fine flower we admire would be quite different, or would not be at all. (106–07)

These observations once again recall the earnest efforts of Symonds to set aside "luxury" and to limit masculine loves to the form of pedagogic relations. As an intellectual relation, homosexuality is acceptable; as a sexual relation it is reprehensible. Corydon comes back to emphasize this point at the end of the book: "I am saying that this love, if it is authentic, tends toward chastity . . . and that for the child it can be the best incentive to courage, to exertion, to virtue" (124). The older lover might even cure the younger of a taste for masturbation: "I am also saying that an older man can understand an adolescent boy's troubles better than a woman can, even one expert in the art of love; indeed, I know certain children excessively addicted to solitary pleasures, for whom I consider this kind of attachment would be the surest remedy" (124). Further, for the young man (whom Gide deprives of all desire and of all sexuality: "more desirable and desired than desiring"), nothing, Gide insists, could be preferable than "a lover of his own sex. . . . I believe that such a lover will jealously watch over him, protect him, and himself exalted, purified by this love, will guide him toward those radiant heights which are not to be reached without love. I believe that if, quite the contrary, this youth should fall into a woman's hands, this can be disastrous for him" (125). This relation of the lover to his beloved will last "from thirteen to twenty-two," because that is "for the Greeks the age of loving friendship, of shared exaltation, of the noblest emulation." And it is only after this clearly initiatory period that the boy will want to become a man, which means to turn his thoughts "to women—which is to say: to marry" (125–26).

One more important point needs to be made. The third dialogue of *Corydon* is presented as a response to a book by Léon Blum: *On Marriage*. Gide opposes to the sexual liberty that Blum seems to support for women (and which earned him as many insults as Gide would earn for *Corydon*) a serious effort to protect young women. If one is to believe what he writes, there is no doubt that for Gide, the fate of a young girl is to become a wife and provide children to her husband and to society. It goes without saying that under ideal circumstances she will remain a virgin until her wedding. But, given that "the male has much more to expend than is required in order to answer to the reproductive function of the opposite sex and to ensure the reproduction of the species" (104), there needs to be a way for surplus male desire to express itself. This is where pederasty comes in. In order to avoid directing "the anxiety and excess of our male appetites" at young women, Corydon suggests, we would do well to return to the "solution" that "ancient Greece advocated" (105). "If you merely consider the fact that, given our morals," Corydon adds, "no literature has devoted so much attention to adultery as the French; not to mention all the semi-virgins and all the semi-prostitutes. This outlet the Greeks proposed, which outrages you and which seemed so natural to them, you want to suppress. Then make your saints; or else man's desire will corrupt the wife, defile the daughter . . ." (110).

In Gide's world, women ideally would have no desire (unless they want to be described as "prostitutes"). But Gide has to admit that adultery, even if it arises from the excesses of male desire, can only take place with the help of women who have set aside their role as spouse (or, worse, with the help of young women, "semi-virgins," who are willing to engage in debauchery). So "pederasty" would function not only to protect young women from men, but also to protect them from themselves, to shelter them from male desire and thereby restore the morality of the larger society.

It is all too easy simply to laugh at the way Gide, in his apology for pederasty, portrays bourgeois society's desire to protect the virtue of its daughters and its wives. Maybe we should stop at pointing out certain blatant contradictions, such as the one between the idea that pederasty will serve as an outlet for excess male desire and the idea that the relations between the older and the younger man will be chaste. Coherence was probably not what Gide was aiming for. Homophobic discourse itself hardly cares about it. It is riddled with contradictions. Its coherence is that it is consistently homophobic. Likewise, gay discourse is not particularly coherent and historically has never been so. A single book can easily harbor contradictory arguments. The coherence of the heterogenous assertions lies in the will toward legitimation that animates the entire discourse.

11

The Will to Disturb

In *Corydon*, then, homosexuality per se is never really brought up. This is first of all because sexuality itself is rarely brought up (except to condemn it). It is also because relationships between grown men are never really brought up (except so that one can be offended by them). The "defense of pederasty" that the book announces at the outset unfolds imperturbably with reference to the Greeks and to relations between an older man and a younger one, an adolescent. The book presents a fantastical project for social reform that would consist in reinstating an institution that existed in antiquity. Its contents do not include anything that could be thought of as a defense of homosexuality. The younger man, in any case, is destined for heterosexuality, or at least for the marriage that will mark his full transition to manhood. Will he, in his turn, take up the role of the older man, turning his attention to male adolescents, leaving to his wife the job of raising their children and managing their household? That would seem to be the expectation, but we cannot really be sure, for the dialogue ends abruptly at the point at which this might be discussed: the narrator picks up his hat and leaves without pursuing the subject further.

Of course, it can be observed that many of the positions taken in the third and fourth of *Corydon*'s dialogues are in contradiction with what was discussed in the first two dialogues (which had been written much earlier). At the beginning of the volume, Gide had rejected the idea that homosexuality could be "acquired" by an individual (an idea that meant, in the medical and moral discourses of the time, that it could also be unlearned or even prevented). His intention was to show that homosexuality is grounded in the nature of certain people. He repeatedly affirms that he has no intention of convincing anyone to become homosexual. He is simply speaking out in order to lessen the burden of opprobrium under which those who are homosexual have heretofore been obliged to suffer. Yet if this is the case, why would he, at the end of the book, produce the elaborate theoretical and historical construction having to do with a return to pederasty—a social institution that would involve all young men of a certain age, an institution in which doubtless all older men would be intended to take care of the younger men?

Perhaps the reason is that Gide's discourse is entirely under the influence of the homophobic violence against which he wishes to fight. The entire discourse that Gide has his spokesman Corydon express is devoted to responding to different homophobic themes: effeminacy, sickness, decadence, and the betrayal of one's own nation. By organizing his discourse in this way, Gide not only defines what he has to say by reference to those categories, he internalizes them. Far from managing to do away with the terms imposed by homophobic discourse, far from rising up against homophobic habits of thought, he in fact accepts and reproduces them. The best he can do is to try to make an exception for "pederasts" and to include himself in that category. The "defense of pederasty" sets itself up by making a distinction between noble and unhealthy forms of homosexuality and by dismissing the latter. In his *Journal* for 1918, Gide comes back to the arguments of *Corydon* (which has, at that point, only been published in a limited edition) in order to distinguish between "three types of *homosexuals*": "I call a *pederast* the man who, as the word indicates, falls in love with young boys. I call a *sodomite* . . . the man whose desire is addressed to mature men. I call an *invert* the man who, in the comedy of love, assumes the role of a woman and desires to be possessed." He adds that the difference between the three is not always "distinct": "There are possible transferences from one to another; but most often the difference among them is such that they experience a profound disgust for one another, a disgust accompanied by a reprobation that in no way yields to that which you (heterosexuals) fiercely show toward all three."[1] To prove his point, to be "persuasive," as he says, it is important to Gide to let heterosexuals know that pederasts, the noble and pure homosexuals, feel the same disgust for other, inverted homosexuals as do heterosexuals. A few lines earlier, he had called to mind the grandeur of pederasty: "Had Socrates and Plato not loved young men, what a pity for Greece, what a pity for the whole world! Had Socrates and Plato not loved young men and aimed to please them, each one of us would be a little less sensible" (2:246). It is easy to imagine why Proust, when he set out to give a somewhat scientific description of social reality and psychological life, would have been particularly attentive to making fun of those homosexuals who invoked Socrates in order to justify their own vice. If

Gide found Proust's way of speaking of homosexuality in his books to be detestable and degrading, doubtless Proust also detested Gide's way of trying to rehabilitate it, something he would have found, if not ridiculous then at the very least full of mystification.

Gide is perfectly willing to recognize that "homosexuals" have faults. When he broaches this subject in *Corydon*, he has of course already excluded "certain degenerates, people who are sick and obsessed" (120). Yet even among "the others," those he calls "normal pederasts," certain weaknesses of character can be observed. Still, responsibility for these can be laid upon the situation in which they are obliged to live: "For the same thing always happens whenever a natural instinct is systematically thwarted. Yes, the state of our morality tends to make a homosexual inclination an academy of hypocrisy, cunning, and disrespect for law" (120). If the normal pederast breaks laws, if he is hypocritical, it is due to the fact that his character has been shaped by the necessity to be forever hiding who he is. But it is not part of his deepest nature to be opposed to the law. Gide's whole purpose throughout the book is to suggest precisely the contrary, that the normal pederast might well be the most attached to the laws of his land, to social progress, to the greatness of the nation.

⊱ When, in his *Journal*, he comments on *Corydon*, and distinguishes between "three kinds of homosexuals," Gide places "inverts" in a special category: "It has always seemed to me that they alone deserved the reproach of moral or intellectual deformation and were subject to some of the accusations that are commonly addressed to all homosexuals" (2:247). Clearly then, Gide finds sexual inversion, the inversion of sexual roles, to be repugnant. Only masculine homosexuality is defensible. What is acceptable is that a grown man love younger men or that younger men love grown men. (So what Gide refers to as a *sodomite* is not someone who practices sodomy—actively or passively. Rather he is a complement to the pederast, who loves younger men. If Gide's ideological merry-go-round is to spin in balanced fashion, he needs a category for the younger man who is attracted to grown men.) Yet as soon as a sexual relation enters into the picture, especially if it includes passive sodomy, Gide is willing to countenance the accusations "commonly addressed" to homosexuals. That person who "assumes the role of a woman" during the sexual act proves particularly disgusting to Gide, even if the active role in sodomy is also quite upsetting to him.[2]

Gide repeated many times that in his case, sexual pleasure was to be found in the form of caresses. Any idea of penetration was rigorously excluded. Gide's sexuality is one of surfaces ("superficial," he wrote in one of the drafts for *Corydon*, with a heavy insistence on the fact that it should be perfectly clear what he meant by that). If he recognizes something of himself in Whitman, it is precisely because a simple bit of epidermal contact seems to suffice for the "comrades" that Whitman imagines in *Calamus*. Gide makes the connection himself in *If It Die . . .*: "As for myself, who can only conceive pleasure face to face, reciprocal and gentle and who, like Whitman, find satisfaction in the most furtive contact . . ."[3]

We know, thanks to the stories Gide himself tells in *If It Die . . .* (just as we know thanks to Symonds's *Memoirs*), to what an extent the apologetic drive to desexualize homosexuality in order to make it more acceptable, the drive which finds expression in *Corydon*, participates in a project of mystification, even self-mystification. After all, even if he did not practice sodomy (which, active or passive, does really seem to have filled him with repugnance), it cannot be said that his "contacts" with the male youths of Biskra, for example, fit well into the chaste and purely pedagogical framework described by the Platonic doctor in Gide's dialogues on Greek love. The most that can be said is that we see here evidence of the radical dissociation that Gide was always striving to establish between physical sensuality and love. He once observed, "No doubt I already felt that fundamental incapacity for mixing the spirit with the senses, which is, I believe, somewhat peculiar to me, and which was soon to become one of the cardinal repulsions of my life."[4] Still, is it possible to believe, to take only the most obvious example, that he never had any sexual relations with Marc Allégret?[5]

⇥ Gide would insist on the distinction between inversion and pederasty through the end of his life. He takes it up again, for instance, in *So Be It*, written shortly before his death in 1951:

> The great number of confidences I have been in a position to receive has convinced me that the variety of cases of homosexuality is much greater than that of cases of heterosexuality. And, furthermore, the irrepressible loathing a homosexual may feel for another whose appetites are not the same as his is something of which the heterosexual has no idea; he lumps them all together so as to be able to throw them

all overboard at one and the same time, and this is obviously much more expedient. I tried in so far as I could to make the distinction between pederasts in the Greek sense of the word (love of boys) and inverts, but no one deigned to see anything in this but a rather groundless discrimination, and I had to give it up. It's probably better not to try again.[6]

This is obviously a strange way of not trying again, since he seems still in 1951 to be regretful that people did not take up this distinction that was already rather suspect in 1924. And there is more. He adds in the text from 1951: "As for my sexual tastes, I have never hidden them except when they might embarrass others. Without exactly flaunting them, I have let them be apparent. This is partly because I have never thought they were such as to dishonor me." So far, so good. But it is difficult not to be troubled upon reading, shortly thereafter, that he again feels the need to denounce others who inspire in him a disgust that he cannot stop himself from expressing— all in order once again to attempt to legitimate his identity, to distinguish himself from those who live their homosexuality differently: "It is the free-and-easy, self-indulgent yielding to those tastes that dishonors" (161).

Reading these words it is difficult to understand how Gide was able to repeat as often as he did that his books, and especially *Corydon*, were intended to "embarrass" or to "trouble." ("I do not want to move to pity with this book; I want to *embarrass* [gêner].")[7] A reader of today naturally has some difficulty grasping how and to whom such notions could be troubling. They seem so clearly to reveal a desire to conform to the values of the dominant culture.

Yet in fact they were troubling. More than that, they provoked reactions of an extreme violence. This tends to suggest that in the eyes of its opponents, the actual content of homosexual discourse is unimportant. What is important is the act of speaking, of refusing what Adrienne Rich refers to as "compulsory heterosexuality." Gide was not attacked because of the absurd things he said about pederasty. He was attacked for speaking of love between men.

This is doubtless why Gide was able to insist throughout his long career that *Corydon* was among all his books the one he considered the most important, the most useful, the most necessary, indeed, the most subversive, whereas it might seem to us rather far behind other texts in which he makes an effort to express his homosexuality. What a huge distance, for example, between the fever of The Fruits of the Earth, which he would more or less disavow, and the stiff and affected tone of Corydon, whose present-day importance and future relevance he continually reiterated. It thus seems that there are two Gides when it comes to thinking about homosexuality: the Gide who strove to open literature to "homosexual" desire (in The Fruits of the Earth, The Immoralist, Saul, Amyntas, If It Die . . ., The Counterfeiters, and so on) and who on occasion proves amazingly audacious, and then the Gide who sets out to accomplish the laborious self-justifying enterprise that is Corydon, an enterprise that will take him over ten years, only to produce that strange song of praise to classical pederasty that effaces any sexuality or even sensuality in favor of moral and educational duty. There is, on the one hand, the Gide who is like Wilde. On the other, there is the Gide who is like Symonds. We can't even really speak of an evolution from the one to the other. Rather, the two seem to coexist, and to remain relatively autonomous and even to reinforce each other. One can always find in Gide—as in Proust, as we have seen—a text, a sentence, a line that will contradict or undermine the most assertorial statements contained in another text or sentence. This explains the necessity of analyzing such statements as much for the political gesture that lies behind them as for their exact content.

That the heavy-handed demonstrations in Corydon, which seem to us so dated and without interest, should be the aspect of his work that made him a trailblazer in the history of modern homosexuality is perhaps not the least of the paradoxes of Gide's work. He was a trailblazer simply in the fact that he took a position and avoided masking it by this or that artistic detour. At the moment when it was about to be accepted that literature could take up the subject of homosexuality, it nonetheless proved scandalous that a militant discourse could see the light of day. François Porché expressed this crudely in his 1929 response to the critique Gide offered of his book, The Love That Dare Not Speak Its Name—a book in which one rather disagreeable chapter was devoted to Gide. Porché writes: "There is a crucial difference between a work of art and a tendentious work, one conceived as propaganda. . . . An author rarely confuses the two. He knows perfectly well when the drive toward disinterested art has been strongly overruled by an obsessive interest in exercising some immediate influence. . . . It is that desire that I frowned upon. Corydon is nothing other than a political tract."[8]

Even before Corydon was published, Jacques Maritain, who apparently made it a personal project to "save" homosexuals, had visited Gide to urge him not to commit the sacrilege of publishing the book. Gide describes the scene in his *Journal* in December 1923: "I told him that I had no intention of defending myself but that he must be aware that everything he could think of saying to me about this book I had already said to myself, and that a project that resists the trial of war, of personal losses, and of all the meditations that ensue runs the risk of being too deeply anchored in the heart and mind for an intervention like his to hope to change it." Maritain leaves him with the request that he "ask Christ to let you know, directly, whether you are right or wrong to publish this book." Gide replies that he cannot "agree to call on him today as one rings someone up on the telephone."[9]

Maritain's pleas regarding the state of Gide's soul were in vain. It did him no good to emphasize that it might be "dangerous" for Gide to publish what he imagined to be the "truth." Nothing availed him. Gide was committed to his mission: "I protested . . . that this book had to be written, that I was uniquely qualified to write it, and that I could not without a sort of bankruptcy release myself from what I considered my duty" (2:339).

Gide was perhaps not wrong in imagining that his long struggle—with himself, with his friends, with literary circles, with the world around him— over the publication of *Corydon* was the struggle that had demanded the most courage of him, the most obstinate determination, the struggle in which he stood to lose the most.[10] In 1911, he had had twelve copies printed, which were immediately "put away" in a drawer from which they never emerged.[11] His friends had convinced him not to finish the work, which, at the time, was only made up of "the first two dialogues and the first part of the third." The rest was "merely sketched." Still, he emphasizes in 1920, as he prepares a new edition (of twenty or so more copies), that "the considerations I was setting forth in this little book seemed to me of the greatest importance, and I believed it necessary to present them."[12] Ten years had passed, yet Gide remained convinced that "however subversive it might seem," *Corydon* "attacked only falsehood after all and . . . nothing is actually unhealthier, for an individual and for a society, than an accredited lie" (xxiii-xxiv). In 1922, when he composes the preface for what will become the commercial edition of 1924, he reiterates this point:

> Ideas which at first attract and seem to dazzle us fade by the next day or soon thereafter. That is why I have waited so long to write this book and, having written it, to publish it. I wanted to be sure that what I was propounding in *Corydon*, and what seemed to me obvious, I would not soon have to retract. But no: my ideas have merely been confirmed in

the meanwhile, and what I now have against my book is its reserve, its timidity. . . . What I believed before the war I believe more strongly today. The indignation *Corydon* may provoke will not keep me from believing that what I say here must be said. Not that I believe one should say all that one thinks, and say it no matter when—but precisely what I am saying here must be said, and must be said today. (xx)

In 1942, he made a remark in his *Journal* concerning the posterity of his work: "*Corydon* remains in my opinion the most important of my books; but it is also the one with which I find the most fault. . . . I believe I said in that book just about everything I had to say on this most important subject that had not been said before me; but I reproach myself with not having said it as I should have done. None the less, certain attentive minds will manage to discover it there later on." He makes a similar remark again in 1946, when he mentions the possibility of his election to the Académie Française: "The Academy? . . . Yes, perhaps, accept becoming a member if I can do it without making solicitations, groveling, paying visits, etc. And immediately afterward, as my first act as an Immortal, a preface to *Corydon*, declaring that I consider that book to be the most important and the most *serviceable* of my writings."[13]

In 1949, during his recorded conversations with Jean Amrouche, he returns once again to "the capital importance that will little by little be recognized" in this text. He insists: "Not only do I not regret writing this book, but at the moment during which I was writing it I had no idea how right I was to be writing it, and this is why my manner in writing it was a bit timid and ironical." He also recalls that he had written *Corydon* out of a "kind of moral obligation." "I considered that it was indispensable for me to say these things, things only I could say."

Amrouche asks him: "Was the drama of Oscar Wilde an incitation to write this book?"

Gide replies: "Yes, of course, among other things."[14]

12

The *"Preoccupation with Homosexuality"*

One might say that Gide decided to publish *Corydon* because the necessary conditions had been met so that such a book could be published. In 1922, Proust had published *Cities of the Plain* (*Sodome et Gomorrhe*), a book that brought more public attention to homosexuality than had perhaps even been the case during the period of the Eulenburg affair. Around the same moment, Roger Martin du Gard—perhaps the only one of Gide's friends who did not try to dissuade him from publishing his dialogues—notes in his *Journal* that "the books of Proust, the movement of ideas in Germany and in Italy . . . the theories of Freud will all bring about very quickly a moment when one will regard with a completely different eye sexual deviance; there will no longer be anything courageous about throwing off the mask."[1]

Yet surely Gide was not only concerned about being overtaken by changing ideas and changing mores. He also wanted to dispute the medicalized representations of homosexuality that were being propagated by Hirschfeld and by Proust. Hirschfeld's motives were those of an activist. (His motto was *Per scientiam ad justiciam*, "Through Science, Justice.") Proust's goals, on the other hand, were literary and his portrayals derogatory. Clearly the great difference between Proust and Gide as regards homosexuality, or as regards the relation of their work to homosexuality, is that Gide speaks either implicitly or explicitly as a homosexual (thus the necessity to ennoble homosexuality by transforming it into pederasty), whereas Proust speaks as if he were heterosexual. In one case, the task is to describe in the manner of an apologia the makeup of the personality and the emotions of the person who is writing. In the other case, it is a question of revealing—either comically or tragically—novelistic characters who are apparently subject to observation by a "moralist." In a note to the preface to *Corydon* that is dated November 1922,

Gide explains what it is that in his eyes justifies his public intervention despite all the objections of his friends:

Certain books—Proust's in particular—have accustomed the public to be less alarmed by, and to consider more deliberately—what it previously pretended or preferred to ignore. For how many of us suppose they can suppress what they ignore! . . . But such books have greatly contributed, I fear, to our current confusion. The theory of the woman-man, of the *Sexuelle Zwischenstufen* (intermediate degrees of sexuality) advanced by Dr. Hirschfeld in Germany quite some time before the war—and which Marcel Proust appears to accept—may well be true enough; but that theory explains and concerns only certain cases of homosexuality, precisely those with which this book does not deal— cases of inversion, of effeminacy, of sodomy. And I realize today that one of my book's shortcomings is in fact its failure to deal with them, for they turn out to be much more frequent than I previously supposed. Even granting that Hirschfeld's theory accounts for these cases, his "third sex" argument certainly cannot explain what we habitually call "Greek love": pederasty—in which effeminacy is neither here nor there. (xx)

Caught off-guard by the evidence that "inverts" and "effeminate" men are more numerous than he had believed when he began writing the book in 1908, caught off-guard as well by the appearance of activist or literary discourses on homosexuality, Gide makes it clear that he intends for his voice to be heard in the defense of a point of view that could only seem outdated given both the audacities of Proust and the expanding visibility of a gay subculture in Paris, one no one could miss—one that was immortalized by Brassaï in a famous series of photographs from the early 1930s.[2] Perhaps it was also because Gide was so fully aware that the image made available by the presence and visibility of this gay culture was the one from which he was so eager to distance himself that he became so insistent that pederasty had nothing to do with the "monsters" portrayed by Proust or with the individuals in drag or the more ostentatious inverts who could be found in the cabarets and the balls of the time. Also we should at this point be wary of an understanding of the transformations within gay culture or within representations of homosexuality that is too evolutionary, that conveys too much a sense of some "progress" being involved in which older forms are relegated to the past. After all, the construct that Gide was defending has perhaps never entirely disappeared. It continued to coexist with new ways of being homosexual or of thinking oneself to be such. The history of homosexuality is not an evolution from one representation to another, one manner of being to another. It is the unstable and often conflictual cohabitation of ways of life, images, and discourses that have no stability and no coherence either individually or among themselves.

It is amusing to note, for example, that even though Gide rejected outright all of Hirschfeld's theses, he insisted on visiting Hirschfeld's Institute (devoted to research on sexuality) during a trip to Berlin a few years after *Corydon* was published. Christopher Isherwood was there that day and describes the Francophobic impulse he experienced upon witnessing this "sneering, culture-conceited frog" looking about with a haughty smile on his face, "judiciously fingering his chin." Isherwood immediately did a mental about-face: "Suddenly he loved Hirschfeld—at whom he himself had been sneering, a moment before—the silly solemn old professor with his doggy mustache."[3]

⌖ We might note that Gide, in his way of opposing himself to Hirschfeld, startlingly resembles the "masculinist" tendency within the German homosexual movement, one which preached more or less the same themes found in *Corydon*: a "bisexuality" based on the one hand on masculine friendships that fall within the pederastic framework and, on the other, heterosexual marriages destined to reproduce the species.[4] In opposition to the idea of a "third sex," for instance, Benedict Friedländer became the advocate for pederastic relations that took place alongside family life, and Adolf Brand set up an opposition between "the Greek side of things" and Hirschfeld's theories. If we are considering only the description of Greek culture or of the redeeming potential of male sociability for civilization, the texts of these German "masculinist" theorists are more or less identical to those of Symonds or Gide.

Brandt and his collaborators on the journal *Der Eigene* thought that by insisting on the idea of a third sex Hirschfeld was limiting homosexuality to a minority definition, one dictated by nature, and was rendering it impossible to imagine propagating homosexuality or homoeroticism throughout the social body, a propagation that was the basis of their idea of social reform.[5] This universalizing conception made for a much more radical calling into question of the heterosexual norm than the one contained in the minoritizing conception of Hirschfeld. It was nonetheless still based on the absolute principle of male domination. This universalizing conception also reached in the direction of certain other ideological currents developing at that time in Germany, currents that were at the opposite end of the spectrum from the socialist and progressive views of Hirschfeld, and were also quite distant from the opinions of Gide and Symonds. Symonds, as we have seen, belonged to an intellectual tradition of liberal and democratic social reform. Gide, in the 1920s and 1930s, was very clearly engaged on the left and involved in anticolonial struggles.[6]

Gide's and Symonds's texts unquestionably bear the mark of an intolerable misogyny, but we should remember that their apologia for masculine camaraderie never leaves the realm of ideological fantasy or of grandiose oratory about culture. They should be read not as architects of authentic social projects, but as writers proffering discourses intended to legitimate certain relations between men. The texts of the German masculinist homosexual theorists, on the other hand, were violently antifeminist and were meant to help establish a concrete political program having to do with the elevation of masculine sociability as a principle of social regeneration. Friedländer was obsessed by the idea that the feminine influence on culture was a menace to civilization, and he called upon masculine and martial friendship to help restore the moral strength and devotion to sacrifice on which the state should be based.[7] He died in 1908, but in the 1910s and 1920s discourses that mixed together ultranationalism, militarism, antisemitism, and homoeroticism proliferated in this sector of the homosexual movement. Certain partisans of these discourses would find themselves close to National Socialism, in which they perceived the realization of the *Männerbund* they had been dreaming of.

Hasty generalizations are not helpful. There is no reason to think that there was a self-evident link between certain ways of thinking about homosexuality and fascism or Nazism. One finds a great deal of heterogeneity within the "masculinist" current: conservatives, anarchists, socialists, ultranationalists all coexisted in the same journals—notably in Brand's *Der Eigene.* Brand understood that homosexuals had every reason to fear Nazism. Indeed, when in 1928 he sent out a questionnaire to different political parties asking them to state their positions about homosexuality, the National Socialist Party was quite clear: they brutally condemned homosexuality on the grounds that the public interest had to come before private ones. (This is one of the major recurring themes in homophobic discourse. It can still be heard today, even from the most "liberal" and "progressive" representatives of homophobia.) The response to Brand was the first public position announced by the National Socialist Party: it stated that homosexuality was incompatible with the prosperity of the German people.[8] This would not stop Brand from writing in 1932 that such public declarations contradicted the true reality of the historical foundations of Nazism, yet he would keep his distance from the Nazi movement. The same cannot be said of all the people who collaborated at his journal.[9]

Finally we should note that this masculinist homosexual current was fond of extolling the "image of man" more or less as it was found in Winckelmann's writings on Greek sculpture.[10] The very same image was endorsed by prefascist and fascist movements. It seems both paradoxical and troubling that Winckelmann could have served both to provide a justification for people who were striving to create a homosexual discourse—be it Pater (!) or Friedländer—and for those who, in the 1930s, would use this canon of male beauty in an effort to annihilate anything that might in their eyes damage the "health of the race," any seed of dissolution in the social body—Jews, homosexuals, and so on.

Hirschfeld, we should not forget, represented the most important current of the homosexual movement, one diametrically opposed to the masculinist tendency. He was Jewish and was denounced as such by both the masculinist homosexuals and by Nazi agents. Hirschfeld's Scientific-Humanitarian Committee was firmly situated on the left and actively engaged alongside the feminist movement.[11] Hirschfeld was a socialist, and on November 10, 1918, he would stand up and speak at an assembly of several thousand people to celebrate the arrival of the republic and of democracy shortly before monarchist officers would open fire on the crowd. As a Jew and a homosexual, it is easy to understand why he was a target for the Nazis. From the 1920s onward, his lectures were brutally disrupted (by gunshots and fistfights, with people in the audience seriously wounded). He was attacked several times by militant Nazis, and on one occasion in Munich in 1920 was so violently beaten that his assailants left him for dead. In May 1933, his institute was attacked and ruined by Nazi assault troops and his library was burned. Hirschfeld was in Switzerland at that moment. He did not return to Germany and so managed to escape the terrible fate that would have awaited him along with thousands of other homosexuals—sent to camps wearing a pink triangle.

❯❯ It is worth emphasizing once again that nothing in Gide's or Proust's discourse would implicate them in what happened in Germany. If there are resemblances between the writings of Gide and of the German masculinists, even sometimes striking ones, this does not mean that there is any ideological or political kinship between them. Nonetheless, we should emphasize that the representations of homosexuality that Gide and Proust strove to put forth turned around a central point: its relation to issues of masculinity and femininity. Whatever fundamental differences in emphasis there may be between Gide's carefully crafted apologetics and Proust's elaborate entomological project, the two writers have one thing in common: they both perpetuate homophobic values, notably the valorization of masculinity. In the essay opening Cities of the Plain (Sodome et Gomorrhe) Proust himself also gives the impression of being disgusted as he describes homosexuals in whom "the woman is not only inwardly united to the man but *hideously visible*, convulsed as they are by a hysterical spasm. . . ." For Proust, as we have seen, homosexuals are, at least in theory, women who desire men. But when this interior reality rises too clearly to the surface, when a "shrill laugh . . . set their knees and their hands trembling," the spectacle becomes simply revolting, and those responsible for producing that spectacle are rejected by other homosexuals who have "sought to efface" those "special marks."[12]

Proust, we know, not only took great care to hide his homosexuality, he was also quite sensitive around the issue of effeminacy.[13] In May 1908, just at the moment he was beginning to think about his project regarding the "race of aunties," he complained to his friend Emmanual Bibesco that Bibesco had joked in front of someone Proust didn't know about Proust's "salaïsme," a word they used between them to designate homosexuality. In October of the same year, he complains in letters to Georges de Lauris and to Louis d'Albufera about "all the inept calumnies that people have accused me of in the past."[14] We shouldn't forget that in 1897, Proust challenged Jean Lorrain to a duel after Lorrain, openly and even ostentatiously homosexual himself, had slipped into an article on Proust's Les Plaisirs et les jours a reference to Proust's relationship with Lucien Daudet. The two adversaries met, pistols in hand, in the woods of Meudon, where each fired into the air to be sure not to hurt the other.[15] Yet Proust seems to have retained throughout his life a feeling of great pride regarding the way he carried off this bit of ridiculous theater. When, twenty-three years later, the critic Paul Souday, writing in Le Temps in

1920, accused Proust of snobbery and of being feminine, Proust reacted violently. Doubtless he would not be justified in accusing the critic of any malicious intent, wrote Proust in a letter to Souday. Yet he reproached him for offering cover for anyone else who, given that Proust was just about to "speak of Sodom" in Cities of the Plain (Sodome et Gomorrhe), would feel no hesitation about making the same accusation out of more disagreeable ulterior motives. Proust reminded Souday of his glorious duel: "From 'feminine' to 'effeminate' is only one short step. Those who served me as seconds in my duel will tell you whether I have the softness of effeminates."[16]

On the other hand, we know from other sources—from stories Gide tells—that Proust enjoyed discussing his homosexuality with those he knew shared his tastes and his practices. In his Journal, Gide describes an evening spent with Proust in May 1921, noting that "far from denying or hiding his uranism, he exhibits it, and I could almost say boasts of it." From Gide's pen comes the surprising portrait of a Proust who (while in Cities of the Plain making fun of those "inverts" who "regard homosexuality as the appurtenance of genius" and wish to claim all the great names of history, art, and literature for the club) is insistent about his claim that Baudelaire was a practicing homosexual.[17]

A similar phenomenon can be observed in the way in which, after making fun of homosexuals who, having at first believed themselves to be alone in the world, gradually convince themselves that everyone is like them and that the "normal" man is the exception, Proust then reproduced this attitude in his novel. For by the end of it, the reader has learned that nearly everyone belongs to that "accursed race." Homosexuality seems to have thrived as the pages go by to such an extent that it retrospectively invades the entire novel, comes to give it its overall color, and without a doubt provides it with one of its most fundamental meanings.

Their correspondence from the year 1914 clearly shows that Gide and Proust were both convinced that their own and the other's literary project were inextricably tied to their desire to write about same-sex love in their books. Even the shape they wished to give to their projects and the aesthetic innovations to which they aspired can only be understood in relation to this shared desire. For example, in March 1914, Proust writes to Gide to tell him that he is "enviously captivated and overjoyed" by his reading of Gide's The Vatican Cellars (Les Caves du Vatican).[18] He adds, "in the creation of Cadio [sic], no one has been objective with that much perversity since Balzac and Splendeurs et misères."[19] A few days later he writes again to ask if "all Cadio's 'uncles' are 'aunties.' "[20] For his part, Gide would write, after reading the passages of Proust's novel that were published in the *Nouvelle Revue Française* that the portrayal of Charlus is "simply marvellous."[21] Proust in reply undertakes to explain the character he has created: "I was trying to portray the homosexual who is fascinated by virility because he is, without realizing it, a Woman. I do not pretend to claim that this is the only kind of homosexual. But it is certainly an interesting kind, and one which, I believe, has not been described previously. Like any homosexual, moreover, he is different from other men, in some ways worse and in others infinitely better."[22] Gide then replies: "M. de Charlus makes for an admirable portrait. But by painting it you have contributed to the confusion that is ordinarily made between the homosexual and the invert. For people will not grant the kind of distinctions that you lay out in your letter. Charlus is only an individual, but he will be taken as typical. He will give rise to generalizations."[23] As Michael Lucey has aptly put it: "Their claims on literary posterity, their claims to be working within and to be advancing the tradition of the European novel rely in part on their innovative use of sexuality, and reciprocally, they intend their aesthetic success to legitimize their representation of that sexuality."[24]

It is, of course, difficult not to agree with J. E. Rivers when he analyzes Proust's way of presenting homosexuality in his work as the manifestation of a certain self-hatred and a hatred of people like him. Proust describes much the same phenomenon in the case of his characters. Such a hatred is finally not that different from the hatred demonstrated by Gide in all the texts in which he goes out of his way to demonstrate his difference from the inverts. Still, whatever precautions they took, both of them consciously and deliberately participated in the bringing into discourse of homosexuality mentioned by Roger Martin du Gard. Despite all their forms of prudence and their forms of controlled audacity, despite their fears of being associated with certain things from which they wished to distinguish themselves, Proust and Gide became the names around which (in France at least) debates concerning homosexuality became focused. One the one hand, there were virulent attacks upon the visibility of homosexuality Gide and Proust helped enable; on the other hand, they became reference points for a collective consciousness. This becomes clear in 1926, when the journal *Les Marges* publishes a questionnaire concerning "homosexuality in literature." After Gide's *The Counterfeiters* appeared in 1925, Paul Souday (the same critic at *Le Temps* whom Proust had dealt with) declared in exasperation, "This is becoming unbearable." He reminds his readers that "progress happens through a process of differentiation" and asserts that "this time things have gone far enough." Eugène Montfort, the founding editor of *Les Marges* thereupon decides to send out a questionnaire to a number of writers, asking them if in their opinion the "preoccupation with homosexuality" has grown since the war ended. The questionnaire also asks if, in their opinion, this literary evolution might have an influence on people's behavior, and if it might be "damaging to art."[25] Henri Barbusse is content simply to send a brief reply that denounces the "social and moral decadence of a certain part of contemporary society." He calls for a proletarian revolution that will do away with all that (20–21). Other respondents take more account of the actual questions the journal has asked. Gérard Bauer speaks of a "fashion" that has been spreading for the past few years and mentions the "victorious and liberated homosexuality thanks in part to the talent of Marcel Proust." He adds:

> Marcel Proust has been a kind of Messiah for this small people and has, through his genius, liberated them from slavery. It is not that his work preaches on behalf of homosexuality, but it provides it with titles of nobility. He was the first in the contemporary modern world to approach the problem head on, and to speak of it without embarrassment or reticence. He opened the way for those who had not yet dared to set out. The case of M. Gide stands out as an example of these hesitations. They are apparent throughout the series of prefaces to *Corydon*, a book it would have been better for his reputation not to have published.

For Bauer, "contagious homosexuality in literature begins with Marcel Proust." Further, "there is no doubt that this intellectual preoccupation has subsequently had an influence on people's behavior" (21–22).

Henriette Charasson also finds that "this preoccupation has developed at an outrageous rate since the war, and this is quite vexatious." She attributes this "obsession to the desire of certain people to market themselves, whatever the cost, for we know there will always be a public for disgusting books, and also to the desire of others to create a scandal and to be talked about." For Charasson as well, "the excessive intrusion of characters who are inverts into literature, and especially into the novel, could well have an influence on people's behavior by publicizing certain anomalies, and by allowing minds to become accustomed to them. The theater and the novel shape people's behavior and have an influence on the generation that follows" (28–29).

For his part, Louis Martin-Chauffier responds that "there is no doubt that homosexuality has become a fashionable literary theme since the war. There is also no doubt that since the war the damages due to homosexuality have increased. It is easy to understand that the war contributed a great deal to the development of this vice, a most odious one, totally contrary to nature." He continues by noting that once "a vice has become widespread enough to affect society and customs and to become a characteristic of a given moment, it legitimately becomes part of literature. Literature cannot ignore it. . . . Yet literature also has no right to alter it either. Literature is meant to depict, to produce knowledge, to judge (though without it being necessary that this judgment be expressed), so if it chooses to depict a vice, the vice should be depicted as vicious, and literature should castigate and denounce it." But what do we see?

> Exactly the opposite. We are not inundated by literature that is against homosexuality, we are inundated by homosexual literature. Better, by a literature of homosexuals. Here we see that behavior has preceded literary expression. We are surrounded by inverts who no longer bother to hide themselves. There was only one audacity waiting to be taken up: writing about it. Marcel Proust has, by the example of his work, incited Sodom to display its unnatural pleasures in the novel. Others have followed his example without realizing that this was only a detail in his work . . . which, even if it does not think of homosexuality as a vice, at least does not make a virtue out of it, but simply a kind of behavior toward which the analyst directs an attentively penetrating but nonetheless serene gaze.

Martin-Chauffier is struck not so much by the "depiction of homosexuality" offered by literature, but rather by the affirmation of what he calls the "homosexual spirit" that is increasingly present in that literature. How could one not imagine that this would have real consequences? "Literature always has an influence on behavior. Homosexual literature, born out of the development of homosexuality, contributes to the further spread of homosexuality because it depicts it with a certain complacency" (41–42).

More pragmatically (if also more hypocritically) François Mauriac also deplores that things have gotten so far out of hand and worries that we might be on the verge of an expansion of homosexual literature, for "many writers will give way to the attraction of these regions that have been out of bounds for so long, ones they would not have dared be the first to enter." From this point on "all they have to do is follow." As for the influence of "this kind of work on behavior," he also recognizes that it is "certain." Not that such works "could influence towards inversion someone who is not so inclined." All those who "find themselves agitated by such depictions are, unbeknownst to themselves, infected by the same illness." But "many of these sick people who were not aware of their condition have gained that awareness thanks to Gide and to Proust. Many who remained in hiding will no longer do so" (47).

In his conclusion, Eugène Montfort asks how one might go about "combating the shameless proselytism of the inverts." He seems, overall, pessimistic about the possibilities. The most he hopes for is that with the help of the responses to the questionnaire that are being published in his journal, "We will be allowed to remain normal without it being scandalous, to love women without seeming antediluvian, like some old relation from before the war." He ends his peroration by citing one of his contributors: "As Léon-Paul Fargue, cited by M. Lucien Fabre, puts it, the time has certainly come for us to have the right to be talented without having to be a pederast" (58–59).

Today's reader, upon encountering these statements, probably cannot help but be struck by the astonishing familiarity of this homophobic blather. Its formulations have been passed on from century to century and still occur in many contemporary discourses mostly unchanged. We find all the familiar themes (they seem never to wear out) that are still brandished against any form of gay speech even in today's attacks on gay visibility, on "gay" literature, on proselytism, and so on. Yet we also see the role that literature played, not only in unleashing this hostility, but more importantly in establishing the conditions for a collective self-consciousness, a context for self-recognition. We might even say, judging by the reactions we have just seen, that Proust's writings—because they spoke more freely—did even more than Gide's to establish the "preoccupation with homosexuality." (Bauer's phrase is a good one.)

In any case, however opposed the literary strategies of Proust and Gide may have been, they led to the same result. Their work, born out of personal life, became part of wider life. And in conformity with a wish that Gide formulated, art rediscovered its social destination.[26]

Gide always felt strongly that a literary work and a personal life were tightly interwoven. In his article on Wilde's *De Profundis*, he expresses his irritation at the remarks made by a translator who had deemed it appropriate to invite the reader to forget the circumstances of Wilde's conviction. The translator had asked, "If someone were to reveal that Flaubert and Balzac had committed crimes, would we have to burn *Salammbô* and *Cousin Bette*?"

Gide is indignant: "Are we still worrying about that sort of thing! . . . How much more interesting and right is it to understand that 'if Flaubert had committed crimes' it is not *Salammbô* that he would have written, but . . . something else, or nothing at all. . . . No, in order to read his work better . . . let us not pretend to ignore the drama of the man who, though knowing that it wounds, wished, nevertheless, *to address himself to life*."[27]

So, in opposition to the old theme rehearsed in Proust's *Against Sainte-Beuve* ("the man who lives in the same body with any great genius has little connection with him . . . he is only a man and may be utterly ignorant of what the poet who dwells in him wants" or "a book is the product of a self other than that which we display in our habits, in company, in our vices"), Gide continually insists on the opposite, that the truly innovative work is deeply inscribed in the biography of the author. The man of genius, the reformer, he writes in his book on Dostoevsky, always gives expression to "some physiological enigma, some non-satisfaction of the flesh, some disquiet, or anomaly."[28] Not only artistic works are in question here. Gide is interested in linking any attempt to alter the order of things to some kind of misfit in regards to norms and normality. Referring to Nietzsche's vaunted "transmutation of values," Gide is quite insistent on this point: "There lies at the root of every reform a malaise of some kind. The malaise from which the reformer suffers is a form of interior imbalance. Densities, positions, and moral values present themselves to him in different perspectives, so he exerts himself to establish a fresh accord. . . . I do not suggest that lack of balance is the necessary condition for the making of a reformer, but I do contend that every reformer starts out with a lack of balance" (153, translation modified). He further mentions Socrates's "demon," the "thorn in the flesh" of Saint Paul, Pascal's "abyss," and the "madness" of Rousseau and Nietzsche. He knows that he is likely to be accused of perpetuating well-known stereotypes, those of Nordau and Lombroso. But he defends himself from this accusation. He admits that there have been some geniuses, such as Victor Hugo, who are "sane and whole." But Rousseau? "Without his madness, he would be nothing but an indigestable Cicero" (154, translation modified).

Perhaps Gide is in fact wrong to believe himself so distant from the medical ideology with which he fears being associated. In the end, what differentiates him from the psychiatrists (the ones we saw being mocked by Wilde) is that he turns their assignment of values around. Gide is looking for innovation; he is moved and agitated by those constitutional weaknesses, by those personal instabilities that open the door to creativity. He is interested in the energy that gives rise to innovation, dissidence, "transmutation," and says as much quite clearly: the "malady" of genius is its salvation. "It is pointless to lament the infirmity but for which he would never have sought to resolve the problem raised by his own anomaly or find a harmony which would not reject his discord. . . . The man whose inner balance is perfect may well contribute reforms—but reforms which touch only the outer man." Whereas the other, "the individual who is abnormal cannot be captured in preestablished codes" (154, translation modified).

⋈ Sartre was, of course, not mistaken when he wrote that "all works of the mind contain within themselves the image of the reader for whom they are intended." He added: "I could draw the portrait of Gide's Nathanaël on the basis of Fruits of the Earth: I can see that the alienation from which he is urged to free himself is the family, the property he owns or will own by inheritance, the utilitarian project, a conventional morality, a narrow theism; I also see that he is cultured and has leisure, since it would be absurd to offer Ménalque as an example to an unskilled labourer, a man out of work, or an American negro."[29] Perhaps Sartre's conception of the posterity of a work of literature was too constrained, as was his conception of the reader to which it might really or potentially be addressed and of the "politics" that it might propose.[30] After all, Gide's readers have been numerous, and quite different from each other: Proust, Genet, Barthes, Foucault, and many others. All have contributed in their own manner to the passing on to more and more Nathanaëls of Ménalque's message—his call for a reinvention of oneself as a free subject.

PART 3

Michel Foucault's Heterotopias

One writes to give life, to free life when it
is imprisoned, to lay down lines of flight.

GILLES DELEUZE

1

Much More Beauty

At the end of his life Michel Foucault was investigating the manner in which we are produced as subjected "subjects" ("*sujets*" *assujettis*) and the ways there might be to escape this "subjection" or "subjugation" (*assujettissement*). This is the period in which he was working on Greece in relation to his *History of Sexuality* project. His thinking turns around the idea from ancient philosophy that it is possible to shape one's own subjectivity through the work one does on oneself. This shaping could happen by way of the creation of "styles of life" by means of which one strives to shake off modes of being and thinking that are passed on by history or imposed by social structures. One could try to reinvent oneself, to recreate oneself.

Thus the question he poses in a 1983 interview, one year before his death, "But couldn't everyone's life become a work of art?"[1] This idea seems quite important to him; he returns to it several times in the course of the interview in question.

Did not Oscar Wilde write an identical sentence some hundred years earlier? "To become a work of art is the object of living."[2] Does not all of Wilde's writing, and even his life, from beginning to end consist of an effort to ask the very question that would come to preoccupy Foucault just before his death? We know, moreover, that Wilde referred both to Hellenism and to the Renaissance in laying out this aesthetics of the self. Foucault would do the same.[3] Whatever the divergences may be between these two authors from such different times and different societies, the parallels between them are also striking. Wilde was trying to forge, if not a new "identity," at least a personage, a role, or, to use a more modern word, a "position" from which it would be possible to create oneself in a way that steered clear of dominant norms. Foucault suggests that we invent new relations between individuals, new modes of life that could be means of resistance to power and could help to further one's own self-reformulation.

The parallels seem even more compelling when we recall that for Foucault the two vectors of the "aesthetic of existence" are what we might call a "politics of friendship," and an "economy of pleasures." The former entails the work of constituting meaningful relations with one's friends, devoting close attention to them day by day; the latter involves the effort to intensify pleasure by means of the maximal eroticization of bodies.[4] Wilde seems close at hand when one recalls, on the one hand, his theories of a new hedonism, and, on the other, the development of (all male) circles in which relations of friendship provide the ground for the invention of a new culture and for resubjectification.[5]

Foucault never mentions this parallel. Perhaps he was unaware of it. If so, it would seem that he spontaneously rediscovered an entire prior history, one that, from Pater to Gide by way of Wilde, consisted in opening up spaces of resistance to subjectivation (to the process in which a subject is produced as subjected to a sexual order that makes him inferior), and in imagining possibilities for self-reinvention as an autonomous subject, a subject constructed against, or at least in divergence from, heterosexual norms. All the themes that one finds put forward by Pater, Symonds, or Wilde can be found again in Foucault, notably in a series of interviews that he gave from the mid-1970s through his death in 1984. They deal with gay issues, and also, more generally, with his writing of the History of Sexuality. One finds references to ancient Greece and the Renaissance, to friendship between men (which is construed as the cultural space in which new forms of existence can be created), to the quest for ways to intensify pleasure, and so on.

If Foucault does not mention Wilde or Pater, he does, it turns out, mention Gide. He compares the moral doctrine of The Fruits of the Earth to the ways in which Greek philosophers shaped their existences: "Sexual austerity in Greek society was a trend, a philosophical movement coming from very cultivated people in order to give to their life much more intensity, much more beauty. In a way, it's the same in the twentieth century when people, in order to get a more beautiful life, tried to get rid of all the sexual repression of their society, of their childhood. Gide in Greece would have been an austere philosopher."[6]

The theme of subjectivation appears in Foucault's work toward the end of his life, but there can be no doubt that the question of resistance was, from the outset, both the motivation for and the object of his entire intellectual enterprise. What had his theoretical objective from the mid-1950s onward been, if not to try to understand how we are "imprisoned"? What had his "politics" been, throughout his entire evolution from *Mental Illness and Personality* in 1954 to the final volumes of the *History of Sexuality* in 1984, if not an attempt to imagine how we could "liberate" ourselves?

This is why Foucault's life and his work cannot be dissociated: they become mixed together in the movement of his thought, they respond to each other, and they transform each other. In his final writings, Foucault explicitly emphasizes the practical effects of philosophy, the self-transformations possible through the exercise of theoretical reflection. But weren't these gestures already at work in his earliest books?

2

From Night to the Light of Day

Foucault read a lot of Gide and Proust when he was young. You might almost say he knew them by heart. They were not only literary touchstones for him, they were also one of the means by which he took part in gay culture. His 1950s correspondence with the musician Jean Barraqué, one of the great loves of his life, shows this quite clearly. There is, for example, the letter fictively dated October 20, 1904 (and really written on October 20, 1954) that offers a pastiche of Gide's *Journal*: "Studied Chopin for two hours this morning, full of inspiration. . . . I had been at work for 3 long and laborious minutes when J.B. telephoned, forever the irascible Corydon. . . . On the way home, somewhere between Barbès and Clichy, I discovered that I had lost my wallet (and all its contents), I don't know how. It was the leather wallet that Wilde had given me the first time we met in Biskra. Goodness me, how one becomes attached to things. Once home, I promised myself never again to give way to vice."[1]

Or there is this undated letter, from around the same time, referring on this occasion to Proust: "If I were morally inclined, my dear Jean, that is to say, if I lived up to the rigorous morality of my immorality, and, further, if I had a chauffeur, I would have him cross the whole of Paris in order to request that M. Barraqué be assured that Monsieur is thinking of him constantly. Rather, I should say, that I would like, like Swann, to stand guard at the entrance to the Verdurin palace until the first rays of dawn appear."[2]

Foucault took palpable pleasure in writing letters such as these. They are a clear source of amusement to him. Further, his literary allusions (and also the mention of what was then a gay cruising area on the Boulevard Barbès in Paris) place him squarely in what must be called a "culture," one with codes, references, a kind of humor, a language.[3] In another letter, for example, he addresses his correspondent in the feminine, "My dear lady," and writes in a style imitated from Madame de Sévigné. Indeed, right up to the end of his life Foucault would often speak in the feminine (about himself or others) when he was in the company of his gay friends. He made notable use of certain traits characteristic of gay conversation, feminizing first names by preceding them with a "la" or using the "la" in front of the surname—and, when possible, giving that surname a feminine form.

His letters to Barraqué reveal a happy Foucault—at least until the break up requested by the musician in 1956, which would cause Foucault great distress. They had met in 1952, and it seems they were friends before becoming lovers. Barraqué introduced Foucault to a world of "bad boys" in which Foucault was able to "take his sufferings for a walk."[4] But soon the friendship would turn into passionate and physical love. There is no doubt that this meeting provoked a "transformation" in Foucault.[5] Before this time, his relationship to his own homosexuality had been painful and conflicted. He had made several suicide attempts (in 1948 and 1950) that Pierre Étienne, the doctor at the École normale supérieure, ascribed to the extreme difficulty Foucault was having accepting his own sexuality.[6] He would often be immobilized by emotional exhaustion for several days running after a nocturnal visit to a gay bar or cruising place. Following a suicide attempt in 1950, Foucault wrote to one of his friends, "Don't make me say anything . . . Let me get used to lifting my head again; let me leave behind the night with which I have grown used to surrounding myself even at midday."[7] There were several occasions on which Dr. Étienne had to intervene to prevent Foucault from taking his own life.[8]

Given all of these circumstances, Foucault's father took him to a psychiatrist. It turned out to be the famous Professor Jean Delay, who must have been working on his psychobiography of André Gide at that time. It is easy to imagine how damaging, how dangerous even, it must have been for a young gay man to find himself in this man's office. The possibility of hospitalizing Foucault at Sainte-Anne was taken under serious consideration.[9] It was probably Louis Althusser, who had gone through such a hospitalization a few years earlier, who talked Foucault out of it. Foucault did consider beginning psychotherapy. (He began therapy, but then dropped it after a few weeks, but he would remain haunted for years by the question of whether an analysis would be a good idea.)

During this same period, Foucault became a serious alcoholic, to the point of needing to go through a detoxification treatment. (People recount that during his time in Sweden there were still moments when he would pass out, stone drunk.) In any case, Foucault suffered deeply with psychological problems. He would never forget them; indeed he may never have entirely freed himself from them. They were in large measure tied to his inability to accept his homosexuality, although his feeling of being extremely ugly may also have contributed to them.[10] Yet that latter consideration too leads us back to his sexuality, to the modalities of gay sexuality (often made up of multiple encounters, of continual cruising, in which one's physical features are of paramount importance). Clearly, Foucault's way of inventing an appearance, a silhouette, his way of creating a personality, and perhaps the idea he would later develop—of taking action on oneself to make changes and to escape from normative violence—are all tied to the problems of his youth and the deep impression they made on him.[11]

It was during this psychologically troubled period, when he was face-to-face with psychiatric medicine embodied in one of its most eminent practitioners, that Foucault chose to direct his education toward psychology and psychiatry. In 1949 he received a diploma from the Institut de psychologie de Paris. In 1952 he received a diploma in psychopathology for which he attended Delay's presentations of patients in the large amphitheater of Sainte-Anne hospital. He had a passionate interest in Rorschach tests. He gave them to all his friends at the École normale, and they became the topic of a course he gave in the 1960s when he was in Clermont. He and his friend Jacqueline Verdeaux worked together as interns in Sainte-Anne's electroencephalography laboratory, part of Professor Delay's department.

It would be a mistake to reduce his interest in psychology to a simple reaction to his own psychological troubles. This interest also needs to be understood in the intellectual and political context of the time. There was a movement in which a certain number of young philosophers of the 1940s and 1950s turned in the direction of the human sciences (Didier Anzieu and Jean Laplanche moving into psychoanalysis, Pierre Bourdieu into ethnology and sociology, and so on). We should also note that in the years after the war France saw an extraordinary spread of psychoanalysis, which contributed to the renewal of intellectual life. The predominant influence of the Communist Party on leftist thinkers in the university (and especially at the École normale) also needs to be taken into account, along with the announced project of Marxist thinkers to develop a materialist psychology in opposition to psychoanalysis. They considered psychoanalysis suspect and denounced it as a "bourgeois" science. Foucault's early writings, especially his first book, Mental Illness and Personality (1954), bear the marks of all of these debates.

Consequently, we might say that Foucault's interest in the scientific aspects of psychology, psychiatry, and psychoanalysis is situated at the crossroads where his personal troubles, his personal questioning, met the kinds of questioning that were agitating the intellectual life of the time.

In any case, psychology would be Foucault's professional specialization for many years. He was hired to teach psychology in Lille in 1952, and he was hired as a psychology professor in Clermont-Ferrand in 1960.[12] All his early works from the 1950s are involved in this area of inquiry: he writes a long preface to Ludwig Binswanger's Dream and Existence (which he and Jacqueline Verdeaux translate); he publishes Mental Illness and Personality (a good portion of which is devoted to Binswanger) and also two contributions to collections of essays, one on "Psychology from 1850 to 1950" and the other on "Scientific Research and Psychology." In these two texts, he reproaches psychology for having forgotten "the negativity of man" and "the contradictions that man encounters in his practices."[13] Psychology will have no future, he writes, if it does not "take these contradictions seriously."[14] Given that psychology has forgotten its "infernal vocation," he concludes, the only way it can save itself is "by a return to Hell."[15]

One rediscovers this idea of an essential human "contradiction" at the heart of Madness and Civilization. There he refers to a "tragic structure," and in another text from the same period to a "tragic split." The very fact that psychology exists means for him that the presence of this tragic dimension has been forgotten.[16]

⊁ Foucault's friends, his fellow students at the École normale supérieure in the late 1940s and early 1950s, were aware of his psychological vulnerability and fragility. That fragility made him seem odd, enigmatic, and sometimes unbearable. His closeness to Louis Althusser, in fact, has as much to do with their shared sufferings as with their intellectual affinities. Althusser, in his posthumous autobiography, described the rapport that grew up between them as they each struggled to maintain their mental equilibrium. Foucault, Althusser says, would be able to heal himself, to rediscover the sun, whereas Althusser would sink deeper into the night of unreason, slowly becoming a "missing person."[17]

The friendship between the two men was never broken off, despite their divergent political evolutions. For example, Althusser would write about Foucault in a 1966 letter to his friend Franca Madonia: "We are a pair of taciturn brothers who communicate by way of our different silences, includ-ing the silences of our afflictions." He goes on to add, "While I was in the hospital, he wrote me a letter that moved me to tears."[18]

If Foucault was able to recover from his psychological problems, it is because he chose flight. In the first part of this book we saw that the impulse to find an "elsewhere" is, for gay people, linked to a kind of malaise, to an uncomfortableness in their very being. The impulse to flee is a way of escap-ing that feeling. Geographic distance, the search for different locations, the effort to inscribe oneself in a new space, are all conditions for reconstructing oneself. Foucault had felt for a long time a desire to leave France, to go into exile. (He uses that word in many of his letters.) He therefore accepted an offer that came from Georges Dumézil in 1954 to take up the functions of lecturer in French and director of the Maison de France in Upsala.[19]

The idea of "exile" returns over and over again in Foucault's letters to Jean Barraqué. In a letter written a month after his arrival in Sweden, for example, Foucault describes all the difficulties associated with his exile, but also the feeling of being able to recognize himself in this in-between sort of existence:

> Frightful pleasures of which I had no inkling rise up in me: those of exile, of a foreign land, of incomprehensible languages, the pleasure of being unnecessary, in excess, something that it is easy to ignore; of being there, among them, a massive presence, but having no attach-ment to them, feeling their glances pass over the surface, like looking through a window at night; and finally, only being held down by the weight of two suitcases. . . . All of this gives me the impression of recognition one sometimes has on rediscovering in the daylight some impression had during the night, in a forgotten dream. In fact that is what my existence and its truth were. They finally rise to the surface of my life with a perfection of which I had despaired.[20]

In another letter: "If you only knew the well-being of mornings in exile, when one is ready to set out into one's day taking the steps of a foreigner up to the solitary peaks. You can see necessity being revealed, like a face on the wet surface of a wall."[21] In yet another: "I'm not blue; it's a different kind of feeling: a very sweet bitterness of which I have always dreamed: not to be there, to be one too many and also absent, running towards a definitively uncertain resting place, being for the people here only the useless trans-parency of a foreigner, and for the people there nothing more than an empty space slowly being filled in; it's marvelous. One feels the cutting edge of life being honed, but for the sacrifice of which existence?"[22] In a letter from August 1955, he tells Barraqué of lunching with the four Frenchmen at the university there, and remarks, "In all of them one finds a parcel of night in which they seal up the secret of their exile. No one asks any questions. No one speaks of Paris, from where we all come. We were immediately complicit in our reservedness, like a bunch of stunned fellows, disheveled, recovering themselves after having all managed to escape over the same wall." Nonetheless, Foucault mentions in the same letter that one of the four men knows "everyone in the Arcadie group."[23] All these descriptions of exile were written in the early days or weeks of his stay in Sweden. The tone of his later letters, especially those to Georges Dumézil, will show him in better spirits.

❧ Foucault only returned to France in 1960, when he took up a teaching post in Clermont-Ferrand, having spent three years in Sweden, a year in Warsaw, and another in Hamburg.

3

The Impulse to Escape

There was another way to fight the repressive violence of normalcy, to effect the necessary work on oneself to escape from it. One could interrogate—through historical inquiry and theoretical reflection—the processes that led to certain divisions, to "social segregation," to the "exclusion" of people with "anomalies," "deviancies," or "sufferings."[1] One could write the history of the dividing lines between the normal and the pathological, thereby calling into question those sciences (most notably psychiatry) that were only able to come into existence after those lines were instituted, those sciences that ratified the lines, making them seem natural. *Madness and Civilization* sets the pattern for this kind of exploration of the past, an exploration undertaken in order to understand and to refuse the present. It is a theoretical act grounded in a personal experience.

Everyone who was present as this enormous book was conceived and then took shape seemed aware of the fact that an entire existence was at stake. Louis Althusser, for example, never separated Foucault's own "madness" from the work that he undertook. In 1962, when Althusser began reading *Madness and Civilization*, he expressed great enthusiasm for a book he called "stupefying, astonishing, the work of a genius, a bit of a mess, but still a beacon with new insights and illuminations, with elements of night and flashes of dawn, a twilight book, like Nietzsche, yet as luminous as an equation."[2]

Throughout Althusser's correspondence with Madonia, one can sense his fascination, even his obsession, with Foucault's book. Clearly these "elements of night" and the accompanying flashes of light resonated with that deepest part of himself that was threatened with madness. Foucault, he says, brings "intimate matters" up to the surface of theoretical reflection, matters in which Althusser doubtless rediscovered his own experience.[3]

Certain of the reflections to which Althusser was inspired by Foucault's book are deeply moving, for instance the page in which he recalls all the unlucky people he has known who have disappeared into silence:

> I am thinking about that entire part of life that makes large numbers of men fall silent. I have frequented, known, or seen many of them. They can be seen when you are in an institution. . . . I had often thought of this, and Foucault's book on madness brought it back to mind. There are those who speak, who move about, use language, enjoy life. These are the ones who are heard and seen, who are taken into account, whose actions matter. . . . This is healthy humanity. But then there are those one never hears speak because they cannot speak. Yet they are alive, or at least they are surviving. Their life is exactly that: waiting for death. Often these people *knew* that they were approaching the edge, that they were about to fall over it. They *saw themselves fall*. Now they are on the other side, where they cannot even kill themselves.[4]

Althusser, in both his autobiography and his correspondence, continually invites us to read *Madness and Civilization* as part of a therapeutic cure by which someone who might have fallen over the edge, maybe even someone who saw himself falling over the edge, who managed to escape from this condition.

Foucault's book is a reflexive work, a turning back on the self, at the same time as it is a turning toward the light. It is a "journey to the end of the night" at the end of which the author is able to rediscover the "sun." It is an "archeology of silence," performed in order to recuperate the possibility of "speech."[5] In the process the book also offers an analysis of those institutions that organize the social topography of daylight and of shadow, a genealogy of the knowledges that have been granted the power to regulate the relations of individuals to the norm, to acts of exclusion, and to a history of relegations.

We see then why Foucault's books are often filled with a tension rarely found in works of history or philosophy: his books are not only about theoretical questions, but also about questions of life and death, of freedom and suffering.

⊁ Gilles Deleuze says something similar (using words that sound like Gide speaking of Dostoevsky) when he speaks of the "vital stammering" of the writer, of the "delicacy of health" and the "frailty of constitution" of the thinker: "It is strange how great thinkers have a fragile personal life, an uncertain health, at the same time as they carry life to the state of absolute power or of 'Great Health.' "⁶ The writer and the philosopher come face-to-face with the forces with which they intersect and of which they are made up. Further, in order for thought to take place, a "crisis" is necessary. In another interview, Deleuze states while speaking about Foucault: "Once you start thinking, you're bound to enter a line of thought where life and death, reason and madness, are at stake, and the line draws you on. You can think only on this witches' line, assuming you're not bound to lose, not bound to end up mad or dead. That's something that always fascinated Foucault, the switching, the constant juggling of what's close and distant in death and madness." A little later he adds, "The question of madness runs right through Foucault's work. Though of course he criticized *Madness and Civilization* for still giving too much weight to an 'experience of madness.' Rather than phenomenology, he preferred epistemology, in which madness is taken up by varying kinds of 'knowledge' from one historical formation to another. Foucault always used history like this. He saw it as a way of avoiding madness."⁷

Foucault often insisted on the ways in which his work was anchored in his biography, and he never hid the important value for him of everything he had to say about the "modes of *implication of the subject* in discourses."⁸ How could things have been otherwise? In a 1981 interview, he states clearly that "every time I have tried to do a piece of theoretical work it has been on the basis of elements of my own experience: always in connection with processes I saw unfolding around me. It was always because I thought I identified cracks, silent tremors, and dysfunctions in things I saw, institutions I was dealing with, or my relations with others, that I set out to do a piece of work—a kind of autobiographical fragment."⁹

A year later, he says almost the same thing: "Each of my works is part of my own biography. For one or another reason, I had the occasion to feel and live those things." He gives the example of *Madness and Civilization* and tells how he had worked in a psychiatric hospital (Sainte-Anne) in the 1950s. "I was free to move from the patients to the attendants, for I had no precise role. It was the time of the blooming of neurosurgery, the beginning of psychopharmacology, the reign of the traditional institution. At first I accepted things as necessary, but then after three months (I am slow-minded!), I asked, 'What is the necessity of these things?' After three years I left the job and went to Sweden in great personal discomfort and started to write a history of these practices."¹⁰

Foucault is here describing a professional relation to the institution. The personal discomfort he mentions is still situated in an exterior register. But in other interviews he brings out a more intimate link. In 1981, for instance, he comments, "It has already been important to me that each of my books be in some way an autobiographical fragment. My books and my personal problems with madness, prisons, sexuality are one."[11]

The objection could always be raised that not all of Foucault's books fit this description. Neither The Order of Things nor The Archeology of Knowledge, for example, seem to fall into this category. It is true, in fact, that Foucault published two kinds of books: those concerned with the history of forms of knowledge and those concerned with the history of institutions. This division is, of course, not absolute, for the books that deal with institutions also investigate the systems of thought that are invested in the institutions. All of Foucault's work can ultimately be thought of as a critique of the human sciences, where we understand the word "critique" in two different ways. The first is the Kantian meaning—an analysis of the historical conditions behind the emergence of certain discursive domains. (Think of the discussion in The Order of Things of general grammar or political economy.) The second involves the political sense of a calling into question of the scientific and normative pretensions of these discursive domains. (Psychiatry is dealt with in this way in Madness and Civilization, and psychoanalysis in The History of Sexuality.) It nonetheless remains difficult to find a personal, biographical reference point for The Order of Things. The book is certainly historically situated, as is any philosophical work. The questions Foucault asks in it concern the transformations in the human sciences in the period after the war, when those sciences were abandoning the notion of "man" and becoming interested in "systems" instead (with Jakobson, Lacan, and Lévi-Strauss each representing one "counter-science").[12] Clearly it is "structuralism" that is being examined, or the evolutions that are being experienced in philosophical and scientific thought. But where are the "personal problems" that we saw referred to in the interviews just cited?

But here is another question we might ask: did Foucault like The Order of Things? Did he like The Archeology of Knowledge? What place do these two books have in his body of work? He would say in 1978 that they were very "technical" works, even "formal exercises." It seems, in fact, that he rapidly ceased to be interested in them, especially after May 1968 had reawakened in him the emotional cord that had vibrated in Madness and Civilization—one that, in addition, made him resonate with the political and cultural movements present in his society. So it is hardly surprising to find that he would go so far as to assert that neither *The Order of Things* nor *The Archeology of Knowledge* were "truly mine." The problems he took up in them, he would say, are not the ones that interested him the most. This is why he was able to oppose these texts, ones he considered "marginal" within his whole work, to the texts that his real "passion . . . runs through," texts that dealt with problems that "really fascinated" him.[13]

One can, of course, take an alternate point of view and consider that all books have their necessary place within the economy of a body of research, within the trajectory of a given body of work. They have at least a small role to play. Even the works that Foucault rejects or thinks of as marginal to his output surely represent moments he had to pass through in order to organize his ways of thinking, in order to deepen this or that aspect of a committed body of work. (So one could say that *The Archeology of Knowledge* grows out of *The Order of Things* in the same way that *The Order of Things* grows out of *Madness and Civilization* and *The Birth of the Clinic*.) They may have responded to problems posed by the theoretical or philosophical context in which Foucault found himself (the context, for example, of the new kinds of questioning opened up by structuralist sciences in the 1960s). In short, we are not required to agree with him in his choice as to which are his "real" books. Gilles Deleuze put it very well when he said, "You have to take the work as a whole. . . . Otherwise you just won't understand it at all."[14]

Still, Foucault did himself sift through his works and separate out those that corresponded to his "real" centers of interest, those that, as he said, dealt with "limit experiences"—"madness, death, sexuality, crime are more intense subjects."[15] There can be no doubt that Foucault always felt a particular sentimental and intellectual attachment to *Madness and Civilization*, which he thought of as in some ways *his* book—a truly innovative book, the one into which he had poured the most of himself, and the one from which all his future research would grow.[16]

When, in the mid-1970s, he took up again his work on the *lettres de cachet* from the Bastille, he wrote a preface for the collection of documents he was intending to publish.[17] It is a magnificent text, entitled "Lives of Infamous Men." In it, he speaks of the emotion ("one of these impressions that are called 'physical'") that he felt upon reading these "'bits of news,' suddenly emerging from two and a half centuries of silence." He says that they "stirred more fibers within me than what is ordinarily called 'literature.'" Then he adds: "A long time ago I made use of documents like these for a book. If I did so back then, it was doubtless because of the resonance I still experience today when I happen to encounter these lowly lives reduced to ashes in the few sentences that struck them down."[18]

This is perhaps the text in which Foucault shows us most clearly, most decisively, the impulse, the theoretical passion, that animates the books that he considers to be truly his. His whole philosophy of history, his whole way of thinking about the individual, and his whole political will surely find themselves encapsulated in these several sentences. In them, he inscribes at the very heart of life, at the very heart of the person, the conflictual arena in which that person's destiny, that person's freedom, is at stake. He is speaking about the struggle that takes place as an individual faces the forces of power: "Is it not one of the fundamental traits of our society, after all, that destiny takes the form of a relation with power, of a struggle with or against it? Indeed, the most intense point of a life, the point where its energy is concentrated, is where it comes up against power, struggles with it, attempts to use its forces and to evade its traps" (161–62).

❧ If Foucault "put his life into his thought," as Gilles Deleuze so aptly said, he never did so as truly, as manifestly, and with such intensity as in the book written between "night" and "daylight." In 1960, when he had just finished writing it, he called it *Madness and Unreason* (*Folie et déraison*). We now know it as *Madness and Civilization* (*Histoire de la folie*).[19]

I do not mean to say that Foucault simply recounts his life in this book, or in any other. There is no "autobiographical confession" to be found here. Foucault always insisted that even if a theoretical work is born out of personal experience, still, the result cannot be a "transposition into knowledge" of that experience. "One's relation to experience must, in the book, allow for a transformation that is not simply my own as a writing subject. That transformation must truly have a value for others as well."[20]

All of this suggests that theoretical work has its point of departure in the personal malaise one experiences vis-à-vis this or that "institution." The malaise is then transformed into a historical problem. Foucault says as much quite clearly in a lecture given to the Société française de philosophie in 1978, in which he defines critical thought as a gesture of "voluntary inservitude" or "reflective indocility."[21] These remarks follow upon an analysis of the development and multiplication of "arts of governing" in the sixteenth century (the art of pedagogy, the art of politics, of economics, and so on), and "of all the institutions of government, in the broad sense that the word government had at this time" (384). He insists on the fact that this process was always accompanied by another that rose up simultaneously in order to oppose it. Its opposition was not some directly contrary affirmation, a simple face-to-face declaration that "we do not want to be governed." Rather it was a kind of perpetual restlessness, an unending calling into question: "How not to be governed *like that*, by that, in the name of these principles, in view of such objectives and by the means of such methods, not like that, not for that, not by them?" (384).

The "art of not being governed" or, as Foucault puts it, the "art of not being governed like that," thus finds itself in opposition to the "arts of governing." This is what Foucault calls a "critical attitude":

> And if governmentalization is really this movement concerned with subjugating [*assujetir*] individuals in the very reality of a social practice by mechanisms of power that appeal to a truth, I will say that critique is the movement through which the subject gives itself the right to question truth concerning its power effects and to question power about its discourses of truth. Critique will be the art of voluntary inservitude, of reflective indocility. The essential function of critique would be that of desubjectification [*désassujettissement*] in the game of what one could call, in a word, the politics of truth.[22]

This explains why Foucault insists on the fact that critique is not to be found primarily in the content of this or that doctrine. It is not a theory. Critique, for Foucault, is above all an "attitude," or, as he will put it a few years later, an *ethos*.[23]

Foucault's entire theoretical project was surely inspired by this critical will, by this "intransigence" that was so firmly rooted in his life and in his body.[24] This same inspiration must also be what allows so many readers to find themselves, in Gilles Deleuze's words, reading "intensely" and entering into "resonance" with Foucault's books.[25] Just as reading Nietzsche often had an overwhelming effect upon his readers, among whom Gide and Foucault hold a prominent place, so coming into contact with Foucault's thought has often been felt as a deeply personal and self-transformative experience.[26]

⋈ The tension present throughout Foucault's work is thus fundamentally tied to the will, or better, to the necessity to free oneself. It is tied to the "impulse to escape [*force de fuir*]" that Foucault describes in his 1973 article on the painter Rebeyrolle.[27] Traveling through history is the means by which one comes to understand the systems of thought that regulate institutions, by which one undoes the sense of self-evident normalcy that inhabits them, by which one breaks the bars that are installed in people's minds by disciplinary technologies.

At the beginning of the text on Rebeyrolle (who paints prisons and the animals that escape from them), Foucault writes: "Prison—as Jackson has testified—is today a political space. That is to say, it is a space in which impulses [*forces*] are born and reveal themselves, a place in which history takes shape and out of which time can arise" (*Dits*, 2:401). In this context perhaps prison should be understood as a metaphor that designates the entire set of principles of subjugation/subjectification. We know, in fact, that two years later, in *Discipline and Punish*, Foucault would demonstrate how the "prison" as an institution appears within the historical context of a huge transformation in the modalities by which power is exercised, in the passage from the public display of sovereignty to the inscription of discipline onto individual bodies, in the passage from the commotion around displays of torture to the subjugated soul—a soul that is both the effect and instrument of this process of incorporation.[28]

We are, then, certainly justified in imagining that it is, in general terms, this interior prison of the soul as it is produced by disciplinary technologies that is being described as the place in which "impulses" toward escape come to manifest themselves. The animals painted by Rebeyrolle are examples of this. Their movements to escape create history, and cause time to happen. A politics is born from these passages, these displacements, these divergences.

Somewhat later Foucault will speak of the "impatience for liberty" as a way of naming the feeling, the transformational energy thanks to which someone undertakes to break out of the web of subjugating constraints and impediments. Slow work in the archives, meticulous work on documents, the genealogical work that seeks out those historic "events" that have constructed us and from which we must disengage ourselves—these are only the means, the method by which we give shape and reality to that "impatience," by which we transform it from a simple feeling of refusal or rejection into a productive and creative act.[29]

4

Homosexuality and Unreason

Would it be possible to read Foucault's *Madness and Civilization* as a history of homosexuality that dared not speak its name? Might we imagine that this book took the place of a work on homosexuality at a moment when it was impossible to choose that subject for a dissertation in the French university system? Is "madness" a metaphor or a "code" meant to express an underground meaning, one hidden by the text of the book yet containing its secret and authentic truth?

Such questions are hard to avoid and perhaps even harder to respond to. For to respond to them would be to interpret Foucault's texts in terms of a problematics of "truth," whereas those texts set out to thwart any such project. It would be to read Foucault's texts in a confessional mode, a practice they intended to challenge. It would be to read them in terms of a "psychological interpretation," something Foucault detested.[1]

It would be, above all, to limit the scope of our interpretation. For when, in *Madness and Civilization*, Foucault seeks to reconstruct the kinds of experience that shaped the appearance of madness in this or that historical moment, or when, in *La Volonté de savoir*, he sets out his "analytics of power," he is making an effort to allow his specific analyses to have as wide a field of applications as possible, to allow them to be useful in the widest range of disciplines. At the very least they should be able to serve as a heuristic grid for other investigations. To tie them down to a single meaning, even a hidden one, would be to impoverish their theoretical power, perhaps even to negate their project.

We also know that Foucault was quite literally obsessed by the theoretical and historical question of madness and of "mental illness." Whatever links there might have been for Foucault between his fascination for madness and his painful experience of homosexuality, it simply is the case that he did set out to study the ways in which the social exclusion of the "insane" came into being, the ways in which the "mentally incompetent" were reduced to "silence." It was in the "lightning flashes" of Artaud, Nerval, Nietzsche, or Hölderlin, in the "transfigurations" of Goya, in all those works that gave voice to the "cries" of madness, that Foucault sought, throughout his work in the 1950s, to ground the possibility of "total contestation" and of a counterattack against psychiatric discourse.[2] He celebrated the idea of the "mad philosopher,"[3] just as he never ceased, throughout the 1960s, to wonder about the links between madness and literature.[4] And when he speaks of the "fundamental experience" of humanity that must be recovered from the oblivion ushered in by the reign of psychology, he invites us to return to the fundamental dialogue between Reason and Madness (notably by way of literary and artistic experiences).[5]

Yet it is necessary to insist that when he speaks of "madness," Foucault speaks simultaneously of other exclusions, notably those related to sexuality. Further, his analysis of "madness" is presented as the first part—a central, but not a unique part—of a group of analyses yet to be written. In the preface to the 1961 edition of Madness and Civilization, Foucault announces that "it will also be necessary to tell the stories of other divisions," in particular, to "write the history—and not only in the terms of ethnology—of sexual interdictions: to speak of the constantly shifting, continually obstinate forms of repression within our own culture" (Dits, 1:161; my emphasis). He thus clearly indicates the necessity of writing a history of sexuality as an obligatory sequel to Madness and Civilization (Histoire de la folie), a continuation without which the earlier work could not be considered complete. The study of madness and the analysis of sexuality form, in Foucault's vision, two fragments of the same inquiry.[6]

For the project of Madness and Civilization, as it is given in the 1961 preface (which Foucault removed from the 1972 republication) was to inaugurate the vast future work of a "history of limits," of gestures that establish borders, "gestures that are obscure and necessarily forgotten once performed, whereby a culture refuses something that will come to function as its Outside."[7]

⊁ Doubtless it would be foolish, and not particularly useful, to try to determine which was the primary, founding interest of Foucault's research: sexuality or madness, madness or sexuality. In fact, it seems that Foucault's intellectual interests always revolved around the same objects—that basically, from the very outset, a set of theoretical problems had presented themselves to him, and he would return to them in all of his future work: madness, sexuality, the penal system, and therefore psychiatry, psychoanalysis, psychology, criminology, and so on.

The question of sexuality had already begun to surface in the introduction Foucault wrote to Ludwig Binswanger's *Le Rêve et l'existence* (*Dream and Existence*), published in 1954, at a time when Foucault was interested in lived experiences of madness viewed through the framework of "existential analysis," as it had been elaborated by Biswanger, a Swiss-German psychiatrist.[8] And during both semesters of the academic year 1956–57, while he was teaching at Uppsala University (that is to say, when he began working on *Madness and Civilization*), he gave a course called "The Conception of Love in French Literature from the Marquis de Sade to Jean Genet."[9] For a long time Foucault was fascinated by Sade's work and greatly admired Genet's writings.[10]

There is another example of Foucault's longstanding interest in the themes that he would turn to in his later books. In 1961, just after the publication of *Madness and Civilization*, the question came up of the republication of his 1954 book, *Mental Illness and Personality*. Foucault expressed some reluctance to Jean Lacroix, the series editor, about republishing what was, in his view, an outdated work. He suggested instead a new study that would have to do with "crime," "penal justice," and "criminology."[11] In the end, he agreed to the republication of the book, but he replaced the second part—too grounded in his Marxism of the early 1950s—with a summary of the theses developed in *Madness and Civilization*. The book would also henceforth be titled *Mental Illness and Psychology*.[12]

Later, in the 1970s, when he was working on *Discipline and Punish*, Foucault devoted a number of courses at the Collège de France to themes that prefigured his *History of Sexuality*, such as, "The Christian Technology of Government and of Individuals." During the same years, he became interested in the discourse of medicolegal expertise, and he combined his interest in psychiatry and in the penal system in the seminar that dealt with a case of parricide in the nineteenth century. That seminar resulted in the 1973 publication of *I, Pierre Rivière. . . .*[13] And in 1975, the year *Discipline and Punish* was published, Foucault's course at the Collège de France had as its subject "The Abnormals."[14]

We might even say that the topic of "abnormality," of the historical construction of the "abnormal" individual, was the central theme around which all Foucault's work was organized. It was part and parcel of the more general theme of the production of the individual and of individuality in Western society (and also of the question of the boundaries being instituted between "normal" and "abnormal" individuals). To put it another way, his guiding concern was with the production of "subjects" and "subjectivities" as subject to "norms" and as socially distributed through divisions and exclusions by those norms.[15]

In any case, from 1956, when Foucault began work on a history of madness in the Carolina Rediviva Library in Uppsala, through his final books in 1984, the question of sexuality (and of homosexuality) was part of his intellectual perspective. It is certainly one of the axes around which his research was structured, an omnipresent theoretical theme—even if sometimes only silently present. It sheds light on a good portion of his work. This is, however, not to suggest that Foucault's work should be understood retrospectively, as if his thought happened to reveal itself slowly over time as an intellectual project or a personal quest that would only fully realize itself in his final books. Instead, one could simply think that in the mid-1970s, when the political context not only authorized, but more importantly impelled him to do so, Foucault came to confront directly a theoretical object that had never been absent from his intellectual preoccupations and had indeed been a focal point from the beginning (as well as part of the biographical background).

⊮ Yet to establish the link between *Madness and Civilization* and *The History of Sexuality* (and therefore the history of homosexuality), would it not suffice to notice that the book from 1961 contains a chapter—central to its argument— on the concomitant invention, in the seventeenth century, of the "personages" of someone who is "mad" and of the "homosexual"? We should not forget that Foucault's dissertation originally had the title *Madness and Unreason (Folie et déraison)*.[16] Indeed, the entire historical demonstration of the work is established in the interrelation of the two notions, that is to say, in the articulation of "madness" with the "sins" linked to sexuality.

In the pages composed in 1962 for *Mental Illness and Psychology*, Foucault summarizes quite clearly the problem he intended to set forth. After having mentioned the Renaissance, a period during which madness was "allowed free rein, . . . formed part of the background and language of everyday life, . . . was for everyone an everyday experience that people sought more to celebrate than to control," he writes:

> About the middle of the seventeenth century, a sudden change took place: the world of madness was to become the world of exclusion. Throughout Europe, great internment houses were created with the intention of receiving not simply the mad, but a whole series of individuals who were highly different from one another, at least according to our criteria of perception—the poor and disabled, the elderly poor, beggars, the work-shy, those with venereal diseases, libertines of all kinds, people whom their families or the king wished to spare public punishment, spendthrift fathers, defrocked priests; in short, all those who, in relation to the order of reason, morality, and society, showed signs of "derangement." (*MIP*, 67; translation modified)

What links all these "deranged people" is that somehow they can be assigned to the category of the "unproductive." At this moment, Foucault is still deeply marked by the Marxism of the 1950s, and his analyses often refer to explanations of an economic order.[17] Internment plays a double role: to reduce unemployment, and to lower production costs by exploiting the labor power assembled in these "forced-labor shops" (*MC*, 54).

But the relation between internment and work is not "entirely defined by economic conditions." It is also the product of a "new sensibility," a "new morality": "A moral perception sustains and animates it" (58). If an entire population of "shiftless" and "useless" people is to be put to forced labor, a population unable "to participate in the production, circulation, or accumulation of wealth," it is also in order to exercise "moral control" (*MIP*, 68). Those who do not respect the "frontiers of the bourgeois order," the "limits" of its work-ethic and of social utility, will find themselves interned behind the walls of the Hôpital Général during the process *Madness and Civilization* designates as "The Great Confinement" (the title of the second chapter of that book).[18]

The mad and all the other outlaws confined with them belonged to a single category that Foucault designated "Unreason." (He often capitalized the word.) It grouped together all those who "no longer could or should belong to society" (*MIP*, 68). Three realms of experience blend into one in this "uniform universe of unreason." They concern either "sexuality in relation to family structure," "profanation in relation to new conceptions of the sacred," or "libertinage." These three realms "together with madness make up, within the space of internment, a homogenous world in which mental illness will take on the meaning that we recognize in it" (*HF*, 97). Its proximity to "vice" will give madness its new meaning: "Madness forged a relationship with moral and social guilt that it is still perhaps not ready to break" (*MIP*, 67). Consequently, "internment played not only a negative role of exclusion, but also a positive role of organization. . . . It brought together into a unified field kinds of people and values between which preceding cultures had perceived no resemblance" (*HF*, 96).

The entire argument of *Madness and Civilization* is contained in these few lines. Madness is not a natural reality that had been waiting around for that happy day in the middle of the nineteenth century, when psychiatry would come along, the fruit of a long history of scientific progress, to assign it its truth as "mental illness." Rather, it is only because madness was constructed as a pathological phenomenon at a given historical moment, only because it was excluded or "exteriorized" from society, that psychiatry was able to come into existence—once its object had been delimited by internment and its consequences.

For one hundred fifty years, people suffering from "venereal diseases," along with other "debauched" folk, would have been confined elbow to elbow with "crazed" people "within the space of the same enclosure." This cohabitation would have inscribed upon the personage of the "mad" person, a sign that would determine how the perception of madness would henceforth be organized (*HF*, 100). Far from being "archaic," such a relation was established only "at the threshold of the modern world." It was produced by "the Age of Reason":

> By inventing, in its imaginary moral geometry, the space of internment, the Age of Reason had stumbled upon both a fatherland and a place of redemption that could be shared both by sins of the flesh and by crimes against reason. Madness became the neighbor of sin. Perhaps it is here that the kinship between unreason and guilt, experienced by the insane person of our time as an unavoidable fate, discovered by doctors as a truth of nature, first takes shape. In this artificial space, cut from whole cloth right in the middle of the seventeenth century, obscure alliances were constructed that more than a hundred years of so-called "positivist" psychiatry have not been able to undo, alliances that in fact were only formed for the first time ever so recently, in the Age of Reason. (100)

But if madness was defined in the seventeenth century by its proximity with moral "vice" and sexual debauchery, by being a "neighbor of sin," inevitably the reverse is also true: areas of experience that were called "sinful" would henceforth be defined and perceived through their relation to madness. Because the "mad" persons were confined alongside those who were "guilty," they came to be thought of as essentially related to "guilt." And, in return, due to their topographical assimilation to those who were mad, the debauched, the libertines, those with venereal diseases were seen as lacking reason and prone to mental disorder.

Given that "homosexuals" figure among these "sinners" of the "flesh" who suffer banishment from the social realm, who have been relegated to mental "homes," it is easy to perceive that for Foucault the conceptualization of homosexuality that psychiatry will produce is in no way scientific. It too arises out of the "perception of unreason in the age of reason" and out of the movement of expulsion of which imprisonment is only a visible symptom. That movement itself arises more profoundly from the coming into being of a particular morality. Psychiatry and psychoanalysis, in their analyses of homosexuality, will be nothing more than the heirs of this "bourgeois morality" that came to prominence in the seventeenth century, the offspring of the moral and social exclusion of homosexuals.

⇥ In the chapter of Histoire de la folie titled "The Correctional World" Foucault can be said to propose a short history of homosexuality.[19] He tells how, in 1726, in Paris, a person was condemned to be burned alive at the Place de la Grève for the crime of sodomy. The execution took place the same day. "This was one of the last executions for sodomy in France," Foucault specifies, for "contemporary feeling was already sufficiently offended by the severity of the penalty that Voltaire would remember it, and refer to it when he wrote the article on 'Socratic Love' for the Dictionnaire philosophique." At that later moment, in the majority of cases, "the penalty, when it isn't banishment to the provinces, is internment at the Hôpital or in a house of detention" (101–2).

But if the penalties are much less severe at the beginning of the eighteenth century, if it is no longer a question of being burned alive, but of being banished or interned, this is because the social and cultural perception of homosexuality underwent a profound transformation during the seventeenth century: "The new indulgence towards sodomy finds its particular significance both in the moral condemnation and in the sanctions provided by scandal that begin to punish social and literary expressions of homosexuality" (102). Thus Foucault can write, "The period in which sodomites are being burned for the last time is also the period in which a lyrical expression of homosexuality, perfectly tolerated by Renaissance culture, is disappearing—as is erudite libertinage" (102). One therefore has the impression:

> that sodomy, formerly condemned under the same rubric as magic and heresy, in the context of religious profanation, is now only condemned for reasons of morality, alongside homosexuality. Homosexuality itself becomes the main focus of the condemnation—added on to sodomitical practices. And at the same time homosexual feelings and desire begin to provoke a new sense of outrage. Two different experiences, previously separate, become confused: the prohibitions on sodomy and the dubious loves of homosexuality [les équivoques amoureuses de l'homosexualité]. A single form of condemnation will now envelope both of them, and will draw an entirely new line of division in the world of feelings. A new moral ensemble is thus formed: it is no longer burdened with older forms of punishment; it has been equalized through internment; it already closely resembles modern forms of guilt. Homosexuality, to which the Renaissance had granted freedom of expression, will from now on pass into silence and cross into the realm of prohibition, heir to the age-old condemnations of a now desacrilized sodomy. (102–3; my emphasis)

Consequently, if "love had, throughout the trajectory of Platonic culture, been distributed across a hierarchy of sublimity which related it either to a blind corporeal madness or to a magnificent intoxication of the soul," in the modern era, "from the Age of Reason onward," a different choice will be offered: between "a love that is within reason" and "a love that is part of unreason." Homosexuality clearly falls into the latter category. Thus little by little, "it comes to occupy a place within the stratifications of madness. It becomes part of the unreason of the modern era, fixing at the heart of every sexuality an unavoidable choice through which our era incessantly reiterates its verdict" (103; my emphasis).

Bourgeois morality is thus not merely a work ethic, it is also a morality of the family, dictating henceforth what society should be and who does or does not fully belong to it: "Family structure works simultaneously as a social rule and as a norm of reason. . . . A new sensibility is substituted for the old forms of love in the western world: a sensibility born of and in the family, a sensibility that excludes as part of unreason anything that fails to conform to its order or its interests" (104–5). Further, "we see in this historical moment the confiscation of sexual ethics by family morality . . ." (100). Society is henceforth ruled by "the great bourgeois, and soon republican, idea that virtue too is an affair of state," and that "decrees can be published to make it flourish."[20]

"New kinds of people," "new personages" thus appear, thanks to a twofold process: on the one hand, the movement to exclude, to relegate an entire "multicolored population" to the far side of a frontier symbolized by the walls of an asylum, with the assistance, on the other hand, of the process of integrating all these disparate individuals under the enormous umbrella of "unreason." Among these disparate individuals, the characteristics of one group have a contaminating effect on the definition of other groups. The "mad" person, by being marked by "guilt," and the "homosexual," by coming to be considered "insane," become hitherto unknown human types:

> From the seventeenth century onward unreason is no longer the world's obsession. Further, it ceases to be the natural dimension in which reason exercises itself. It takes on the appearance of a human fact, of a spontaneously produced variation in the topography of social species. What was formerly an unavoidable peril for humankind's objects and language, its reason and its territory, now takes on the form of a certain kind of person. Or of certain kinds of persons: the people of unreason whom society recognizes and quarantines: the debauched, the spendthrift, the homosexual, the magician, the person with suicidal tendencies, the libertine. Unreason comes to be measured in relation to a certain divergence from the social norm. . . . From the seventeenth century on, an unreasonable person is a concrete type, drawn from a social world, judged and condemned by the society to which that person belongs. (HF, 117–18)

Thus do the "abnormals" make their appearance: those defined by the norms that reject them. The social personage of the homosexual is born. Psychiatry will have this personage in its clutches once internment has "circumscribed the area of a *certain objectification*" by delimiting "a region *already colored by the negative values of exile*" (119; my emphasis).

It is at this point, where madness and sexuality join up within the perception of unreason, that Foucault launches into an attack on psychoanalysis:

In the light of its own naiveté, psychoanalysis was able to see that all madness is rooted in some kind of troubled sexuality; but this makes sense only to the extent that our culture, in a demonstration of the principles of its Enlightenment, places sexuality on the border between reason and unreason. Sexuality has in every period, and probably in every culture, functioned within a system of constraints; but it is only in our culture, and at a relatively recent date, that it has been divided so rigorously between *reason* and *unreason*, and thence reductively transformed into a distinction between *sickness* and *health*, and between *normal* and *abnormal*. (103; my emphasis)

Madness and Civilization thus proposes a radical historicization not only of madness or "mental illness," but also of homosexuality. The personage of the homosexual is not a fixed figure that can be found in any century or any society. Just as madness is perceived and thus produced differently in each age, so homosexuality will not have the same reality in Plato's Greece and in the Europe of the Age of Reason. What psychiatry will call homosexuality is the specific creation of the Age of Reason.

Thus a new species has appeared during the unfolding of the Great Confinement, as a result of the new morality and the various norms that confinement set in place: it is the homosexual, a new kind of being formed in the social and moral spaces of the Age of Reason, shaped by its logic of exclusion. The medical gaze, the psychiatric gaze, and finally the gaze of psychoanalysis will all come to rest on this new species.

And so, just as Foucault says that "psychology only became possible in our world when madness had been mastered" (*MIP*, 87), we could say, following the implications of *Madness and Civilization*, that psychiatry and psychoanalysis only became possible when homosexuality had been banished and excluded from the realm of reason and had been perceived as a social pathology—which would lead, two centuries later, to its perception as a mental pathology or a perversion of desire or of the sexual instinct. For it is clearly as much about homosexuality as about madness that Foucault is speaking when he asks, "Is it not centrally important for our culture that *unreason* could become an object for knowledge only to the extent that it had already been the object of an excommunication?" (*HF*, 119).

5

The Birth of Perversion

La Volonté de savoir (The Will to Knowledge) was published in 1976 as a general introduction to the larger project of a History of Sexuality.[1] Foucault indicated that five volumes would follow.[2] Yet he quickly found himself revising his project. None of the announced volumes would appear, and this programmatic introduction would have to wait eight years for a sequel. For, while he had indicated his intention to study "a good three centuries" in this project (*HS1*, 72), that is, to go back as far as the seventeenth century and to the thematization of the "techniques of the self" established during the Counter Reformation, Foucault found himself drawn by his researches farther and farther back into the long history of Christian discourse, right back to the earliest days of Christianity. He thus began working on a book entitled *Les Aveux de la chair* [*The Confessions of the Flesh*]. The logic of his thinking then led him to become interested in what had taken place before the imposition of Christian morality. He turned to the doctrines of pagan antiquity and thus came to write *The Use of Pleasure* and *The Care of the Self*, dedicated to "practices of the self" as they are expounded in Greek and Roman thought. These latter two volumes were published a few days before his death in June 1984.[3]

La Volonté de savoir is clearly a book linked to events current at the time of its writing. Foucault says as much in his conversations with Paul Rabinow and Hubert Dreyfus in 1983: "My current work is tied to our present moment [actualité] and to my personal experience, just as in the case of the prison, the clinic, etc. Of course it is not the same kind of experience. . . . The book on sexuality is linked . . . with the fact that you could see, in the liberation movements of the 1970s, first of all, people who were looking for a theoretical justification in psychoanalysis or in some theory of desire. Secondly, they were also looking, in a more or less explicit manner, for a new ethics."[4]

There is no question that the strategic intention of La Volonté de savoir—and thus of the whole project of the *History of Sexuality* as Foucault conceived of it when he set to work on it—is deeply embedded in the theoretical and political space defined by the irruption in the 1970s of "sexual liberation" movements—and also by the inflation of psychoanalytic discourse within French intellectual life at that time. To put it concisely, Foucault's political target was Freudo-Marxism, and the works of Herbert Marcuse and Wilhelm Reich, who had become the major theoretical references of the liberation movements. His theoretical target was psychoanalysis.

In just a few years after 1968, in the wake of the huge success of Marcuse's books *Eros and Civilization* and *One-Dimensional Man*, Reich's writings (which had already enjoyed a certain vogue in the 1930s) were translated into French and became the bibles of subversion of the far Left: *The Sexual Revolution, The Invasion of Compulsory Sex-Morality*, and *The Mass Psychology of Fascism*.[5] Beyond Freudo-Marxism and theories of the liberation of "desire," Foucault wanted to call psychoanalysis itself, the theoretical ground of the politico-sexual discourses he wanted to contest, radically into question. Further, he wanted to pursue the project of critical reflection on the human sciences that he had begun in *Madness and Civilization*.

From the first pages of his book Foucault places himself in direct opposition to the theoretical schemas of Freudo-Marxism. In those schemas, bourgeois society represses sexuality in order to channel sexual energies (the libido) into labor power. According to such a historical perspective, it would be sufficient to outsmart the processes of "repression," to transgress taboos, to multiply sexual discourses, in order to liberate people from their shackles and to shake the capitalist order to its roots. Sexual liberation would thus be a political gesture subversive of the entire social order. For Foucault, by contrast, modern Western society, far from imposing silence on sexuality, encouraged constant talk about it. This encouragement could be seen in the very existence of a group of specialists—psychoanalysts—who were paid to listen to people talk to them about their dreams, their secrets, their drives. Of course, the institution of psychoanalysis represents only one of the aspects of the demand that one speak. Yet it is around this particular institution that a certain double-bind is most clearly articulated: the order that you speak of yourself and your sexuality—more particularly of your sexuality as the locus of truth about yourself—while letting it be believed that it is forbidden to speak of any such thing, and that to express yourself you will have to work to overcome the forces of "repression" (both individual and social).

In this book from 1976, then, Foucault tells us that the social incitement to speech dates back to the Counter Reformation. The governing principle of Christian pastoral work as it was established at that time was that "everything had to be told" to one's spiritual director—everything one had done, of course, but also everything one had thought, felt, dreamed, and so on: "A twofold evolution tended to make the flesh into the root of all evil, shifting the most important moment of transgression from the act itself to the stirrings—so difficult to perceive and formulate—of desire" (*HSI*, 19–20). This was perhaps the moment when a particular "injunction, so peculiar to the West, was laid down for the first time, in the form of a general constraint" (20). It was not "the obligation to admit to violations of the laws of sex, as required by traditional penance," but "the nearly infinite task of telling—telling oneself and another, as often as possible, everything that might concern the interplay of innumerable pleasures, sensations, and thoughts which, throughout the body and soul, had some affinity with sex." If this "scheme for transforming sex into discourse had been devised long before in an ascetic and monastic setting," the seventeenth century "made it into a rule for everyone" (20).

For Foucault, then, the task is to understand both why and how—through what historical mechanisms—such an internal transformation in Christian pastoral work was "diffused," as he puts it, throughout society. Indeed, this confessional "technique" could have "remained tied to the destiny of Christian spirituality or to the sphere of individual pleasures if it had not been supported and relayed by other mechanisms. In the first place, by a 'public interest.'" It is not a question of "a collective curiosity or sensibility; not a new mentality," but rather a question of "power mechanisms to whose functioning the sexual discourse became essential" (23; translation modified).

Throughout his book, Foucault works to show precisely which power mechanisms made both this discursive hold on "sex" and the production of what would from then on be called "sexuality" so necessary, so "essential." In the final section of the book he takes on this question directly. He means to show how a shift in forms of power took place: from a form based on exercising power over the life or death of an individual to a form based on managing life and administering populations.[6] He writes, for example:

> The old power of death that symbolized sovereign power was now carefully supplanted by the administration of bodies and the calculated management of life. During the classical period, there was a rapid

development of various disciplines—universities, secondary schools, barracks, workshops; there was also the emergence, in the field of political practices and economic observation, of the problems of birth-rate, longevity, public health, housing, and migration. Hence there was an explosion of numerous and diverse techniques for achieving the subjectivation of bodies and the control of populations. (139–40; translation modified)

One pole of this historical transformation "centered on the body as a machine." Foucault here again sets out the analyses of Discipline and Punish, which had appeared a year earlier, and describes an "anatomo-politics" consisting of procedures of power that in this later book he designates "disciplines": training bodies, optimizing their capacities, extorting their strength, rendering them simultaneously more docile and more useful, and so on (139). The other pole was centered on the "species body," "imbued with the mechanics of life and serving as the basis of the biological processes: propagation, births and mortality, the level of health, life expectancy and longevity . . ." In this instance we see the setting up of a system of "regulatory controls," defined by Foucault as "a bio-politics of the population" (139).

Sex becomes a key issue in the exercise of power precisely because it is situated at the pivot point of "anatomo-politics" and "bio-politics," of body training and population management: "at the juncture of the 'body' and the 'population,' sex became a crucial target of a power organized around the management of life rather than the menace of death" (147). Sex is "a means of access both to the life of the body and the life of the species. Disciplines were molded in response to it; regulations were written with it in mind" (146; translation modified).

⇥ Foucault's proposition is to write the history of sexuality in terms of sexuality's "production," its incitation, and no longer in terms of repression and prohibition. This proposition is best understood in terms of his analysis of the transformations Western society passed through from the seventeenth to the nineteenth centuries, from "a symbolics of blood to an analytics of sexuality" (148; Foucault's emphasis). He does not, of course, deny that certain forms of sexuality are repressed. But he asserts that notions of repression and prohibition will not be useful for thinking about these phenomena within a historical frame. For to speak of repression is to imagine that whatever reality is repressed—be it this or that sexuality, or sexuality in general—would have preexisted whatever discourse seized on it in order to pick away at it or to prohibit it. The "permanent examination" of "peripheral" sexualities, the "infinitesimal surveillances" to which they are subjected (145), cannot be dissociated from the production and multiplication of "perversions," from the creation of categories for them. Nineteenth-century psychiatry contains a veritable "discursive explosion" (38) that produces this *Scientia sexualis*, this science of sex, whose gaze and functioning depend on the demand that people be induced to speak (to tell their symptoms, to recount their memories, to make free associations), and also on the subsequent "interpretation." For if a subject is required to make these confessions, it is because the "truth" they express cannot be known by the subject. Only the person who is granted the expertise to decipher "the truth of this obscure truth" can do that. It is the listener who is "the master of truth," who holds the "hermeneutic" function (65–67).

Thus "sexuality" does not preexist this science of sex. It is produced by it. It is nothing but its "correlative": "For one hundred and fifty years a complicated apparatus [*dispositif*] has been in place for producing true discourses on sex: an apparatus joining two different historical moments in that it connects the ancient injunction of confession to clinical listening methods. Thanks to the workings of this apparatus, it has been possible for something called 'sexuality' to seem to be the truth of sex and its pleasures" (68; translation modified).

It is in the very process of attempting to control that psychiatric discourse has divided, subdivided, and resubdivided "perversions," setting up elaborate taxonomies, giving "strange baptismal names" to those who fall outside the "norm": exhibitionists, fetishists, zoophiles and zooerasts, auto-monosexualists, mixoscopophiles, gynecomasts, presbyophiles, sexoesthetic inverts, dyspareunist women, and so on. This explains why, after providing a sample of these "fine names for heresies," Foucault comments: "The machinery of power that set out in pursuit of this odd lot would intend to do away with it only as it also provided it with an analytical reality that was visible and permanent: it was implanted in bodies, slipped into modes of conduct, made into a principle of classification and intelligibility, established as a *raison d'être* and as the natural order of disorder." Then Foucault asks: "Was it a question of excluding these thousand aberrant sexualities? Hardly. Rather, it was a question of their specification, the regional solidification of each of them. It was a matter, through dissemination, of scattering them throughout reality and incorporating them into specific individuals" (43–44; translation modified).

The power of control and surveillance thus operated by "implantation," by the "incorporation of perversions" and by the "new specification of individuals." The hunt, the pursuit of "heretical sexualities" on which nineteenth-century medicine embarked consisted of acts of naming and of placing individuals in the new species defined by these nominations. But it also consisted of making these new categories part of reality, of giving existence to an entirely new garden of species.

And so the "homosexual" would be born.

» Indeed, among the many new species invented by psychiatric medicine in the nineteenth century, Foucault mentions one in particular that will have an important future. What I cite here again is, of course, one of the best-known passages in *La Volonté de savoir*:

> The sodomy of the old civil and canonical codes was a category of forbidden acts; their author was nothing more than the juridical subject of them. The nineteenth-century homosexual became a personage: a past, a case history and a childhood, a character-type, a form of life; also a morphology, with an indiscreet anatomy and possibly a mysterious physiology. Nothing of that person's total being escapes from sexuality. Everywhere it is present: it underlies every action because it is its insidious and indefinitely active principle, shamelessly inscribed on the face and the body because it is a secret that always gives itself away. It is consubstantial with the person, less as a habitual sin than as a singular nature. We must not forget that the psychological, psychiatric, medical category of homosexuality was constituted from the moment it was characterized—Westphal's famous article of 1870 on "contrary sexual sensation" can stand as its birth certificate—less by a type of sexual relations than by a certain quality of sexual sensibility, a certain way of inverting the masculine and the feminine in oneself. Homosexuality appeared as one of the forms of sexuality when it was transposed

from the practice of sodomy into a kind of interior androgyny, a her-maphrodism of the soul. The sodomite had been a recidivist; the homosexual was now a species. (43; translation modified)

Modern homosexuality thus appears at the moment when psychiatrists begin to describe in terms of "sexual orientation" what had previously been considered as "practices" or "acts." (Thus, as one sees in Westphal's article, acts themselves are no longer necessary to define the orientation—now un-derstood as a pathology—no longer a particular perversity that implies a penchant for this "vice," but a "perversion" that presupposes mental or physiological problems.)[7]

In this light, it is easy to understand why—given that this "perversion" is defined by the "inversion" of one's gender, by a "hermaphrodism of the soul" (a way of looking at things that Proust, as we have seen, would take up)—Foucault will now be particularly interested in the question of hermaphrod-ism in the context of his work on the history of sexuality.[8] Indeed, in a 1978 interview he declares: "Once homosexuality became a medico-psychiatric category in the second half of the nineteenth-century, it is striking to me that it was immediately analyzed and rendered intelligible in terms of hermaphrod-ism. That is how a homosexual, or that is the form in which the homosexual enters into psychiatric medicine, the form of the hermaphrodite."[9]

6

The Third Sex

Thus at the heart of two of Foucault's works, fifteen years apart, lies the question of the "birth" of "homosexuality" and of the "personage" of the "homosexual." Yet in those two works Foucault proposes two different dates: the seventeenth century in *Madness and Civilization*, the nineteenth in *La Volonté de savoir*.

More than the periodization changed between the two works. A process reversed itself. *Madness and Civilization* argued that psychology and psychiatry became possible only when their objects (the mad person and the homosexual) had been shaped for them by the internment process and, more deeply, by a new "moral sensibility" that saw the light of day during the "Age of Reason." It was only because the personages of the mad person and the homosexual had been created through these historical processes—both moral and institutional—that psychiatry was able to lay hold of them. Psychiatry thereby produced the illusion that it represented the scientific end point of some progress in knowledge, an end point at which the truth about what it took to be certain invariable and natural realities was finally revealed. In *La Volonté de savoir*, not only is it two centuries later that the homosexual becomes a personage, but, more importantly, it is psychiatry that invents this new set of conceptual divisions and works to make it part of reality. Psychiatry produces what it was produced by, or at least what it—in *Madness and Civilization*—came after.

One does of course find in *La Volonté de savoir* analyses that are quite close to those of the 1961 volume. For the very project of a *History of Sexuality*, like the project of a *History of Madness*, as the (French) titles indicate, consists precisely of reinscribing in history certain notions and realities that various discourses with "scientific pretensions" (psychiatry or psychoanalysis) had taken as "natural" or as transhistorical. This is why Foucault can claim that his *History of Sexuality* can serve as an "archaeology of psychoanalysis" (*HSI*, 130). By that he means that he intends, on the one hand, to reinscribe the practice of the psychoanalytic session within the historical sequence that includes the Christian practice of confession but also, on the other hand, and more importantly, to show how the "subject of desire" that psycho-analysis is concerned with was born. Psychoanalysis, in its preoccupation with this subject, imagines that it gains access to the deep structures of individuality, whereas all it in fact does is ratify and reproduce the manner in which this individuality was created, at a given historical moment and by means of technologies of power and subjectivation.[1]

We also find in *La Volonté de savoir* one of the central threads of *Madness and Civilization*: the effort to analyze the way in which a system of power whose procedures rely above all on the norm and on "normalization" (89) was put into place: "From that point on, the technology of sex was essentially or-dered in relation to the medical institution, the exigency of normality."[2] Moreover, Foucault insists on the fact that homosexuals, who previously had only been considered "libertines" or "delinquents," would now be perceived as having "a global kinship with the insane," as "suffering from a sickness of the sexual instinct."[3]

A final similarity: one of the great themes running through *Madness and Civilization*, that "normality" relies on the "family" and the "family unit" to advance itself, is taken up once again in *La Volonté de savoir*. Foucault writes: "What has taken place since the seventeenth century can be interpreted in the following manner: the apparatus [*dispositif*] of sexuality which first de-veloped on the fringes of familial institutions . . . gradually became focused on the family."[4]

Still, the differences between the two books should not be minimized. Even if we find at the origin of both *Madness and Civilization* and *La Volonté de savoir* the desire to historicize what psychiatric and psychoanalytic thought tends to naturalize, even if the two works share a theoretical focus in study-ing the development of a power of the norm and of normality, they are sharply distinguished from each other by the fact that, in the latter book, psychiatry defines the "heretical sexualities" (49) and brings them into exis-tence as pathological realities arising from a discourse of health and sick-ness: "The learned discourse on sex that was pronounced in the nineteenth century was imbued with age-old delusions, but also with systematic blind-nesses: a refusal to see and to understand; but—and this is clearly the crucial point—a refusal concerning *the very thing that the discourse was causing to appear and whose formulation it was urgently seeking.*"⁵ We see here a performative productivity of psychiatric discourse. Foucault himself says as much: "The history of sexuality—that is, the history of what functioned in the nineteenth century as a specific field of truth—*must first be written from the viewpoint of a history of discourses*" (69; my emphasis).

⸕ We are now in a position to notice certain difficulties. If it is psychiatry that causes perverse sexualities to proliferate—by making ever more minute conceptual distinctions between them, or by subjecting them to interrogation, by inventorying them in order to build up an illustrated guidebook, by creating a whole new gallery of personages individuated by their sexual desires and practices—then one might wonder how these categories forged by a medical discourse gained access to the bodies and minds of the persons concerned. After all, these psychiatric writings were published in journals or anthologies read only by a few dozen specialists, although a few works, such as Krafft-Ebing's *Psychopathologia sexualis*, were read widely outside medical circles.

Foucault does not, of course, attribute to psychiatry any such performative efficaciousness. On the contrary, he underscores the fact that "confessional discourse," as it is produced by the different technologies that collectively create the demand that one speak—and notably by psychiatry—cannot be imposed from above. "By virtue of the very power structure immanent in it," it can only come "from below, as an obligatory act of speech which, under some imperious compulsion, breaks the bonds of discretion or forgetfulness" (62). The productive force of the injunction to produce discourse is not simply a result of the way in which the injunction pushes one toward speech; this force also resides in the belief produced by the injunction that it is necessary to speak.

Consequently, if psychiatric discourse proceeds by way of incitation and injunction, it causes a certain speech to be born in response, be it via acquiescence or opposition, submission or revolt. It is at this point of contact, this "strategic" meeting place between, on one hand, a way of getting a conceptual hold on things and, on the other, the reactions of those gotten hold of— that "multiple sexualities," circumscribed by psychiatry, enter into reality.

We are dealing, says Foucault, with a mechanism that has "a double impetus: pleasure and power." The two terms of the mechanism circulate within a field of power and resistance: "The pleasure that comes of exercising a power that questions, monitors, watches, spies, searches out, palpates, brings to light; and on the other hand, the pleasure that kindles at having to evade this power, flee from it, fool it, or travesty it. The power that lets itself be invaded by the pleasure it is pursuing; and opposite it, power asserting itself in the pleasure of showing off, scandalizing, or resisting." Thus "confrontation and mutual reinforcement" take place simultaneously (45).

I will come back later to this theorization of power in terms of a "relational" analysis. This is what is most centrally "at issue" (*enjeu*) in the book.[6] It is in fact in terms of this "analytics of power" that one can best understand Foucault's relation to the homosexual movement: the historical importance he accords to it and the need (one he dwells on) to move beyond it and to transform its intellectual and political presuppositions. The crucial point here is to note that the mechanism of implantation, of incorporating perversion into subjects, functions by means of a process in which those individuals appropriate for themselves the categories to which they have been assigned, whether they do so to submit to norms, to take pleasure in speaking about what they are, or to resist the "policing of sex."

❧ But is it possible to entertain the idea that no one would have thought of themselves as possessing a particular sexual "nature" if psychiatry had not come along and put together its whole conceptual apparatus? Is it possible to entertain the idea that it was only in reaction to these scientific discourses that individuals who had heretofore only practiced "homosexual acts" began to consider themselves "homosexual persons" and came to see the totality of their being as shaped by their sexual desires, thus acquiring all at once a "past," a "history," and a "childhood" (43)? Is it possible to believe that what had until then been nothing but a habitual sin turned into a secret nature? And could that be because individuals designated in this new way turned around the weapon that psychiatry had forged against them? Foucault says as much in several interviews published shortly after the first volume of the *History of Sexuality*: "You have only to see [that] the notion of homosexuality [appears] in 1870 and . . . to remark that the great debate around homosexuality . . . gets under way in the next twenty years to understand that we have here *an absolutely correlative phenomenon*. The idea was to capture people within this notion of homosexuality. Naturally people turned the weapon to their own ends. People like Gide, Oscar Wilde, Magnus Hirschfeld, and so on."[7]

It is, of course, impossible to ignore that psychiatry exercised a profound influence on homosexuals of both sexes, if only because it inspired representations that were spread by militant movements and by certain literary works. One might mention the way in which in France Armand Dubarry used psychiatric literature to write a series of novels, *Les Déséquilibrés de l'amour* (*Loves out of Balance*) including the 1896 volume called *Les Invertis (Le Vice allemand)* (*Inverts—The German Vice*).[8] Yet the most influential literary works came quite a bit later: Proust's *Remembrance of Things Past* only began to appear in 1913, whereas what one could define as a "gay culture" (whatever name one gives it) existed long before that. And if Radclyffe Hall's novel, *The Well of Loneliness*, which uses the categories of psychiatric medicine to describe its protagonist (that is to say, as an example of "sexual inversion"), had enormous repercussions for the self-representation of lesbians, it was published only in 1928, at which point lesbian modes of life had been well developed for quite a while.[9]

Indeed, it seems strange that in *La Volonté de savoir* Foucault takes an interest only in elite culture, as if the transformations affecting homosexuality in the nineteenth and twentieth centuries were limited to a space circumscribed by psychiatrists and writers. Of course certain themes ceaselessly circulated between psychiatric discourse and literature, and literature fixed, froze, and disseminated psychiatric representations in the social world. But popular culture—its ways of life, its forms of sociability—played without a doubt an even more considerable role in the elaboration of a "self awareness" or of a "collective self awareness." George Chauncey demonstrates this fact admirably. It is within the framework of a dynamic specific to the "gay world," in the interactions between individuals (inside and outside this world), that identities are formed and transformed. The "invert" and the "normal man" were "popular discursive categories" before they were "elite discursive categories."[10] And evolutions happen in different ways in different social classes, as Chauncey shows in reference to a shift that happened a few decades earlier in the middle classes than in popular classes: the idea of a homosexual considered as an "invert" seeking "normal men" giving way to a model of "homosexuality" (in which both partners are thought of as homosexual). Or not totally giving way, since in both groups of classes the category of the invert or the "fairy" survives to this day, "uneasy, contested, and disruptive" (27). According to Chauncey's analysis, the modern model of homosexuality managed to impose itself in a general fashion only in the second half of the twentieth century.[11] But what is the case for New York is most likely not the case for European cities, where the model of homosexuality had established itself much earlier. In France, for example, as we have seen, the idea of homosexuality began to spread as early as 1907, in the aftermath of the Eulenburg trials, accounts of which filled the German press. It was to perpetuate the model of inversion against the newer model that Proust put forward his theory of the man-woman (which was the theory of Ulrichs and Hirschfeld as much as of any psychiatrist)—although he also talked endlessly about homosexuality and homosexuals in ways that totally contradicted his own theory.[12]

Chauncey sets himself the task of demonstrating how the "gay world" created itself and how within that world the different discursive categories through which sexual relations between men could be thought about and spoken about were produced and modified. Gay New York can thus be read as putting into question the idea that medical discourse produced these representations and that gays did nothing other than take them on for their own ends. Chauncey works instead to reinscribe the medical discourse within the general context of the evolution and transformation of social practices and of the ways in which gays perceived themselves and were perceived by others in the context of urban life.[13]

Indeed, how is it possible to imagine that all those who frequented the cabarets, the "Molly Houses," the balls, the restaurants, and the like, throughout the eighteenth or the nineteenth century never thought of themselves as possessing a certain identity? Perhaps it was not a homosexual identity according to our contemporary usage, but surely it was an identity all the same.[14]

Similarly, it seems impossible to maintain that there can be found no trace of identities in literary and scholarly discourse before psychiatry came on the scene. Symonds, Pater, Wilde, and Gide, as we have seen, are all cases to the contrary, even if it is clear that their ways of conceiving of homosexuality or of perceiving themselves correspond neither to what we today call homosexuality nor to what the psychiatrists called sexual inversion. Symonds and Gide, for example, defended the "virile" idea of a "pederastic" friendship that had no room for either inversion or homosexuality, even if their own sexual desires and practices might differ enormously from the conceptions they put forth in an effort at legitimation.

There is no doubt that Symonds considered himself a different kind of person from other people, not because of acts he committed, since for a long time he did not commit any, or because of his "sins," which were only imaginary. Rather it was because of the feeling he had about his "sexual orientation" and the fact that this orientation completely shaped his being, as it had shaped his childhood, his past, his history.

The same is true for many other people who had a clear sense of themselves as different in kind from other people from childhood onward and a clear sense that their particularity colored their entire personality and psychology. Krafft-Ebing, after the publication of his *Psychopathia sexualis*, received numerous letters from people who told him of having recognized themselves in his descriptions and analyses, who offered him accounts of their lives, introspective narrations of their feelings, and even, on occasion, detailed accounts of their sexual practices. Even if we decide that psychiatric discourse set in motion this epistolary wave of autobiographical writing, it remains clear that the way in which these individuals perceived themselves, the ways in which they thought of themselves as defined by their sexual orientation, had preexisted the establishment of the categories of inversion and homosexuality that medical discourse performed.[15]

Moreover, Foucault seems to overlook the fact that when Hirschfeld spoke of the "third sex," he was not referring only to the categories of psychiatric medicine. For one of the earliest theorizations of sexual inversion—and even the very invention of the word *homosexuality*—was the work not of psychiatrists hostile to homosexuals and out to cure or intern them, to "medicalize" or "pathologize" them, but of jurists and men of letters (Ulrichs, Kertbeny), who wanted to legitimate loves between persons of the same sex. For Hirschfeld it was not enough to turn the psychiatric discourse "strategically" back on itself in order to found a homosexual discourse and a homosexual movement. Hirschfeld explicitly claimed to be a follower of Ulrichs, to whom he often payed homage as a pioneer in the struggle to which Hirschfeld too was dedicating his life.[16]

Indeed, when Ulrichs invented the model of "hermaphrodism of the soul" at the beginning of the 1860s, when he described "uranists" as individuals with "a woman's soul in a man's body," his aim was the decriminalization of homosexuality. For Ulrichs, "uranists" really did make up a third sex, a particular category of persons with inborn sexual inclinations. Having emphasized this point, and thus also the fact that "love between men" was a natural phenomenon, Ulrichs concluded that each person should be able to live his or her own life, without being "struck by the sword of injustice," as "heretics, Jews, and witches" had been.[17] As early as 1865 he had sketched out a charter for a "uranist organization" whose goal was to break down the isolation in which individuals condemned to silence (and blackmail) lived and to create real "solidarity" between them, to struggle for the abolition of repressive laws and to further the development of a "uranist literature."[18] In 1869, Ulrichs put the final touches on the first (and only) issue of what had been announced as a monthly publication, one that he had dreamed of since 1866 and that finally appeared in January 1870: *Uranus*.[19]

The medicalization of inversion took Ulrich's theory as a point of departure and as something to work against.[20] Referring to Ulrichs, all the while sharply distinguishing himself from him, Westphal wrote, in 1869, that the "perverse inclinations" that drew individuals to persons of their same sex belonged to the field of medicine.[21] Westphal accepted the idea that sexual inversion was innate and thus thought it regrettable that it was subject to legal repression. He nonetheless deduced that inversion was a sickness, a "pathological phenomenon," a fact of which, he added, those individuals afflicted by it were perfectly conscious. It seemed to Westphal that an invert such as Ulrichs, who refused to admit the pathological character of his condition, was even more seriously ill than those who did admit it. Ulrichs was pleased by this "scientific" point of view, of which he saw only the desire for homosexuality to be decriminalized. He went on categorically rejecting the idea that uranism belonged to the field of mental illness.

Even Krafft-Ebing elaborated his theory to a great extent by reference to and in opposition to Ulrichs's theory. In fact Ulrichs, always on the lookout for support in the scientific world, had sent Krafft-Ebing a number of his brochures during the 1860s, and Krafft-Ebing wrote to him much later that they had led him to take a close interest in sexual inversion. One might imagine Ulrichs's subsequent regret at ever having mailed them.[22]

As for the word *homosexuality* itself, it was coined in 1869 by Karl Maria Kertbeny, an Austro-Hungarian man of letters who was also struggling for the repeal of laws penalizing homosexual acts with imprisonment. In letters to Ulrichs he opposed to any notion of effeminacy and inversion a "virile" vision of love between men. Even though he always denied it, Kertbeny was probably homosexual himself.[23] In any case, he worked for what we would call the "gay cause." Thus the word *homosexual* was invented with an aim favorable to gay people, before Krafft-Ebing took it up in 1887 for the second edition of his *Psychopathia Sexualis*.[24]

7

Producing Subjects

From the very first pages of *La Volonté de savoir* we find Foucault ironizing about the Freudo-Marxist ideology of sexual liberation and about the psychoanalytically inspired leftist boilerplate that held up shimmering images of the happiness that tomorrow had in store for us, promising that "tomorrow sex will be good again." But he does not take the trouble to specify who his adversaries are; he relies on circumlocutions such as "they tell us" or "the story goes" or "it would seem" or "we are informed." There was no particular reason to be more specific: anyone reading at the time would have understood of whom and of what he was speaking. These discourses could be found everywhere. Toward the end of the book, Foucault mentions Wilhelm Reich (*HS1*, 131)—respectfully we might add. But at the outset he attacks those contemporary discourses, a generalized Reichianism in fact, that colored the political vision of the far left.[1]

Still, it is hard to shake off the strange impression that the entire critique Foucault undertakes in these celebrated pages is nothing but a critique of, well, Foucault. However sarcastic his intent may be, every sentence seems aimed at something that he himself has written earlier. In the second paragraph on the very first page he says: "At the beginning of the seventeenth century, *so they tell us*, a certain frankness was still common. Sexual practices had little need of secrecy; words were said without undue reticence, and things were done without too much concealment; one had a tolerant familiarity with the illicit" (*HS1*, 3; my emphasis, translation modified). On the next page: "These are the characteristic features attributed to repression, which serve to distinguish it from the prohibitions maintained by penal law: repression operated as . . . *an injunction to silence, an affirmation of nonexistence*" (4; my emphasis). Or, a little farther along: "This discourse on modern sexual repression holds up well, owing no doubt to how easy it is to uphold. A solemn historical and political guarantee protects it. By placing the advent of the age of repression in the seventeenth century, after hundreds of years of open spaces and free expression, one adjusts it to coincide with the development of capitalism: it becomes an integral part of the bourgeois order" (5). And what are we to think upon noticing that the very "they," whose discourse Foucault ironically recreates for us, are said to inform us that "if repression has indeed been the fundamental link between power, knowledge, and sexuality since the classical age, it stands to reason that we will not be able to free ourselves from it except at a considerable cost: nothing less than a transgression of laws, a lifting of prohibitions, an irruption of speech . . ." (5)?

In this theatrical preamble, which establishes a distance between the author and a group of indeterminate speakers whose discourse is so well known that it needs no specific attribution—in this series of sentences that seem to describe the state of a theoretical field that needs to be left behind, it is striking that each proposition we are meant to oppose or leave behind might as well be drawn from *Madness and Civilization*. The thematic focus is identical: it can be characterized as the large opposition between, on the one hand, repression and imposed silence and, on the other, speaking for oneself and transgressing prohibitions.

This problematic that animated the analyses of *Madness and Civilization* (and that we might call the "repressive hypothesis") was one that Foucault kept in place long after that book—right through the beginning of the 1970s. It is true that, when he defines his historical and theoretical work in *The Archaeology of Knowledge* in 1969, he emphasizes that his goal is to treat discourses "as practices that systematically form the objects of which they speak."[2] That seems a precise announcement of the project that he will develop a few years later in *La Volonté de savoir*. Yet toward the end of the 1960s, Foucault was still thinking in terms of a limitation and a "scarcity" of discourses. Indeed that is one of the major avenues he follows in *The Archaeology of Knowledge*, in which he sets out to respond to some of the objections raised in response to *The Order of Things*.[3]

Foucault places at the heart of his analyses the system that defines, in a given epoch, what is thinkable and sayable and the rules of formulation and circulation that govern discourses. So when he evokes in *Archaeology*, yet again, the possibility of a history of sexuality, he clearly imagines it as an analysis of discourses and not of the object of those discourses:

Instead of studying the sexual behavior of men at a given period . . .,
instead of describing what men thought of sexuality . . ., one would ask
oneself whether, in this behaviour, as in these representations, a whole
discursive practice is not at work; whether sexuality . . . is not a group
of objects that can be talked about (or that it is forbidden to talk about),
a field of possible enunciations . . ., a group of concepts. (193)

Yet Foucault still anchors this archaeology of discourses in the framework of
an investigation into systems of "prohibitions and values" (193).

In 1970, in his inaugural lecture at the Collège de France, Foucault is still
asking himself about the "anxiety" provoked by discourses when they are
"manifested materially, as a written or spoken object." He wonders: "What
is so perilous, then, in the fact that people speak, and that their speech
proliferates? Where is the danger in that?"[4] To respond to that question,
he puts forward a "hypothesis" that will help establish, he says, the "terrain"
or the "provisional theatre" of the research he plans to undertake: "I am
supposing that in every society the production of discourse is at once
controlled, selected, organised and redistributed according to a certain
number of procedures, whose role is to avert its powers and its dangers, to
cope with chance events, to evade its ponderous, awesome materiality"
(216).

First Foucault distinguishes three "great systems of exclusion": "prohibited words, the division between reason and madness, and the will to
truth" (219; translation modified). After analyzing these external "procedures" of limitation on discourses, he turns to "internal procedures,"
meaning cases "where discourse exercises its own control" (220). He mentions the "author function" in literature and the sciences (221–22).

Throughout this lecture, which lays out and defines his research projects
for the coming years, Foucault is thinking in terms of a theory of "scarcity."
The "excluding" principles that reject certain forms of discourse and the
"figures" that organize forms of discourse from the inside (author, scientific discipline, etc.) work together to determine a "negative activity of the
cutting-out and economizing of discourse" (229; translation modified).
Moreover, when Foucault announces here that he intends to work on a
history of sexuality, it is hardly surprising to find him once again describing
it as a study of the "taboos" [interdits] that weigh on it (233):

We could attempt an investigation of a system of linguistic prohibitions
bearing on sexuality from the sixteenth to the nineteenth century. In

doing this, we would *not* be concerned with the manner in which this system has progressively—and fortunately—disappeared, but rather with the way it has shifted and rearranged itself, from the practice of confession, in which forbidden behaviors were identified, categorized, and ranked, in explicit detail, to the belated, initially hesitant appearance of the topic of sexuality in nineteenth-century psychiatry and medicine. (232; translation modified)

If all regions of discourse are subject to constraint, it is in the cases of "sexuality and politics" that the "web is most tightly woven," and it is in these places that "danger spots are most numerous" (216).

So, in this text from 1970 the "order of discourse" is essentially linked to a principle of rarefaction both of possible enunciations and of possible modes of enunciation, and even of possible speaking subjects. And the historical filiation between Christian confession and nineteenth-century psychiatry, which Foucault begins to emphasize at this moment, is presented as a perpetuation of linguistic prohibitions.

» One can only be astonished, then, by what Foucault writes at the beginning of *La Volonté de savoir* as he defines what he means to accomplish through the analysis of discourse he will undertake in his *History of Sexuality*: "In short, I would like to disengage my analysis from the privileges generally accorded the economy of scarcity and the principles of rarefaction" (*HS1*, 12). The question seems unavoidable: For what reason did Foucault move, in such a short time—only a few years—from a thematic of "rarefaction" to one of "proliferation," from a theory of the prohibitions on language to a theory of the incitement to speech? Such an evolution seems all the more remarkable given Foucault's insistence that those who think in terms of prohibition and transgression are trapped in ways of thinking that have been put in place by technologies of power: "One has to be completely taken in by this internal ruse of confession in order to attribute a fundamental role to censorship, to taboos regarding speaking and thinking" (60).

One could propose explanations for Foucault's shift on many levels. The first has to do with the political situation in France at the beginning of the 1970s, with Foucault's own commitments, and with the new way in which his work was being received. As I have already mentioned, his book from

1961, *Folie et déraison*, was republished in 1972 with the title *Histoire de la folie* (*Madness and Civilization*). Between those dates that work had acquired an increasingly direct political meaning: it had been swept up in the currents of the antipsychiatric movement, becoming a sort of breviary in the struggle against "repression."[5] In the new edition, Foucault replaced the original preface with a much shorter one that explained that it is not up to the author to dictate the reception of a book. He knew perfectly well that his book had been assigned meanings he had never thought of. Yet he did not set out to challenge them, first, because a book belongs to those who read it, and second, because the political content retrospectively read into those pages by post-May 1968 movements might already have been there, as unperceived potential. The book was already political in the sense that it proposed a critical discourse on subjectivation by the norm and normality. These themes were central to post-May 1968 struggles. In fact one might say that the book bore within it preoccupations that had not been constituted as political when Foucault wrote it but that became so in later years. In a 1974 interview Foucault was asked, "Is *Madness and Civilization* political?" He responded, "Yes, but only now." Then he clarified himself: "The frontier of the political has shifted, and so now subjects such as psychiatry, internment, or the medicalization of a given population have become political problems. After all that has happened in the last ten years, certain groups have been obliged to include these areas in their activities, and thus we have come into contact, they and I—not so much because I have changed, but because in this case I can say that politics came to me, or rather it has colonized areas that had been almost political yet not recognized as such."[6]

In any case, his 1961 book had found itself, at the beginning of the 1970s, at the center of the "antirepressive" ideology that Foucault himself tried to call into question in his book from 1976. This explains why the later book in a certain way disturbed his readers and has often been misread or disliked. When questioned in 1978 about *La Volonté de savoir*'s mostly unfavorable reception, Foucault explained: "That it surprised so many people has perhaps to do with the simplistic quality of my previous positions, and with the fact that I was easily associated with an enthusiastic and wide-eyed conception of the struggle against all forms of repression, whenever and wherever they were. I think that there was a kind of a sense of a "shift," if you will, in relation to positions that people believed to be mine or that were those of this or that other person."[7]

» Here is a second level of explanation for Foucault's shift: if he comes to feel it necessary to call into question the use that political movements make of *Madness and Civilization*, it is because he is, in the 1970s, working to elaborate his thoughts about power. In his courses at the Collège de France and in *Discipline and Punish*, he is inquiring into the production of "subjects and individuals." He sets out this theme quite clearly in his courses for 1975–76 (published as *Il faut défendre la société*), when he begins the analyses that will be elaborated in *La Volonté de savoir*. (Foucault's courses at the Collège de France often served as the testing ground for his books.) He distinguishes two "large hypotheses" behind most analyses of power. The first, which "I will call, for the sake of convenience, Reich's hypothesis," holds that "the mechanism of power is repression." The second, which, again for the sake of convenience, he calls "Nietzsche's hypothesis," asserts that "the basis of a relation of power is the bellicose confrontation of forces" (17). These two systems are not, of course, irreconcilable, but it is the second that Foucault will spend the entire year of 1976 exploring. And it is the opposition between "Nietzsche's hypothesis" and "Reich's hypothesis" (or, more exactly, the way in which "Nietzsche's hypothesis" reworks "Reich's") that will be the guiding thread of the book Foucault will publish several months later.

Foucault sets out in his courses for 1975–76 to show that the idea that a power mechanism proceeds via repression is part and parcel of "a deciphering of power in terms of 'sovereignty.'" There will be on one side an instance of sovereignty (the State, the Law, the Dominant Class, etc.), and on the other side subjects on whom power is imposed, whereas Foucault's analyses of the "operators of domination," notably those found in *Discipline and Punish*, led him to believe that subjects do not preexist power. It is not a question of having individuals on one side and power on the other. Rather it is a question of a relation of domination that "determines the elements involved in it" (38). Subjects and individuals exist, then, only in and through subjectivation. That is to say, they are the historical products of effective, concrete, and multiple relations of domination.[8]

It is thus perfectly clear that Foucault is trying to understand how individuals are produced by power. The individual is not an autonomous and preexisting reality on whom power is exercised through repression. Quite the contrary: "If a body, its gestures, its discourses, its desires come to be identified and considered as individual, that very fact is one of the first effects of power" (27). Power does not repress, it produces.

⊮ There is yet another level of explanation to consider. Foucault wants to decouple the analysis of power from economic analysis.[9] Given the historical context, this decoupling implied important political consequences. It implied working against all the current Marxist discourses to establish that a certain number of struggles could be undertaken, and a certain number of results achieved, without necessarily staging a revolution or a social change, without addressing politics in its most general form. Given that relations of domination are multiple and concrete, both theoretical critique and action are partial and local. It is not necessary to imagine what a future society might be in order to work, for example, to throw off models to which sexuality is subjected.

In the specific domain of the sexual, there is power, and there is resistance. It must be possible to think this without imagining that it will topple capitalism or bourgeois society.[10]

8

Philosophy in the Closet

If we want to understand why Foucault shifted from an analysis in terms of repression and rarefaction of discourses to an analysis in terms of production and the incitement to speech, doubtless we must also consider his "personal experience." In the 1950s and 1960s his desire to write a history of sexuality was, as we have seen, strongly tied to the actual situation of homosexuality and homosexuals, obliged to live in shame, silence, and secrecy. When he evoked this theme, he always used a group of words that referred to "banishment." He spoke of prohibitions, of taboos, of dark corners in the system of discourses. It is hardly surprising that the project of a history of sexuality was conceived—in the preface to *Madness and Civilization* and in later texts through the beginning of the 1970s—as an archaeology of the "gestures" through which boundaries and exclusions were established.

But when Foucault finally settles down to do the theoretical and historical work for this project, the situation is entirely different. Homosexuality is no longer denied access to speech, reduced to a silence that can be transgressed only by a few brilliant bolts of lightning (such as Genet). The homosexual cause is no longer limited to a few organizations that offer a forum for a certain "gay culture" all the while preaching "discretion," "respectability," and "dignity" in order to gain "social acceptance."[1]

By the mid-70s everything was different: here and there throughout the world, in the wake of the revolts of 1968, the feminist struggle, and the post-Stonewall appearance of the Gay Liberation Front in the United States, gay speech had burst onto the public scene.[2] In France, 1971 saw the creation of the FHAR (Homosexual Front for Revolutionary Action), one of whose first spectacular actions was to interrupt a radio broadcast concerning "The Painful Problem of Homosexuality." Subsequently the FHAR would make a point of participating in the May Day parade of French unions. Guy Hocquenghem, one of the FHAR's organizers, wrote an article for a major French news-weekly in 1972, and in the same year also published a groundbreaking book, *Homosexual Desire*, largely inspired by Gilles Deleuze and Félix Guattari's *Anti-Oedipus*.[3]

Did Foucault feel that he was about to be deprived of a project that had been close to his heart for so long? At the very least it was clear to him that such a project could no longer claim to be audacious. Above all, there could be no doubt for him that whatever impulse had been pushing him so strongly toward this project, it was now wrongly oriented: he had intended to denounce certain prohibitions, to break a certain silence, yet the situation had changed to such an extent that people were speaking for themselves everywhere, including in newsmagazines. Hadn't Hocquenghem written in *Le Nouvel Observateur*: "We are all somehow deformed in an area of our lives we all know to be crucial, the area known as sexual desire or love. We must begin to uncover these desires that we have been forced to hide. No one else can do it for us"?[4]

⇥ This is the political and intellectual context in which we must come to understand *La Volonté de savoir*. It is astonishing that Foucault never cites Hocquenghem in his book, for it would seem that *Homosexual Desire* helped launch his own thinking. Indeed, in *Homosexual Desire*, Hocquenghem had already described the "recent" invention of homosexuality as a category produced by medical discourse:

> Capitalist society manufactures homosexuals just as it produces pro-letarians, constantly defining its own limits: homosexuality is a man-ufactured product of the normal world. . . . What is manufactured is a psychologically repressive category, "homosexuality": an abstract divi-sion of desire which allows even those who escape to be dominated, inscribing within the law what is outside the law. The category under discussion, as well as the term indicating it, is a fairly recent invention. The growing imperialism of a society seeking to attribute a social status to everything, even to the unclassifiable, created this particular form of disequilibrium: up to the end of the eighteenth century, people who denied the existence of God, who could not speak, or who practiced sodomy, were locked up in the same prisons. Just as the advent of psychiatry and mental hospitals demonstrates society's ability to invent

specific means for classifying the unclassifiable (see Foucault's *Madness and Civilization*), so modern thought creates a new disease, homosexuality. According to Havelock Ellis (*Sexual Inversion*), the word "homosexual" was invented in 1869 by a German doctor. Dividing in order to rule, psychiatry's modern pseudo-scientific thought has turned barbarous intolerance into civilised intolerance. (50–51; translation modified)

Thus Hocquenghem not only refers to the Foucault of *Madness and Civilization*, but also presages the Foucault of *La Volonté de savoir*. Hocquenghem, in adding that "the establishment of homosexuality as a separate category goes hand in hand with its repression" (55), is probably closer to the Foucault of 1961 than to the Foucault of 1976. Nevertheless there is a striking resemblance between the long passage just cited and the famous page that Foucault consecrates, in *La Volonté de savoir*, to the birth of the homosexual.

The major difference is that Hocquenghem imagines there to be, beneath all the "categorizations" of sexuality, a sort of pure desire, an "unbroken and polyvocal flux," of which both homosexual and heterosexual desire are "arbitrarily frozen frames" (50). He certainly does not imagine a return to some originary "bisexuality"—although many contemporary leftist discourses inspired by Freud did (even those favored by the FHAR). In Hocquenghem's eyes, to speak of bisexuality was once again to situate oneself in the "oedipal" space of categories.[5] For him what was important was to call norms and normality into question, to challenge the idea that there could be a good sexuality (heterosexuality) and a bad one (homosexuality): "More than anything else, the very idea of normality has oppressed us. . . . Everything that is normal is tied to what oppresses us. Any kind of normality rubs us the wrong way. . . . We know that the true revolution will banish normality."[6]

Hocquenghem also refuses to allow the multiple forms of homosexual sexuality and the plural expressions of homosexual desire to be pigeonholed in a unifying category of homosexuality.[7] This explains why he is so careful at the beginning of his book to distinguish between "homosexual desire" and "homosexuality." In their dispersion, their heterogeneity, even their multiplicity, homosexual practices (made up of numerous fleeting encounters, of expressions of sexuality in parks, etc.) call into question a grounding of sexuality in the family or in the "private" realm. Given that homosexuality proceeds by way of simple "connections" (like the meeting of Charlus and Jupien at the beginning of Proust's *Cities of the Plain*), and given that the homosexual system of "cruising" sexualizes daily life, "homosexual desire" represents for Hocquenghem an encouragement to a generalized political contestation of the social forms of capitalist civilization—of which the family is a central pillar. In his eyes, the goal of the "homosexual struggle" is not to gain rights for a minority or to affirm the pride of an oppressed group,[8] but to act on the entire social body by way of a "crude sexualisation" of politics and society, by a "sexualisation of the world" that would threaten "patriarchy" and "phallocratism."[9]

Hocquenghem thus announces the coming into being of a "desirous social struggle," and the homosexual movement is assigned a mission of radical destabilization: it challenges both those forms of civilization that are founded on "normal" sexuality and whatever forces of repression guarantee that sexuality's normality.[10]

⊁ Surely Foucault must have wanted to respond to Hocquenghem's book when he began to write his History of Sexuality. Hocquenghem himself had referred to Foucault's Madness and Civilization, and thus it was Foucault's own influence that he himself would have to move beyond. In La Volonté de savoir— how can there be any doubt?—Foucault is inspired by the analyses in Homosexual Desire to return—via the elaboration of his "analytics of power," and in a kind of underground way to this whole question: repression is not the apt notion for thinking about the categories through which power produces "categories"; there is no form of desire in some raw state that is repressed or constrained by way of conceptual divisions. Foucault in fact takes the questions Hocquenghem addressed and redoes his arguments at a deeper level, both rejecting the "naturalism," or even the "biologism," that marked the discourse of "sexual liberation," and trying to disengage the resistance to sexual norms from the political struggle against bourgeois society.[11]

The first volume of The History of Sexuality was written in reaction to Hocquenghem's book, but of course also as a response to Deleuze and Guattari (and perhaps even more as a response to Guattari's own writings, which clearly evidenced a Reichian point of view) and, more generally, as a response to the diffuse ideology of sexual liberation and the revolution of desire. (In that diffuse ideology one would certainly include the films of Pasolini: Teorema from 1968 as well as the trilogy including The Decameron, The Canterbury Tales, and The Arabian Nights from 1971 to 1974.)[12]

But Foucault also meant to respond to the actions and practices of the new political movements that incarnated these ideologies, notably the FHAR, whose militants, while rejecting the categories of established sexuality, frequently had recourse to a veritable terrorism of their own in demanding that one "avow" what one was. Not only did these proponents of a subversive radicalism virulently reject all previous modes of gay life; they also frequently demanded that all homosexuals openly and publicly declare themselves as such and denounced as "shameful" and "closeted" anyone who did not give in to their demand.

In the eyes of the new activists, an organization such as Arcadie instantiated the horror of "bourgeois homosexuality" as much as it instantiated self-closeting and the interiorization of shame. All the glories of that organization and its publication—"literary" homosexuality, references to Gide, endless articles on ancient Greece, lists of famous homosexuals, and so on— would be swept away as outdated products of repression. They were to be replaced by a more directly sexual discourse that violently rejected any idea of integration or assimilation.

Thanks to the work of historians, it is now possible to revalorize those forms of culture as spaces of freedom, as modes of life whose inventiveness and vitality rival contemporary realities. Chauncey, for example, cautions us not to view the history of homosexuality as a march toward freedom and progress, and not see in past cultural forms merely the first steps toward or the prefigurations of contemporary life. Above all, he insists that "the history of gay resistance must be understood to extend beyond formal political organizing to include the strategies of everyday resistance that men devised in order to claim space for themselves in the midst of a hostile society."[13]

This was certainly not the way in which the militants of the FHAR saw older forms of gay culture. Indeed, in *Homosexual Desire*, Hocquenghem denounces the "Proust-Gide-Peyrefitte sequence," which he compares to the "Freud-Adler-*France-Dimanche* sequence."[14] The revolutionary movements of the 1970s constructed their discourses in opposition to earlier forms of gay culture (apparently unaware that they did not themselves arise out of nothing, that they existed only because an entire culture, a subcultural life, and a whole set of discourses preceded them). They had no intention of doing any historical work of rediscovery and rehabilitation. Instead they wanted to sweep away the stuffier forms of that culture, whose goal of "respectability" and whose relationship to secrecy or discretion seemed unbearable, especially as their goal was now to encourage homosexuals to "stop hiding in the shadows" [*cesser de raser les murs*].[15]

It is obvious that Foucault belonged to the pre-Stonewall, pre-May 1968 generation. In historical terms, he was doubtless closer to Arcadie than to the FHAR. Arcadie was founded in 1954, the very year Foucault was writing the letters to Barraqué cited earlier. Even if Foucault never joined the organization, he most likely attended events that it sponsored or at least knew certain of its members. In a 1955 letter, written while he was living in Sweden, Foucault tells Barraqué about a discussion of Arcadie that he had had with other French expatriates. Moreover, he was in regular contact with the organization's president, André Baudry—over a long enough period that in 1979 he would deliver an address at Arcadie's annual meeting—even if that contact diminished after 1968. As Baudry tells it:

> From 1960 to 1968, I saw Michel Foucault on many occasions. He asked me questions about the 'Arcadians,' about their lives, their problems. Several times during these years he referred his friends or acquaintances or correspondents to me when they were in need of our assistance. Because of the nature of the events of 1968, we lost sight of each other until later Maurice Pinguet brought us back in touch. So several times I had occasion to have dinner with him on the rue de Sèvres, at Maurice Pinguet's. Our relations became cordial again, if irregular.[16]

In 1982, when Baudry felt left behind by new forms of gay activism and decided to dissolve his organization, Foucault expressed a desire to write something on the man and the history he was involved in, which obviously interested him—or had interested him—greatly.[17]

The example of Baudry demonstrates how much confusion the eruption of a radical gay movement could create for those who were familiar with the completely different conditions that prevailed prior to 1968. How could such people, who had lived with the idea that speech was not allowed, not have been troubled by the arrival of a movement that demolished the very manner in which they had constructed their existences and their personalities, forging conditions for living out their homosexuality in spite of a generalized hostility? They had been obliged to hide themselves and to silence themselves. Now they were to be subjected to the violent critiques of the new militants, to be reproached for their discretion. It is said that Foucault himself was violently taken to task by the militants of the FHAR at one public meeting. Perhaps we might see in this event one point of departure for the historical critique of "confession" that he would elaborate in La Volonté de savoir.

If so, we might even go so far as to ask if the thematic of the "production of discourses" by technologies of power that is developed in that book is not somehow traversed by what might be thought of as a "logic of the closet."[18] Could it not be that the elaborate production mounted by Foucault to set off the famous page on which he announces, so dogmatically and with so little historical support, that the homosexual did not exist before 1870 and is only an invention of psychiatry—could it not be that this is a result of a desire to transform a profound personal malaise into a theoretical and political response? Such a malaise was felt at the outset of the 1970s, after the eruption of a revolutionary homosexual discourse, whose reshuffling of the politico-sexual deck had called into question both his person and his very being. Doubtless Foucault was not displeased to be able to respond to the most radical of these militants, the ones lecturing him about his politics, that they were themselves the dupes of the power they thought they were combating.

9

When Two Guys Hold Hands

One has only to read the book of conversations between Foucault and Thierry Voeltzel to understand to what an extent Foucault's theoretical project during the 1970s was enmeshed in such a political (and eminently personal) situation. In the conversations, published in 1978 but recorded in 1976—just as he was finishing *La Volonté de savoir*—Foucault is questioning a young man, twenty years old, and a portion of the conversation has precisely to do with what changed at the outset of the 1970s regarding possible and actual ways of living out one's homosexuality.[1] In the questions and comments Foucault provides throughout the book it is clear how deeply the problems taken up in *La Volonté de savoir* resonate with the most intimate levels of lived experience, notably with the experience of moving from one moment to another in the history of homosexuality.

After listening to Voeltzel recount his sexual life, Foucault states:

> Basically you were able to practice homosexuality now and then, when you wanted, episodically, in phases, without ever having to say to yourself: "my goodness, why I must be homosexual, given that I'm doing homosexual things." That kind of deduction—that one *used* to have to make, that *was* so telling, that psychologically *used* to be so difficult to accept, whose consequences *used* to be so heavy—well you never drew that conclusion, felt those consequences, and there was no need for you to do so. The category of homosexuality was only developed quite late. It didn't always exist; what existed was sodomy, that's to say, a certain number of sexual practices which were themselves forbidden, but the homosexual individual didn't always exist. For me what is striking, in you and what you say, is the fact that your generation actually recovered the possibility of engaging—even predominantly or exclusively—in homosex, with-

out ever having to ask yourselves, "Am I homosexual?" (33–34; my emphasis)

Voeltzel immediately qualifies Foucault's conclusion, emphasizing that this was not the case for everyone. He mentions a boy in his class with whom he had had a sexual experience yet who insisted that it remain secret and that he was in no way homosexual. Voeltzel adds that even for himself things were not quite so simple and that he had sometimes felt guilty after having sex with another boy.

It is also unavoidably clear that Voeltzel knows he is being taped, and speaks accordingly. (His discourse does not in fact always hold together all that well, although to be fair we should remember that we are speaking of a taped conversation made when he was only twenty years old.) Foucault is quite conscious of the gap between the things Voeltzel says that he knows will be published and what he says when the microphone is switched off. He says as much: "There's something funny here. Once we turn the tape recorder off you always start saying that of course it's much more complicated than that, that things are difficult, that things are simple only in exceptional cases; then the tape starts running again and suddenly everything becomes . . . [laughter]."[2]

Yet the eagerness with which Foucault turns the young man's words into near truths or prophecies cannot fail to surprise us. Even setting aside his evident fascination with the young man, one would think that Foucault would be rather likely to distance himself from the kinds of things being said. Voeltzel, for example, does not hide the inspiration he takes from Reich.[3] He is also steeped in the leftist ideology of an original and universal bisexuality that is to be rediscovered behind all the repressions and prohibitions applied to sexuality.[4] This particular fantasy, drawn from Freud's work, is one Foucault had never subscribed to and had even challenged rather strongly. Indeed, he states:

In all of this literature of the Antinorme type . . . there is a particular theme that has struck me, perhaps because it appears so frequently, but also because it seems outright utopian; it's this idea that what makes homosexuality different, what gives it its specificity is in reality only the result of certain forms of alienation, socio-political constraints, etc., and that a liberated sexuality should be as much homosexual as heterosexual and that consequently there will come the happy day when finally we'll go back to loving women just like everyone else. (28)

A bit later, Foucault describes this idea of universal bisexuality as a "purely tactical and political discourse thanks to which one can build alliances with the feminist movement or with liberal heterosexuals." He adds: "So tactically this discourse amounts to saying 'just wait and see, when we are free we too will start to love women' [laughter]; this ridiculous and utopian discourse has nonetheless been quite effective, has been one of the conditions for the acceptance of homosexuality within all these political groups."[5]

What Foucault seizes on in Voeltzel's discourse are the elements that allow him to draw a line of transition between a period that he wants to believe is now over—one in which he had lived out his twenties—and a period corresponding to "today" in which his interlocutor will live out his own twenties. We can find something of Foucault's autobiography in this opposition between a then and a now. That he even asks Voeltzel the following question speaks volumes: "Have you ever seen fellows who had what are called problems, that's to say who seemed to have what psychologists or psychiatrists or psychoanalysts would consider signs of neurosis or depression . . . linked to their sexual lives, or suicidal tendencies?" (43).

↣ Voeltzel's stories send Foucault back to his own history. It is his own history that he invokes in the sentence cited above, when he speaks of "that kind of deduction—that one *used* to have to make, that *was* so telling, that psychologically *used* to be so difficult to accept, whose consequences *used* to be so heavy. . . ." The past tenses of the verbs in Foucault's turns of phrase indicate that he is referring to his own experience. A little bit later he says again:

> But it seemed to me, when I met you, that there was a huge difference between someone from your generation and people from earlier generations. For those from earlier generations, the discovery that you were homosexual was always a solemn moment in life, both a revelation and a rupture; it was a kind of magic, the day you realized that that is what pleasure was, and at the same time there was the feeling that you were marked, the black sheep, and that that would be the case until the end of our days. . . .

Foucault ends this thought with a question: "Was it like that for you?"[6]

Raising the issue of people's ages, Foucault states:

It used to be that one of the mechanisms people used to protect them-selves from the idea that they were homosexual was the question of age differences. Before age sixteen, whatever you did couldn't yet be homo-sexuality, it was just the agitation of puberty. If you played around with a friend of the same age, okay, those were sort of forbidden games, a kind of mutual narcissism, but it still wasn't homosexuality. Then there was the fact that when you were finally twenty years old, and really began having sex with people leading a homosexual life, the fact of having sex with someone ten, fifteen, or twenty years older, that was quite a difficult step to take, one which brought you into a kind of closed, secret, and slightly damned freemasonry. (34–35)

The terms Foucault uses ("secret," "damned" [maudit], "freemasonry") inevitably call to mind Proustian homosexuality. It is also clear that in the end it is not "sexual liberation" that bothers Foucault, if by that one under-stands the way of living one's sexuality after 1968. Far from it. Rather, he seems enchanted by all these transformations, by this new freedom, and specifically by the fact that a multiplicity of feelings no longer need fit into the single model of "love." "I wonder if the most liberating thing—of course, I'm not very fond of that word, liberating—but I wonder if the most liberating thing isn't that you no longer have only this single label, love, to apply to all these sensations, all these feelings" (48). A few pages later, he comments, "The fact that the monotonous signifier, love, has been exploded is very important" (52). At the end of the book, Foucault, summarizing the conversations, states: "All of these binary divisions—being one of us, not being one of us; making love, not making love; being in love, not being in love—all of these binaries have to be done away with; they are only part of a system of constraints" (211).

⍒ Right in the middle of this book, there is a strange passage in which several of Foucault's preoccupations are brought together and it prefigures what he will be thinking about in the years ahead. He mentions a letter he has read in Libération. During these years, that newspaper regularly published a wide-open and free-ranging page of letters to the editor, in which readers recounted their experiences and set out their points of view on a whole range of subjects. It was, Foucault says, the best thing about the paper.[7] In the letter in question, a young heterosexual man tells how he and a group of other young men and women set off on a vacation trip together. Foucault retells the story like this:

> They were all camping in a tent. Then one day two other guys showed up to see them and, as things turned out, he [the letter writer] slept one night in the same sleeping bag or the same bed as one of those guys. . . . The next morning they got up and it was clear from the way they behaved that they had made love. Not only that, but they were in love, as they showed throughout the rest of the day, and quickly the others in the group began having reactions of intolerance—even though they were leftist, liberated—guys and girls slept together, there weren't any prohibitions. The negative reactions escalated to the point that they kicked the two guys out. (123–24)

If the letter writer seems to say that the "homosexual act the group refused to admit was the real reason for kicking them out," Foucault on the contrary thinks that

> the point that caused the resistance in the others wasn't that they had slept together or, to put things crudely, that one of them had fucked the other, that wasn't what was intolerable; it was that the next morning they held hands, that they kissed each other at breakfast, that they couldn't keep apart; it was a whole series of pleasures having to do with being together, bodily pleasures, pleasures in looking. . . . And that particular economy of pleasures is what is so unbelievably badly accepted. . . . That's what the prohibition is directed at, that's the most insidious form of prohibition, the most widespread, the one that is never spoken yet that ultimately bans a whole series of things from homosexual lives, makes existence a burden, however tolerated the sexual act may be, for I'd say that tolerance for the act does exist today to a certain degree. (124–25)

Voeltzel is reasonably skeptical and responds: "More or less; that's to say that generally homosexuals keep themselves hidden so everything is sort of fine. As you say, it's their way of conducting themselves that bothers people." Foucault replies, "It's the pleasure that people see, not the pleasure that's hidden" (125).

The thoughts in this exchange seem, of course, to contradict those expressed at the beginning of the conversation, claiming that it is no longer necessary to ask oneself, if one practices homosexual acts, whether one is or is not homosexual. In the reflections that the letter in Libération gives rise to, Foucault says this quite clearly: in his eyes, it is a question not just of homosexual acts but of the whole social perception of homosexuality. Homophobia is directed less at the practices themselves, notably sodomy, than at everything implied in the fact of being together and displaying love. It is not sexuality itself that is targeted, but what Foucault calls the "economy of pleasures." These remarks would seem to shed a new light on the call made in La Volonté de savoir to base the counterattack against the apparatus [dispositif] of sexuality on "bodies and pleasures" and not on "sex and desire."

But all this also announces Foucault's reflections in the years to come. Against the discourse of sexual liberation, against Reich, who exalted the "orgasmic function," against the idea that genital sexuality, once it is disencumbered of mutilating repressions, will be the privileged avenue of individual development, Foucault will repeatedly return, in more or less identical terms, to the figure of two fellows holding hands. From this, he will slowly gain conviction in his thoughts about a "gay mode of life" and a "gay culture" based on new forms of relations between individuals. Thus in a 1978 interview he states: "If people see two guys go off together to sleep in the same bed, that's tolerable, but if the next morning the two get up smiling, if they hold hands, that's unforgivable. It's not leaving to go have fun together that's unbearable, it's getting up happy the next morning."[8] In 1982 he says the same thing, but he has replaced the expressions "being happy together" or "economy of pleasures" with the notion of a "style of life": "I think that what most bothers those who are not gay about gayness is the style of gay life, not sex acts themselves."[9]

From this point on, Foucault will thus oppose the trend of "always more sex" and "always more truth in sex" with a movement that consists not of "rediscovering" but of "fabricating other forms of pleasure, of relationships, coexistences, attachments, loves, intensities."[10] In 1981, when he denounces the "great myth" of the lack of difference between homosexuality and heterosexuality that had been propagated in leftist discourse in the 1960s and 1970s, he insists once again that what makes homosexuality "troubling" is "the homosexual mode of life, much more than the sexual act itself." He adds, "To imagine a sexual act that doesn't conform to law or nature is not what disturbs people. But that individuals begin to love one another—there's the problem."[11] He clarifies this by adding:

> One of the concessions one makes to others is not to present homosexuality as anything but a kind of immediate pleasure, of two young men meeting in the street, seducing each other with a look, grabbing each other's asses and getting each other off in a quarter of an hour. There you have a kind of neat image of homosexuality without any possibility of generating unease, and for two reasons: it responds to a comforting canon of beauty, and it cancels everything that can be troubling in affection, tenderness, friendship, fidelity, camaraderie, and companionship, things that our rather sanitized society can't allow a place for without fearing the formation of new alliances and the tying together of unforeseen lines of force. (136)

Against Hocquenghem, against the discourse of sexual liberation, Foucault affirms that it is not so much in the "sexualization" of society, of cruising, of public sex—not in the multiplication of partners, and so forth—that we should look for the mechanism that destabilizes the established order. Rather, we should look to the invention of new modes of life, to new modes of relation between individuals: "The affirmation that to be a homosexual is for a man to love another man—this search for a way of life runs counter to the ideology of the sexual liberation movements of the sixties. . . . Homosexuality is a historic occasion to reopen affective and relational virtualities, not so much through the intrinsic qualities of the homosexual but because the "slantwise" position of the latter, as it were, the diagonal lines he can lay out in the social fabric allow these virtualities to come to light" (138). It is to the invention of some such "relational system" (137) that one should look to discover the possibility of reinventing oneself or of escaping from subjugation at the hands of social norms.

10

Resistance and Counterdiscourse

At the outset of the 1970s, Foucault's political commitments were focused in the area of the "seizure of speech" [*prise de la parole*], conceived of in the light of his earlier works. When he created the GIP (Group for Information about Prisons) in 1971, he presented the movement's goals in the following way: "The GIP does not propose to speak on behalf of the inmates of various prisons. Instead, it proposes to give them the possibility of speaking about themselves and about what goes on in prison. The goal of the GIP is not a reformist one. We do not dream of some ideal prison: our wish is that the prisoners should be able to express what is intolerable in the system of penal repression. We will try to broadcast as quickly and as widely as possible the revelations of the prisoners themselves."[1]

We are not far from the way in which Guy Hocquenghem presented the April 1971 *Tout* special issue on sexuality: "As for fags, dykes, women, prison inmates, women who have had abortions, people who have been declared asocial or mad . . . no speaking for them. They have begun to speak for themselves, based on their desire, based on their oppression. They demand the right to do as they please with their bodies."[2] In fact, the FHAR and the GIP would often be involved in the same political protests, as, for example, in the 1972 protest at the death of Gérard Grandmontagne, an inmate who had been placed in solitary confinement because of his homosexuality and who had killed himself there.[3]

In 1973, while he was participating in the founding of the newspaper *Libération*, Foucault proposed in the same vein that committees be set up to collect information and pass it along to the paper's writers and editors, who would be responsible for diffusing it. In his eyes, these committees were to be in direct communication with the feminist movement, the gay movement, and others. Foucault also wanted the paper to establish a "chronicle of the memory of the working class" that would have collected recollections of various struggles and then "recounted" them.[4]

Even after the publication of La Volonté de savoir Foucault would not totally abandon this politics of "speech" [la parole]. For example, "Lives of Infamous Men," which belongs to this line of thought and which might seem more closely related to Madness and Civilization than to the History of Sexuality, was published in 1977. We could remark the same thing about the collection Foucault launched in 1978, "Parallel Lives." In the text presenting the collection, Foucault wrote:

> The Ancients liked to display lives of famous men in parallel fashion. One could hear these exemplary shades converse across centuries. Parallel lines, I know, meet at infinity. Let us imagine others, which would always diverge—no meeting point nor any place for them to be collected. Often their only echo is that of their condemnation. We would have to grasp them in the force of the movement that separates them; we would have to rediscover the dazzling, momentary wake left behind as they rushed into an obscurity from which "nothing more is heard," and where all "fame" is lost.[5]

The first volume of this short-lived collection (there would only be two volumes) would be made up of the memoirs of the nineteenth-century hermaphrodite, Herculine Barbin.

⹔ What transformations would come about in Foucault's political thinking, especially about gay issues, as a result of the theoretical work done in La Volonté de savoir? It would be worth first making the point that Foucault obviously intended no critique of the legitimacy of the gay movement when he wrote that the "personage" of the "homosexual" was invented only in 1870. Quite the contrary. The analytics of power that he elaborated in this book is based on the idea, as he put it in his teaching at the Collège de France in 1975–1976, that "politics is war continued by other means."[6] This conveys Foucault's intention to substitute for a model of power based on organized repression by a sovereign one based on the idea of "a mobile field of force relations."[7] Power is everywhere, in every social relation, at all levels of society. But any instance of power immediately encounters resistance, or better, "resistances" (HS1, 96). Power is effective and has meaning only because it finds points of "support" in various points of resistance. Yet it must immediately be added, and the two levels cannot be dissociated, that power, immediately upon being exercised, causes points of resistance to come into being. In short, power relationships are "strictly relational" (95).

In this context, Foucault presents what he refers to as the "rule of the tactical polyvalence of discourses." He means by this that there is not, on one side, the discourse of power, and, on the other, the discourse of resistance, but rather "a multiplicity of discursive elements that can come into play in various strategies." Thus a given enunciation will function differently in a given field of power relations depending on who gives voice to it. "Identical formulas" can be subjected to "shifts and reutilizations . . . for contrary objectives" (100). At this point, Foucault introduces the notion of "reverse" discourse that is so essential to his analytics of power, and he does so in reference to the analyses performed earlier in the volume regarding the invention of the "homosexual":

> There is no question that the appearance in nineteenth-century psychiatry, jurisprudence, and literature of a whole series of discourses on the species and subspecies of homosexuality, inversion, pederasty, and "psychic hermaphrodism" made possible a strong advance of social controls into this area of "perversity"; but it also made possible the formation of a "reverse" discourse: homosexuality began to speak in its own behalf, to demand that its legitimacy or "naturality" be acknowledged, often in the same vocabulary, using the same categories by which it was medically disqualified. There is not, on the one side, a discourse of power, and opposite it, another discourse that runs counter to it. Discourses are tactical elements or blocks operating in the field of force relations; there can exist different and even contradictory discourses within the same strategy; they can, on the contrary, circulate without changing their form from one strategy to another, opposing strategy. There is no point in mainly asking questions as to what implicit theories these discourses rely on, or what moral constructs they are perpetuating, or what ideology—dominant or dominated—they represent; rather we must question them on the two levels of their tactical productivity (what reciprocal effects of power and knowledge they ensure) and their strategical integration (what set of circumstances and what distribution of power make their utilization necessary in a given episode of the various confrontations that occur). (101–02; translation modified)

This means that "resistance" may consist in giving a new meaning to a given enunciation or a given discourse. Power may find "support" in points of "resistance," but resistances often gain strength by strategically turning around what power has done. "Reverse" discourse or counterdiscourse is thus not necessarily another discourse, an opposite discourse. It might be the same discourse, relying on the same categories, but turning them around or transforming their meaning. What takes place might be a reappropriation of the meanings power has produced in order to transform their value. Judith Butler has aptly referred to this as a process of "resignification." An enunciation or a discourse never has its meaning defined once and for all: the meaning varies according to the strategic functions it is meant to fulfill. The same discourse can have different, even opposite, meanings, just as discourses that initially seem to be opposed might have the same meaning. In any case, resistance can never be exterior to power relations. It is always situated, always contextual.[8] One might say, paraphrasing the title of one of Foucault's articles, that there is no "thought from outside." Action always takes place within a strategic configuration in which it happens according to rules of transformation for which it is in part responsible; but it can never escape from the mobile, shifting, always relational system of power relations.

⊁ Oddly enough, toward the end of his book, Foucault seems to leave behind his own definitions. This happens at a moment when he turns to the political ideas of Wilhelm Reich:

> Thus between the two world wars there was formed, around Reich, the historico-political critique of sexual repression. The importance of this critique and its impact on reality were substantial. But the very possibility of its success was tied to the fact that it always unfolded within the apparatus [dispositif] of sexuality, and not outside or against it. The fact that so many things were able to change in the sexual behavior of Western societies without any of the promises or political conditions predicted by Reich being realized is sufficient proof that this whole sexual "revolution," this whole "antirepressive" struggle, represented nothing more, but nothing less—and its importance is undeniable—than a tactical shift and reversal in the great apparatus of sexuality. But it is also apparent why one could not expect this critique to be the grid

for a history of that very apparatus. Nor the basis for a movement to dismantle it. (131; translation modified)

Does this imply that it would be possible to "dismantle" the "apparatus" of power? Does it imply that historical critique could be the basis of a political movement situated in an external relation to the strategic field of force relations and of "tactical shifts"? That "resistance" could undo the system it confronts, but in which it is also caught up? When, in the final pages of his book, Foucault attempts to specify what this dismantling might be, he does return to the vocabulary of strategies: "It is the insistent presence of sex that we must break away from, if we aim—through a tactical reversal of the various mechanisms of sexuality—to counter the grips of power with the claims of bodies, pleasures, and knowledges, in their multiplicity and their possibility of resistance. The rallying point for the counterattack against the apparatus of sexuality ought not to be sex-desire, but bodies and pleasures" (157; translation modified).

All of Foucault's thinking will unfold in this interlocking set of problematics, between, on one hand, the necessity (one constitutive of the very idea of "resistance") of struggling within a particular strategic field, and, on the other, the possibility of a critical and historical interrogation that would allow for the dismantling of an apparatus and also for a political activity that would consist in the invention of "other spaces." Thanks to these other spaces, one could escape, to whatever extent possible, from a system of power relations and also from the opposition between technologies of power and strategic reversals, between discourse and counterdiscourse. Foucault's "gay politics" is mapped out in this double movement, in the double gestures of resistance and of "heterotopia": the invention, perhaps within urban geographies, perhaps within individual or collective consciousnesses, of new possibilities existing outside established systems. The entire thematic of subjectivation, of practices of the self, of the stylization of life, of the construction of a gay culture, belongs to the second movement, to the heterotopical gesture, to the idea of establishing a divergent relation to the system of subjugation.[9]

⊁ Perhaps linked to this double movement is the development at the end of the 1970s and into the 1980s of a tension in Foucault's thought about homosexuality. On one hand, there is the idea that homosexuality is not a natural given, that it is not unchanging throughout the centuries, that it is something that appeared in the nineteenth century. On the other is the evidence that throughout history there have been conscious identities, both individual and collective, that formed around the fact that certain individuals practiced a particular or a minority sexuality. On this latter point, Foucault refers to the book by John Boswell, Christianity, Social Tolerance, and Homosexuality.[10]

It is worth insisting on this tension, because English language scholarship is today largely founded on the idea of a radical rupture with Boswell (the target of many attacks), one it is taken for granted that Foucault enabled. The pages in La Volonté de savoir that are devoted to the invention of the personage of the homosexual in the nineteenth century have, in effect, given rise to what has come to be called the "constructionist" approach.[11] Boswell set out to look for "gay subcultures" or "gay people" in the Middle Ages.[12] The historicization by Foucault of sexuality categories does seem to turn its back on this "essentialist" way of conceiving things.[13] But Foucault's readers rapidly forgot that the page in La Volonté de savoir on the "invention of the homosexual" was first of all, and above all, a polemical statement, a strategic intervention, that needed to be situated in the theoretical context in which it was made. As for Foucault himself, if he did in fact seem himself to adhere to the idea of a historical rupture provoked by psychiatry in 1870, he soon nuanced his position, especially once he had read Boswell's book. Unfortunately, that page of La Volonté de savoir has taken on doctrinal status on the American side of the Atlantic, where endless books and articles repeat that there were no "identities" before the end of the nineteenth century, but rather simply acts occurring between people of the same sex.[14] Further, it is rather astonishing to note that no one among all those who go on repeating the dogma about the invention of homosexuality in 1870 ever mentions, even dismissively, Foucault's markedly different analyses in Histoire de la folie, analyses that seem to have been completely overshadowed by La Volonté de savoir.[15] But Foucault mentioned his agreement with Boswell many times.

Before developing this point any further, it might be useful to note that Foucault rapidly became aware that the periodization he proposed in La Volonté de savoir was dubious. If he had to abandon the project as he had initially conceived it, perhaps it was because the historical turning points he had set out could not stand up under scrutiny. As we have seen, at the heart of his book is the idea (one without which the thematic of confession [l'aveu] is incomprehensible) that desire was inscribed into the very personhood of individuals as their true nature, their deepest truth. "Sexuality" is a "histor-ical apparatus." But when was it formed? When was it set in place? In the 1981 text called "Sexuality and Solitude," Foucault describes the discussions he had with the historian of antiquity Peter Brown, whom he met in Berkeley, and whose work was to become important for Foucault: "Recently, Professor Peter Brown stated to me that what we have to understand is why it is that sexuality became, in Christian cultures, the seismograph of our subjectivity. It is a fact, a mysterious fact, that in the indefinite spiral of truth and reality in the self sexuality has been of major importance since the first centuries of our era. Why is there such a fundamental connection between sexuality, subjectivity, and truth obligation?"[16]

Brown's work in fact shows clearly how this process of the personal interiorization of sexuality, of desire can be located at least as far back in time as the earliest years of Christianity.[17] Was it because of meeting this historian that Foucault changed the direction of his research? In any case, Foucault quickly realized that it would not be sufficient simply to go back three hundred or so years in order to locate the origin of the contemporary appara-tus of sexuality in the confessional techniques that were issued during the Counter Reformation. He would have to go even further back, to the earliest days of Christianity.[18] This explains why Foucault set to working on St. Augustine for his volume Les Aveux de la chair (The Confessions of the Flesh), which he began to write once he had given up on the initial plan for his work. Is it really possible to imagine that the theoretical and historical rethinking to which Foucault was led by the internal logic of his own research was applica-ble only to sexuality in general, and not also to homosexuality?

In his later reflections, Foucault would frequently refer to two books on the history of homosexuality that were of particular interest to him: Boswell's book, as I have already mentioned, and also Dover's Greek Homosexuality. When commenting on Dover's book, he tends to emphasize the dissolution of the category of "homosexuality" by "historical nominalism." When dis-cussing Boswell, he emphasizes the incontestable fact that there have been "gay cultures" throughout history. Yet in his eyes, the two books have a common ground; henceforth for Foucault it will be part of the same project to claim both that "homosexual" loves cannot be understood as some kind of anthropological constant and that they have throughout history served—for individuals attracted to others of the same sex—as a basis for a consciousness of belonging to a specific minority. In 1982, in an article devoted to the appearance of the French translation of Dover's book, he writes:

Dover clears for us an entire landscape that had been rather cluttered. There will, of course, always be those friendly folk who think that basically homosexuality always existed. Cambacérès, the Duke Crequi, Michelangelo, or Timarchus all prove that. To such naive people, Dover offers a strong lesson in historical nominalism. A relation between two individuals of the same sex is one thing. But to love someone of the same sex as you, to take your pleasure with that person, is something else; it is an entire experience, with objects and their values, with the subject's ways of being and the subject's consciousness of self. It is a complex experience; it is diverse; its forms change. There is an entire history to be written of "the other of the same sex" as an object for pleasure. This is what Dover has done for classical Greece.[19]

He will comment on Boswell's book in almost identical terms in an interview for the French journal *Masques* that appeared in 1982:

His idea is the following: if men have sexual relations among themselves, whether between an adult and a young man in the city or in the monastery, it is not only because of the tolerance of others vis-à-vis a certain form of sexual act; it implies necessarily a culture, that is to say, modes of expression, valorizations, etc., and thus the recognition by the subjects themselves of the specific nature of these relations. One can admit this idea as long as it doesn't imply a constant sexual or anthropomorphic category, but a cultural phenomenon that changes in time while maintaining itself in its general formulation: a relation between individuals of the same sex that entails a mode of life in which the consciousness of being singular among others is present.[20]

In another interview from the same year that Foucault published in the United States, he also speaks of Boswell:

Sexual behavior is not, as is too often assumed, a superimposition of, on the one hand, desires that derive from natural instincts, and, on the other hand, of permissive or restrictive laws that tell us what we should or shouldn't do. Sexual behavior is more than that. It is also the consciousness one has of what one is doing, what one makes of the experience, and the value one attaches to it. It is in this sense that I think the concept "gay" contributes to a positive (rather than a purely negative) appreciation of the type of consciousness in which affection, love, desire, sexual rapport with people have a positive significance.[21]

He adds a bit later in the same interview, "Homosexual consciousness certainly goes beyond one's individual experience and includes an awareness of being a member of a particular social group. This is an undeniable fact that dates back to ancient times" (142–43).

It is precisely because this individual and collective consciousness not only exists and perpetuates itself from century to century, but also "changes over time and varies from place to place" (143)—and so can be transformed and reinvented—that such an idea becomes the basis for Foucault's "gay politics."

11

Becoming Gay

In the years between the publication of *La Volonté de savoir* and his death in 1984, Foucault frequently had things to say about the gay movement and gay issues in general, most notably in a series of interviews given both in the United States and in France.[1] These texts make up not so much a coherent set of reflections as a set of variations on a theme and notes for further research.[2] Foucault often formulates what he has to say hypothetically and he frequently contradicts himself. Sometimes he seems to be thinking out loud in front of his questioners without having any particularly fixed ideas about the matter at hand.[3]

All these texts are closely tied to the work Foucault undertook in those years in order to write the later volumes of his *History of Sexuality*. They clearly grow out of Foucault's thinking in *La Volonté de savoir*, yet also—given the shift in what is strategically at stake from the 1970s to the 1980s—mark a profound break with that book. For example, in these interviews, Foucault sketches out a history of the "repression"—or better, the "surveillance" and the "inspection" of homosexuality: "It's a very complicated history, and I would say that it has three stages."[4]

About the first stage he observes: "From the Middle Ages, there existed a law against sodomy, which carried the death penalty, but it was seldom applied." He continues:

> The second aspect is the practice of the police in regard to homosexuality, very clear in France in the mid-seventeenth century, an epoch when cities actually exist, where a certain type of police surveillance is in place and where, for example, one observes the arrest, relatively massive, of homosexuals—in the Jardin du Luxembourg, Saint-Germain-des-Près, or the Palais Royal. One observes dozens of arrests; names are

taken down, people are arrested for several days or are simply released. Some remain "in the hole" without trial. A whole system of traps and threats is set up, with cops and police spies, a little world is put into place very early, in the seventeenth and eighteenth centuries. . . . This is all inscribed within the framework of a surveillance and organisation of a world of prostitutes—kept women, dancers, actresses—fully developing in the eighteenth century. But it seems to me that the surveillance of homosexuality began a little earlier. (369)

Finally, the third stage in this history "is obviously the noisy entry of homosexuality into the field of medical reflection in the mid-nineteenth century. It had happened more discreetly during the eighteenth and at the beginning of the nineteenth centuries" (369; it is clearly a typographical error that the text reads "seventeenth" instead of "eighteenth" century here). Foucault concludes these remarks by specifying that it is a question of "a social phenomenon of great scale, more complicated than a simple invention of doctors."[5]

In any case, Foucault will henceforth emphasize the "repression" of homosexuality, doubtless in order to counteract what he perceived as an incorrect reading of La Volonté de savoir. In a 1982 interview, for instance, he would insist that "in a society like ours . . . homosexuality is repressed, and severely so," and in the same interview he would declare that "in Christian culture of the West, homosexuality was banished."[6] This is why he repeatedly emphasizes the importance of the sexual liberation movements of the 1970s, just as he did at the end of La Volonté de savoir, where he mentioned the important role played by Wilhelm Reich. He consistently came back to this point in his interviews from these years.[7] Looking back on those movements, he insists on their important achievements: "It's quite true that there was a real liberation process in the early seventies. This process was very good, both in terms of the situation and in terms of opinions."[8] He explains in this same interview why he had critiqued the notion of "sexual liberation":

What I meant was that I think what the gay movement needs now is much more the art of life than a science or scientific knowledge (or pseudo-scientific knowledge) of what sexuality is. Sexuality is a part of our behavior. It's a part of our world freedom. Sexuality is something that we ourselves create—it is our own creation, and much more than the discovery of a secret side of our desire. We have to understand that with our desires, through our desires, go new forms of relationships, new forms of love, new forms of creation.[9]

This rejection of "biologism" and of "naturalism" make sense in the light of the direction of Foucault's thinking; what he says here about sexuality could be understood as one example of the articulation in his thought between theoretical work (whose goal is to find the "contingency" of the "historical event" lurking beneath the seeming naturalness of the most quotidian institutions and gestures) and a political project that would invite one to free oneself of certain burdens that history had left behind.[10]

This can be seen as well in the "fraternal" critique that Foucault directs at the theses of the thinkers of the Frankfurt School. Whatever common sources of inspiration might link Foucault to Horkheimer and Adorno, Foucault insists on the essential point of disagreement between them: "I don't think that the Frankfurt School can accept that what we need to do is not to recover our lost identity, or liberate our imprisoned nature, or discover our fundamental truth; rather, it is to move toward something altogether different."[11]

It is in this light that one should understand certain formulas that are repeated throughout these interviews, such as this one from 1981: "Homosexuality is not a form of desire but something desirable. Therefore we have to work at becoming homosexuals and not be obstinate in recognizing that we are."[12] Or, again, in 1982, when he is asked about what he meant in his comment from 1981:

> I wanted to say, "we have to work at being gay," placing ourselves in a dimension where the sexual choices made are present and have their effects over the whole of our life. I also meant that these sexual choices must at the same time be creative of ways of life. To be gay means that these choices spread across a whole life; it's also a certain way of refusing life paths that are set out for us; it is to make one's sexual choice the pivot of a change of existence. Not to be gay is to say: "How am I going to be able to limit the effects of my sexual choice in such a way that my life doesn't change in any way?" I would say: one must make use of one's sexuality to discover, to invent new relations. To be gay is to be in a state of becoming. To respond to your question, I would add that one should not be homosexual but should work to be gay.[13]

⊁ But to "become gay," it is first necessary to be "homosexual." Foucault always insists on this point: the battle for rights, for freedom, is a necessary, primary task. This is why he gives as the primary goal of the gay movement the achievement of freedom of choice: "It is important, first, to have the possibility—and the right—to choose your own sexuality. Human rights regarding sexuality are important and are still not respected in many places. We shouldn't consider that such problems are solved now."[14]

Yet while he never ceases to reaffirm that we should be "intransigent" on this point, Foucault has no intention of limiting his approach to the attainment of rights that already exist and to the possibility of gaining access to modes of life that are already established: "We should consider the battle for gay rights as an episode that cannot be the final stage." This is first of all because he knows that a legal right, "in its real effects, is much more linked to attitudes and patterns of behavior than to legal formulations. There can be discrimination against homosexuals even if such discriminations are prohibited by law."[15] But it is above all because it seems necessary to Foucault to move beyond the stage of making demands that, however essential, will be limited to the effort to open "already existing cultural fields" to same-sex loves. He does of course support, if reticently, the struggles already underway at the time for the legal and social recognition of homosexual couples, the right to adoption, and so on. Asked about marriage, Foucault replies that this struggle is "very interesting," yet emphasizes that it will be "difficult work." And indeed he was right! But he makes a point of insisting that this could only be a first step: "If you ask people to reproduce the marriage bond for their personal relationship to be recognized, the progress made is slight. We live in a relational world that institutions have considerably impoverished. . . . We should fight against the impoverishment of the relational fabric. We should secure recognition for relations of provisional coexistence, adoption." His interviewer interjects the question, "Of children?" Foucault replies, "Or—why not?—of one adult by another."[16]

Foucault is most interested by the struggle for the social and legal recognition of these different and multiple forms of relations, of these "other spaces" of relational and emotional life: "The fact of making love with someone of the same sex can very naturally involve a whole series of choices, a whole series of other values and choices for which there are not yet real possibilities."[17] It is therefore necessary "to imagine and create a new relational right that permits all possible types of relations to exist and not be prevented, blocked, or annulled by impoverished relational institutions" (158).

Basically Foucault proposes a reversal of the procedure in which one takes for a model the social norms of heterosexuality and asks for the right of access to them:

> Rather than saying what we said at one time, "Let's try to re-introduce homosexuality into the general norm of social relations," let's say the reverse—"No! Let's escape as much as possible from the type of relations that society proposes for us and try to create in the empty space where we are new relational possibilities." By proposing a new relational *right*, we will see that nonhomosexual people can enrich their lives by changing their own schema of relations.[18]

Instead of modeling their aspirations on heterosexual ways of life, gays should rather consider that their own inventiveness in the way of modes of existence and of relation could aid in the renewal of laws and institutions—a renewal from which heterosexuals might profit as well, in order to escape from the yoke of conjugal normality and the limitations it places on possible relations.[19]

❥ It is clear that from whatever angle Foucault considers the question of homosexuality in the 1980s he always comes back to the idea of the invention of new possibilities, of new modes of life, of new relations between the individuals involved: "Not only do we have to defend ourselves, but also affirm ourselves, and affirm ourselves not only as an identity but as a creative force." It is truly a question of "creating culture."[20]

Foucault always remains evasive about what this "new culture" or these "cultural creations" might be. This is hardly surprising: his point is not to propose a program, for that would curb inventiveness. "The idea of a program of proposals is dangerous. As soon as a program is presented, it becomes a law, and there's a prohibition against inventing. There ought to be an inventiveness special to a situation like ours and to this longing that Americans call 'coming out,' that is, showing oneself. The program must be wide open."[21]

This refusal to prescribe a vision of the future, to define ahead of time what kinds of new possibilities there might be, is quite consistent with Foucault's theoretical and political thought more generally. It is no surprise that it turns out to be at the end of an interview on homosexuality that he launches into a long critique of the very idea of a political program, emphasizing to what an extent it was important that the social movements of the

1960s and 70s ("sexual liberty, ecology, prisons," he says) were able to exist and develop without being answerable to specific programs. Foucault had many reservations about political parties, about the "party function." His refusal of programs or platforms is deeply linked to what was for him a central idea, that action is above all resistance, or better, a multiplicity of partial resistances whose coherence in the face of their diversity is "strategic" (by which he means that struggles are defined by that which they oppose). His refusal is also tied to the idea that resistances do not always proceed through a gesture of refusal, but could just as well take on the form of experimenting with new practices and new modes of existence:

> Since the nineteenth century, great political institutions and great political parties have confiscated the process of political creation; that is, they have tried to give to political creation the form of a political program in order to take over power. I think what happened in the sixties and early seventies is something to be preserved. One of the things that I think should be preserved is the fact that there has been political innovation, political creation, and political experimentation outside the great political parties, and outside the normal or ordinary program. It's a fact that people's everyday lives have changed from the early sixties to now, and certainly within my own life. And surely that is not due to political parties but is the result of many movements. These social movements have really changed our whole lives, our mentality, our attitudes, and the attitudes and mentality of other people—people who do not belong to these movements.[22]

⊮ Even if Foucault does not formulate a program, he does give a few general indications about what "gay culture" might be. It is in this context that he offers some reflections on friendship. Indeed, when he speaks of a new "culture" that will invent "ways of relating, types of existence, types of value, types of exchanges between individuals which are really new and are neither the same as, nor superimposed on, existing cultural forms," he nearly always refers to "relations of friendship" as they existed in Greek and Roman antiquity. These were, he says, relations inscribed within an institutional framework that was "supple" even if "it was sometimes constraining." The framework constructed "a system of obligations, tasks, reciprocal duties." Foucault does not suggest a return to this model, but suggests that we can see in it an example of a system that was "supple and relatively codified" and that permitted "important and stable relations, which we now have great difficulty defining."[23]

The theme of friendship returns as a constant preoccupation throughout the interviews Foucault gives at the beginning of the 1980s: "One thing that interests me now is the problem of friendship," he states in 1982 in the interview "Sex, Power, and the Politics of Identity."[24] He remarks once again in this extremely important text that "for centuries after antiquity, friendship was a very important kind of social relation: a social relation within which people had a certain freedom, a certain kind of choice (limited of course), as well as very intense emotional relations. There were also economic and social implications to these relationships—they were obliged to help their friends" (170).

This type of friendship, Foucault adds, disappeared in the sixteenth and seventeenth centuries, "at least in the male society." At that same moment, certain authors began to critique friendship as "dangerous." Foucault offers the following hypothesis:

> Homosexuality became a problem—that is, sex between men became a problem—in the eighteenth century. We see the rise of it as a problem with the police, within the justice system, and so on. I think the reason it appears as a problem, as a social issue, at this time is that friendship had disappeared. As long as friendship was something important, was socially accepted, nobody realized men had sex together. You couldn't say that men didn't have sex together—it just didn't matter. It had no social implication, it was culturally accepted. . . . Once friendship disappeared as a culturally accepted relation, the issue arose: "What is going on between men?" And that's when the problem appears. . . . The disappearance of friendship as a social relation and the declaration of homosexuality as a social/political/medical problem are the same process. (171)

That explains why Foucault asserts that having undertaken to write the history of sexuality, "now we should study the history of friendship, or friendships" (171).

12

Among Men

For the Foucault of the beginning of the 1980s, the idea of friendship represented more than a historical detour that allowed him to evoke new kinds of relations between individuals. It also allowed him to imagine a "relational system" that could become the principle of a differentiation internal to a society: the "gay mode of life" could thus become a divergence, an "other space" in which individuals would produce themselves as a social group thanks to a common sexuality.

Foucault made no secret of the fact that his reflections were inspired by his acquaintance with gay "communities" in the United States, in New York, and especially in San Francisco, an acquaintance begun enthusiastically in the mid-1970s, when he began giving courses at a number of universities, notably Berkeley.[1] He says in 1981, while giving a description of gay life in big American cities, "In the United States . . . the interest in friendship has become very important; one doesn't enter a relationship simply in order to be able to consummate it sexually, which happens very easily; what people are drawn to is friendship." He then asks, "How can a relational system be reached through sexual practices? Is it possible to create a homosexual mode of life?" Then he goes on: "This notion of mode of life seems important to me. Will it require the introduction of a diversification different from the ones due to social class, differences in profession and culture, a diversification that would also be a form of relationship and would be a 'way of life'? A way of life can be shared among individuals of different age, status, and social activity."[2] One sees clearly that Foucault acts here as the theoretician of a form of sociability that neoconservative discourse in France today polemically labels "homosexual separatism": a way of life chosen and constructed by a group of individuals, one that, as Foucault puts it, "can yield a culture" (138).

What Foucault calls "gay culture" is closely linked to what we today call "gay communities," to the existence of bars, clubs, bathhouses, sexual meeting places—for alongside this "new system of relations" that he ardently wished for, Foucault also insisted on a second direction in which gay culture should move in order to escape from regimes of social and sexual normality: "the intensification of pleasures."

There is no doubt that Foucault is thinking of San Francisco when he gives this series of interviews in the 1980s. One has only to read what he says of sadomasochistic practices as the crucible in which a subculture with new personal identities is forged:

> The idea that S&M is related to a deep violence, that S&M practice is a way of liberating this violence, this aggression, is stupid. We know very well what all those people are doing is not aggressive; they are inventing new possibilities of pleasure with strange parts of their body— through the eroticization of the body. I think it's a kind of creation, a creative enterprise, which has as one of its main features what I call the desexualization of pleasure. The idea that bodily pleasure should always come from sexual pleasure as the root of all our possible pleasures—I think that's something quite wrong. These practices are insisting that we can produce pleasure with very odd things, very strange parts of our bodies, in very unusual situations, and so on. . . . The practice of S&M is the creation of pleasure, and there is an identity with that creation. And that's why S&M is really a subculture. It's a process of invention.[3]

Foucault finds in gay communities spaces in which new ways of life are invented, yet obviously that does not imply that he will always necessarily approve of what is produced there. "Danger" is everywhere, for Foucault, and all groups give off the effects of power toward which one should always show a certain "distrustfulness."[4] This general attitude of distrust must continually be transformed into a "critical practice" and elaborated as a "critical analysis." The role of the intellectual is therefore always "negative."[5] Yet when the sociologist Robert Bellah asks him if, in the struggle against certain instances of state power, one couldn't imagine a certain "participation with others, if not a party, perhaps a part of a party, if not a church, at least a congregation, in any case some kind of context in which the individual would not feel entirely alone," Foucault responds to him:

When I speak of this attitude of suspicion, it's only a general attitude. Because there is no relation to power, in any society, that is not dangerous, that is not on the level of [here some words are missing], of sexual relations, of small communities, and so on. This is why I think general suspicion is necessary. I don't think we can oppose a good kind of community to a bad kind of community. They are all dangerous, but each represents a particular kind of danger and also a particular degree of danger, so we can't always react in the same way. Sometimes we should use the support of this or that kind of community in order to resist a greater danger from another community. . . . These strategies and shifts in strategy are very important. So the general attitude of suspicion is not necessarily a solitary attitude.[6]

One could conclude from these remarks that for Foucault the gay "community" is in no way free from "danger," for all communities, of any kind, bring danger with them. Yet the constitution of these communities remains for him an important, even a fundamental part of the struggle to invent new forms of existence and to invent new styles of life—all in order to escape from the much more serious looming danger of the rigors of the norm and of the totality of a "disciplinary" society.[7]

↦ Given that Foucault always thinks of "gay ways of life" within the horizon of sexuality (for him the link between the individuals who participate in the culture is first of all and primarily a shared sexuality, that is to say, homosexuality), his reflections on the "culture" to be invented are always circumscribed by monosexuality.

One might well be surprised by this. For even if bars or meeting places (not to mention bathhouses), and therefore a large section of the "gay way of life" of which Foucault is speaking, are necessarily monosexual, it is hard to understand why friendship and the "culture" founded on friendship should also be so. In his insistence on the idea of monosexuality, Foucault contradicts what he endlessly affirms about the necessity not to prescribe what a future culture might be, not to pose limits, but rather to open it out onto the improbable or the unthinkable.

It will not do to imagine that he proceeds in this way through inadvertence or because he was thinking only of the example of gay neighborhoods in the United States. Monosexuality is not something he has observed; it is something he has thought about; it is a politics. He insists on this explicitly when asked about the fact that since the 1970s many bars have ceased to be "private clubs." His interviewer sees in this the effect of a new situation characterized by the greater freedom of the new moment. "Absolutely," Foucault replies. But he hastens to add that this also has something to do with the fact that gays themselves are "uneasy about monosexuality." A bit later on he returns to this point:

> In the often-negative response some French people have toward certain types of American behavior, there is still that disapproval of monosexuality. So occasionally we hear: "What? How can you approve of those macho models? You're always with men, you have mustaches and leather jackets, you wear boots, what kind of masculine image is that?" Maybe in ten years we'll laugh about it all. But I think in the schema of a man affirming himself as a man, there is a movement towards redefining the monosexual relation. It consists of saying, "Yes, we spend our time with men, we have mustaches, and we kiss each other," without one of the partners having to play the role of the *éphèbe* or the effeminate, fragile boy.[8]

There are several reasons for this insistence on monosexuality. The first recalls the considerations mentioned in earlier chapters about guys holding hands: the life of men among themselves, gay neighborhoods, gay ways of life all constitute spaces in which such gestures are possible without the participants risking violence or insult. To affirm that being gay means being able to hold hands also implies that one creates the means for holding hands.

There is also very clearly a second reason. Foucault continues in his interviews from the 1980s to critique the idea of a natural bisexuality or polysexuality—an idea that had, as we have seen, haunted the sexual liberation movements of the 1970s. Monosexuality as a way of life is the exact opposite of the myth of a great fusion of all individuals into an undifferentiated sexuality: "The promise that we would love women as soon as we were no longer condemned for being gay was utopian. And a utopia in a dangerous sense . . . because it was at the expense of monosexual relations."[9] Yet these discourses on polysexuality had mostly ceased to be of any interest in the 1980s, so much so that it is surprising that Foucault takes the trouble to challenge them. There must be deeper reasons for his apology for monosexuality.

In point of fact, whether Foucault is speaking of a future gay culture or of a historical model of friendship, what interests him is what happens among men: what kinds of feelings they can experience, what kinds of relations they can construct.

Yet, in order to show that intense affective links can exist between men thanks to a shared sexuality, Foucault always has recourse to examples in which it is not sexuality that is important. In the interview "Friendship as a Way of Life," he comes back to the idea that masculine monosexuality has been nearly impossible since the eighteenth century, except when imposed by outside circumstances such as the army or a war. He takes as his example the life of soldiers in the trenches during World War I:

> You had soldiers and young officers who spent months and even years together. During World War I, men lived together completely, one on top of another, and for them it was nothing at all. . . . And apart from several remarks on camaraderie, the brotherhood of spirit, and some very partial observations, what do we know about these emotional uproars and storms of feeling that took place in those times? One can wonder how, in these absurd and grotesque wars and infernal massacres, the men managed to hold on in spite of everything. Through some emotional fabric, no doubt. I don't mean that it was because they were each other's lovers that they continued to fight; but honor, courage, not losing face, sacrifice, leaving the trench with the captain—all that implied a very intense emotional tie. It's not to say: "Ah, there you have homosexuality!" I detest that kind of reasoning. But no doubt you have there one of the conditions, not the only one, that has permitted this infernal life. (139)

This reference to emotional ties between men in the trenches doubtless owes a great deal to Dumézil.[10] Called up in 1916, at the age of eighteen, Dumézil spent two years of his life immersed in the horrors of the war, yet he also experienced a kind of freedom that at the time was only possible in such extreme situations. This explains why he was fond of saying that he had never been so happy as at that moment of his life, a fact also attested to by the dedication to his book, *Mythe et épopée* (Myth and Epic), which speaks of "the noisy parties we had in our twenties."[11] These deep emotional and homoerotic feelings, born under fire in the horrible circumstances of war, were celebrated by many English poets: Siegfried Sasson, Wilfred Owen, Robert Graves, and others.[12] It seems more than likely, as historians of homosexuality have argued, that these wartime experiences had an important influence on the development of gay culture in Europe (and especially in France) in the 1920s. Allan Bérubé has similarly argued that the ties that developed during World War II played a decisive role in the organization of gay life in the 1950s.

Foucault mentioned on several occasions his plan to begin working on a history of war once he had finished his *History of Sexuality*. More precisely, he was interested in a history of armies. It is clear that the military forms of masculine sociability, soldierly forms of male "friendship," would have been one of the topics he would have investigated.

In the interviews he gave in the 1980s about gay issues, however, his main focus was contemporary politics and not history. Two ideas are always collapsed together in these interviews: first, the idea that a sexuality that is common to a disparate group of individuals is capable of uniting them in a shared "culture"; second, that emotional ties between men can exist in the absence of any sexual relation. All the historical examples Foucault mentions fall into the second category. These examples are what enable him to begin to imagine what new kinds of relations between men there might be after the creation of new gay modes of existence. The set of relations Foucault imagines will take root in homosexuality, but some forms of relation that develop will have no necessary link with that sexuality. His way of putting things makes this quite clear: "Homosexuality is a historic occasion to *reopen* affective and relational virtualities."[13]

In this light we can better understand why, in order to support his suggestions regarding the lives of men together, Foucault refers on several occasions to Lillian Faderman's *Surpassing the Love of Men*, which is, after all, a book about the lives of *women* together.

> There is a book that just appeared in the U.S. on the friendship between women. The affection and passion between women is well documented. In the preface, the author states that she began with the idea of unearthing homosexual relationships—but perceived that not only were these relationships not always present but that it was uninteresting whether relationships could be called "homosexual" or not. And by letting the relationship manifest itself as it appeared in words and gestures, other very essential things also appeared: dense, bright, marvelous loves and affections or very dark and sad loves. (138)

In fact Faderman's book postulates that emotional relationships between women can hardly be reduced to sexuality and that in the end, as Foucault saw, answering the question as to whether or not the women she studies, from the sixteenth to the twentieth centuries, engaged in sexual relations is not all that important. We should also note that this set of historical problems was rooted in a separatist feminist tradition, one that now seems a bit dated, a tradition that held to the idea (developed by Adrienne Rich in a well-known article) of a "lesbian continuum" that ranged from simple friendship between women to sexual relations.[14]

This idea of a continuum has been strongly critiqued by women historians and theoreticians, precisely because it amounts to a desexualization of lesbianism,[15] whereas it was precisely this desexualization that was of interest to Foucault. Faderman's historical analysis permitted Foucault to imagine that a whole range of relations might be possible between people of the same sex. The suggestiveness of Faderman's analysis, together with his own remarks about life in the trenches, led Foucault to the idea that this mono-sexual culture (women alone together and men alone together) could provide the basis for a culture that was yet to be invented. Faderman's book thus becomes for him a kind of metaphor for discussing gay male culture: he is simply trying to suggest that very deep relationships, ones involving no sexual relations, can be cultivated between men. Even so, it is a common sexuality (homosexuality) that holds together this new relational network—one that creates a new principle of differentiation within society.

Foucault is perhaps moving a bit too quickly here in his conceptualization of what a "gay culture" might be. He seems to think of it only from the male point of view and as something that only concerns men. Of course he allows for the separate development of a lesbian culture. But he does not pose the question of how the two cultures might meet up. In this sense, even though queer theorists are fond of relying on his work, Foucault seems much closer to gay ways of life from the 1970s and 1980s than to today's "queer" culture, which calls gay and lesbian separatisms into question.

We might even go a step further and wonder if what Foucault is presenting as a new system of relations does not fundamentally resemble some extremely traditional gay ways of life: multiple sexual encounters that sometimes lead to friendships, circles of friends composed of former lovers and their lovers and former lovers, male sociability, links between men of different ages and different backgrounds, visits to gay male bars, cafes, and restaurants. This does not seem far distant from the way many gay men led their lives in the twentieth century.

The gay culture of which Foucault speaks seems thus to be an expansion on a previously unimagined scale of traditional gay male culture, a culture that was, for various obvious reasons, primarily monosexual. Certainly the extraordinary expansion and visibility of these ways of life in the past twenty or thirty years has caused considerable transformation in them. Foucault, as someone who saw all this happen in person, must have been quite struck by the emergence of this phenomenon. But is it not, after all, the same "gay culture" found throughout the century? Finally, is not the only really innovative idea put forth by Foucault that of creating a new legal standing for these relations, one that would allow for the institutionalization of certain specific ties between people of the same sex (the adoption of one adult by another or a kind of domestic partnership that would not be concerned with whether or not the individuals involved had sexual relations)?[16]

Foucault's expressed support for monosexuality can thus be seen as part of a long history; it certainly has a lot do to with his own past. A few years ago, I wrote that, as regards the history of homosexuality, Foucault seemed to me closer to Dumézil than to contemporary gay life.[17] One of the most notable characteristics of the cultural proximity of the two men would doubtless be a certain kind of "misogyny," one that is characteristic of gay men whose forms of sociability were picked up in the years prior to the 1970s.[18] Foucault himself emphasizes the personal basis of his preference for monosexual forms of sociability: "As far back as I remember, to want guys was to want relations with guys. That has always been important for me. Not necessarily in the form of a couple but as a matter of existence: how is it possible for men to be together? To live together, to share their time, their meals, their room, their leisure, their grief, their knowledge, their confidences? What does that mean, to be among men?"[19]

⋫ And so, at the end of this look at Foucault's writings, we find ourselves back at our starting place: where personal experience is the crucible for theoretical and political inspiration. In that crucible we can surely find explanations for the various hesitations, evolutions, and limitations of Foucault's thought on gay issues. We can also understand something of their ability to startle us: what is played out in his thought is the existence of individuals shaped by the entire history of homosexuality, a history of subjugation, but also of resistance and of a consistent heterotopic impulse that encourages gay people to invent different, improbable, unforeseen ways of life—or at least to be continually wondering about their invention.

13
Making Differences

Foucault taught us that we can never situate ourselves outside of politics. "Other spaces," Foucault's heterotopias, to the extent that they move beyond the incantatory stage of subversive utopias, will necessarily be located in a social world whose norms and disciplinary technologies will constrain, dominate, and subjugate or subjectify. We are not, for all of that, condemned to be trapped by power, conquered by its ruses, powerless to escape from its knots and its nets. If the act of dissenting is always relative, if victories are only partial, local, and uncertain, fragile and provisional, that doesn't mean that we are always the losing party. The mythology of all or nothing needs to be set aside. We can, by way of a never-ending critical effort, alter the limits imposed upon us and expand the possibilities for freedom. "We have to move beyond the outside-inside alternative," Foucault wrote in providing his definition of a critical stance. "We have to be at the frontiers. Criticism indeed consists of analyzing and reflecting upon limits."[1]

In opposition to the metaphysics of the subject and to the project of emancipation offered by various famous prophetic philosophical discourses, and also in opposition to all the orders to submit, all the calls to resignation, we can place the idea of "subjectification": the work of transforming and inventing oneself. Such work can be thought of in Foucault's terms, as "a practical critique that takes the form of a possible crossing-over [du franchissement possible]."[2] It is not, after all, simply the point of view of historical studies that Foucault is thinking of as he describes what a critical stance would be. It's not simply a question of studying the past that has made us what we are. It's also a question of breaking the grip of that past, to whatever extent possible. Thus the critical stance is taken up through an "experimental" practice. "This work done at the limits of ourselves must . . . put itself to the test of reality, of contemporary reality, both to grasp the points where change is possible and desirable, and to determine the precise form this change should take" (316).

This experimental practice is always thought of by Foucault as an activity limited to particular domains, to specific and delimited struggles. He never speaks in general terms, but always about "very specific transformations." He gives as examples those "that have proved to be possible in the last twenty years in a certain number of areas which concern our ways of being and thinking, relations to authority, relations between the sexes, the way in which we perceive insanity or illness" (316).

In this perspective, Foucault's remarks often take on a rather Sartrian cast. "We cannot jump outside the situation, and there is no point where you are free from all power relations. But you can always change it."[3] Unlike Sartre, however, Foucault does not believe that our task is necessarily to rediscover some authenticity, as if any such thing could preexist the act of self-transformation, or as if it were the only possible form of relation to oneself:

> The theme of authenticity refers, explicitly or implicitly, to a way of being for the subject that is defined by some relationship of adequacy to oneself. Now it seems to me that one's relation to oneself should be able to be described according to a multiplicity of forms, and authenticity is only one of the modalities that might be possible. It is necessary to imagine that a relation to oneself is structured as a practice with models, conformities, variants, and also creativity. The practice of the self is a complex and multiple domain.[4]

And when Foucault claims to be closer to Nietzsche and to the saying from The Gay Science according to which "one should create one's life by giving style to it through long practice and daily work," it is easy to understand that subjectification is an act that must be constantly renewed, and whose content cannot be dictated in advance.[5] Quite the contrary, each individual and each group will have to choose what form to give it.

Such a political conception, we might add in passing, is surely crucial if we want to move the gay movement beyond the endless struggles by which it is bedeviled, concerning what the "right" path might be: to seek for integration or remain marginalized, to advocate open sexuality or couples and marriage. If subjectification is a form of self-reinvention, then it can only be thought in terms of multiplicity and plurality.

⇉ "To take oneself as object of a complex and difficult elaboration"—is this not, Foucault wonders, the same thing that Baudelaire, in the language of his moment, called dandyism? Indeed, Foucault writes, "Modern man, for Baudelaire, is not the man who goes off to discover himself, his secrets and his hidden truth; he is the man who tries to invent himself. This modernity does not 'liberate man in his own being'; it compels him to face the task of producing himself."[6]

Pierre Hadot is thus surely correct when he offers the reproach that Foucault presents the ancient philosophers too much in the light of nineteenth-century aestheticism and dandyism, and without sufficient attention being paid to the historical truth of their own moral conceptions.[7] This might reveal that the work Foucault devotes to Greece in the last two volumes of his *History of Sexuality* is less motivated by his interest in the Greeks themselves than by his contemporary preoccupations. Foucault is interested in "us, today," what we are, and what it is possible for us to do.[8] It is certainly not the case that he wanted to portray Greece as a golden age that we should try to rediscover. Greece is assuredly not a model for us. In any case, Foucault was not writing a history of solutions that we might think of applying, but rather a history of problems, a history of the ways in which certain areas of human experience have been thought about and organized at different times. So Greece offers us one example of a way in which experience can be problematized, a way that allows us to imagine the invention of a morality and a politics in the light of an aesthetic of existence, that enables us to consider that "the work we have to do" is "principally that of our life and ourselves."[9]

It is, in fact, more than obvious that when Foucault describes the "asceticism" of the sexual morality of Greek Antiquity as an "aesthetic of existence," as an "elaboration and stylization" of oneself, he is not merely laying out a historical theme.[10] He is inquiring into the posterity of these "arts of existence," and this is why he can affirm that "the study of the problematization of sexual behavior in antiquity" is merely "a chapter—one of the first chapters—of that general history of the 'techniques of the self' " (11). He will point out the resurgence of this history during the Renaissance by way of a reference to Burckhardt's studies: "In the Renaissance, you also see—and here I refer to Burckhardt's famous text on the aesthetics of existence—the hero as his own work of art."[11] He rediscovers this same history in the nineteenth century, with Baudelaire; finally, in order to demonstrate that this interest in the "culture of the self" has not disappeared in the twentieth century, he mentions Walter Benjamin's study of the author of *Flowers of Evil*.[12]

Foucault's thinking is thus oriented to the contemporary world, to a political activity we could take up, especially when it comes to the creation of gay culture. So it is that he comes back to the question of ascesis in the interview on "Friendship as a Way of Life": "Asceticism as the renunciation of pleasure has bad connotations. But ascesis is something else: it's the work that one performs on oneself in order to transform oneself or make the self appear which, happily, one never attains. Can that be our problem today? We've rid ourselves of asceticism. Yet it's up to us to advance into a homosexual ascesis that would make us work on ourselves and invent—I do not say discover—a manner of being that is still improbable" (137). Here one sees that ascesis, self-invention, the creation of new forms of life, of new kinds of relations—everything that Foucault includes in the idea of "subjectification"—has nothing to do with "private life." It refers, to cite Gilles Deleuze one more time, to "the way individuals and communities are constituted as subjects on the margins of established forms of knowledge and instituted powers."[13]

The idea of "subjectification" thus has nothing to do with the so-called return to the subject that some have claimed to see in the late Foucault. Far from calling us to a hermeneutics of subjectivity, he invites us to think about the very possibility of a subject as something produced only provisionally, to be continually remade, in the work of self-creation, be it individual or collective. In Foucault's books from the 1960s, the subject only existed as a form of experience subjugated to repressive forces and to mechanisms of power, or else as a voice that burst out to break a monotonous and oppressive silence. In the 1970s, it was conceived of as a geometrical point constituted by power relations—the body and the "soul" were traversed by disciplinary technologies at the same time as they were foyers of resistance. In his final books, it also becomes the locus of a process of self-reformulation, a locus in which to create new forms of "experience." In all these instances the "free" subject is never given; it is always in the making and in need of being remade.

Thus the "resistance" to "subjugation," the "critical stance" and the "creation of new modes of life" are simply synonymous expressions. They all refer to the concrete exercise of the freedom which allows individuals and groups to move from subjection to subjectification, to shape their specific existences by cultivating their differences.

Foucault's final texts reverberate with something he wrote in the 1960s, when he praised in a single sentence "these differences we are" and "these differences we make."[14] They reverberate with the verse from René Char that he places at the end of the preface to *Folie et déraison*.[15]

> *Développez votre étrangeté légitime.*
> Let your legitimate strangeness unfold.

Addendum: Hannah Arendt and "Defamed Groups"

FOR JOHN

Perhaps the reader will be surprised at finding an addendum on Hannah Arendt at the end of this book. What rapport could there be between her work and gay issues or even between her work and questions of discrimination and minority subjectivities? It is true that French discussions of her work often use it as a scaffolding on which to hang various neoconservative varieties of thought, often those precise varieties that suggest to minority voices that they keep quiet in order not to disrupt the "common world" in which we should all be living.

But this biased way of using Arendt's work is hardly the most pertinent; one might even think that it seriously distorts a thought that is much more complex than first appearance might suggest. It is, in any case, more complex than certain French acolytes seem to appreciate. They find in it (as is their wont with many thinkers) little more than a bunch of slogans.¹ In certain of Arendt's writings one does in fact find careful reflection on discrimination, and this might encourage us to rediscover in her work a certain richness or potential of which certain of her more zealous commentators would deprive us. How interesting that her thought on these matters should take shape precisely around the question of the right to marriage, which was for Arendt a cornerstone of legal equality!

Arendt makes a distinction between two types of discrimination: social discrimination and legal discrimination. In one of her more surprising texts, "Reflections on Little Rock," she suggests that it is unquestionably necessary to struggle for an end to legal discrimination and yet probably useless to hope to do away with discrimination in the social realm. Such social discriminations, she says, are the price we pay to maintain a society made up of a plurality of cultures. In this article, which deals with the effort to bring an end to segregation in American schools, Arendt asserts that educational institutions are not the appropriate battleground for such a struggle.[2] She emphasizes instead the form of discrimination that seemed to her most serious: marriage discrimination—the prohibition of mixed marriage in the South. "The right to marry whoever one wishes is an elementary human right," she states. In her eyes, the right to attend an integrated school, the right to sit anywhere one pleases on a bus, the right to stay in a hotel or use a recreation area are "minor" questions compared to the fundamental right to be able to construct one's life and one's happiness. Arendt goes so far as to claim that "the right to vote, and nearly all other rights enumerated in the Constitution, are secondary to the inalienable human rights to 'life, liberty and the pursuit of happiness.'" She concludes that it is "to this category [that] the right to home and marriage unquestionably belongs" (236).

Arendt was aware as she wrote (the article was written in 1957, but only published in 1959) that her priorities were not those that had been set by the organizations working for civil rights and against racial discrimination. She brushes aside this objection with the observation that "oppressed minorities were never the best judges on the order of priorities in such matters and there are many instances when they preferred to fight for social opportunity rather than for basic human or political rights." Where laws are concerned, she adds, "the order of priorities . . . is to be determined by the Constitution, and not by public opinion or by majorities" (232).

Arendt's article was, of course, violently attacked at the time. Ralph Ellison, for example, would criticize her for her ignorance of the daily realities of segregation and of the battles being fought by people whose most basic rights were not being recognized, and Arendt would in turn write to him to say that he was correct, that she had not understood the real nature of the "bodily fear" produced by segregation.[3]

One can only applaud Ellison for his reaction. Arendt's manner of dictating from some philosophical place above the fray what the priorities of African Americans should be, what struggles they should or should not engage in, was nothing if not detestable. Yet the main interest of her analysis is not to be found in her discussion of the priorities of activists. Rather, we could remark, if we set aside the historical context for the moment, that Arendt was attempting to reverse the order of priorities in a struggle against discrimination for a particular and simple reason. She wanted to make a clear distinction between discrimination on a juridical level, which was for her unacceptable, and discrimination at the social level, which was for her inevitable. From here she is able to offer ideas that might lead her reader to begin to question some of the things often taken for granted in struggles for democracy and justice. Vacation resorts provide her with one of her examples:

> It is common knowledge that vacation resorts in this country are frequently "restricted" according to ethnic origin. There are many people who object to this practice; nevertheless it is only an extension of the right to free association. If as a Jew I wish to spend my vacations only in the company of Jews, I cannot see how anyone can reasonably prevent my doing so; just as I see no reason why other resorts should not cater to a clientele that wishes not to see Jews while on holiday. (238)

While the first part of this argument might seem obvious to a reader of today, that same reader will most likely find the second part nearly intolerable. Still, Arendt insists on thinking the two parts together. She is quite insistent on this point: "There cannot be a 'right to go into any hotel or recreation area or place of amusement,' because many of these are in the realm of the purely social where the right to free association, and therefore to discrimination, has greater validity than the principle of equality" (238). Clearly there is something strange about thinking about hotels and recreation centers in terms of association, and from there deducing that the "right of free association" could justify the denial of access to these places to a certain category of persons—especially when Arendt specifies that such cannot be the case for museums and theaters, in which, apparently, people do not assemble in order to associate. One cannot help wondering who is to decide in which places association happens and thus from which places it is legitimate to exclude certain categories of people.

Yet Arendt's goal was to emphasize the fact that "without discrimination of some sort, society would simply cease to exist and very important possibilities of free association and group formation would disappear" (238). It would seem that "conformism" is a greater danger in her mind than discrimination, a conformist society being one that would refuse to recognize itself as composed of a cultural plurality, that would refuse to acknowledge the existence of different groups.[4] Now cultural pluralism within a given society and the resulting cohabitation of different groups necessarily produce certain forms of discrimination, the minimal level of which would be the desire to associate within a group that is closed to "others." This is, Arendt says, the price one pays for plurality. Thus she insists on defining very strictly the appropriate intervention of the political and the juridical orders into the social order: "While the government has no right to interfere with the prejudices and discriminatory practices of society, it has not only the right but the duty to make sure that these practices are not legally enforced" (240).

⊁ How could an analysis such as this be useful to us today? We can see that for Arendt (indeed this seems to be the central point of her argument) the existence of groups that affirm their differences is what guarantees cultural pluralism and thereby the very life of society. Not only can this pluralism not be maintained without certain forms of discrimination, but it is the case that the self-affirmation of a given group might even contribute to strengthening this discrimination. Far from frightening Arendt, this prospect seems to her preferable to conformism, that is, to homogeneity. In the end, it is the struggle against legal discriminations (especially those concerning the right to marriage) that should take priority over all others, for there is where equality is really at stake. The priorities should come, not via consensus or the wishes of the majority, but from what the law and the Constitution demand. So the argument advanced by certain opponents of the right to marriage of same-sex couples (and they seem to be numerous among Arendt's "disciples," at least in France), the argument that asserts that since most gay men and lesbians are not asking for that right it should not be granted amounts simply to invoking the logic of the majority to the detriment of the logic of legal equality.

To sum up, we can see that Arendt's position, once it is isolated from the polemics that tie it to its historical context, consists in *defending simultaneously the idea of political and juridical equality and the idea of cultural difference or differentiation.*[5] Obviously those French essayists who use her work to justify refusing to extend equal rights and refusing the right to cultural difference to lesbians and gay men claim erroneously that she says precisely the opposite.

Thus, as one might have imagined, the things Arendt has to say about our "common world" turn out to be considerably more complex than what certain ideologically minded commentators, ones too biased to be honest in their presentation, would have us believe.[6] As we have seen, the large question that is at the center of Arendt's thinking is precisely how to arrange things so that a plurality of points of view is able to exist within a society. Only in that situation is a democratic way of life possible. The "common world" is thus never a given, but something always under construction. This construction is based on the coexistence of multiple and different perspectives. What Arendt calls the "common world" is not some transcendent reality that would be imposed on individuals and on groups from the outside. To the contrary, it is something these groups construct together; they must be working continuously to ensure its existence. The idea of the "common world," far from being contradictory to the existence of groups with markedly different and heterogeneous points of view, presupposes such groups. If Arendt offers such a severe critique of racial segregation, it is, of course, because it is a morally reprehensible system, but also because it destroys the very possibility of a plurality by reducing certain groups to silence. And such a plurality is, according to the principles of her political philosophy, the necessary condition of a "common world." This explains why she thinks that the principle political goal to be achieved by the elimination of violence is an expansion of this plurality.[7]

It is therefore the case both that the "common world" makes no sense in the absence of a respect for differences and diversity *and*, even more fundamentally, that such a plurality is the very condition for the existence of any such "public space." That public space is, in fact, nothing other than the result of the crisscrossing of all these different perspectives. Arendt here uses the metaphor of a group of people seated at the same table, a table which, as she says, unites them as much as separates them. One might sometimes choose to emphasize the unity and sometimes the separation. This idea is one Arendt holds to so deeply that, as she puts it with a certain polemical violence in her article on Little Rock, she claims she would prefer social discrimination to the elimination of differences.

It would be worth pausing over the antidemocratic potential present in the idea of a "common world," one in which the social sphere is held separate from law and politics. Such an idea seems to authorize an individual (in this case a philosopher) to decide for others (in this case African Americans, but it could be any minority group) what their aspirations and their struggles should be. Be that as it may, it still remains impossible to interpret the idea of a common world as a tool in the struggle against the affirmation of cultural difference. Indeed, in Arendt's thought, this idea's function is to justify such differences. What Arendt rejects—and how strongly she does so!—is rather the idea of "unanimity." Unanimity would indicate to her, in the words of one commentator, that "people had ceased to think."[8] For Arendt, there is clearly a great danger in refusing divergent points of view in the name of some unique truth that would be opposed to arbitrariness and multiplicity. Different people see the world differently, and that is what constitutes the public domain. "The reality of the public realm relies on the simultaneous presence of innumerable perspectives and aspects in which the common world presents itself and for which no common measurement or denominator can ever be devised."[9] Arendt also claims that "under the conditions of a common world, reality is not guaranteed primarily by the 'common nature' of all men who constitute it, but rather by the fact that, differences of position and the resulting variety of perspectives notwithstanding, everybody is always concerned with the same object" (57–58). So the common world is as much endangered by "radical isolation, where nobody can any longer agree with anybody else, as is usually the case in tyrannies," as by "conditions of mass society or mass hysteria, where we see all people suddenly behave as though they were members of one family, each multiplying and prolonging the perspective of his neighbor" (58). Following on from this, Arendt is able to conclude that "the end of the common world has come when it is seen only under one aspect and is permitted to present itself in only one perspective" (58). So the disappearance or the occultation of a point of view, of one of the visions of the world that is offered by "a group of men on the basis of their specific place in the world" and that "no one else could reproduce," would thus be a mutilation of the "common world."[10] In sum, Arendt here calls into question, and in quite a radical way, the ideology of abstract universalism. In her advocacy of a concrete universalism she is in the end—and despite appearances to the contrary—quite close to Sartre.

❧ What "public space" offers is the possibility of different perspectives coming into confrontation. This is, in fact, what allows citizens to obtain a kind of "enlarged thought," an expression Arendt borrows from Kant's Critique of Judgment. It is true that the distinction she proposes in a number of different texts between "private life" and "public space" would seem to indicate that she does not consider that what we refer to as "sexual politics" could form one of the differentiated "perspectives" that together constitute the common world. Indeed, a certain number of feminists have severely criticized Arendt for defining the common world in such a way that access to it seems reserved to men. For example, when, in The Human Condition, she analyzes what she refers to as the vita activa, Arendt does seem (as Adrienne Rich has pointed out) to relegate women to the private world of the home.

Arendt seems not even to recognize that domestic labor is labor. She does not seem to take into account the ways in which women contribute to the work sphere (even if it is only by the way they have throughout history, via their performance of the daily tasks of housekeeping, continually recreated the conditions that enable men to go to work).[11] Still, we can also accept Seyla Benhabib's response to Rich's criticisms, in which she suggests that we try to avoid anachronism while reading Arendt and thus avoid criticizing her for her failure to respond to political and social questions that preoccupy us today, but that were not yet being posed, or only barely, at the moment she was writing.[12] After all, it is possible to imagine that the plurality of perspectives making up the common world is not given once and for all. To the contrary, the definition of that plurality is open to the effects of the expansion of thought that cannot help but be produced by the advent of new ways of looking at the world. Feminism is part of this expansion. Moreover, as Benhabib reminds us, one can find in Arendt's texts a certain number of moments that suggest a move in this direction. One example would be the biography of Rahel Varnhagen, an early text in which she traces Varnhagen's destiny both as a Jew and as a woman. In other words, there is no reason not to enlarge the way Arendt views the "enlarged thought" that results from the coexistence of a plurality of points of view. In fact, freedom as it is envisioned by Arendt implies that a certain number of individuals can together undertake an action whose goal is to bring something entirely new into existence, "to call something into being which did not exist before."[13] To put it slightly differently, it is not possible to think of "public space" and the problems with which it is concerned as being defined once and for all, because freedom is defined by spontaneity and by the ability of a certain number of actors to produce new and unforeseen points of view. So if, as Benhabib's rereading of Arendt suggests, it is possible to think that women as a group and as a point of view on the world are justified in taking part in the shaping of public space, then it is just as legitimate to think that gay men and lesbians could henceforth also constitute a point of view (or several points of view) that would contribute to "enlarging" thought.

It is quite striking, moreover, to remark that Arendt herself seems quite explicitly to have authorized us to make this latter inference. We know to what a degree thinking about the "Jewish question" was central to her project—in particular, thinking about the ways in which Jews could and should constitute a point of view in the public arena. In one of the chapters of The Origins of Totalitarianism, Arendt herself makes a point of comparing

Jews and homosexuals.[14] In that book, her analysis of the transformation of the situation of European Jews in the nineteenth century is supported in part by her reading of Proust, and notably of the volume *Cities of the Plain* (*Sodome et Gomorrhe*), a work in which, as we have seen, Proust set out to describe the "accursed race" that he considered homosexuals to form, using a comparison with Jews to do so. Arendt takes up Proust's comparison, but turns it around; she takes Proust's descriptions of homosexuals as "an example of the role of Jews in non-Jewish society" (80). The commentary she offers of *Remembrance of Things Past* is meant to demonstrate that the process by which certain Jews were accepted into various aristocratic salons, far from indicating that they were no longer being thought of as foreign beings, indicates rather that their difference was undergoing a kind of incorporation, an embodiment in individuals as a set of "psychological characteristics." Proust had already posed the question as to whether or not society was becoming "secretly more hierarchical as it became outwardly more democratic."[15] Aristocrats who began extending invitations to Jews and homosexuals had certainly not abandoned their profound antipathy for both groups. If Jews received invitations to the salons of the Faubourg Saint-Germain, according to Arendt it was due to the phenomenon of an attraction-repulsion that was being experienced toward something that was both strange and foreign, due to a taste for something exotic and dangerous.[16] This is the ground for the comparison, borrowed from Proust, with "inverts," who represent another incarnation of "monstrosity." As it moved from being a crime punishable by law to being a vice that was simultaneously alluring and horrifying, homosexuality became fashionable in the salons. Yet it also became the condition from which every "normal" man was then required to distinguish himself— perhaps precisely because it had become more approachable. The end result of this process was, for the homosexual as for the Jew, the production of a sort of "typical personality" or a "psychology"—one that corresponded to this situation of simultaneous tolerance and rejection:

> Such were the conditions from which arose the complicated game of exposure and concealment, of half-concession and lying distortions, of exaggerated humility and exaggerated arrogance, all of which were consequences of the fact that only one's Jewishness (or homosexuality) had opened the doors of the exclusive salons, while at the same time they made one's position extremely insecure. In this equivocal situation, Jewishness was for the individual Jew at once a physical stain and

a mysterious personal privilege, both inherent in a "racial predestination." (82)

The process by which "Jewishness" is transformed in something that is inborn, a set of "shared . . . psychological attributes" (66), is, in Arendt's analysis (one that strives to make a strong distinction between modern antisemitism and anti-Jewish sentiment in other historical periods) a major consequence of the secularization of Judaism and of Jewish assimilation.[17] As she puts it: "Jewish origin, without religious and political connotation, became everywhere a psychological quality, was changed into 'Jewishness,' and from then on could be considered only in the categories of virtue or vice. If it is true that 'Jewishness' could not have been perverted into an interesting vice without a prejudice which considered it a crime, it is also true that such perversion was made possible by those Jews who considered it an innate virtue."[18] Proust's descriptions would seem intended to show that assimilation, far from producing an effacement of difference or differentiation, in fact made differences more salient, more crucial for those who would only accept someone Jewish if that person renounced being a Jew. Yet these same people always kept in mind that such a person was Jewish, and they would never allow that person to forget it either. Arendt concludes by insisting on the fact that the very society that had transformed a "crime" into a "vice" would itself soon turn criminal in order to eradicate the vice.

Throughout the chapter in question, Arendt is preoccupied with understanding how Jews managed to stay out of politics as Jews. She presents two figures produced by the double logic of assimilation and exclusion: there is the "parvenu," who tries to assimilate, and the "pariah," who is excluded. Arendt refers to this condition of exclusion as "worldlessness," an absence of participation in the "world," which is to say, a failure to participate in politics as the representative of a Jewish point of view on the world.[19] Yet Arendt is also interested in those people who represent a resistance to the political situation of the Jews, and thus in those people who proposed different ways of escaping from this "worldlessness." There were first of all literary attempts, notably those of Heine and Kafka, who, perhaps without knowing it, breathed life into the tradition of Jewish culture. There were also specifically political efforts, such as those of Bernard Lazare, who embodied the strategy Arendt seems inclined to favor: someone who is conscious of his position as a pariah and rebels against it, someone who is uninterested in assimilation and yet not content to be excluded from politics. Here is someone who engages in politics as a Jew and thus participates in a common world, helping to build and define it by putting forth a specifically Jewish point of view.[20]

Arendt holds that the response to antisemitism is necessarily political. She points out, at the end of the first part of The Origins of Totalitarianism (entitled "Antisemitism") that the sole political response come up with by Jews is Zionism. Whatever criticisms and reservations Arendt may have had about the political programs that went under the name of Zionism, she never gave up the idea of a specifically Jewish politics. As she wrote in 1946, in a letter to Karl Jaspers, who had asked her if she thought of herself as Jewish or as German, "To be perfectly honest, it doesn't matter to me in the least on a personal and individual level. . . . Politically, I will always speak only in the name of the Jews whenever circumstances force me to give my nationality."[21]

We can see what a degree of resemblance there is between these reflections of Arendt's (even if they are not always perfectly clear or perfectly coherent when taken together) and Sartre's thought. Arendt was, of course, always severely critical of him—perhaps due to a personal hostility to Sartre and Beauvoir. Be that as it may, the figure of the conscious pariah, of the militant pariah, a figure Arendt values so highly, is in the end quite close to what Sartre calls the authentic Jew, who "lives to the full his condition as Jew," as opposed to the "inauthentic Jew," who, on the contrary, tries to efface that condition through a process of assimilation, to the point of becoming antisemitic or at least hostile to nonassimilated Jews.[22]

Like Sartre, Arendt describes the psychology of the Jew—both the parvenu and the pariah, the assimilated and the excluded—as defined by antisemitism, by the situation of exclusion in which Jews as a group find themselves. This is, in fact, the case for all defamed groups. As Arendt puts it: "As long as defamed peoples and classes exist, parvenu- and pariah-qualities will be produced anew by each generation with incomparable monotony."[23] The psychology, the "character" of both the parvenu and the pariah are the products of defamation. Only those representatives of the group who make an effort to speak as conscious pariahs, as rebellious ones, will be in any position to escape from their predetermination and to work against the absence of the group as such from the historical and political arena. For Arendt, as Martine Leibovici puts it, it is crucial to preserve "the existence of social groups that determine distinct social identities."[24] Above all, one must intervene in the political arena, not in order to escape as an individual from the group to which one belongs, but rather to speak and act as an individual who "represents this group."[25] This does not imply that any given individual will speak for all the others. It means that such a person will situate her or his political commitments in the perspective of a defense of the values, the rights, the culture, of the group from which she or he comes.

So, Arendt explains, if the existence of defamed groups is constitutive of the psychological traits written into the very hearts of the individuals belonging to those groups, it is also the origin of a kind of political action in which the members of these groups intervene in public space in order to propound their own vision of the world and their own culture. This is why we can take Hannah Arendt to be the philosopher of the gay movement.

Notes

Preface

1. Eribon, *Michel Foucault, 1926–1984*. The English translation, published by Harvard University Press and Faber and Faber, appeared in 1991.

2. David Halperin was notable among those who critiqued me in this way—in the second part of his book *Saint Foucault*, for instance. Halperin's book and American gay and lesbian studies and queer theory have all nourished my recent thinking on Foucault, even if in the present book my goal has been to construct an alternative (perhaps even an opposing) approach.

3. Eribon, *Michel Foucault et ses contemporains*.

4. See Eribon, *Dictionnaire des cultures gays et lesbiennes*. I am also indebted for some of these insights to work-in-progress by Michael Lucey, especially his lecture "Contexts for Colette," delivered at the École des hautes études en sciences sociales in Paris on April 1, 2003.

5. A good indication of the climate in which I wrote this book can be seen in the fact that a book as preposterous as Frédéric Martel's *Le Rose et le noir: Les Homosexuels en France de 1968 à nos jours* (Paris: Seuil, 1996)—a book that provoked only indignation, anger, and hilarity among participants in the French lesbian and gay movement, among French AIDS activists, or among French scholars working on these questions—could have been advertised in the press (across the whole political spectrum from the left to the extreme right) as the "noble" gesture of a "courageous" gay man who took it upon himself to reveal the danger that Lesbian and Gay Pride and gay "separatism" represented for society as a whole. The book would not even be worth mentioning were it not for the fact that the media blitz that surrounded its publication in France led to its translation into English (*The Pink and the Black: Homosexuals in France since 1968*, trans. Jane Marie Todd [Stanford: Stanford University Press, 1999]). (Oddly enough, Martel is presented on the cover of the American edition as having written for the gay press. This is not mentioned on the cover of the French edition, where he is rather presented in a way that distances him

from the gay and lesbian movement: as a contributor to the journal *Esprit*, well known for its harsh hostility to that movement. No mention is made on the cover of the American edition that when Martel was president of a gay and lesbian student organization, or when he wrote for the gay press, he used a pseudonym. At the time he stated that "homosexuality is something one can only live out in pain and sorrow.")

Enormous errors abound in this book. Guy Hocquenghem is presented as the founder of FHAR (Front homosexuel d'action revolutionnaire), which is not the case. At one point the book asserts that Hocquenghem had read Foucault prior to 1968, but a hundred pages later it is stated that Hocquenghem discovered Foucault only in 1976. The book reproaches Hocquenghem for never having had an HIV blood test done, whereas Hocquenghem's partner found after his death the results of a test Hocquenghem had done in 1985, the very year such tests became available. Martel makes fun of Monique Wittig who, he claims, exiled herself to the United States in order to be able to call herself an "écrivaine." [Translator's note: traditionalists in French language use insist that the noun for writer only has one form, which is masculine: *écrivain*. All women who write and all men who write must be called *un écrivain*. More recently some French speakers have been insisting on using a new feminine form of this word—*une écrivaine*—to refer to women writers. This new usage remains controversial in certain circles.] But to make such a claim, Martel must obviously be unaware of the fact that all of Wittig's work is constructed in opposition to the very notion of the assignment of a gender, against the idea of an *écriture féminine*. She left France precisely because of the violent attacks against her on the part of differentialist feminists.

The hatred Martel feels for the people whose history he claims to be writing can also be seen in the vulgar terms in which he insults a transsexual activist who later became a well-known journalist. That journalist in fact sued Martel, obliging him to remove the offending passage from later editions of his book, a passage in which he had described her as "hysteria tempered by hormones."

Many different scholars have pointed out that on every page, in every line, one finds errors that range from conflicting details to huge absurdities. (On one page he claims that it was the gay movement that was successful in bringing Mitterand to power in 1981 [!?], whereas he also asserts that in 1981 the French gay movement had more or less ceased to exist.) Yet what journalists found so appealing in this book is that it repeated everything they wanted to hear in condemnation of "gay identity politics," in condemnation of the idea that gay people might establish themselves as a separate community, and thus in condemnation of the collective visibility of lesbians and gay men. (The closing page is telling on this point, describing how the homosexual individual should melt into society and thereby disappear.)

The book's thesis is simple: given that certain gay activists denied the existence of the AIDS epidemic at its outset, the gay movement was responsible for the spread of AIDS, and so it should be abolished. Of course such a thesis completely misses the complexity of the range of reactions to the new illness. (For a rigorous history, see the book edited by Patrice Pinell, *Une Épidemie politique*.) In interviews given in newspapers, Martel went so far as to demand that the government cease subsidizing organizations that were fighting the AIDS epidemic, on the grounds that they were "run by homosexuals" and that it was homosexuals who were infecting each other. The book's combined homophobia and stupidity can be seen in passages such as the one in which it is claimed that gay activists invent homophobia in order to feel that they exist, or, more profoundly, in the passage where Martel asserts that gay people cannot really consider themselves to be the victims of Nazi persecution given that there were kapos in the camps who were themselves homosexual.

Add that Martel, as several people have commented, copies entire sentences from other books without including either quotation marks or references. But finally, to understand the level on which the book is written, it would suffice to mention the sentence where he says that "the women's liberation movement created a culture that was fundamentally monogamous." He meant to say "monosexual" but used the wrong word. This is the intellectual level of a book that was praised by conservatives from the left as well as from the right. The simple fact is that the book allowed them to use a token homosexual to denounce the lesbian and gay movement—the obedient colonized person who acts as a spokesperson for colonialist discourse. They paid no attention to the quality (or absence thereof) of the book.

6. Eribon, *Une Morale du minoritaire*. See also Eribon, *Hérésies*.

7. *Le Monde* refused to publish the letters sent by certain of the conference participants to protest the absurd misrepresentations printed about them. Pierre Bourdieu then wrote a response to the article and, given his status in the French intellectual world, *Le Monde* could not avoid printing it. Bourdieu upbraided *Le Monde* for the way it had allowed eminent foreign scholars to be defamed in the pages of an important French newspaper, and he lamented that *Le Monde* had portrayed a field of study that was being developed in universities around the world as a homosexual conspiracy to attack culture itself.

8. In order to help American work become better known in France, I translated Halperin's *Saint Foucault* and Chauncey's *Gay New York*. Further, Françoise Gaspard and I have invited people such as Judith Butler, David Halperin, Michael Warner, Carolyn Dinshaw, George Chauncey, Leo Bersani, Sharon Marcus, and others to visit our seminar.

9. David Halperin, for example, is himself presently working to analyze "gay

subjectivity" and the modalities of cultural identification that accompany it. See notably his "Homosexuality's Closet," 21–54.

10. In this book I employ the term "subjectivities," a somewhat loose term, precisely because it is sufficiently imprecise so as to leave open the possibility of mixing different kinds of analysis and different levels of analysis. It allows one to elude the extremely problematic opposition between conscious and unconscious. Yet I also know that the word "subjectivity" itself makes reference to the idea of a "subject," and that we do well to be wary of the ideological, metaphysical, or even mythological (and especially psychoanalytic) charge that is sometimes attached to this word. Obviously, I could have used the Bourdieusian term, *habitus*, for it too undoes the opposition between the conscious and the unconscious; it allows one to think about the permanence and the persistence beyond its moment of formation of the being that is produced via the apprenticeship of the world, even when a radical rupture has occurred; it allows one to think about how there is no present without a past, no future without traces of the past, no "pride" without "shame," no escape from what one is without a self-recomposition from the elements of what one has been, and so on. Yet I preferred not to use this term, for it would have implied, on one hand, a totalizing notion of the individual, and on the other, a gay habitus in opposition to a heterosexual one. The idea of subjectivity seems to me to avoid this idea. It leaves the door open for the idea of a class of individuals who—in certain ways, and only in those certain ways—share and have shared experiences that have shaped their minds and their beings as regards one important aspect (yet only this one aspect) of their relation to the social world.

Introduction: The Language of the Tribe

1. Proust, *The Captive*, in vol. 3 of *Remembrance of Things Past*, 39. Hereafter cited as *RTP*. [Translator's note: There are now a number of different English versions of Proust's novel in print, and titles of the novel as a whole and of its various volumes differ from translation to translation. It was first translated as *Remembrance of Things Past*, but is also titled *In Search of Lost Time*—which is a more literal translation of the French *À la recherche du temps perdu*. (The older version had as one of its advantages that it was alliteratively closer to the French.) One of the volumes of the novel from which Eribon cites most frequently is called in French *Sodome et Gomorrhe*. It exists in English translation under two different titles: *Cities of the Plain* and *Sodom and Gomorrah*.]

2. In *Cities of the Plain* (*Sodome et Gomorrhe*), we are specifically told that M. de Vagoubert is "one of the few men (possibly the only man) in society who happened to be in what is called in Sodom the 'confidence' of M. de Charlus" (*RTP*, 2:666). Yet

one finds this remark contradicted in *The Captive*, where Charlus in the course of an evening exchanges "furtive remarks" (3:244) with two dukes, a general, and so on.

3. Isherwood, *Christopher and His Kind, 1929–1939*, 16.

4. Goffman, *The Presentation of Self in Everyday Life.*

5. Goffman, *Stigma*, 78.

6. Scott, "The Evidence of Experience," 779.

7. See Butler, *The Psychic Life of Power*, 12–17.

8. See Adam, *The Survival of Domination.*

9. [Translator's note: The decision of the editors in the first two volumes of the English language edition of the *Essential Works of Foucault* was to use "subjectivation" as a translation for *assujetissement* and "to subjectify" as a translation for *assujetir*. In volume three of the *Essential Works of Foucault*, *assujetissement* is rendered by "subjugation." It could also be translated by "subjection." *Assujetir* could be rendered by "to subjugate" or "to subject." I will make use of all these options.]

10. Bourdieu, *Masculine Domination.*

11. I employ the notion of "symbolic violence" as it is defined by Bourdieu in "Sur le pouvoir symbolique," 405–11.

12. See Butler, *Bodies that Matter.*

13. Bartlett, *Who Was that Man?*

14. Derrida, *Spectres de Marx.*

15. [Translator's note: The French title was not used for the English translation, which is simply known as *The History of Sexuality, Volume 1: An Introduction*. Hereafter cited as *HSI*. I will keep the French title in the text.]

16. [Translator's note: Eribon is here referring to a chapter from Foucault's *Histoire de la folie à l'âge classique*, which has never been translated into English. The published English translation, *Madness and Civilization: A History of Insanity in the Age of Reason*, was made from an abridged version of the French text.]

17. [Translator's note: Sartre wrote a book called *Réflexions sur la question juive*. It was translated into English under the title *Anti-Semite and Jew*. It was therefore not possible to preserve the parallelism between Eribon's and Sartre's titles in English.]

18. Chauncey, *Gay New York.*

19. [Translator's note: the socio-lexical situations in France and in the United States are different enough to pose some problems for the translator. "*Homosexuel*" is probably more widely used by gay men and lesbians in France than "homosexual" would be in the United States, where many would avoid using it to refer to themselves. This is not the case in France, where the word is used much more freely. The word "gay," on the other hand, as Eribon is here making clear, still perhaps seems to some like an American importation to France, and so can raise various kinds of red flags for many French speakers. This is in part palpable in the

indecision as to whether it should be used with an American/English spelling (*gay*), or converted into French (*gai or gaie*). The word *queer*, still contentious among some English speakers, is even more so in France, where there is no easy French equivalent, linguistically or socio-historically speaking. I will, of course, always translate *gay* as "gay" in the pages ahead. I will also frequently translate *homosexuel* as "gay man."]

20. Amnesty International, *Breaking the Silence*.

PART 1   A World of Insult

1. The Shock of Insult

1. Jouhandeau, *De l'abjection*, 145.

2. As Genet puts it in one of his poems, "a dizzying word, arriving from the foundations of the world, destroyed its happy order [un mot vertigineux, venu du fond du monde, abolit le bel ordre]." See Genet, "La Galère," in *Poèmes*, 51. Sartre cites this verse in his book on Genet, whose second chapter is called precisely, "A Dizzying Word." See Sartre, *Saint Genet*, 17. Hereafter cited as *StG*.

3. Austin, *How to Do Things with Words*.

4. Austin, *How to Do Things with Words*, 4–6.

5. See Goffman, *Stigma*.

2. The Flight to the City

1. Take, for example, three of the most important works of gay literature of recent years: Hollinghurst, *The Swimming Pool Library*; Peck, *Martin and John*; Bartlett, *Ready to Catch Him Should He Fall*.

2. See Hirigoyen, *Le Harcèlement moral*.

3. Schiltz, "Parcours de jeunes homosexuels dans le contexte du VIH," 1503.

4. "San Francisco is a refugee camp for homosexuals. We have fled from every part of the nation, and like refugees elsewhere, we came not because it is so great here, but because it is so bad there." Wittmann, "A Gay Manifesto," 330.

5. Bérubé, *Coming Out Under Fire*.

6. D'Emilio, *Sexual Politics, Sexual Communities*.

7. See Chauncey, *Gay New York*, 233–35, 271–73.

8. Ibid., 271.

9. On this point, see Bech, *When Men Meet*, 148–51.

10. On Germany, see Isherwood, *Christopher and His Kind*. For a more general view, see Tamagne, *Recherches sur l'homosexualité dans la France, l'Angleterre et l'Allemagne*

du début des années vingt à la fin des années trente, 1:105 ff. [Translator's note: Since the publication of Eribon's book, Tamagne's dissertation has been published as a book: *Histoire de l'homosexualité en Europe: Paris, Londres, Berlin* (Paris: Seuil, 2000).] On Foucault and Dumézil, see Eribon, *Michel Foucault*, 29–30, 73–98, 187–98; *Michel Foucault et ses contemporains*, 105–38, 266–87; and *Faut-il brûler Dumézil?*.

11. Bech, *When Men Meet*, 98.

12. Hirschfeld, *Le Troisième sexe*, 5–6.

13. On the moment of arrival in the city, see the opening pages of Bartlett's *Who Was That Man?*

14. See Chauncey, *Gay New York*. On Berlin, London, and Paris in the 1920s and 30s, see Tamagne, *Recherches sur l'homosexualité dans la France*, esp. 1:242–96.

15. Hirschfeld, *Le Troisième sexe*, 5.

16. Chauncey's entire book can be read as a history of these fluctuations, of this give and take—partly deliberate, partly enforced—between secrecy and openness.

17. Descriptions of Paris's gay subculture at the end of the nineteenth and the beginning of the twentieth centuries can be found in the novels of Jean Lorrain and the autobiographical texts of Francis Carco.

3. Friendship as a Way of Life

1. Goffman, *Stigma*, 100.

2. Sedgwick, *Between Men*, ix.

3. Rich, "Compulsory Heterosexuality and Lesbian Existence," 23–75.

4. It is hard to know in which category to place the normative violence one finds in so much of the psychological or psychoanalytic literature: all the methods they suggest to inhibit boys from becoming too "effeminate" or girls too "masculine," all the discussions about "roles" and "identifications" (for boys, identification with a father), about the necessity of "gender difference," etc., all the pseudo-therapeutic advice given to help bring "deviant" children back to the correct hetero-sexually normative developmental path, back to orthodox gender behavior, are of a piece with the insults (to be experienced by such children a bit later) that are directed at "fairies" and "fruits" or "dykes." For an analysis of this "soft" discursive violence, see Sedgwick, "How to Bring Your Kids Up Gay," 154–64.

5. Bech, *When Men Meet*, 116–17.

6. Discretion had, of course, already lost a lot of ground. Proust speaks of "extremists who allow a bracelet to slip down from beneath a cuff, or sometimes a necklace to gleam in the gap of a collar, who by their persistent stares, their cooings, their laughter, their mutual caresses, oblige a band of students to depart in hot haste" (*RTP*, 3:642).

7. See Chauncey, *Gay New York*, 133. Analogous remarks can be found in a great number of medical or police documents in France from the end of the nineteenth century and the beginning of the twentieth.

8. It has always seemed to me (perhaps I am wrong) that the ideas used by Pollak in his extremely important book, *Les Homosexuels et le sida*—which, ten years after its publication, remains one of the few books published in France in which one finds a rigorous analysis of the lived experiences of gay men in the 1970s and 1980s— emerge from what we might call a "dominated point of view" on homosexuality, the point of view of those who accept without questioning them the representations produced by domination itself. To speak as he does of a "fated grouping" ("for lack of a better term," he adds, without wondering what that "better" might be), amounts to a neglect of or an underestimation of certain parts of the process in question: both the creative energy (first of all *self*-creative) and the collective and individual constructive force put into identities and subjectivities. It also seems impossible to present the ways of life constructed by gay people as a fate or a destiny unless one considers that heterosexuality and family life are the normal and legitimate ways of life. For what is in fact at stake for gay people is an escape from the fate or destiny they had been assigned in a world to which they could not fully belong. It also does not seem possible to describe as a "freely chosen segregation" something that is rather the result of concentrations and mixtures—temporary and volatile ones—in the same place (neighborhoods, bars, and so on) of individuals who live out their homosexuality in quite different ways. What is the precise nature of the "group" that they form? This is a question that needs to be asked. It is strange, for example, to find Pollak using the word "ghetto" without ever asking about the ideological baggage attached to such a word once it is imported into social scientific discourse—especially given that the reality such a word is meant to refer to only involves a minority of (self-identified) gay people. Pollak never asks if all those who frequent the "ghetto" have the same relation to whatever it is that the word designates.

This nonanalytical way of employing rather suspect notions is all the more surprising given that Pollak himself insisted on the ways in which the sociology of homosexuality had evolved since the 1960s, leaving behind ideas such as "deviancy," "stigmatization," or "marginality" (the concepts used by Erving Goffman or Howard Becker), but especially by replacing the question "why?" by the question "how?"—that is, by turning away from studies of the etiology of sexual orientation to analyses of ways of life. In an article written at the same time as his book, Pollak writes that it should be a question of studying homosexuals and their ways of life not simply in terms of the "interiorization of social constraints weighing upon them," but rather in terms of a "relatively autonomous sociability." As he so rightly puts it, "they are as much a self-construction as a social one." See Michael Pollak,

"Un Sujet inclassable," 12. This raises a further problem: the descriptive sociology of "ways of life" that are considered in terms of self-constructions has become a crucial part of the understanding of gay sociability (due in large measure to the fact that these new works were to a large extent produced by gay people); yet it has in turn largely abandoned the question of "subjectivation," limiting itself to purely descriptive approaches to practices and behaviors.

This is why it is necessary to return to Goffman's notions, to examine them in the light of "constructivist" conceptions, as opposed to abandoning them to the history of the social sciences. (The notions of "stigma," "stigmatization," and "stigmatizable" seem to me particularly useful.) If the works of Eve Kosofsky Sedgwick or Judith Butler (among others) seem so important to me, it is because they help us to escape from the false alternatives Pollak presents (if not "interiorization of social constraints" then "self-construction"), because in fact those two levels of gay and lesbian reality are inseparable and need to be thought together. It is precisely this kind of false alternative that all of Bourdieu's work has tried to go beyond. (This is particularly clear in *Masculine Domination*.) One can only regret that Pollak's work, so indebted to Bourdieu's, was brought to a halt before being able to develop a general anthropology of homosexuality, something he would certainly have been able to achieve had he used the Bourdieu of both *The Logic of Practice* and *Distinction*.

9. Robert Park, "The City: Suggestions for the Investigation of Human Behavior in the Urban Environment" (1916), cited in Chauncey, *Gay New York*, 134.

10. See Chauncey, *Gay New York*, 133.

11. The studies done in Chicago by Gilbert Herdt and Andrew Boxer show how the collective visibility present in big cities allows young gays and lesbians to assume their homosexuality at an earlier age. See Herdt and Boxer, *Children of Horizon*.

12. See Lynch, "Nonghetto Gays, 165–201.

4. *Sexuality and Professions*

1. Sedgwick, "Queer Performativity," 4.

2. Proust, "Esquisse I" for *Sodome et Gomorrhe*, in *A la recherche du temps perdu*, 3:933. Hereafter cited as *Recherche*.

3. *Recherche*, 3:931. One finds a modified version of this theme in the published versions of *Cities of the Plain*, in *RTP*, 2:646–47. We might also note here, while speaking of Proust, that the whole beginning of *Remembrance of Things Past* bears a strong resemblance to the paradigmatic story of a gay childhood.

4. See, in Paul Monette's autobiography, the story of a small-town adolescence filled with a true passion for female movie stars, whose lives and acts he follows in

the newspapers: *Becoming a Man*, 66–67. See also the novel by Josselin, *Quand j'étais star*. It is thus a bit surprising to find Proust writing, in one of the variants of *Cities of the Plain*, that if the Baron Charlus, when he was an adolescent, decorated his bedroom with photographs of actresses, it was perhaps because he was not yet homosexual or did not yet realize that he was. It would make more sense to think, given Proust's own descriptions, that he did this precisely because he was homosexual: the women in question were not objects of desire, but objects of identification. (See *Recherche*, 3:1283–84: "I later learned from the rest of this family that I came to know so well that when M. de Charlus was an adolescent, the mirror and the walls of his bedroom were hidden under chromolithographs of actresses. Must one then place at the beginning of this life a taste that would not be found in its later periods, as when dark-haired men can show childhood photographs of themselves in which they were blond?")

A few lines later, Proust will end up referring to this "purely esthetic love for women" (1284). Perhaps the simplest explanation for it is that it is the only available way for an adolescent boy, in a world in which the heterosexual norm is so strong, to express for himself and in the presence of others his attraction for men, as Proust's reference to Ivanhoe so well illustrated. But it is also true that the identification with certain highly theatrical feminine "roles" seems to have been, through many historical periods, so characteristic of certain homosexual behaviors (those certain behaviors being scorned by many other homosexuals who detest these phantasmagorics), and so permanent a feature that it would be worth studying seriously.

5. See, on this point, and on homosexuality in general as an important factor in the choice of a profession, Pollak, *Les Homosexuels et le sida*. For more recent updates of his observations, see Schiltz, "Parcours de jeunes homosexuels dans le contexte du VIH," and also the works cited in the bibliography to her article. Pierre Bourdieu (in *Homo Academicus*) speaks of a masculine pole and a feminine pole within the field of academic disciplines. It would be interesting to investigate in what ways gay men and lesbians are distributed along the axis running between these two poles.

6. George Chauncey evokes this phenomenon when he describes the arrival of newcomers in the city: those who preceded them advise them not only about gaining access to the gay subculture, but also more generally as to their professional and social lives. The "gay world" fills the functions of a mutual assistance network, without ever being organized or thought of as such. It goes without saying, of course, that these helpful acts only rarely correspond to the celebrated literary representations that may have been given of them, as in the pact Vautrin proposes to Lucien de Rubempré in *Lost Illusions* or the proposition to serve as his guide in life that Charlus makes to the narrator of *Remembrance of Things Past* in *The Guermantes Way*.

7. I obviously do not mean to suggest that every gay man avoided sports as a child or an adolescent. My goal is to define the structuring polarities that permit one to recognize certain phenomena (and only certain ones) that have been attested to by sociological or historical studies or by studies of ideas or representations. It goes without saying that these phenomena do not cover all the available sets of experiences that define homosexuality at a given moment or in a given social space.

8. Hocquenghem, L'Amphithéâtre des morts, 23.

9. Of course there is no single, unique set of experiences that captures the case of every gay man. The preceding considerations of the city and of occupations cannot apply to everyone who engages in same-sex practices. If it is possible to describe a certain number of phenomena (statistically attested ones), one must always be aware that, alongside what one is describing, other forms coexist that cannot be explained in the same terms. I am perfectly aware, for instance, that working-class gay men exist. (Who could think the contrary?) Yet that does not, on its own, invalidate the statistical findings of the sociologists nor the kinds of stories attested to in various autobiographies. We could even think of studying the differentiations that exist in regard to culture between working-class gay men and straight ones.

5. Family and "Melancholy"

1. See Derrida, Feu la cendre.

2. See Freud, "The Dependent Relationships of the Ego," chapter 5 of The Ego and the Id, 38–49.

3. See Butler, Bodies That Matter, 112–13, and The Psychic Life of Power, 132–98.

4. Bourdieu, "The Space of Points of View," in Bourdieu et al., The Weight of the World, 4.

5. Surely these wounds and this "melancholy" combine together to compose the feelings of sadness, of "spleen," that many gay men claim to experience so regularly. Perhaps they also explain the draw of tragic figures in art and literature or of artists who sing of tragedy and distress. (Think of the admiration for Callas, for example, or for the French singer Barbara, whose performances drew crowds of gay men.)

6. Butler, The Psychic Life of Power, 137.

7. See, on this point, the analysis of Prieur and Halvorsen, "Le Droit à l'indifférence," 6–15. See also Prieur, "Le Mariage homosexuel est-il concevable?" 72–79.

8. See, for example, stG: "I maintain that inversion . . . is a solution that a child discovers when he is suffocating" (78). See also Sartre, "De la vocation d'écrivain": "Literature, like pederasty, is a virtual solution, invented in certain situations, and not even envisioned in others in which it would be of no assistance" (697).

6. The City and Conservative Discourse

1. See, as mentioned earlier, Wittmann, "A Gay Manifesto."

2. Chauncey, *Gay New York*, 26. See also the entirety of chapter 5, 131–49.

3. The idea of such an "ecological niche" is the starting point of an intellectually rather impoverished book by Gabriel Rotello—a rather detestable one, as well, given its revolting moralism and its hate-filled puritanism in regards to gay sexuality and gay ways of life. Yet its initial observation is hard to argue with. Rotello, *Sexual Ecology*.

4. See Pinell and de Busscher, "La Création des associations de lutte contre le sida," 316–23. See also Fillieule, "Mobilisation gay en temps de sida," 81–96. Already in 1988, Michael Pollak was calling attention to the fact that even if certain gay "activists" (notably certain journalists writing for the gay press) had demonstrated great reticence before admitting that there was an epidemic (something that can be explained in large measure by the explosion of homophobia unleashed at the outset of the epidemic), it was still among those reading that press, gays involved in the gay subculture, that prevention measures were adopted most rapidly. See, for example, the chart published on the final (unnumbered) page of his book, *Les Homosexuels et le sida*.

5. Aron clearly expressed this sentiment in his public "confession" a year before he died: "Mon sida," *Le Nouvel Observateur*, October 30, 1987.

6. Lucey, "Balzac's Queer Cousins and Their Friends," 177.

7. On the relationship of the city (notably Berlin) to gay movements, see Steakley, *The Homosexual Emancipation Movement in Germany*. For the United States, see D'Emilio, *Sexual Politics, Sexual Communities*.

8. Chauncey, *Gay New York*, 132.

9. Walter C. Reckless, "The Distribution of Commercialized Vice in the City: A Sociological Analysis," in *The Urban Community*, ed. Ernst W. Burgess (Chicago: University of Chicago Press, 1926). Cited in Chauncey, 132.

10. See Burleigh and Wippermann, *The Racial State*, especially the second part, "The 'Purification' of the Body of the Nation," 75–197.

11. Mirbeau, *La 628-E-8* (Paris: Fasquelle, 1907), cited in Patrick Cardon's "Présentation" to *Le Troisième Sexe*, by Magnus Hirschfeld, viii.

12. For example: "All these antennas one sees in the large cities are like hairs that stand up on a head. They are asking for demoniacal connections." Or, "As soon as we enter into a room bathed in mechanical music it is as if we have entered into an opium den." Ernst Jünger, *Jardins et routes, pages de journal, 1939–1940* (Paris: Plon, 1951), 50–51, cited in Bourdieu, *L'Ontologie politique de Martin Heidegger*, 27.

13. Heidegger, "Pourquoi nous restons en province," 149–53.

14. Mirbeau, *La 628-E-8*, viii.

7. To Tell or Not to Tell

1. [Translator's note: In French, the letters P D would be pronounced the same way as the word *pédé*, which is more or less equivalent to the American insult "faggot."]

2. Régis Gallerand, *Homo sociatus*.

3. Kissen, *The Last Closet*. "Outing" is the political gesture of publicly revealing the homosexuality of certain people who are still in the closet, notably when those people spend their time denouncing homosexuality. It has been practiced in England (and rightly so, in my view) against conservative elected officials who were voting in favor of repressive laws directed at gays and lesbians and against religious figures who officially denounced the abomination of homosexuality (which they then went home and practiced). On the other hand, it seems to me less justifiable in the case of actors or singers, on the pretext of encouraging a wider public acceptance of homosexuality. While that may be the end result, nonetheless, as long as the actors or singers in question are not publicly condemning homosexuality in order to better hide their own, I have a difficult time seeing by what right one can demand individuals, even famous ones, to declare what they are—even if one may well deplore their preference for saying nothing.

4. Cf. Goffman, *Stigma*, 77–78.

5. Gide, *Oscar Wilde*, 30–31.

6. Goffman, *Stigma*, 86–87.

7. See Adam, *The Survival of Domination*, 93.

8. Despite all the criticisms it drew (and merited), the film *In and Out* had the advantage of showing how a gay man can be known as such by others or be subject to ostracism without himself knowing or admitting that he is gay.

9. Bourdieu, *Masculine Domination*, 116–17.

10. See Herdt and Boxer, *Children of Horizons*.

11. For an analysis of this point see Sedgwick, *Epistemology of the Closet*, 65–90.

12. See Sedgwick, "Proust and the Spectacle of the Closet," in *Epistemology of the Closet*, 212–51.

8. Heterosexual Interpellation

1. Butler, *Excitable Speech*, 5–6, 2.

2. Louis Althusser, "Ideology and Ideological State Apparatuses," 174.

3. See Bourdieu, *The Logic of Practice*.

4. Althusser, "Ideology and Ideological State Apparatuses," 182.

5. For the history of these daily, permanent microstruggles see the works of John D'Emilio and George Chauncey.

6. See Bartlett, *Who Was That Man?* xxi-xxii.

7. Nicole Brossard, "Ma continent," in *"Amantes" suivi de "Le Sens apparent" et "Sous la langue,"* 116.

8. Sartre, *The Family Idiot*, 1:3, translation modified. The ideas that the world and language exist prior to us and take hold of us and that human freedom consists in giving meaning to the world and to language are central themes in Sartre's work.

9. Riggs, *Tongues Untied*.

10. See Franz Fanon's comments in *Black Skin, White Masks*: "As long as the black man is among his own, he will have no occasion . . . to experience his being through others" (109).

11. All this is portrayed magnificently in the 1955 novel by Green, *The Transgressor*.

9. The Subjected "Soul"

1. I do not mean to suggest that everyone who becomes homosexual only later on in life is a person who was unable to recognize earlier what he or she was. Such is the case in a great many instances, but people also change their sexuality (in both directions) at this or that moment in life, or move from one sexuality to another, not to mention those who live out several sexualities at the same time. Sexual identities are plural and any statement that purports to be some kind of "general" reflection must include an implicit qualification that it cannot in itself truly encompass all experiences. On the other hand, I also do not believe that there are as many identities as there are individuals, to the extent that it would become impossible to designate classes of experience—even if each person who can be included in this or that class will also obviously have distinguishing characteristics.

2. Bourdieu, "Remarques provisoires sur la perception sociale du corps," 53n10.

3. Perhaps we should here make a distinction between men and women, for if the insult "faggot" is widespread, the insult "dyke" is less so. To make fun of the effeminacy of a boy is to make an absolute and violent condemnation, whereas to point out that a girl is a "tomboy" is not always pejorative. Further distinctions need to be made, however, for the other forms of violence that can be exercised against an effeminate boy (in his family, at work, at school) can in a similar way be exercised against a masculine girl or woman. Moreover, the repertory of insults that can be directed at women who are perceived not to be respecting sexual norms is much larger than for men ("bitch" or "slut," and so on, in English, or "*pute*" and "*salope*," and so on, in French), and so "dyke" (*gouine*) is much less necessary than "faggot" (*pédé*), given the large number of other words available to express a call to order.

4. See Herdt and Boxer, *Children of Horizon*, 111, 120–21, 200, 207–209, 245.

5. For the distinction between "discredited" and "discreditable," see Goffman, *Stigma*, 4, 41–42.

6. "The soul is the effect and instrument of a political anatomy; the soul is the prison of the body" (Foucault, *Discipline and Punish*, 30).

7. Isherwood, *Christopher and His Kind*, 162.

8. Lewin, *Resolving Social Problems*.

9. Kardiner and Ovesey, *The Mark of Oppression*.

10. Caricature and Collective Insult

1. Numerous examples of antihomosexual caricatures can be found in the volume published by the Cahiers Gai-Kitsch-Camp that brings together the work of John Grand-Carteret, *Derrière "Lui*," first published in 1908, and the work of the American historian James Steakley, "Iconography of a Scandal." These two texts, along with the historical documents associated with them, deal with the caricatures published in the German press during the Eulenburg affair. (Eulenburg was a German aristocrat close to the Emperor who, when accused by a journalist of being homosexual, sued him for defamation.) The series of ensuing trials produced a proliferation of articles and books throughout Europe. For images in film, see Russo, *The Celluloid Closet*, of which a film has also been made.

2. Freud, *Five Lectures on Psycho-Analysis*, 30–31.

3. See Kris and Gombrich, *Caricature*. See also Gombrich and Eribon, *Ce que l'image nous dit*, 44.

4. In one of the columns he published in *L'Autre Journal*, Michel Cressole discussed in these terms the witticisms of television comics who, day after day, allow themselves to make incredibly rude jokes about gay people: "For them, the position of being outspoken on television amounts to speaking about gays in ways Jacques Médecin would never dare use in speaking of Jews." Cressole concludes with a concise, brutal, and probably quite justifiable statement: "It is as if one were hearing Le Pen talking at the dinner table" (Cressole, *Une Folle à sa fenêtre*, 9). The discursive register of television jokes is very close, if not identical, to that of cabaret singers, of whom many songs find their inspiration in the crudest forms of homophobia. (Examples can be found on the disk put out by the Gais Musettes organization, *Chansons interlopes* [Illicit songs], which collects songs written between 1908 and 1936.)

5. See the drawings reproduced in Grand-Carteret, *Derrière "Lui*," 105.

6. My attention was drawn to these caricatures of Cambacérès thanks to a lecture by Darcy Grimaldo Grigsby at the University of California, Berkeley, on April 18, 1998: " 'The Effects of Hunger': Cannibalism and Other Intimacies of Empire." Reproductions of some of these caricatures can be found in Clerc, *La Caricature contre Napoléon*.

7. Foucault, "Des caresses d'hommes considérées comme un art," in *Dits et écrits*, 1954–1988, 4:315–317. Hereafter cited as *Dits*.

8. Here, I speak only of male homosexuality. Love between women doubtless needs an entirely different analysis. In *The Use of Pleasure*, we should add, Foucault does clearly emphasize this form of transhistorical permanence. He speaks of a "typical portrait" to be found in nineteenth-century texts of the homosexual or the invert as invariably effeminate, and he calls attention to the fact that this "stereotype" was already "clearly delineated in the Greco-Roman literature of the imperial age." He adds that "the long history of this image still needs to be written" (Foucault, *The Use of Pleasure*, 18–19, translation modified).

9. See Adam, *The Survival of Domination*, 31.

10. One can find some thoughts on collective stigmatization of Jews (one which links each member of a group to a set of derogatory characteristics) in the ninth chapter of book IV of Dickens's *Our Mutual Friend*.

11. Here is how the character in the Dickens novel concludes that it is impossible to escape from stigmatizations: "I reflected—clearly reflected for the first time, that in bending my neck to the yoke I was willing to wear, I bent the unwilling neck of the whole Jewish people" (Dickens, *Our Mutual Friend*, 726).

12. Sartre, *StG*: "Shame isolates. As does pride, which is the obverse of shame" (41n). It should be noted that the individual (and individualist) pride (*orgueil*) mentioned here by Sartre, which consists in feeling superior to other gay people and in scorning them, is precisely the opposite of the notion of pride (*fierté*), developed since the 1970s, which is consistently thought of as necessarily collective, as having the goal of founding this "reciprocity" between gay men (and lesbians, whom Sartre forgets to mention), this "solidarity" which in 1952 Sartre thought to be impossible.

13. See Bourdieu, "Le Paradoxe du sociologue," 86–94. See also *Masculine Domination*: "The dominated apply categories constructed from the point of view of the dominant to the relations of domination, thus making them appear as natural" (35).

14. The organizing of gay men and lesbians still provides, as it has always provided, an occasion for a proliferation of homophobic discourses, from all parts of the political spectrum. These discourses would naturalize, would claim as ontological, the current social order. They know what it should be (because it has "always" been that way) and they know what it cannot be (because that would "destroy the very foundations of civilization" or of the "symbolic order" by way of which one enters into human culture). For examples of, and a devastating critique of, these discourses, see Fassin, "Ouvrir le mariage aux homosexuels, 22; Fassin, "L'Illusion anthropologique"; and Iacub, "Le Couple homosexuel, le droit et l'ordre symbolique," 111–24.

15. Gide, *Corydon*, 28–29.

11. *Inversions*

1. Butler, *Excitable Speech*, 51–52.

2. See Bourdieu, *Masculine Domination*. The extension of the schemas that apply to male-female relations to heterosexual-homosexual relations (at least for men) is suggested by Bourdieu himself in his "Quelques questions sur la question gay et lesbienne," 45–50. Bourdieu took up and reworked these remarks as an appendix to *Masculine Domination*.

3. See the analyses and the texts cited by Rosario in *The Erotic Imagination*, 88.

4. Tamassia, "Sull'inversione dell'istinto sessuale" (1878), cited in Rosario, *The Erotic Imagination*, 86. On relations between women and the different ways in which they can be perceived as contravening the natural law of the "difference between the sexes," see Faderman, *Odd Girls and Twilight Lovers*, 38–61.

5. Freud, *Three Contributions to the Theory of Sex*, 11.

6. See also 928: "More often than not having to content themselves with the roughest approximation. . . ." See also *Cities of the Plain*, *RTP*, 2:638.

7. On this point, see Tadié, *Proust*, 86–92, and Lindon, "Être Proust," in *Je t'aime*, 75.

8. Proust, "Esquisse XI," in *Recherche*, 3:1022: "I had seen the Marquis de Gurcy [Charlus's name in the drafts of the novel] talking arm in arm with a soldier. . . . The soldier had more the air of a painted pierrot covered in powder and make-up than that of a real soldier. . . . I had noticed Gurcy's face with great curiosity, but without recognizing him. I was thinking with admiration of how the combination of necessity and the hope for pleasure can cause even the most startlingly different bit of reality to come to resemble our ideal—so that M. de Gurcy, hungry for virility, sickened by effeminate men, could have come to believe himself meeting a real young man in that small *tante* disguised as a soldier."

9. When Proust speaks of his "girlish air enshrined in his masculine beauty [air de fille au milieu de sa mâle beauté]" (*RTP*, 2:1040), he is referring more to the fact that he is interested in the baron's money than to any effeminacy. The word *fille* here carries the meaning of "prostitute."

10. It is in one of the variant readings provided in the Pléiade edition of the novel that Proust wrote: "The homosexual . . . believes himself to be identical to what he desires, just as a snob believes himself to be noble" (*Recherche*, 3:1279).

11. See *RTP*, 2:653.

12. Of course Proust, or his narrator, does say, at the beginning of *Cities of the Plain*, that his "theory" is going to evolve. Just before presenting the idea of the man-woman who will only be able to satisfy his desire with other inverts, he offers the following hesitation: "according at least to the first theory which I sketched in outline at the time, which we shall see subjected to some modification in the sequel" (*RTP*, 2:638).

13. Letter from Marcel Proust to Paul Souday (1920), cited in the reference matter by Antoine Compagnon to *Recherche*, 3:1254.

14. On the relation between Proust's theory and Ulrichs's (which Proust undoubtedly knew of thanks to the texts of Hirschfeld and Krafft-Ebing), see Rivers, *Proust and the Art of Love*, 185–87.

15. See Kennedy, *Ulrichs*, 170.

16. Cited in Kennedy, *Ulrichs*, 50.

17. See ibid., 73–75.

18. Proust uses the phrase "third sex," citing Balzac as his source. See "Esquisse IV" in *Recherche*, 3:955.

19. "To describe men, even if the results were to make them resemble monsters," is the account he gives of his project on the final page of his novel (*RTP*, 3:1107).

20. Gide, *The Journals of André Gide*, 2:267. [Translator's note: The phrase "shades of young women" (à l'ombre des jeunes filles) recalls the title of the second volume of Proust's novel, *A l'ombre des jeunes filles en fleurs*, which has in some editions been given the English title *Within a Budding Grove*. *Sodom* refers to the volume of the novel called *Sodome et Gomorrhe*, which has in some editions been given the English title *Cities of the Plain*.]

21. On the reception of Proust, see Ahlstedt, *La Pudeur en crise*.

12. On Sodomy

1. See Bard, "Lectures de *La Garçonne*," 78–95. See in particular 88–92.

2. Mosse, *The Image of Man*, 190.

3. Pollak, *Les Homosexuels et le sida*, 45–47. One can detect a real phobia regarding fairies, queens, and effeminacy in the discourse of many gay men, notably in the rag bag of popular books on gays that have appeared recently, whose authors, not bound by any kind of scholarly rigor, allow themselves to reveal their personal prejudices in a much cruder and naive form than does Michael Pollak.

4. On playing with femininity, see the classic book by Newton, *Mother Camp*.

5. [Translator's note: the insult being referred to is *enculé*, for which there is no easy English equivalent. It means, literally, someone who has "taken it up the ass." English has a parallel insult that is roughly the equivalent of the French *enculé*, though it refers to a different sexual act: "cocksucker."] If *enculé* is an extremely common insult, the same is also the case for "*se faire enculer*" (to take it up the ass), which means to have been tricked or duped, just as the expression "*baisser son pantalon*" (to drop one's trousers) means to lack courage or fortitude.

6. [Translator's note: in French, when one speaks of oneself as a "top," the word one uses is *actif*. When one speaks of oneself as a bottom, *passif*.] On the various

cosmologies founded on the opposition between the "masculine" principle and the "feminine," see Bourdieu, *Masculine Domination*, especially the pages devoted to an ethnology of Kabylia. See also the study called "Irresistible Analogy" in *The Logic of Practice*, 200–70, and also, in the same book, the appendix titled "The Kabyle House or the World Reversed," 271–83.

7. See Grand-Carteret, *Derrière "Lui."*

8. See the helpful commentary by Sedgwick, *Epistemology of the Closet*, 219–20.

9. Prieur, *Mema's House, Mexico City*.

10. See Mendes-Leité, *Bisexualité, le dernier tabou*.

11. Bourdieu, *The Logic of Practice*, 146. See also *Masculine Domination*, 5ff.

13. Subjectivity and Private Life

1. Isay, *Being Homosexual*, 137.

2. Cocteau, *The White Book*, 21.

3. Isherwood, *Christopher and His Kind*, 3.

4. Genet, from an interview in *Playboy*, April 1964. Cited in Pucciani, "Le 'Dialogue infernal' de Genet et Sartre," 87. The BBC interview is cited in Pucciani, 88.

5. Monette, *Becoming a Man*, 61.

6. Goffman, *Stigma*, 88.

7. See ibid., 100–102.

8. See Bartlett, *Who Was That Man*: "Our first experience of talking as gay men is the experience of lying" (84).

9. See, on this point, Goffman, *The Presentation of Self in Everyday Life*.

10. Habermas, *The Philosophical Discourse of Modernity*, 296–97.

11. See Adam's analyses in *The Survival of Domination*, 96.

12. See the classic analysis of MacKinnon, "Feminism, Marxism, Method and the State," 515–44.

13. Dunning, "Sport as a Male Preserve," 274–75.

14. See Sedgwick, *Epistemology of the Closet*, 186, and *Between Men*, 88–89.

15. Bourdieu, *Masculine Domination*, 20.

16. Ibid., 50.

17. Goffman, *Stigma*, 128–29.

18. See Halperin, *Saint Foucault*.

19. On "theatricality," see Butler, "Critically Queer," in *Bodies That Matter*, 232. She presents theatricality as a way to expose "the homophobic 'law' that can no longer control the terms of its own abjecting strategies."

20. See also Sedgwick, "Queer Performativity," 5. Along with the escape from shame, there may be another closely related factor to consider when trying to understand the reasons for this play with self-presentation: the feeling of being

"separate" or "different" and the isolation that implies create for many gay men an imaginary life filled with images and fantasies (drawn from books, magazines, films, people observed in the world, and so on) that can then be exteriorized in their own gestures, their own personal theater, once they have decided to reveal the secret that previously had caused them to play at discretion and the imitation of heterosexual models.

14. Existence Precedes Essence

1. Pollak, *Les Homosexuels et le sida*. Such a finding leads us back to the issue of the over-representation of college-educated people in the spontaneously produced samples often used in sociological studies. But this, in turn, should not lead us to neglect the important phenomenon of upward mobility. Together, these two issues might lead us to a more complex vision of the causality Pollak lays out: it will not be sufficient to say that it is only gays with a higher degree of cultural capital who are best positioned to self-identify as gay. Rather, prior to that, it is the impulse to be able to self-identify as gay (in whatever way that might be, even by way of a temporary refusal of one's self) that leads one (but how exactly?) to pursue education even to advanced levels.

2. Nietzsche, *The Gay Science*, 219–20.

3. Consider, for example, the character Daniel in the series of novels called *The Roads to Freedom*. For Sartre's homophobia, one can also consult the text in which he described those men who collaborated with the Germans during the Second World War as "cowardly," that is to say, "feminine," that is to say, "homosexual." As corroboration of his opinions, he noted that "Parisian homosexual circles provided many brilliant recruits to the collaboration" (Sartre, "Qu'est-ce qu'un collaborateur?" 58). We see here the traditional topos of the gay man as traitor to the nation (Sartre would certainly have known that people had frequently invoked it in attacking Gide), a topos we find Sartre using again when we see Daniel cheering the arrival of German troops in Paris. (Charlus, in Proust's *Time Regained*, proves to be another Germanophile, revealing a certain consistency across time in the representation of gay men.) On Simone de Beauvoir's homophobia, see her correspondence with Nelson Algren, in which she jokes endlessly about "fairies" and "pansies" (Beauvoir, *A Transatlantic Love Affair*).

4. See his interview with the gay magazine *Gai Pied Hebdo*. In that interview he states that "I think that for the moment, homosexuality is obliged to remain fairly isolated, to be a group within a prudish society, a marginal group that cannot be integrated into society. It must reject that society and even, in a certain way, hate it. Homosexuals are obliged to refuse that society, and the only thing that they can

hope for at the present time is, in certain states, a sort of free space where they can find each other, as happens in the United States, for example."

5. Sartre, *Anti-Semite and Jew*, 69.

6. After having remarked that Zionism is in a certain sense a "counterideology" to antisemitic ideology, Arendt adds, "This, incidentally, is not to say that Jewish self-consciousness was ever a mere creation of antisemitism; even a cursory knowledge of Jewish history, whose central concern since the Bablyonian exile has always been the survival of the people against the overwhelming odds of dispersion, should be enough to dispel this latest myth in these matters, a myth that has become somewhat fashionable in intellectual circles after Sartre's 'existentialist' interpretation of the Jew as someone who is regarded and defined as a Jew by others" (Arendt, *The Origins of Totalitarianism*, xv). This criticism (based on a naive reading of Sartre's text) does not really seem pertinent, for Sartre is obviously not trying to say that there is no Jewish cultural tradition, but rather that there is no "nature," no "essence," to "being Jewish." Consequently, to be Jewish is to be defined as such within a given society. Sartre did, of course, later (in an interview in 1966) recognize that he should have included historical specifics in his argument. Yet in the same interview he insists that in his own eyes the description he had given of the structural opposition between "authenticity" and "inauthenticity" remained perfectly valid (cited in Contat and Rybalka, *Les Écrits de Sartre*, 140).

7. Sartre, *Anti-Semite and Jew*, 67.

8. Ibid., 93. He also writes: "Many inauthentic Jews play at not being Jews" (96). That might recall for us the definition of "bad faith" given in *Being and Nothingness*: "The first act of bad faith is to flee what it cannot flee, to flee what it is" (Sartre, *Being and Nothingness*, 115).

9. Sartre, *Anti-Semite and Jew*, 108.

10. Sartre, "Textes politiques," 23.

11. David Halperin has also written of "an identity without an essence" in *Saint Foucault*.

12. Bech, *When Men Meet*, 97. See also Halperin, *Saint Foucault*.

15. Unrealizable Identity

1. See the comments by Sedgwick in *Epistemology of the Closet*, 68.

2. Bech, *When Men Meet*, 96.

3. Shoshana Felman has pointed this out in *The Literary Speech Act*.

4. See Derrida, "Signature Event Context": "Could a performative utterance succeed if its formulation did not repeat a 'coded' or iterable utterance, or in other words, if the formula I pronounce in order to open a meeting, launch a ship or a

marriage were not identifiable as *conforming* with an iterable model, if it were not then identifiable in some way as a 'citation'?" (18).

5. [Translator's note: Domestic partnership legislation (the PACS, Pacte civil de solidarité) was adopted in France in fall 1998. The first French edition of this book was published in spring 1999.]

6. See Barthes, *Roland Barthes by Roland Barthes.*

7. Sports are obviously a location where homosexuality is forbidden (and unspeakable). It is sometimes offered as a reproach to organizers of the Gay Games or of other gay and lesbian sports organizations that such a form of separatism is incomprehensible. Sports are neither gay nor straight, it is said. Such critics choose to forget or to ignore that sports are deeply heterosexual and that a self-declared gay man or lesbian would only with difficulty be able to continue as a member of a team. (There is an exemplary case of an English soccer player who was slowly pushed out of the professional circuit. One could also think of the scandal that broke out when Martina Navratilova came out, an act she could permit herself, already being at the top of her sport. That did not, however, prevent hate-filled reactions from other players.) It is not difficult to understand the pleasure that is involved in being able to be openly gay or lesbian within an athletic context, and we might also recall that these organizations and their competitions are open to bisexuals, transsexuals, and heterosexuals as well as to people of all ages.

8. See Sartre, *Being and Nothingness,* 675–80. I use this notion somewhat freely here, straying a bit from the precise meaning given to it by Sartre.

9. See Halperin, "The Queer Politics of Michel Foucault," in *Saint Foucault,* 15–126.

10. Foucault, "Friendship as a Way of Life," in *Ethics: Subjectivity and Truth,* 136, translation modified. This volume will hereafter be cited as *Ethics.* I will return to this text and others in the third part of this book.

11. Bersani, *Homos.*

12. Joan Scott has analyzed this insurmountable paradox in the context of the feminist movement in *Only Paradoxes to Offer.*

13. One could think here of the elitist circle of Stefan Georg in Germany in the 1920s or the "masculinist" wing of the German homosexual movement of the same moment.

14. On the Mattachine Society, see D'Emilio, *Sexual Politics, Sexual Communities,* especially chapter 4, "Radical Beginnings of the Mattachine Society" (57–74) and chapter 5, "Retreat to Respectability" (75–91). See also the biography of Harry Hay, the founder of this movement, by Timmons, *The Trouble with Harry Hay;* see also the anthology of writings by Hay, *Radically Gay.*

15. See Steakley, *The Homosexual Emancipation Movement in Germany,* 22–69.

16. See Altman, *Homosexual: Oppression and Liberation*; and Hocquenghem, *Homo-sexual Desire*. This theme can also be found in the book that had so much influence on Hocquenghem: Deleuze and Guattari, *Anti-Oedipus*.

17. On the queer movement, see Sedgwick, "Construire des significations *queer*," 109–16. On the importance of Guy Hocquenghem, see Moon's introduction to *Homosexual Desire*.

16. Perturbations

1. Bersani, "Trahisons gaies," 67.

2. Foucault, "Le Départ du prophète," cited in Eribon, *Michel Foucault et ses contemporains*, 280–81. My aim is not to present Arcadie as more subversive than the FHAR. Far from it! But it does seem to me that "subversion" is always relative, always historically, culturally, and politically situated. It must always be thought of in relation to that situation.

3. See Faderman, *Surpassing the Love of Men* and *Odd Girls and Twilight Lovers*. For a look at a more specific period, see Benstock, *Women of the Left Bank, Paris 1900–1940*.

4. See "Dana International, la Queen de Sabbat," *Libération*, June 8, 1998. Jennie Livingston's film, *Paris Is Burning*, about drag balls in Harlem, could lead to the same kind of reflections: the ideal that the participants in the contests that take place at these balls strive to imitate is that of a well-to-do white woman. Further, even those competitors who live day-to-day as transvestites, such as the wonderful Xtravaganza, have as their ideal to find a husband and set up house. The same aspirations can be found in the Mexican transvestites interviewed by Annick Prieur in *Mema's House*.

5. A Jew can be racist; a black person can be antisemitic; a gay person can be racist and antisemitic, and so on. The paradigm of this absence of solidarity among the oppressed can be found in the attitudes of August von Platen and Heinrich Heine. The former denounced the latter as a Jew. The latter mocked the former for his homosexuality. See Mayer, *Les Marginaux*, 220–37.

6. Goffman, *Stigma*, 138.

7. Bourdieu, *Masculine Domination*, 93.

8. Bell and Weinberg, *Homosexualities*, 157.

9. Adam, *The Survival of Domination*.

10. Pierre Herbart said of Gide: "As for that anarchical force that he harbored, and that occasionally makes an appearance in his work—a body of work that is, for those with the eyes to see it, imbued with that very force—he only knew how to make good use of it in his life, due to a shadowy struggle that our 'morals' helped him to undertake." (Herbart, "André Gide," 78).

11. On Gide's proximity to the Action Française, see Hanna, "What Did André Gide See in the Action Française?" 1–22. On his evolution toward the left, see Lucey, *Gide's Bent*.

17. The Individual and the Group

1. *RTP*, 2:639–40. The entire passage is worth reading in this regard.

2. For Proust, "race" does not always carry a biological meaning. If he sometimes describes homosexuality in quasi-physiological terms as an error of nature in placing a woman's soul in a man's body, he also uses the notion of race as a metaphor to describe the "collective" that gay men form despite themselves as a historical product, a product of the social hostility that they face and that has determined them: "brought into the company of their own kind by the ostracism to which they are subjected, the opprobrium into which they have fallen, having finally been invested, by a persecution similar to that of Israel, with the physical and moral characteristics of a race . . ." (*RTP*, 2:638; my emphasis). In the first draft of this passage, the historicization of the notion of race was even clearer: "Other apologists of their race sing its praises back to its origins . . . similar to those Jews who insist that 'Jesus Christ was a Jew,' without realizing that sin, even original sin, has a historical origin and that it is reprobation that produces shame" (*Recherche*, 3:933; my emphasis). Or again: "In the end, given the shared opprobrium of an undeserved abjection, they took on common characteristics, the look of a race" (*Recherche*, 3:924).

3. Sartre, *Critique of Dialectical Reason*. It is obviously not my intention here to reconstruct all the complexities of Sartre's thought on this question, and notably on all the different levels of "groups" that he is at pains to define. My goal is simply to see how the general idea of the passage from "seriality" to a "group" can be useful in thinking of the "gay question."

4. Sartre, "Textes politiques," 43.

5. Ibid., 79.

6. Ibid., 43. These articles by Sartre, with titles such as "Maoists in France" or "Elections: Fool's Gold," are profoundly marked by the problematics and the vocabulary of the far left of the early 1970s. Yet it is striking to what an extent, once they are stripped of their far-left rhetoric, they seem to be written as a response to the questions posed by the political and cultural organizing of today. It is true that Sartre does not speak only of workers in these texts, but of "struggles" in general. Indeed, one finds in the text from 1971 on the Burgos trial and the Basque question, extremely interesting comments on the opposition between "abstract universalism" and a concrete and "singular universal." See 21–37, esp. 24–25.

7. Sartre, *Critique of Dialectical Reason*, 676.

8. See *StG*, 54–55, 58.

9. Sartre, *Black Orpheus*, 62. Franz Fanon critiqued rather severely this Hegelian idea of a stage of revolt leading to an ideal society, a process that apparently proceeds by way of the laws of some historical necessity that would impose some preexisting meaning on the origins of these movements of revolt: "And so it is not I who make a meaning for myself, but it is the meaning that was already there, preexisting, waiting for me. . . . The dialectic that brings necessity into the foundation of my freedom drives me out of myself. . . . I am not a potentiality of something, I am wholly what I am. . . . My Negro consciousness does not hold itself out as a lack. It *is*. It is its own follower" (*Black Skin, White Masks*, 134–35).

10. Sartre, *Black Orpheus*, 61. He says more or less the same thing at the end of *Anti-Semite and Jew*, where he writes that "the authentic Jew who thinks of himself as a Jew" is not hostile to assimilation. He "simply renounces *for himself* an assimilation that is today impossible; he awaits the radical liquidation of anti-Semitism for his sons." The "access of consciousness" of the Jew as Jew and the "war" he must wage are nothing other than a step toward that "radical liquidation of anti-Semitism" that will be produced by the "socialist revolution" (150).

11. Sartre, *The Words*, 255.

12. Hirshman, *Bonheur privé, actions publiques*.

13. See Adam, *The Rise of a Gay and Lesbian Movement*.

14. See on this point, D'Emilio, "Capitalism and Gay Identity," in *Making Trouble: Essays on Gay History, Politics, and the University* (New York: Routledge, 1992), 3–16.

15. Many other such examples can be found in George Chauncey's book or Florence Tamagne's dissertation.

16. "The achievements which surround us and which we want to change are old victories that have rotted" (*STG*, 189).

PART 2   *Specters of Wilde*

1. How *"Arrogant Pederasts"* Come into Being

1. Hyde, *The Trials of Oscar Wilde*, 339. Ellmann, *Oscar Wilde*, 477–78.

2. Wilde, *De Profundis*, 938.

3. Ibid., 894.

4. See Bartlett, *Who Was That Man?*

5. Forster, *Maurice*, 159.

6. On Magnus Hirschfeld, see Wolff, *Magnus Hirschfeld*. On Virginia Woolf, see Vanita, "The Wildeness of Woolf," in *Sappho and the Virgin Mary*, 186–214, esp. 186–89.

7. See Pollard, *André Gide*, 3; and Martin, *André Gide ou la vocation du bonheur*, 553.

8. Gide, *If It Die . . .*, 280–87. On Gide's relations with Wilde in Paris, see Martin, *André Gide*, 160–62, and on Algeria, 250–51.

9. See Martin, *André Gide*, 309–10.

10. See Gide, *Oscar Wilde: In Memorium*.

11. Delay, *La Jeunesse d'André Gide*, 2:547. If Delay does not hold Wilde fully responsible for Gide's homosexuality, it is because he has two other explanations to provide: too frequent masturbation and a temperament marked by a notable "nervous weakness" (526). It is difficult to understand how a work such as this, which provides a condensed version of all the homophobic stupidity to be found in psychiatric discourse, could still be considered today as a "masterpiece." For a (devastating) critique of the book, see Lucey, *Gide's Bent*, esp. 120–21.

12. The journalist Maximilian Harden had accused two aristocrats who were close to the Emperor—Prince Philipp Eulenburg and Count Kuno Moltke—of being homosexual. The libel trials begun by those two aristocrats in 1907 and 1908 lasted for years, with many ups and downs. They were covered widely all over Europe. Of course, the lives and careers of the two aristocrats (and of several others) were ruined. The fact that Magnus Hirschfeld came to testify for Harden to the effect that Moltke was homosexual (with the crazy idea that in such a forum he would be able to defend the idea that homosexuality was inborn, that it was found even in the highest social levels, and thereby advance the cause of its decriminalization) had disastrous long-lasting effects for the German homosexual movement. On Eulenburg and the "Affair," see Hull, *The Entourage of Kaiser Wilhelm II, 1888–1918*, 45–145. On Hirschfeld's role in the various trials, see Wolff, *Magnus Hirschfeld*, 68–85.

13. Gide, *Corydon*, 3.

14. Cited in Pollard, *André Gide*, 416.

15. On homosexuality in Proust's work in general, see Rivers, *Proust and the Art of Love*. On Proust's interest in the Eulenburg affair, see 112–37. See also Antoine Compagnon's "Notice" for the 1988 Pléiade edition of *Sodome et Gomorrhe*, which documents quite precisely the relation of the Eulenburg affair and its coverage in France to the genesis of Proust's novelistic project (*Recherche*, 3:1196–1202).

16. Cited by Compagnon, in *Recherche*, 3:1201.

17. The letter is from August 1909. See Proust, *Correspondance*, 9:155.

18. See "Esquisse IV" (*Recherche*, 3:955) and "Esquisse I" (*Recherche*, 3:919).

19. *RTP*, 2:979. In one of the drafts for the novel, Charlus is very close to one of those accused in the affair (see *Recherche*, 3:1202). Proust also mentioned the Eulenburg scandal in a draft composed in 1910–1911 (see *Recherche*, 3:952).

20. In Wilde's novel, *The Picture of Dorian Gray*, the hero is "poisoned by a book" (in *The Complete Works of Oscar Wilde*, 115). The book, which he reads over and over again, and from which he "could not free himself" (102), is none other than Huysmans's *Against Nature*. Dorian identifies with the novel's main character, Des Esseintes. Huysmans's inspiration for that character was Montesquiou.

21. The book from 1908 that I mentioned earlier (Grand-Carteret, Derrière "Lui") was devoted to this subject. The trials are also discussed in a book by Weindel and Fischer, L'Homosexualité en Allemagne, that also appeared in 1908. It was also in 1908 that the book by Hirschfeld, Le Troisième Sexe was first published in French.

22. See Proust's letter to Louis d'Albufera in May 1908, in Correspondance, 8:112–13.

23. See Proust's letter to Robert Dreyfus in May 1908, in Correspondance, 8:122–123. See also Antoine Compagnon's "Notice" in Recherche, 3:1198. And also Rivers, Proust and the Art of Love, 145–51.

24. Gide, Corydon, 7.

25. See Sibalis, "The Regulation of Male Homosexuality in Revolutionary and Napoleonic France, 1789–1815," 80–101.

26. This growth toward the assumption of the right to speak is helpfully traced in Lepape, André Gide, le messager.

27. Sedgwick, Between Men, 114.

28. Sedgwick, Epistemology of the Closet, 49. Gide should, of course, be added to the list. To speak of "modern homosexuality," by which one understands "as we know it today," poses its own set of problems, especially to the extent that it allows one to assume there to be some unique, unitary form of homosexuality and that we could take account of it by simply looking around us. But this would leave out, of course, all the forms that we do not "know," that we do not see, all the forms that do not fit within the "homosexual/heterosexual" duality. Obviously the modern way of thinking of "gay identity" has not brought about the disappearance older ways of thinking of relations between people of the same sex (the Freudian model of bisexuality, classical "pederasty," and so on) that have continued to cohabit with more recent forms. See, on all these points, Sedgwick's Epistemology of the Closet, 46–47, and her remarks at a colloquium at the Centre Pompidou, "Construire des significations queer," 109–16, esp. 111–12.

2. An Unspeakable Vice

1. Dumézil, preface to L'Homosexualité dans la mythologie grecque, by Bernard Sergent. Republished as Homosexualité et initiation chez les peuples indo-européens, 9.

2. On Dumézil and World War I, see Eribon, "Georges Dumézil, un homosexuel au XXe siècle," 31–32.

3. One historian has recently suggested that it was thanks to the experience of the war and of the period just after the war that real gay culture was able to emerge. (See Tamagne, Recherches sur l'homosexualité dans la France, vol. 1, 45–52.) One should probably qualify Tamagne's assertions a bit. In her remarkable work she shows a

tendency to emphasis ruptures too much, at the expense of continuities that should be equally obvious. It would probably be better to think in terms of reorganization or of development rather than of emergence or creation.

4. Dumézil, preface to *Homosexualité*, 9.

5. Ibid., 9. He is referring to the article by E. Berthe that appeared in 1907 in *Rheinisches Museum für Philologie*, no. 62, 438–75.

6. One finds what must surely be that same will to legitimation by way of the claim of a relation to a glorious past in Boswell's book, *Same-Sex Unions in Premodern Europe*.

7. Forster, *Maurice*, 51.

8. See, on this subject, Halperin, *One Hundred Years of Homosexuality and Other Essays on Greek Love*, 2–3.

9. Cited in Crompton, *Byron and Greek Love: Homophobia in 19th-Century England*, 290.

10. On Bentham, see Crompton, *Byron*, 48.

11. Cited by ibid., 39.

12. See Halperin, *One Hundred Years of Homosexuality and Other Essays on Greek Love*, 4.

13. See ibid., 4. On Ulrichs and Plato, see Kennedy, *Ulrichs*, 50.

14. See Kennedy, *Ulrichs*, 167.

15. Freud, *Three Contributions to the Theory of Sex*, 4–5.

16. For an idea of this cultural efflorescence, see the anthology edited by Reade, *Sexual Heretics*. See also the analyses of Dellamora in *Masculine Desire*.

17. The full text of the poem can be found in Reade, *Sexual Heretics*, 360–62. Reade also reprints another poem by Douglas, "In Praise of Shame," which ends with the verse: "Of all sweet passions, Shame is the loveliest" (362).

18. See Ellmann, *Oscar Wilde*, 386, 427–28.

19. Ibid., 386.

20. Merle, *Oscar Wilde ou la "destinée" de l'homosexuel*, 72.

21. On all these points see Dowling, *Hellenism and Homosexuality in Victorian Oxford*.

22. See ibid., 80.

3. A Nation of Artists

1. Here I am following the analysis of Dowling in *Hellenism and Homosexuality in Victorian Oxford*, 5–11, and citing 5. On English Republican discourse, see the classic study by Pocock, *The Machiavelian Moment*, which Dowling cites on many occasions.

2. See Halperin, *One Hundred Years of Homosexuality and Other Essays on Greek Love*, 3.

3. See chapter 3 of Boswell, *Same-Sex Unions*, esp. 55–62.

4. Boswell, *Same-Sex Unions*, 57. Even Halperin, who, contrary to Boswell, insists on the fact that it is impossible to transpose the experience of ancient Greece into the terms of today's homosexuality (because the relations of people of the same sex were always structured by relations of age or of class), notes that there existed in Greece and in Rome the practice of male prostitution about which the texts tell us very little (Halperin, *One Hundred Years of Homosexuality and Other Essays on Greek Love*, 94). More importantly, he criticizes the true "political agenda" that is hidden within the idea that pederasty was only ritualistic, that is to say, that it did not include the expression of any real desire between the younger and the older man, as if it were necessary to sustain the idea—the fiction—of a primary heterosexuality (ibid., 61). We might add that Henning Bech has identified the same implications in the ways the ideas developed by Halperin (and by Foucault)—according to which, in the Ancient World, it was not the sex of the partner that mattered but rather the active or passive role in the sexual relation—have been taken up and understood by others. Some have gone so far as to say that for men in the active (and socially superior) position, there was an indifference to the partner's sex. (See Bech, *When Men Meet*, 71, 236n126.) Bech sees here a perhaps implicit will—especially odd when it is formulated by gay men—to assert that when a Greek man had relations with a younger man, he might as well have been having relations with a woman—which amounts to a refusal of the specificity and the reality of homosexual desire. As I just indicated, David Halperin had already explicitly dissociated his own analysis from any such reading (*One Hundred Years of Homosexuality and Other Essays on Greek Love*, 33–34).

5. Dumézil, preface to *Homosexualité*, 11. During a conversation I had with him when Sergent's book was published, Dumézil expressed his reticence more clearly, telling me, "Bernard Sergent tends to believe too easily that what he finds in the texts allows him to know what was going on in reality."

6. Symonds's *Studies of the Greek Poets* is reprinted in the collection of his texts edited by Lauritsen, *Male Love*, 12–145. This note is on 144.

7. The sentence from Plato is at *Laws* 636 c.

8. Symonds, *The Memoirs of John Addington Symonds*, 239.

9. See Bartlett, *Who Was That Man?*, 199.

10. Wilde, *The Portrait of Mr. W. H.*, in *The Complete Works of Oscar Wilde*, 1175. On Platonism and love in the *Symposium*, see 1174. The other author to whom Wilde makes frequent reference in this work is none other than Walter Pater, from whom Wilde borrows his theory of aesthetic experience.

11. Cited by the editors of Wilde, *Lettres*, 44.

12. Symonds, *The Greek Poets*, cited by Ellmann, *Oscar Wilde*, 33.

13. Bartlett, *Who Was That Man?*, 199.

14. Wilde, *The Picture of Dorian Gray*, 113.

4. Philosopher and Lover

1. Pater, "Diaphaneitè," in *The Renaissance*, 154–58. See the commentary by Dowling in *Hellenism and Homosexuality in Victorian Oxford*, 83.

2. Dowling, *Hellenism and Homosexuality in Victorian Oxford*, 81.

3. See ibid., 101n14.

4. Pater, *The Renaissance*, 122–23. (The first edition of this book in 1873 was titled *Studies in the History of the Renaissance*. Pater changed the title for the 1877 edition, choosing *The Renaissance: Studies in Art and Poetry*. It is this later edition that is available today.)

5. In *Art and Illusion*, Gombrich insists on the fact that these statues were sculpted according to the strictest criteria, according to imposed schemas.

6. Pater, *The Renaissance*, 152–53.

7. Solomon's paintings represent androgynous figures who sometimes recall John the Baptist or Leonardo da Vinci. Solomon was a homosexual who, in 1873, was arrested while out cruising and given a prison sentence.

8. Cited in Ellmann, *Oscar Wilde*, 84.

9. Cited in ibid.

10. See Dowling, *Hellenism and Homosexuality in Victorian Oxford*, 104–14.

11. Cited in Ellmann, *Oscar Wilde*, 176. "Charlotte-Ann" or "Mary-Ann" are expressions by which one designated effeminate homosexuals or, indeed, all homosexuals. "Fairy" or "fruit" might be contemporary equivalents. There is also a play on words with *charlatan*.

12. See ibid., 169. "Epicene" refers to gender ambiguity, as opposed to the vigor and robustness of "sturdier minds," that is to say, their virility.

13. Ibid., 29–30.

14. See ibid., 42–43.

15. The photographer Cecil Beaton went through something similar in the 1930s: showing up wearing a bit too much make-up to a ball given by the Count of Pembroke, Beaton was thrown into some water by a group of "virile" young men. See Hoare, *Serious Pleasures*, 85–86, cited by Tamagne, *Recherches sur l'homosexualité dans la France*, 1:250.

5. Moral Contamination

1. On the Wilde trial, see Ellmann, *Oscar Wilde*, 440–78, and also the recent book by Folsy, *The Trials of Oscar Wilde*. See also Hyde, *The Trials of Oscar Wilde*.

2. Cited in Ellmann, *Oscar Wilde*, 447, 449.

3. Cited in ibid., 463.

4. Cited in ibid., 477.

5. Cited in Hyde, *Trials*, 253.

6. Gide, *Oscar Wilde*, 1. Gide also comments that Wilde was not so much a great writer as a "great *viveur*," and he adds that, "like the philosophers of Greece, Wilde did not write but talked and lived his wisdom" (x).

7. Ellmann, *Oscar Wilde*, 453.

8. Henri de Régnier, "Souvenirs sur Oscar Wilde," 86.

9. Gide, *Oscar Wilde*, 17.

10. *RTP*, 2:638. In *Against Sainte-Beuve*, Proust also discusses Wilde's fate as a kind of destiny of which Wilde himself would have had a premonition. He recalls a witticism of Wilde's stating that the greatest sorrow of his life was the death of Lucien de Rubempré in *Splendeurs et misères des courtisanes*. He goes on: "There is something peculiarly dramatic moreover about this predilection and compassion in Oscar Wilde, at the height of his success, for Lucien de Rubempré's death. He felt compassionate, no doubt, because he saw it, like all readers, from Vautrin's point of view, which is also Balzac's point of view. From which point of view, moreover, he was a peculiarly choice and elect reader to adopt this point of view more completely than most readers. But one cannot help reflecting that a few years later he was himself to be Lucien de Rubempré. The end of Lucien de Rubempré in the Conciergerie, when he has seen his brilliant career in the world come crashing down after it has been proved he had been living on intimate terms with a convict, was merely the anticipation—as yet unknown to Wilde, it is true—of exactly what was to happen to Wilde" (65).

11. See Ellmann, *Oscar Wilde*, 108, 426–27.

12. See ibid., 450–51, 462.

6. The Truth of Masks

1. Wilde, *The Picture of Dorian Gray: Authoritative Texts*, 232.

2. Wilde, *The Picture of Dorian Gray*, in *The Complete Works of Oscar Wilde*, 93.

3. See Richard Ellmann, *Oscar Wilde*, 322.

4. Wilde, *The Picture of Dorian Gray*, in *The Complete Works of Oscar Wilde*, 29, 32.

5. Ibid., 104. Even if very few readers today recognize Pater's name, it could still be said that, by way of Wilde, he has been one of the most influential authors for gay intellectual and literary culture and for "gay culture" more generally. He may have given eloquent expression to rather than actually inventing his ideas about seizing the moment, about the "pulsations" that one should seek to multiply, about the need to be forever seeking out new sensations, about finding ways to renew one's passions, and so on. But these ideas are certainly among the most remarkable constants of gay life, or at least of the representations that gay people like to give of their lives. *The Picture of Dorian Gray*, given that it was one of the most read books

among gay men (often the first gay book they would read), could hardly help having deep and lasting effects on gay self-representation and self-perception—for instance, with the idea of the necessary youthfulness of the gay man. Is this not also one of the most generalized representations within received wisdom? An aging gay man, or, even more markedly, an elderly gay man, is surely the target of the most violent insults, all the more violent for the obscene sarcasm that often characterizes them. The old queen (or the old dyke) as a grotesque figure or a figure of ridicule is certainly one of the least examined of homophobic images, and one of the most widespread—even among gay people themselves.

6. Cited in Ellmann, *Oscar Wilde*, 47, 83.

7. See ibid., 83–85.

8. Wilde, *De Profundis*, 917–18.

9. See Ellmann, *Oscar Wilde*, 83–84.

10. See ibid., 60–61.

11. Wilde, "Wasted Days," in *The Complete Works of Oscar Wilde*, 732.

12. Wilde, "Madonna Mia," in ibid.

13. Isherwood, *Christopher and His Kind*, 42.

14. Ibid., 184–87.

15. Ibid., 78.

16. In *Christopher and His Kind*, Isherwood finally gives the real reason, hidden in *Lions and Shadows*, for his trips to Germany: he was able to live out his homosexuality freely there (ibid., 2–3).

17. He would still publish, in 1924, his masterpiece, *A Passage to India*, a book he had begun writing much earlier, but had given up on for a good number of years. See Furbank, *E. M. Forster: A Life*, 2:132.

18. See the chapter "Proust and the Spectacle of the Closet," in Sedgwick, *Epistemology of the Closet*.

19. Gide, *The Journals of André Gide*, 2:409–10.

20. See Ellmann, *Oscar Wilde*, 320.

21. Johnson, "In Honorem Doriani Creatoisque Eius," cited by Ellmann, *Oscar Wilde*, 323–24. On the rhetoric of flowers, omnipresent in gay literature and a veritable part of the counter-discursive "code," see the chapter entitled "Flowers" in Bartlett, *Who Was That Man?*, 39–59. Flowers were not only a figure of discourse or a part of a literary or poetic code, they were also, in the real world, a sign to be recognized, a way of displaying what one was. At the premier of his play, *Lady Windermere's Fan*, on February 20, 1892, Wilde and all his friends wore a green carnation, which became a kind of sign of homosexuality (see Bartlett, 50). A book even appeared on this subject, called *The Green Carnation*. When Gide published *Corydon*, Jérôme and Jean Tharaud exclaimed, "Whom will M. Gide convince that one should prefer green carnations to roses?" (cited by Gide in the appendix to

Corydon, 135). There was an equivalent for lesbians. Maurice Sachs, in *Au temps du Bœuf sur le toit*, 199, describes "the ever so slightly lesbian ladies who wear violets in their buttonholes to identify themselves" (cited in Bard, *Les Garçonnes*, 22).

7. The Greeks against the Psychiatrists

1. Foucault, "The End of the Monarchy of Sex," in *Foucault Live*, 217–18. Hereafter cited as *FL*. The interview first appeared in *Le Nouvel Observateur*, March 12–21, 1977.

2. Symonds, *The Letters of John Addington Symonds*, 3:394.

3. Symonds, *A Problem in Modern Ethics*, 34.

4. See Dover, *Greek Homosexuality*, and Halperin, *One Hundred Years of Homosexuality and Other Essays on Greek Love*.

5. Lauritsen, introduction to *Male Love*, by Symonds, ix.

6. Symonds, *The Letters of John Addington Symonds*, 3:691.

7. Symonds, *A Problem in Modern Ethics*, 57.

8. Symonds to Carpenter, December 29, 1892, reprinted in Symonds, *Male Love*, 149.

9. Ibid., 150–51. In *The Artist* of April 2, 1894, Charles Kains-Jackson, who doubtless had received a copy of *A Problem in Modern Ethics* from Symonds, issued a call for a new order of chivalry that would be held together by the exaltation of the ideal of masculine youth—just as the older order of chivalry, that of a nascent, still imperfect civilization, had been oriented toward the ideal of feminine youth. The colonial power of England, Kains-Jackson wrote, protects it from French or German invasion, and so there is no longer any need to be concerned about the need for population growth. (See Charles Kains-Jackson, "The New Chivalry," in *Sexual Heretics*, ed. Brian Reade, 313–19.) Of course the manner in which these pleas on behalf of love between men are characterized not only by a profound misogyny but also by ideologies of national regeneration—and, more generally, by nationalist and colonialist ideologies needs to be looked into. Just as the rehabilitation of the Dorians by German intellectuals in the first half of the nineteenth century was able to resonate with the racial ideology of German superiority, so, upon its importation into England, it became linked to the ideology of England's national and imperial greatness. This was not the case for Pater, who had left the warrior aspect of the discourse aside, but was certainly the case for Symonds. On this subject, see Dellamora, "Dorianism," in *Apocalyptic Overtures*, 43–64. In the text by Kains-Jackson, the themes central to Symonds in his early period—the reference to Sparta, the praise of the joys of the *palaestra* and also of pederasty, both occasions for older men to pass on their experience to adolescents—can be found alongside more Whitmanian themes which are closer to Symonds in his later period: descriptions of male youths

on river banks, in forests, descriptions of the pleasure of physical life and of life in nature, and so on.

8. *The Democracy of Comrades*

1. From a letter to Leonard Smithers, dated December 11, 1897. Wilde, *The Letters of Oscar Wilde*, 695.

2. Nordau, *Degeneration*, 320. The book was published in German in 1893. The first part is subtitled "Fin de siècle."

3. Nordau, *Degeneration*, 537, 557–59.

4. See Ellmann, *Oscar Wilde*, 503.

5. Wilde, *The Letters of Oscar Wilde*, 695.

6. Cited in Ellmann, *Oscar Wilde*, 550. Although I have no particular justification for saying this, Wilde's witticism has always made me think of Michel Foucault (the early Foucault, the Foucault of *Madness and Civilization*), who could easily have spoken those very words.

7. Wilde, *De Profundis*, 902.

8. Symonds, *The Memoirs of John Addington Symonds*, 246, 189.

9. Cited in Schmidgall, *Walt Whitman: A Gay Life*, 303–4.

10. Symonds, *The Memoirs of John Addington Symonds*, 189.

11. Symonds's letter to Whitman is dated September 5, 1890, and is cited in Reynolds, *Walt Whitman's America*, 396–97.

12. Ives's journal is cited by Ellmann, *Oscar Wilde*, 171.

13. Schmidgall, *Walt Whitman*, 303.

14. See Symonds, *A Problem in Modern Ethics*, 115–25.

15. See, for example, the account of a visit to Gide in 1948 in Gore Vidal's autobiography, *Palimpsest*, 182–84.

16. Forster, "Terminal Note," *Maurice*, 249.

17. Carpenter's letter to Whitman of July 12, 1874, is cited in Rowbotham, "Edward Carpenter: Prophet of a New Life," in Rowbotham and Weeks, *Socialism and the New Life*, 34–35.

18. Whitman, "One's-Self I Sing," in *Leaves of Grass, Complete Poetry and Collected Prose*, 165. This poem was written in 1860, and is included in the third edition of *Leaves of Grass*, published that same year, in which the "Calamus" section was also included. It is either this edition or that of 1867 that was read by Symonds, Wilde, and Carpenter. The poems were revised for the final edition of 1892 which appeared shortly before Whitman's death.

19. Whitman, "Starting from Paumanok," in *Leaves of Grass, Complete Poetry and Collected Prose*, 179.

20. Whitman, "For You O Democracy," in *Leaves of Grass* (edition of 1891–92), 272.

21. Whitman, *Democratic Vistas*, in *Leaves of Grass, Complete Poetry and Collected Prose*, 927–94.

22. On Carpenter, see Rowbotham, "Edward Carpenter," 25–138.

23. Whitman, preface to "Democratic Vistas With Other Papers—English Edition," in *Leaves of Grass, Complete Poetry and Collected Prose*, 1195.

9. *Margot-la-boulangère and the Baronne-aux-épingles*

1. Wilde, The *Picture of Dorian Gray*, 112.

2. See Weeks, *Coming Out*, 37, 42.

3. The letters are cited in Kennedy, *Ulrichs*, 116.

4. See ibid., 59.

5. See the chapter titled "Molly" in Bray, *Homosexuality in Renaissance England*, 80–114. See also Trumbach, "The Birth of the Queen," 129–40, and "Sodomitical Subculture, Sodomitical Roles, and the Gender Revolution in the Eighteenth Century," 109–21.

6. See Bray, *Homosexuality in Renaissance England*, 89–91.

7. Bartlett, *Who Was That Man?*, 142. On the entire affair, see 128–43. Jeffrey Weeks offers a different explanation. He underscores the fact that the concept of homosexuality was not yet well formed in 1871. It was not their "homosexuality," he suggests, that was a problem, but rather their transvestism and the fact that they solicited men while dressed as women. See Weeks, *Sex, Politics, and Society*, 101. Yet this "constructionist" or even nominalist qualification does not seem convincing to me. Above all, it changes nothing about what is essential here.

8. Cited by Bartlett, *Who Was That Man?*, 94.

9. See Ellmann, *Oscar Wilde*, 474. See also the story Pierre Louÿs told Gide and that Gide prints in *If It Die . . .*, 272–73.

10. See Rey, "Parisian Homosexuals Create a Lifestyle, 1700–1750," 179–91.

11. Ibid., 186–88.

12. See Peniston, "Love and Death in Gay Paris," 128–45.

13. Ibid., 133.

14. Wilde, *De Profundis*, 938. On Wilde's gay life much information can be found in Ellmann's biography, but see also Schmidgall, *The Stranger Wilde*, especially chapter 9, "Ass-Thete: Lover of Youth," 169–97.

15. Tardieu, *Études médico-légales sur les attentats aux mœurs* (Paris, 1862), cited in Thompson, "Creating Boundaries," 115.

16. Symonds, *The Memoirs of John Addington Symonds*, 254.

17. Cited in Weeks, *Coming Out*, 41.

18. Citied in ibid.

19. See Isherwood, *Christopher and His Kind*. On Auden, see the biography by Carpenter, *Auden*.

20. Schlumberger, *Madeleine et André Gide*.

10. From Momentary Pleasures to Social Reform

1. Gide, *The Fruits of the Earth*, 40, translation modified.

2. Ibid., 63–76.

3. Painter, *André Gide*, 33. Gide's house was located at Cuverville in Normandy.

4. Gide, *The Immoralist*.

5. Gide, *The Fruits of the Earth*, 65–66.

6. Ibid., 185 (my emphasis), translation modified. *New Fruits*, a compilation of fragments composed over a twenty-year period, was published in 1935. (The English translation includes *The Fruits of the Earth* and *New Fruits* in the same volume.) Yet near the end of *The Fruits of the Earth*, Gide was already writing "Nathanaël, how I wish I could take you back with me to those love-filled hours of my youth when life flowed in me like honey." This comes from a page that also mentions Athman, who will be so important in Gide's life (172). On the place sexuality holds in the way that Gide imagines the posterity of his work, see Lucey, "Practices of Posterity, 47–71.

7. Gide, *The Fruits of the Earth*, 196.

8. Gide, *Journal 1887–1925*, 272. [Translator's note: this is one of the passages in Gide's *Journal* that was restored in the most recent French edition. It is not part of the English translation by Justin O'Brien published in the 1940s.]

9. Corydon is the name of a shepherd in Virgil's second eclogue.

10. Gide, *Corydon*, 4.

11. Ibid., 5. In 1914, Gide would translate nine poems from *Leaves of Grass* for the *Oeuvres choisies* [*Selected Works*] of Whitman published by the NRF. See Gide, *The Journals of André Gide*, 2:29–31.

12. See Pollard, *André Gide*, 63. Pollard's book is a detailed study of Gide's sources for *Corydon*.

13. Gide, *Corydon*, 118, 19.

14. See Hull, *The Entourage of Kaiser Wilhelm II, 1888–1918*, 108–45.

15. See Weeks, *Coming Out*, 126–27.

16. It is striking to see to what an extent the theme of the ridicule to which a nation can be subjected is omnipresent. Eulenburg makes his nation the laughingstock of the French and Gide renders his nation "ridiculous." On the attacks on Gide, see Ahlstedt, *André Gide et le débat sur l'homosexualité*.

17. Gide, *Corydon*, 87–88, 90.

11. The Will to Disturb

1. Gide, The Journals of André Gide, 2:246. The italics are Gide's.

2. See the description of his feelings upon watching the scene of sodomy between his friend Daniel and Mohammed in If It Die . . .: "I could have screamed in horror" (286).

3. Ibid., 287.

4. Ibid., 144.

5. See the ironical comments by Michael Lucey about French Gidians who spend their time explaining that Gide never had sex with Allégret, or only a little, or with Athman, and so on (Lucey, Gide's Bent, 12, 64). Of course it is also important to think about Gide's relation to the "Orient" and to the colonial situation in which his sexuality was at this moment grounded. On this subject as well the commentaries by certain French Gidians are remarkable for their astonishing naivete. Éric Marty, for example, wishes only to see in Gide's (sexual) voyages to North Africa an attempt to rediscover the mythical Arcadia of Virgil, assuming thereby that Gide never stops thinking about Greece in metaphoric relation to the Orient. (See Marty, André Gide, 55–60.) It is true that Marty wishes to convince us that Gide was subject to no form of "perversion": "Gide is not perverse in the sense that he did not choose the pathological." Goodness me! And supposing he had chosen it? Marty continues: "If one does feel it necessary to employ the term perversion, it must be entirely redefined: one should simply see in it the part of desire that is exempt from the trivialities of sentimentalism and its corruptions" (Marty, 60–62; my emphasis). Here we find that the categories of thought of Professor Delay have lived on! Fortunately, there are more complex analyses to be found (politically more lucid and also less homophobic) of the relation between Gide's sexuality and colonialism. See Said, Culture and Imperialism, and Lucey, Gide's Bent, esp. 43ff and 143ff.

6. Gide, So Be It or The Chips Are Down, 163–64.

7. Gide, The Journals of André Gide, 2:248.

8. "Réponse de François Porché," in Gide, Corydon, 153. [Translator's note: Porché's response is not published in the English translation of the book.]

9. Gide, The Journals of André Gide, 2:339–40. On Maritain's relentless efforts to reform homosexuals (Cocteau, Crevel, Green, Mauriac, Sachs, and others), see Barré, Jacques et Raïssa Maritain. Although the book is written from a point of view close to that of Maritain, it is filled with interesting information. It allows one to see to what a degree the struggle against homosexuality was a central preoccupation of Catholic intellectuals of the time. Claudel, for example, never missed an occasion to express his hatred for Gide. We might also recall that in 1952, thirty or so years after Maritain's visit, a year after Gide's death, the Vatican would place all of Gide's books on the Index.

10. In the preface to the 1924 edition of *Corydon*, Gide wrote: "My friends insist that this little book is of the kind which will do me the greatest harm. . . . I do not believe I value greatly what it will rob me of: applause, decorations, honors, entrée into fashionable circles are not things I have ever sought out" (xix).

11. Gide says twelve copies in the preface written for the 1920 edition of the book (xxiii). Claude Martin sets the figure at twenty-two (*André Gide ou la vocation du bonheur*, 555). The book was published under the title C.R.D.N. with no author's name given.

12. Gide, *Corydon*, xxiii. In 1920, Gide has twenty-one copies printed, with the full title, but still without the name of the author (Martin, *André Gide ou la vocation du bonheur*, 556).

13. Gide, *The Journals of André Gide*, 4:130–31, 256.

14. Gide, "Entretiens avec Jean Amrouche," in Marty, *André Gide*, 289–93.

12. The "Preoccupation with Homosexuality"

1. Martin du Gard, *Journal*, 2:295–96, cited in Lucey, "Practices of Posterity," 56–57. It should also be emphasized that Gide also felt released from a certain duty to be secretive out of respect for his wife, for in 1918 she destroyed all the letters he had written to her over a period of twenty years at the moment he left on a trip to England with Marc Allégret, telling her that he was "rotting away" at her side. See Schlumberger, *Madeleine et André Gide*, 189–90. In his journal he notes on November 24, 1918, "At least now nothing prevents me any longer from publishing both *Corydon* and the Memoirs in my lifetime" (Gide, *Journal 1887–1925*, 1077). [Translator's Note: this passage from Gide's *Journal* was not present in the version translated by Justin O'Brien in the 1940s.]

2. Brassaï, *Le Paris secret des années trente*. On the gay subculture in Paris, see Barbedette and Carassou, *Paris Gay 1925*, and Tamagne, *Recherches sur l'homosexualité dans la France*, volume 2.

3. Isherwood, *Christopher and His Kind*, 17.

4. See Steakley, *The Homosexual Emancipation Movement in Germany*, 42 ff. See also the texts brought together in Oosterhuis and Kennedy, eds., *Homosexuality and Male Bonding in Pre-Nazi Germany*. See also Hewitt, *Political Inversions*.

5. See Oosterhuis, "Male Bonding and Homosexuality in German Nationalism," 241–63.

6. It should nonetheless be noted that, at least in France, the invocation of Greece and classical culture, the kind one sees magnified in *Corydon*, was often linked, at least before the war, to Action Française, a right-wing nationalist group known to have influenced Gide during his youth. See Hanna, "What Did André Gide See in the Action Française?"

7. See Oosterhuis, "Political Issues and the Rise of Nazism," 183–90.

8. Ibid., 188.

9. See Ibid., 189. It might be wondered if it was not equally the allegiance to masculinist values (or the recognition of masculine superiority that went along with their desire to disassociate themselves from the social roles traditionally assigned to women) that led members of certain lesbian circles (notably in Paris) to support explicitly profascist opinions in the 1920s and 1930s. If feminists were in the majority antifascist, a certain number of lesbians were, to the contrary, drawn to those ideologies. Djuna Barnes, Nancy Cunard, Colette, Sylvia Beach, and Adrienne Monnier were without question extremely hostile to the totalitarian regimes that were emerging in Europe after the First World War. The same cannot be said of Gertrude Stein, Alice Toklas, Romaine Brooks, Radclyffe Hall, and Natalie Barney. Barney, like Liane de Pougy, was notably antisemitic, as was Gertrude Stein (despite the fact that she was herself Jewish). Of course, one needs to take into account first of all their class backgrounds: aristocrats or upper class bourgeois women, they often tended toward fascism because of their horror of communism. Yet one should also not fail to take into account the role played by their involvement in artistic modernism, nor the one played by their sexual politics. See Benstock, "Paris Lesbianism and the Politics of Reaction, 1900–1940," 332–46.

10. See Mosse, *The Image of Man*.

11. Hirschfeld defended the principle of the equality of men and women, even if he was unable ever to give up the idea of a certain kind of masculine superiority. See Wolff, *Magnus Hirschfeld*, 86–99, 148, 153, 169.

12. *RTP*, 2:643 (my emphasis). See the commentary by Bersani and Dutoit, *Caravaggio's Secrets*, 11–12.

13. See Rivers, *Proust and the Art of Love*, 38.

14. The letters are cited by the editor Antoine Compagnon, in *Recherche*, 3: 1198.

15. Lorrain was trying to come up with an explanation for why Léon Daudet, the famous critic from *L'Action Française*, and the father of Lucien, would have shown so much kindness to such a mediocre writer. See Tadié, *Marcel Proust*, 286. On dueling as a practice meant to reaffirm masculinity, see Nye, *Masculinity and Male Codes of Honor in Modern France*.

16. Cited in Rivers, *Proust and the Art of Love*, 32.

17. Proust, *RTP*, 2:643. Gide, *The Journals of André Gide*, 2:265.

18. [Translator's note: This novel has also been translated as *Lafcadio's Adventures*.]

19. Proust, *Correspondance*, 13:107. The letter is dated March 6, 1914.

20. Ibid., 13:139. Letter of April 6 or 7, 1914.

21. Ibid., 13:235. Letter of June 6, 1914.

22. Ibid., 13:247. Letter of June 10 or 11, 1914. This letter sets out the theme of a

difference in sensibility between Charlus and his brother, but does not yet present the idea of the man-woman as a general theory.

23. Ibid., 13:249. Letter dated June 14, 1914.

24. Lucey, "Practices of Posterity," 56.

25. The "Enquête sur l'homosexualité en littérature," published in *Les Marges* in March and April 1926, has been reprinted by the *Cahiers Gai-Kitsch-Camp*, edited by Patrick Cardon. The questionnaire, which cites Souday's article, can be found on 19.

26. "It was a dangerous thing for art to separate itself from life. . . . The artist who is no longer in touch with his public is led not to a failure of production, but to the production of works with no destination." These words are from a lecture by Gide, titled "On the Importance of the Public." Cited in Lepape, *André Gide, le messager*, 198.

27. Gide, *Oscar Wilde*, 42–44. Gide's emphasis.

28. Proust, *Against Sainte-Beuve*, 39, 12. Gide, *Dostoevsky*, 152–53, translation modified.

29. Sartre, *What Is Literature?* 73.

30. See Lucey, "Practices of Posterity," 62–63.

PART 3 *Michel Foucault's Heterotopias*

1. Much More Beauty

1. Foucault, "On the Genealogy of Ethics," 261. In the original transcript of this interview, Foucault says "Why couldn't everyday life, everyone's life, become a work of art?" Hubert Dreyfus and Paul Rabinow, "Discussion with Michel Foucault, April 15, 1983," transcription in the archives of Paul Rabinow.

2. Cited in Ellmann, *Oscar Wilde*, 310.

3. See, for example, Wilde, *The Soul of Man Under Socialism*, 1079–1104.

4. I discuss these matters in more detail in *Michel Foucault et ses contemporains*, 285–86.

5. The descriptions of Walter Pater cited earlier come to mind immediately, for example, when one reads what Paul Veyne wrote in his journal in 1983. (Veyne would often stay in a studio adjoining Foucault's apartment when he came to Paris from his home in the south of France to give his courses at the Collège de France.) In describing the atmosphere that reigned in the "large apartment with white ceilings and walls" on the rue de Vaugirard, Veyne notes: "The kinds of conversations that were preferred consisted entirely of fantasies, sincere confidences, and, of course, complete freedom of expression, meaning that all forms of libertinism

were allowed. In fact the most libertine conversations were heard and appreciated. There were no cold glances. Indeed, people smiled at what would have horrified the bourgeois or the academician. On the other hand, few bourgeois gentlemen or academicians would have been able to sustain the level of elegance or of impertinent nonchalance that was required of those admitted to this salon, one secretly more elitist than that of the Guermantes. The guests were carefully screened, and the screening criteria were quite esoteric. . . . I remember an appearance made by X. . . . If I mentioned the subject of the conversation, even quite unchaste ears would blush. Yet the style and the manners exhibited showed a libertine refinement of quite an eighteenth-century variety." (Consulted with the permission of the author. I have removed the name of the person mentioned.)

6. Foucault, "On the Genealogy of Ethics," 261. This interview was done in English by Paul Rabinow and Hubert Dreyfus. Foucault made slight modifications to it when preparing the French translation. See "A propos de la généalogie de l'éthique," 4:616. This passage caught the eye of David Halperin, who has asked if we would be justified in making the opposite inference, that Seneca, were he living in San Francisco today, would be a gay man into leather. See Halperin, *Saint Foucault*, 103.

2. *From Night to the Light of Day*

1. Letter from Michel Foucault to Jean Barraqué, dated October 20, 1904 (1954). Archives of Jean Barraqué.

2. Undated letter from Michel Foucault to Jean Barraqué. Archives of Jean Barraqué.

3. In a later letter, one still written in the esoteric language that is characteristic of this moment in his life, Foucault writes, "The only thing missing, as you know, when I am vertical and parallel to you, is homosexuality, whose surface area permits an infinite, definitive, and reciprocal destruction of the myth of comedy. I am certainly to blame, for it is up to people like me—who else?—to preserve the traditions of exile, and to raise up before dawn in places where no one tarries altars that will never be used for sacrifices." The letter is dated January 2, 1956.

4. "His erudition in the matter of bad boys is nearly encyclopedic," wrote Foucault to a friend in 1952. "I am totally taken aback to find myself invited by him to explore a world I didn't even know existed, in which I can take my sufferings for a walk." Cited in the "Chrononogie" of *Dits*, 1:18.

5. That is the word used by the recipient of the letter cited in the previous note to describe Barraqué's effect on Foucault. See ibid., 1:18.

6. I interviewed Dr. Étienne when I was writing my biography of Foucault. He was certain of himself on this subject, having spoken about it at length with

Foucault, whom he would often have admitted to the infirmary at the École. [Translator's note: the École normale supérieure is one of the most prestigious institutions of higher learning in France. Entrance is by an extremely competitive examination.]

7. Letter dated May 23, 1950, and cited in the "Chronologie" of Dits, 1:16. The recipient's name is not given. In 1954 he would write to Jacqueline Verdeaux, "A great Husserlian ascesis has led me to lands that are so strange and unexpected that I am not even sure if it is possible to breathe there. After having considered becoming a monk or else turning in the direction of the paths that lead into the night, I have decided to make the effort to live. But I have only taken the first few breaths. I am keeping an eye on the mirror to make sure I don't turn blue." Letter to Jacqueline Verdeaux, August 19, 1954.

8. See Eribon, Michel Foucault, 26–27.

9. [Translator's note: Sainte-Anne is a psychiatric hospital in Paris.]

10. See "Chronologie," in Dits, 1:15.

11. A comparison again seems called for between this art of playing with one's physical appearance, theatricalizing it, making something new—something of one's own—out of it and Wilde's way of shaping his appearance. It could also be compared to the general theatricalization involved in gay self-affirmation. For it is always a question of reinventing one's gestures, one's appearance, one's very being in the eyes of others—reinventing everything that goes into what Goffman has called the "presentation of self."

12. See Eribon, Michel Foucault, 41–49, 128–30, 138–40.

13. Foucault, "La Recherche scientifique et la psychologie," 1:158, and "La Psychologie de 1850 à 1950," 1:136.

14. Foucault, "La Psychologie de 1850 à 1950," 1:137.

15. Foucault, "La Recherche scientifique et la psychologie," 1:158.

16. See his preface to Madness and Civilization, ix-xii; hereafter cited as MC. See also the formulations he gives in Mental Illness and Psychology, 88; hereafter cited as MIP. [Translator's note: the full text of Foucault's 1961 preface to Madness and Civilization was not printed in all subsequent editions, and only a truncated version is present in the English translation. The full version can be found in Dits, 1:159–67. The volume was published under a slightly different title in 1961: Folie et déraison: Histoire de la folie à l'âge classique (Paris: Plon, 1961). Future French editions would have the shorter title Histoire de la folie à l'âge classique.]

17. See the passage in which Althusser describes himself as a "missing person" and where he says that Foucault wrote about himself: " 'in the bright sunlight of Polish freedom,' once he felt himself cured." Althusser, The Future Lasts Forever, 23, translation modified. Althusser is here referring to a sentence from the 1961 preface to Madness and Civilization in which Foucault writes that his book was "begun during

a Swedish night" and "finished in the stubborn bright sunlight of Polish freedom" (*Dits*, 1:167). In this same text Foucault mentions a future work he plans to write "under the sun of the great Nietzschean project" (1:162). The opposition between "night" and "sun," between shadow and light, and so on, is one of the structuring principles of *Madness and Civilization*.

18. Letter from Althusser to Franca Madonia, dated February 28, 1966, in Althusser, *Lettres à Franca, 1961–1973*, 660. I discuss Foucault's relations with Althusser at greater length, focusing especially on this period, in *Michel Foucault et ses contemporains*, 314–50.

19. For more details on this nomination and on Foucault's meeting with Dumézil (a meeting that was to have immense importance in Foucault's life, his career, his work, and so on), see Eribon, *Michel Foucault et ses contemporains*, 105–83.

20. Letter from Michel Foucault to Jean Barraqué, dated September 25, 1955. Archives of Jean Barraqué.

21. Letter from Michel Foucault to Jean Barraqué, dated November 13, 1955.

22. Letter from Michel Foucault to Jean Barraqué, dated September 20, 1955.

23. Letter from Michel Foucault to Jean Barraqué, dated August 1955, with no day given. More information on Arcadie follows in the pages ahead.

3. The Impulse to Escape

1. For this vocabulary, see Foucault, "Madness Only Exists in Society," 8, and "Médecins, juges et sorciers au XVIIe siècle," 1:753.

2. Letter from Althusser to Franca Madonia, dated September 25, 1962, in *Lettres à Franca 1961–1973*, 215.

3. "It is only in Foucault's book that I have experienced this rising to the surface of intimate matters." Letter from Althusser to Madonia, February 28, 1966, in ibid., 659.

4. Letter from Althusser to Franca Madonia, dated September 28, 1963, in ibid., 455. Emphasis in original.

5. Immediately after *Madness and Civilization*, Foucault had the idea of publishing a series of documents retrieved from archives. Here is how the work, which was never published, was announced in advance publicity: "Madmen: From the Bastille to Hôpital Sainte-Anne, from the seventeenth to the nineteenth centuries, Michel Foucault recounts the journey to the end of the night. Forthcoming." See Eribon, *Michel Foucault*, 144. Foucault describes *Madness and Civilization* as an archeology of silence in its preface. See *MC*, xi.

6. Deleuze and Parnet, *Dialogues*, 5.

7. Deleuze, *Negotiations 1972–1990*, 103–4, translation modified. The three texts on Foucault assembled in this volume (83–118) strike me as one of the best com-

mentaries available of his work and also of its guiding gesture. See also Deleuze, *Foucault.*

8. Foucault, "My Body, This Paper, This Fire," in *Aesthetics, Method, and Epistemology,* 416. This volume is hereafter cited as *Aesthetics.* [Translator's note: this essay was originally published as an appendix to a later French edition of *Histoire de la folie* (*Madness and Civilization*). It is not present in the English translation of that volume.]

9. Foucault, "So Is It Important to Think?" in *Power,* 458, translation modified. This volume is hereafter cited as *Power.*

10. Martin, "Truth, Power, and the Self: An Interview with Foucault," 11. On these questions, see Eribon, *Michel Foucault et ses contemporains,* 62–63.

11. Foucault, "L'Intellectuel et les pouvoirs," 4:747–48.

12. See Eribon, *Michel Foucault et ses contemporains,* 233–64.

13. The citations in this paragraph are taken from a 1978 interview with Ducio Trombadori, first published in 1980: "Interview with Michel Foucault," trans. Robert Hurley, in *Power,* 267.

14. Deleuze, *Negotiations,* 85. He also comments in this passage: "When you admire someone you don't pick and choose; you may like this or that book better than some other one, but you nevertheless take them as a whole, because you see that some element that seems less convincing than others is an absolutely essential step in his exploration, his alchemy." For more on the coherence of Foucault's works across all his "crises" and "reorientations," see ibid., 104–5.

15. "Interview with Michel Foucault," 267. [Translator's note: the published English translation omits the word "death" which is present in the French version. See *Dits,* 4:67.]

16. One day in the early 1980s I asked him which of his books was his favorite, and he replied without hesitating: *Madness and Civilization.* He added, "Of course it would be different if I wrote it today, but I think that book had something totally new to contribute."

17. [Translator's note: *Lettres de cachet* were warrants issued by the throne during the *ancien régime* under which a person could be imprisoned indefinitely, and without specific cause.]

18. Foucault, "Lives of Infamous Men," 158. This text first appeared in 1977, but the anthology it was to preface was not published, and Foucault would not include this text when, together with Arlette Farge in 1982, he published a collection of *lettres de cachet* from the archives of the Bastille entitled *Le Désordre des familles.*

19. Deleuze, *Negotiations,* 106.

20. I am citing from the original transcript of Foucault's 1978 interview with Ducio Trombadori.

21. Foucault, "What Is Critique?," 386.

22. Ibid., 386. See Eribon, *Michel Foucault et ses contemporains*, 66–67.

23. "What I would like to speak to you about is the critical stance as a general virtue," he said at the beginning of his lecture ("What Is Critique?," 383; translation modified). On critique as *ethos*, see Foucault, "What Is Enlightenment?," 303–19.

24. On "intransigence," see Foucault, "So It Is Important to Think?"

25. "When people follow Foucault, when they're fascinated by him, it's because they're doing something with him, in their own work, in their own independent lives. It's not just a question of intellectual understanding or agreement, but of intensity, resonance, musical harmony." Deleuze, *Negotiations*, 86.

26. Among the most notable examples of this, we might mention the sentence in which David Halperin identifies with Foucault as a "gay intellectual"—understood both as a political position and as a condition of social vulnerability: "Michel Foucault, c'est moi." See Halperin, *Saint Foucault*, 8. See also, in an entirely different perspective, the very beautiful book in which Maria Inés Garcia Canal attempts to grasp the effects her reading of Foucault had on her life, her thought, and her political commitment: *El loco, el guerrero, el artista*.

27. Foucault, "La Force de fuir," 2:401–5.

28. Foucault, *Discipline and Punish*. Gilles Deleuze is quite right to point out that for Foucault the prison played the role of an analogical model. (See Deleuze, "Postscript on Control Societies," in *Negotiations*, 177.)

29. Foucault defines critical work as "a patient labor giving form to our impatience for liberty." See "What Is Enlightenment?," 319.

4. Homosexuality and Unreason

1. See Foucault, *Death and the Labyrinth*, 164.

2. On the "lightning flashes," see *MC*, 278. On Goya see *MC*, 279–81. On the "cries," see *MIP*, 87–88: "And when, in lightning flashes and cries, [madness] reappears, as in Nerval or Artaud, Nietzsche or Roussel, it is psychology that remains silent, *speechless*, before this language." On "contestation," see *MC*, 281.

3. See the dialogue that follows his talk "Nietzsche, Freud, Marx" (1964), in *Dits* 1:579. [Translator's note: The talk, but not the following dialogue, can be found in *Aesthetics*, 269–78.] See also "A Preface to Transgression," *Aesthetics*, 69–87.

4. See, e.g., "La Folie, l'absence d'oeuvre," 1:412–20; or "Introduction to Rousseau's *Dialogues*," 21–51. See also *Death and the Labyrinth*.

5. See the preface to the original 1961 edition of *Madness and Civilization* in *Dits*, esp. 1:159, and also the closing sentences of *Madness and Civilization*, which mention Nietzsche, Van Gogh, and Artaud (289). Foucault would rapidly abandon the idea

of an "original experience" of madness that could be recovered outside history. For more on this topic, see Eribon, *Michel Foucault et ses contemporains*, 139–61.

6. "A long inquiry that aims to confront the dialectics of history with the immobile structures of the tragic," Foucault wrote, from within the same perspective he occupied when he still postulated the idea of an "originary experience of madness" that was to be rediscovered through the historical forms that had captured it (*Dits*, 1:162).

7. *Dits*, 1:161. In *Mental Illness and Psychology*, Foucault insists on the construction of mental illness as a "deviancy," a "departure": "Mental illness takes its place among the possibilities that serve as a margin to the cultural reality of a social group" (62, 63). To show that such illnesses are not viewed as such in every culture, he gives the example of the *berdaches* of the North American Dakota people: "These homosexuals have a religious status as priests and magicians" (62).

8. Foucault, introduction to *Le Rêve et l'existence* by Ludwig Binswanger, 1:65–115.

9. It was also in 1956 that the publisher Jean-Jacques Pauvert was prosecuted in Paris for republishing Sade's writings (whose publication the court would refuse to ban). Foucault would return to a more traditional theme for the academic year 1957–58: "The Religious Experience in French Literature from Chateaubriand to Bernanos."

10. Later, Foucault distanced himself from Sade, to the point of calling him a "sexual policeman" in a 1975 interview ("Sade, Sergeant of Sex," 223–27). His admiration for Genet did not last either. Toward the end of his life he could speak quite sarcastically of Genet's work. When Patrice Chereau put on *The Screens* at the Amandiers Theater in Nanterre in 1983, Foucault attended a performance in the company of Daniel Defert, Mathieu Lindon, Hervé Guibert, and Guibert's companion, Thierry Junot. Foucault found the production exasperating and repeatedly expressed a desire to leave before it was over. In subsequent days he frequently commented harshly on Genet's works. I remember making the objection one evening when we were having dinner together that "what you say may be true for the plays, which are really unplayable now, but it certainly isn't true for the novels." Foucault replied, "It's clear you haven't read them for a while. Read them again and you'll see."

11. Foucault wrote to Lacroix: "I had set out to write what was primarily a book for students, to present the state of a certain field of study. But the state of knowledge has changed and it would seem to me to be taking advantage of readers to republish such outdated stuff. Don't you think we could ask some young psychopathologist to write a slightly more "up to date" [in English in the original] book? For my part—and only if you are interested of course—I'll try to write something else for you on a subject I'm more familiar with, on, for example, crime, criminol-

ogy, penal justice, etc." (August 1, [1961]). Foucault did in fact give a course on penal justice at the University of Clermont-Ferrand. In a later letter to Lacroix, Foucault wrote: "I don't know how to give you an answer as far as the title goes. I'm planning to spend several years giving seminars on the penal system. . . . Could we just use "criminology" for the time being?" (October 20, [1961? 1962?]).

12. Foucault, *Maladie mentale et psychologie*. Foucault opposed future republications of even this second edition. It was only ten years after his death that it once again became available (Paris: PUF [Quadrige], 1995). Strangely, this reprinting bears the copyright date of 1954, whereas the first edition of *Maladie mentale et psychologie* is from 1962. The publication date of *Maladie mentale et personnalité* is 1954.

13. In introducing that volume Foucault wrote: "We had in mind a study of the practical aspects of the relations between psychiatry and criminal justice. In the course of our research we came across Pierre Rivière's case" (*I, Pierre Rivière, having slaughtered my mother, my sister and my brother*, vii).

14. Those courses have recently been published: Foucault, *Les Anormaux*.

15. In a letter written in July 1973, while he was composing *Discipline and Punish*, Foucault describes the book as a study of "the great *techniques of individualization*: clinical medicine, psychiatry, pedagogy, criminology" (quoted in the "Chronologie" of Dits, 1:44; my emphasis). On the notion of the norm as a focal point of his analyses, see Foucault, *Histoire de la folie*, 96. [Translator's note: The passage in question is not available in the English translation, which is of an abridged version of the original edition. Much of Eribon's demonstration in the following pages is based on a chapter of *Histoire de la folie* that has never been translated into English. References are necessarily to the French edition and are indicated *HF*.] See also the "course description" from the Collège de France for the academic year 1974–75: "Since 1970, the series of courses has dealt with the slow formation of a knowledge and power of *normalization* based on the traditional juridical procedures of punishment." (In *Ethics*, 55; my emphasis.)

16. [Translator's note: *Déraison* has a wide range of meanings that would include lunacy or folly, so that the word could be used to characterize behavior (including sexual behavior) perceived as irregular or dissident.]

17. In a 1971 lecture, Foucault speaks of the "essentially economic reasons" for the process of internment that marked the seventeenth century (cf. "Madness and Civilization," delivered at the Club Tahar Haddad in Tunis, March 24, 1971. I have published some excerpts from this lecture in *Michel Foucault et ses contemporains*, 323–24). Yet his argument is already quite clear in *Madness and Civilization*, 49–54, esp. 53–54.

18. *MC*, 58. The chapter called "The Great Confinement" can be found on 38–64.

19. *HF*, 93–123. [Translator's note: this is one of the chapters missing from the English translation of the abridged edition.]

20. *MC*, 61. See also *HF*, 88, and *MC*, 61, where internment is described as "the underside of the bourgeoisie's great dream and great preoccupation in the classical age: the laws of the State and the laws of the heart at last identical." This question will ceaselessly preoccupy Foucault. It leads, starting with *Madness and Civilization*, to the idea of the family as a participant in the operation of power, given that it is often the father, the husband, the wife, and so on, who ask that this or that "deviant" individual be interned (see *HF*, 105). It is one of the principal reasons for Foucault's renewed interest in the 1970s and 80s in the *lettres de cachet* of the Bastille. He wondered how ordinary people addressed the powers that be to ask for their intervention in family conflicts. While the Bastille and the *lettres de cachet* were generally perceived as the very epitome of an arbitrary exercise of power, Foucault wanted to show that that arbitrariness depended on a link between power and its object, a link that might just as well be one of complicity as one of resistance. He thereby posed, of course, the question of the participation of dominated people in their own domination. But above all he wanted to demonstrate the entanglements of public and private orders and the insinuation of administrative and political apparatuses into the space of the family. (See his comments in Farge and Foucault, *Le Désordre des familles*, 345–48.) Foucault's study of the *lettres de cachet* (begun for *Madness and Civilization* and resumed at the beginning of the 1970s, leading up to the publication of *Le Désordre des familles*) is probably the starting place for his conception of a power that also comes from "below," that is to say, from the fact that subjugated individuals give power existence by calling on it. It may have been during this investigation that the idea of power's capillarity, of its penetration throughout the social body—an idea developed in *Discipline and Punish*—was born. Foucault's analyses in terms of a "microphysics of power" will by that time be specifically directed against the theories of Althusser, as will the formulations in *La Volonté de savoir* that declare that all conceptualizations of power as "monarchical" should be discarded—formulations directed as much against Althusser and his "State" as against Lacan and his "Law."

5. The Birth of Perversion

1. [Translator's note: As mentioned in the introduction, the French title was not used for the English translation, which is simply known as *The History of Sexuality, Volume 1: An Introduction*. I will keep the French title in the text.]

2. The titles were announced as: *The Flesh and the Body; The Children's Crusade; Women, Mothers, and Hysterics; Perverts; Populations and Races*. On the general project and its revisions, see Eribon, *Michel Foucault*, 269–76.

3. Thus *Les Aveux de la chair* was written before *The Use of Pleasure* and *The Care of the Self.* But Foucault wanted to rewrite it based on the work he had done for the volumes on Greece and Rome. He had just begun this rewriting when he died. This final part was left unfinished and remains unpublished. This is regrettable, given that in a certain way, despite being unfinished, it contains the key to the whole undertaking.

4. Hubert Dreyfus and Paul Rabinow, "Discussion with Michel Foucault, April 15, 1983," transcription in Paul Rabinow's personal archive. This passage is not included in the published versions of the conversations with Dreyfus and Rabinow.

5. Marcuse, *Eros and Civilization* and *One-Dimensional Man.* Reich, *The Sexual Revolution, The Invasion of Compulsory Sex-Morality,* and *The Mass Psychology of Fascism.* On Marcuse, see Raulet, *Marcuse.* On Reich, see Plon and Roudinesco, *Dictionnaire de la psychanalyse,* 888–93. On the influence of Reich in France, see Roudinesco, *La Bataille de cent ans,* 58–61, 64–69, 486–88, and also 501 (on his influence on Deleuze and Guatarri's *Anti-Oedipus*).

6. See "Right of Death and Power over Life," chap. 5 of *HSI,* 135–59. See also the "cours du 17 mars 1976," in Foucault, *"Il faut défendre la société,"* 213–35.

7. David M. Halperin has recently emphasized this point: at least one case on which Westphal founds his theory of "contrary sexual feeling" is a man who never had (or claimed he never had) sexual relations with other men ("How to Do the History of Male Homosexuality," 108).

8. Shortly after *La Volonté de savoir,* Foucault organized the republication of the memoir of a nineteenth-century hermaphrodite. (See Foucault, *Herculine Barbin.*) I have analyzed more fully elsewhere the relation that Foucault established between the question of sexual identity and the history of hermaphrodism. See Eribon, *Michel Foucault et ses contemporains,* 265–87.

9. Foucault, "Le Gai Savoir," 48–49. Only partial versions of this interview had been published until the version published in *La Revue h. Dits* fails to include any version of the interview.

6. The Third Sex

1. "The truthful confession was inscribed at the heart of the procedures of individualization by power" (*HSI,* 58–59). See also *HSI,* 159 (the final page of the book, an indication of how central the critique of psychoanalysis is to the project of the *History of Sexuality*): "The good genius of Freud had placed [sex] at one of the critical points marked out for it since the eighteenth century by the strategies of knowledge and power; how wonderfully effective he was—worthy of the greatest spiritual fathers and directors of the classical period—in giving a new impetus to the secular injunction to study sex and to bring it into discourse."

2. *HSI*, 117. It is important to remark that Foucault inscribes the origins of modern racism—of which the twentieth century will see the monstrous result—in these very discourses of the "normal" and the "pathological," of "health" and "sickness." One finds a very clear formulation of the link between the "society of normalization," "social hygiene," and "state racism" in the "Cours du 17 mars 1976," in *"Il faut défendre la société,"* 225.

3. Foucault, "The End of the Monarchy of Sex," 218.

4. *HSI*, 110; translation modified. For the entire passage in question, see *HSI*, 108–11. Foucault speaks of the "interpenetration of the apparatus of alliance and that of sexuality in the form of the family" (108). This explains why the "family" soon ran to "doctors, educators, psychiatrists, priests, and pastors, to all the 'experts' who would listen to the long complaint of its sexual suffering" (111).

5. *HSI*, 55; my emphasis, translation modified. See also 53–54.

6. The first chapter of the fourth part of *La Volonté de savoir* is entitled "Enjeu" (*HSI*, 81–91). [Translator's note: The English translation gives "Objective."] It is there that Foucault develops the idea of an "analytics of power."

7. Foucault, "Le Gai Savoir," 43.

8. See Rosario, *The Erotic Imagination*, 10–11, 181, 215.

9. Lillian Faderman remarks that "lesbianism as the sexologists viewed the phenomenon was an infrequent theme in American fiction until the publication in the United States of *The Well of Loneliness*" (*Odd Girls and Twilight Lovers*, 57). The model of "romantic friendships" was predominant before that. It is true that Faderman wishes to corroborate the model that assumes the invention of homosexuality by psychiatric discourse. But the dates that she provides for this transformation imply the existence of lesbian communities and lesbian ways of life well before the psychiatric model was influential. (Chauncey contests Faderman's argument in *Gay New York*, 381n61.) It is worth adding that the model of sexual inversion accepted and popularized by Radclyffe Hall was immediately and vigorously rejected by many lesbians.

10. Chauncey, *Gay New York*, 27.

11. Ibid. See also Chauncey, "Genres, identités sexuelles et conscience homosexuelle dans l'Amérique du XXe siècle," 97–107.

12. Cf. Proust, *The Captive*, in *RTP*, e.g. 3:214–15.

13. See Chauncey, *Gay New York*, esp. 26–27; see also Chauncey's two important articles "From Sexual Inversion to Homosexuality," and "Christian Brotherhood or Sexual Perversion?"

14. One need only read samples of the judicial, medical, and police literature dealing with "pederasts" and "queens" that proliferated (well before Westphal) from the outset of the nineteenth (and even the eighteenth) century. It can be seen that the existence of places for social interaction and the repression that targets those places give police agents, magistrates, and doctors the occasion to express

their points of view. Their descriptions do not bring into existence what they describe, but, just the opposite, derive their existence from it. We might remember that Balzac, in *A Harlot High and Low* (1847), was already speaking about a "third sex" and about "queens" [*tantes*]. This latter word also figured in the work by the police agent Vidocq, *Les Voleurs* (1837). See Pierre Hahn, *Nos ancêtres les pervers*, 35.

15. On the ways in which homosexuals turned to medical literature, both to find information and explanations about themselves and to find a certain titillation, see Rosario, *The Erotic Imagination*, 10.

16. See Wolff, *Magnus Hirschfeld*, 102–3.

17. See Kennedy, *Ulrichs*, 57.

18. See ibid., 87–88, 167. It is important to remember that Symonds began corresponding with Ulrichs in 1889, and visited him in 1891 in Aquila, Italy, Ulrichs's place of retirement since 1880, when, discouraged, he had abandoned his lifelong struggle (216–18). In a letter to Edward Carpenter in 1893 Symonds recalled this meeting and described Ulrichs as "the true origin of the scientific outlook on these questions" (218). In 1909 Hirschfeld would also take a trip to Italy, a kind of pilgrimage, to see the places where Ulrichs had lived and died (in 1895) (see Wolff, *Magnus Hirschfeld*, 102).

19. Kennedy, *Ulrichs*, 167.

20. It would be useful here to be able to reconstruct the entire history of medical discourse on homosexuality in nineteenth-century France and Germany (taking note especially of Casper and Tardieu). Ulrichs himself did not know any of these texts when he began writing.

21. Ibid., 130.

22. See ibid., 71. Ulrichs often complained bitterly that Krafft-Ebing had never publicly acknowledged his debt to him, had never cited him in his writings, and thus had claimed for himself ideas borrowed from Ulrichs (222–23).

23. See Herzer, "Kertbeny and the Nameless Love," 1–26.

24. Halperin, "Homosexuality," 451.

7. Producing Subjects

1. See also the "Cours du 7 janvier 1976," in "*Il faut défendre la société*," 3–20. That text gives the clearest description by Foucault himself of the theoretical context for the writing of *La Volonté de savoir*, which would appear in November of that year. He writes there of the reference, however "vague and fairly distant, however blurry, to Reich and Marcuse," that inspired the struggles against "traditional morality and traditional sexual hierarchies" (7).

2. See Foucault, *The Archaeology of Knowledge and The Discourse on Language*, 49; hereafter cited as *Archeology*.

3. See ibid., 118: "The analysis of statements and discursive formations . . . sets out to establish a law of scarcity" (translation modified). On the connection between *Madness and Civilization* and *The Order of Things*, see the preface to the latter (Foucault, *The Order of Things*, xxiv).

4. That lecture is published as an appendix to *Archeology*, under the title *The Discourse on Language*, trans. Rupert Swyer. This citation is from 216. [Translator's note: the title of this lecture in the English translation is "The Discourse on Language," but the French title is "L'Ordre du discours" (the order of discourse).]

5. On the history of the reception of *Madness and Civilization*, see Eribon, *Michel Foucault*, 116–27.

6. Foucault, "Prisons et asiles dans les mécanismes du pouvoir," 2:524. Foucault often insisted in later years that his work, along with a whole group of movements of political and theoretical critique, had contributed to the expansion and transformation of the definition of the political. (See, e.g., a 1982 interview that was published posthumously, "Pour en finir avec les mensonges," *Le Nouvel Observateur*, June 25, 1984.)

7. Foucault, "Le Gai Savoir," 42. In a 1977 interview with Alessandro Fontana and Pasquale Pasquino, Foucault states that he has had "a great deal of difficulty getting rid of" the notion of repression: "When I wrote *Madness and Civilization*, I made use, at least implicitly, of this notion of repression. I believe that I imagined then a kind of madness that was lively, voluble, and anxious, and that mechanisms of power and psychiatry managed to reduce to silence. Whereas it seems to me that in point of fact the notion of repression is perfectly inadequate to account for all that is productive in power" ("Entretien avec Michel Foucault," 3:148).

8. "Instead of taking as a point of departure the subject (or even subjects) and the elements that would be prior to the relation and localizable, the point of departure will be the very relation of power, of domination in its effective and factual elements, to see how this relation itself determines the elements involved in it. It is not a question of asking subjects why, by what right, they can accept being subjected, but of showing how the relations of subjection produce subjects" ("*Il faut défendre la société*," 38–39). Moreover, "We must grasp the material instance of subjection as the constitution of subjects . . ., must study the bodies constituted as subject by the effects of power" (26–27).

9. See "*Il faut défendre la société*," 28, where Foucault provides two examples of what he intends to critique: the idea that mad people were locked up because they were not useful for industrial production (he fails to mention that he himself developed this argument), and the idea (developed by Reich, he says) that infantile sexuality was repressed to direct energies toward work. See also his interview with Fontana and Pasquino ("Entretien avec Michel Foucault," 3:146–47).

10. See "*Il faut défendre la sociéte*," 7–8. A few years later, when the political context

had again shifted enormously, Foucault would make similar remarks, but in the opposite direction. He would say again that there is no necessary ("analytical" is the word he uses) link between, on the one hand, our daily life, our sexual life, and, on the other hand, large moral, economic, and social structures. But this time he is not directing his remarks toward "revolutionaries" to tell them that one need not change the whole social order to shift the sexual order. He is speaking to neo-conservatives who worry about the dangers to the social and political order that may result from changes to the sexual order. In 1983, Foucault would say that we must "get rid of" the idea that "we couldn't change anything, for instance, in our sex life or our family life, without ruining our economy, our democracy, and so on" ("On the Genealogy of Ethics," 261).

8. Philosophy in the Closet

1. *Respectability* and *discretion and dignity* were catchwords of Arcadie, an important organization in France from the middle of the 1950s to the end of the 1970s, whose president, André Baudry, was forever dressing down anyone who failed to exhibit polite behavior. He denounced "eccentric behaviors," "swishy walks," "make-up," "effeminacy," and so on. (See a December 1967 document cited in Girard, *Le Mouvement homosexuel en France, 1945–1981*, 53.) The correct program was to request "tolerance" while conforming to established norms, which were, of course, never to be contested. The organization's discourse was irreconcilably divided between two conflicting conceptions: one that considered the "homophile" (to use the lexicon one finds in the organization's publication) as "different" from others, and, together with his peers, as forming a separate "people" and another discourse that demanded that the "mass of homophiles" live "blended into society" such that "no one could notice any difference" (see ibid., 39–73).

2. In the early hours of June 28, 1969, the clients of a gay bar in New York rebelled against a police raid—a common event, one of the typical dangers of gay life of the period. The clash escalated into three days of rioting. The commemoration of that historic day a year later (a commemoration that gave birth to Gay and Lesbian Pride parades) can certainly be thought of as the starting point of the contemporary gay and lesbian movement. (See D'Emilio, *Sexual Politics, Sexual Communities*, 231ff. See also Duberman, *Stonewall*.)

3. Guy Hocquenghem, "La Révolution des homosexuels," *Le Nouvel Observateur*, January 10, 1972, and *Homosexual Desire*; Deleuze and Guattari, *Anti-Oedipus*. On the FHAR, see Girard, *Le Mouvement homosexuel en France*, 81–111; d'Eaubonne, "Le FHAR, origines et illustrations," and "FHAR, la fin d'un mouvement." See also the FHAR documents collected in *Rapport contre la normalité*. On Hocquenghem, see Marshall, *Guy Hocquenghem*; Weeks's preface to Hocquenghem's *Homosexual Desire*,

23–47; and Schérer's postface to Hocquenghem's *L'Amphithéâtre des morts*, 111–47. It is regrettable that there exists no serious general overview of the French gay movement, either of the life of organizations or of the currents of thought, notably from 1968 to the present.

4. See Guy Hocquenghem, "La Révolution des homosexuels," *Le Nouvel Observateur*, January 10, 1972. See also Hocquenghem, "Pour une conception homosexuelle du monde," in FHAR, *Rapport contre la normalité*, 76: "Class struggle is also the struggle to express desire, the struggle to communicate, and not merely political and economic struggle."

5. See Hocquenghem, *Homosexual Desire*, 138–39. It was against the utopian idea of a generalized bisexuality that Hocquenghem wrote "Pour une conception homosexuelle du monde," which in no way defends the idea of a gay identity. Rather, it develops the idea that the specificity of homosexual sexuality and of the place of homosexuals in society gives them a kind of detachment, thanks to which it should be possible to reexamine politics.

6. Hocquenghem, "Pour une conception homosexuelle du monde," 71–77.

7. Hocquenghem, *Homosexual Desire*, 148.

8. "It is no longer a matter of justifying, or vindicating, or even attempting a better integration of homosexuality within society. I shall now be discussing the way in which recent gay movements, linked up with left-wing activism, have changed or overturned the commonly acknowledged relation between desire and politics" (ibid., 133).

9. Ibid., 144–45. See also Hocquenghem, "Pour une conception homosexuelle du monde": "We want nothing to do with a homosexuality that would be accepted alongside heterosexuality, because in our societies, heterosexuality is the rule, the norm, and the norm cannot coexist with abnormality. The two are necessarily in struggle. We want an end to heterosexuality in the sense in which heterosexuality in the current moment is necessarily a relation of oppression" (75).

10. Obviously this conception of homosexual desire as the agent of a generalized subversion of the social order is a bit of a fantasy: you do not become revolutionary just by transgressing racial and class boundaries when you are out cruising or by practicing a sexuality that is not couple-based or family-based. As Leo Bersani puts it (in his telling critique of "queer thought," which—strikingly—often reads like nothing so much as a rediscovery of themes advanced by Hocquenghem or other theorists of the 1970s), the same people who practice "subversive" sexuality at night might be racist or fascist during the day or might simply behave, being an employer or a landlord, precisely as any other employer or landlord would. There is no continuity between sexuality and political positioning, and if there is any relation between the two registers, it is evidently too complex to be captured by the idea of social or political subversion. ("Is the Rectum a Grave?" 197–222.) Indeed, Hoc-

quenghem was perfectly conscious of this fact, but his way of conceptualizing homosexual desire did not allow him to think of the effective production of homosexual individuals as subjected subjects except to imagine that as soon as they failed to conform to his "revolutionary" model, they had to be denounced as servants of the established order and of oedipal structures. Thus he was quickly drawn to denigrate actual homosexuals, their ways of living their lives, and the homosexual movement itself. Within his antinormative rhetoric there lies a profound normativity, consisting of accepting only certain kinds of homosexual lives and denouncing all the others as bourgeois. That is why after his book in 1972, he spent his time deploring—sometimes bitterly, sometimes humourously—everything that had to do with the homosexuality around him; he regarded even his own earlier writings quite severely. In 1974, when he republished some of them, he described "Pour une conception homosexuelle du monde" as "the tight-laced armature of a homosexual thirsty for dignity, at the height of his totalitarian dream"; he also commented, "How fucking stupid to be proud of being one of us, which makes you miss the chance literally to get off on the words of a sentence that takes the form of a hard-on" (*L'Après-mai des faunes*, 157, 149). A condensed version of his critiques of homosexuals can be found in his story, "Oiseau de nuit" (in Bory and Hocquenghem, *Comment nous appelez-vous, déjà?* 139–200). In the afterword to that text he cites *La Volonté de savoir*, noting, probably perfidiously, that "Foucault, *like others before him*," tells us that the words "homosexual" and "homosexuality" were created at the end of the nineteenth century (203, emphasis added).

11. Still, Foucault never moves truly far away from Hocquenghem, in whom we already find the idea that power is exercised through categories, given that it is through their mediation that the desiring fluxes are divided into sexualities and fixed into identities. One even finds in *Homosexual Desire* a critique of confession (89–92) and an analysis of the "prohibition-transgression" dyad. (Hocquenghem speaks of "perverse integration" and of the focus of desire "on what is supposed to be forbidden, so that anyone who wants to ignore the prohibition can have a taste of the transgression" [143].)

12. On the way in which Pasolini fits into the sexual liberation movement, see Duflot, *Entretiens avec Pasolini*. In 1975, Pasolini recanted his work in his "Trilogy of Life" and the ideological position it represented. In his opinion the politicosexual struggle it was part of had been "overtaken and neutralized by the decision of consumerist power to grant a kind of tolerance as wide as it was fallacious." (See Pasolini, "Documents de travail," in Gérard, *Pasolini ou le mythe de la barbarie*, 123–25.) Pasolini's 1975 film, *Salo, the 120 Days of Sodom*, manifests this break. The sexuality hitherto conceived as a form of resistance to capitalism will now be perceived as an obligation and a duty organized by neocapitalist society. Foucault is known to have been enormously interested in Pasolini's films.

13. Chauncey, *Gay New York*, 5; see, in general, 1–29, esp. 8–9.

14. Hocquenghem, *Homosexual Desire*, 91. See also Deleuze's preface to *L'Après-mai des faunes*: "There are no longer homosexual subjects, but rather homosexual productions of desire and homosexual agencies productive of enunciations that are buzzing around everywhere: SM, transvestism, as much in relations of love as in political struggles. There is no longer any Gide-subject, carried away or divided, nor even any Proust-subject forever guilty . . ." (16). Hocquenghem also attacks *Corydon* and the attempt to "base the form of desire on nature" (*Homosexual Desire*, 62). But in referring to the pages that Deleuze and Guattari devote to Proust in *Anti-Oedipus*, he emphasizes that one finds in *Cities of the Plain* (*Sodome et Gomorrhe*) a "language of flowers" whose "biological aspects" particularly interest Proust and open onto a different conception of homosexuality, as a pure connection of desiring machines (Hocquenghem, *Homosexual Desire*, 90–91; Deleuze and Guattari, *Anti-Oedipus*, 68–70). [Translator's Note: *France-Dimanche* is a popular weekly magazine that covers the lives of famous personalities.]

15. FHAR, *Rapport contre la normalité*, 7.

16. Baudry to the author, May 30, 1994. See Eribon, *Michel Foucault et ses contemporains*, 274–76.

17. Foucault's text on Arcadie and Baudry was published in *Libération* on July 12, 1982. At the last minute, he decided that he preferred not to sign it, and asked me if I would. The article thus appeared under my initials (D. E.). For the text itself, for further information on the conditions of its publications, and for a fuller discussion of Foucault's relations with Arcadie, see Eribon, *Michel Foucault et ses contemporains*, 265–87.

18. Sedgwick, from a quite different perspective, has already offered a reading of *La Volonté de savoir* as a "drama of the closet." See her "Gender Criticism," 271–302, esp. 278–85.

9. When Two Guys Hold Hands

1. Voeltzel, *Vingt ans et après*. Foucault's name does not appear in the book. In the preface, Claude Mauriac, who edited the series in which the book appeared and who commissioned it, simply comments: "A very young man, Thierry, speaks in front of an older friend" (7). On the book, see Eribon, *Michel Foucault*, 281–82. Voeltzel had participated in the group called Antinorme (which had grown out of the FHAR) and in the founding of the magazine *Gai Pied* in 1979. It was to please Voeltzel that Foucault published an article, "Un Plaisir si simple," in the first issue of that magazine.

2. Voeltzel, *Vingt ans et après*, 51. See also 37: "I [Foucault] came to understand, according to everything you had told me, that, for you, homosexuality was quite

simple. And now you've just told me, while the tape recorder was turned off, that while it had become simple, all the same it was complicated."

3. Ibid., 22. Foucault makes a point of saying that when Reich speaks of homosexuality, "he says ignominious things" (18).

4. Ibid., 29. Voeltzel himself emphasizes, however, that all the discourse about bisexuality had little to do with the sexual practices of the individuals concerned.

5. Ibid., 30. A few years later, in 1981, Foucault came back to this question, speaking in an interview of "the great myth of saying: There will no longer be any difference between homo- and heterosexuality." He opposed to this utopia of undifferentiation the idea of a gay "way of life," and insisted that "this search for a way of life runs counter to the ideology of the sexual liberation movements of the sixties" ("Friendship as a Way of Life," 138).

6. See Voeltzel, *Vingt ans et après*, 32. Foucault seems satisfied when Voeltzel tells him not only that he does not "think of himself as homosexual" but that at the same time he thinks that in the future he will be exclusively homosexual in his practices (38–39).

7. Needless to say, as *Libération* followed the process of institutionalization in the 1980s, this space for free speech disappeared, replaced by an "Opinions" page similar to the ones found everywhere else.

8. Foucault, "Le Gai Savoir," 48.

9. Foucault, "Sexual Choice, Sexual Act," 153; translation modified (originally published in *Salmagundi* 58–59 [fall 1982–winter 1983]: 10–24). Leo Bersani uses these remarks as the starting point for the critical discussion of Foucault developed in *Homos*, 77–112, where he reproaches Foucault for desexualizing both homophobia and the transgressive aspect of homosexuality.

10. Foucault, "The End of the Monarchy of Sex," 218. He offers as a sign of this "anti-sex grumbling" Guibert's *La Mort propagande.*

11. Foucault, "Friendship as a Way of Life," 136–37.

10. Resistance and Counterdiscourse

1. From the presentation (written but not signed by Foucault) of the brochure *Intolérable*, no. 1 (Paris: Champ libre, 1971). I cite from these documents at greater length in *Michel Foucault*, 227–28. Foucault adds, after having laid out the kinds of inquiries that should be undertaken in the justice system, the health care system, and so on (each one of them "the first episode in a struggle"): "These inquiries are not done from the outside by a group of technical experts. Those making inquiries are those about whom the inquiry is being made. It is for them to seize speech, to break down their isolation, to formulate what is intolerable. It is for them to take charge of the struggle that will prevent the exercise of oppression."

2. Hocquenghem, "Notre corps nous appartient," *Tout*, no. 12 (April 1971), reprinted in *L'Après-mai des faunes*, 143–44.

3. See Foucault, *Intolérable*, no. 4, *Suicides de prison* (Paris: Gallimard, 1973). See also, Eribon, *Michel Foucault*, 228–29. See also Hocquenghem, "Novembre noir," *Actuel*, no. 26 (December 1972), reprinted in *L'Après-mai des faunes*, 34–35. It was at the moment of the protests around this affair that Foucault was strongly criticized by the activists from the FHAR, especially by Hocquenghem, who accused him of leaving in the background the role homosexuality played in the affair. (Conversation with Hélène Hazera, September 15, 1998.)

4. See, on all these points, Eribon, *Michel Foucault*, 251–54. On Foucault's political activities in the 1970s, see also Mauger, "Un Nouveau Militantisme."

5. The text can be found on the back cover of the first edition of both volumes of the collection, "Les Vies parallèles," which includes the memoir that Foucault edited, *Herculine Barbin dite Alexina B.*

6. See "*Il faut défendre la société*," 16. See also *HSI*, 102.

7. *HSI*, 102. We should not forget that Foucault's intention is to offer a critique not only of Freudo-Marxism, but also of Althusser's theory of power and of "Ideological State Apparatuses."

8. Resistance, Foucault says, "is never in a position of exteriority in relation to power" (95).

9. Foucault introduced the notion of heterotopia in an article from 1967, which he allowed to be reprinted only in 1984: "Of Other Spaces." Foucault's analyses in the article do not have exactly the political meaning that I give to them here by reading them in the context of his thought in the 1980s. Yet one clearly sees in the article the extent to which his analyses privilege thinking about space over thinking about time.

10. The full title in English is *Christianity, Social Tolerance, and Homosexuality: Gay People in Western Europe from the Beginning of the Christian Era to the Fourteenth Century*. The title given to the French translation was *Christianisme, tolérance sociale et homosexualité: Les Homosexuels en Europe occidentale des débuts de l'ère chrétienne au XIVe siècle.*

11. There were, of course, "constructionist" approaches before Foucault, notably that of Mary McIntosh, proposed in her 1968 article, "The Homosexual Role."

12. The French publisher seems absurdly to have insisted that Boswell give up this vocabulary and substituted "*les homosexuels*" where Boswell had, by writing "gay people," intended to emphasize the anachronism in the usage. Boswell was interested precisely in portraying the history of people who were conscious of their erotic inclination for people of the same sex. He did not want to limit himself to a consideration of sexual practices. For this reason, he nearly decided not to allow his book to appear in French translation. He finally allowed the translation to appear,

but included a discussion of matters of terminology at the beginning of the French edition.

13. For an excellent discussion of the opposition between essentialism and constructionism, see the anthology edited by Stein, *Forms of Desire*. This volume notably includes a text by Boswell, "Concepts, Experience, and Sexuality" (133–74), as well as the article by Mary McIntosh mentioned in note 11 (25–42).

14. On the influence of Foucault on historical research in the United States, see Eribon, "Traverser les frontières," and Fassin, "Politiques de l'histoire."

15. Of course a simple reason for this presents itself: the chapter in *Histoire de la folie* that contains the pages on homosexuality that I discussed earlier is not included in the English and American editions of *Madness and Civilization*. Those editions reproduce the abridged version of *Histoire de la folie* published in paperback in 1964. Moreover, given that few people in France have shown any interest in these questions up till now—French gay and lesbian history is still in its infancy—these contradictions in Foucault's work have never been called to our attention.

16. Foucault, "Sexuality and Solitude," in *Ethics*, 179.

17. Brown's analysis of these matters can be found in a book that appeared after Foucault's death: *The Body and Society*.

18. Of course, in *La Volonté de savoir*, Foucault indicates that the act of confessing to one's spiritual director was already practiced in the "ascetic and monastic tradition," but what was of interest to him at that moment was the fact that "the seventeenth century made it into a rule for everyone" (20; translation modified).

19. Foucault, "Des caresses d'hommes considérés comme un art [Men's caresses considered as an art]," 4:316. The review first appeared in *Libération* on June 1, 1982.

20. Foucault, "History and Homosexuality," 369–70.

21. Foucault, "Sexual Choice, Sexual Act," 140–41.

11. *Becoming Gay*

1. Most of these texts have been collected in *Dits et écrits*. See principally, in volume 3, the texts numbered 200 and 206, and, in volume 4, texts 293, 311, 313, 314, 317, 349, and 358. The interview called "Le Gai Savoir" published in the Netherlands in a disputed version in 1978 should also be mentioned. Because of disputes about the text it was not included in *Dits et écrits*. The full transcription has been published by the journal *Revue h*, no. 2 (autumn 1996). [Translator's note: Eribon's list includes the following texts available in *Ethics*: "Friendship as a Way of Life," "Sexual Choice, Sexual Act," "The Social Triumph of the Sexual Will," "Sex, Power, and the Politics of Identity." A few of these texts are also found in *Foucault Live*, along with several others in Eribon's list: "The End of the Monarchy of Sex"

and "History and Homosexuality." Eribon's list also includes "Le Jeu de Michel Foucault," an interview that originally appeared in the French Lacanian journal *Ornicar?* and has been translated by Alain Grosrichard as "The Confession of the Flesh"; a 1981 interview, "Interview de Michel Foucault," by J. François and J. de Wit; and "Des Caresses d'hommes considérées comme un art," Foucault's review of the French translation of Dover's *Greek Homosexuality*.]

2. I offered an earlier commentary on these texts in *Michel Foucault et ses contemporains*, 265–87. Another analysis of them can be found in Halperin, *Saint Foucault*. Halperin is the first person I know of to have taken them together as a corpus from which a certain number of theoretical and political orientations can be deduced. In *Michel Foucault et ses contemporains*, I offered a certain number of criticisms of the second half of Halperin's *Saint Foucault*, which is devoted to the question of Foucault's biography. Perhaps I did not give enough emphasis to the importance of Halperin's analyses in the first part of his book, analyses that are essential to an understanding of Foucault's "gay politics" as a kind of "positionality." By that I mean a systematic effort to diverge from the norm, a strategy of resistance that seeks to evade any stable and fixed content, any "identity." This is what Halperin calls "the queer politics of Michel Foucault."

3. This can be seen clearly in the transcript of the interview "Le Gai Savoir." Foucault begins his responses with exclamations such as "Wow, that's complicated. I don't have a clue [C'est archi-compliqué. Je n'y vois que du feu]" (48). Obviously, such spontaneous oratorical qualifications are normally removed from published versions—with the result that statements made in them come to seem intended to be more definitive than they probably were.

4. Foucault, "History and Homosexuality," 368.

5. Ibid., 369. Foucault will suggest in a number of interviews around this time that the surveillance of homosexuality began in the seventeenth century. For example, in 1982: "For four centuries, homosexuality has been much more the object of repression, surveillance and interventions at the hands of police agencies than at the hands of the judiciary. A certain number of homosexuals have suffered from judicial interventions, from laws. But it's quite a limited number in comparison with police repression. For example, it's not true that homosexuals were burned in the seventeenth century, even if it happened a few times. On the other hand, they were arrested by the hundreds in the Luxembourg Gardens or at the Palais-Royal" (Foucault, "Non aux compromis," 4:336). In another interview, given in 1981, but only published in 1984, Foucault also speaks of the seventeenth and eighteenth centuries: "One sees that hundreds of homosexuals were arrested each year in the Luxembourg Gardens or around the Palais-Royal. Should we call this repression? This system of frequent arrests cannot be explained by the law or by an intention to

repress homosexuality. In the normal course of things, they are only arrested for twenty-four hours. How should we understand that? My idea is that we see being introduced a new kind of relation between homosexuality and political, administrative, and police power. . . . We see a restructuring of technologies of the self around sexuality. In all parts of society, sexuality becomes the general apparatus that explains the unity of human personality" (Foucault, "Interview de Michel Foucault," 4:660). It would seem then that Foucault had, by the beginning of the 1980s, abandoned the idea of the "invention of the homosexual" by nineteenth-century psychiatry. In these interviews, what links homosexuality to the individual and inscribes it as the truth of one's personality is the new hold of politico-administrative structures—in the seventeenth and eighteenth centuries—on sexual life. This kind of periodization seems closer to *Madness and Civilization* than to *La Volonté de savoir*.

6. Foucault, "Sexual Choice, Sexual Act," 146, 149. In his preface to the German edition of *La Volonté de savoir*, Foucault mentions the criticisms that were made of the volume. See "Sexualité et vérité," 3:136–37. He also mentions them in "Le Gai Savoir," 42.

7. In 1978, for example, when he insists that his way of proceeding is "in no way a rupture with those struggles" but "on the contrary, simply a suggestion that such struggles take on a wider character, and that there could be a shift in the basis of such struggles, a reorientation" ("Le Gai Savoir," 44).

8. Foucault, "Sex, Power and the Politics of Identity," 164. This interview was conducted in Toronto in June 1982 and first published a few weeks after Foucault's death.

9. Ibid., 163. See also his comments in "Friendship as a Way of Life": "Another thing to distrust is the tendency to relate the question of homosexuality to the problem of 'Who am I?' and 'What is the secret of my desire?' Perhaps it would be better to ask oneself, 'What relations, through homosexuality, can be established, invented, multiplied, and modulated?' The problem is not to discover in oneself the truth of one's sex, but, rather, to use one's sexuality henceforth to arrive at a multiplicity of relationships" (135).

10. On the rejection of biologism and naturalism, see "Le Gai Savoir," 44. On the question of history see "Nietzsche, Genealogy, and History," 369–91; and "So Is It Important to Think?"

11. Foucault, "Interview with Michel Foucault," 275. On Foucault and the Frankfurt School, see Eribon, *Michel Foucault et ses contemporains*, 296–311.

12. Foucault, "Friendship as a Way of Life," 136.

13. Foucault, "History and Homosexuality," 369–70. See also "Interview de Michel Foucault," 4:656.

14. Foucault, "Sex, Power, and the Politics of Identity," 164.

15. Foucault, "The Social Triumph of the Sexual Will," 157.

16. Ibid., 158. Elsewhere, however, Foucault states: "I don't mean that the legalization of marriage among homosexuals should be an objective; rather, that we are dealing here with a whole series of questions concerning the insertion and recognition—within a legal and social framework—of diverse relations among individuals which must be addressed" ("Sexual Choice, Sexual Act," 143–44). I recounted in *Michel Foucault* Sylvia Lacan's recollection of a dinner she gave in the 1960s at which Foucault was in attendance, and during which he declared: "There will be no civilization as long as marriage between men is not accepted" (154). We should not forget that almost all the interviews bearing on these questions were for publication in gay newspapers or reviews, or, as in the case of "Sexual Choice, Sexual Act," for a special issue on homosexuality. Foucault was thus addressing a gay public, and so the thoughts he expresses in these contexts might not reveal the whole of his position. It is easy to imagine that in other contexts he would have dwelt on his support for those claims that in other respects he wanted to challenge. (One can easily support certain demands while nonetheless remaining critical of them or while pushing to enlarge them.) Foucault never ceased insisting that one should never "stabilize oneself in a position; one must define the use that one makes of it according to the moment" ("History and Homosexuality," 369). Position taking is always strategic; there is no fixed or unique response to a question— for example, to the question as to whether one should state or refuse to state one's homosexuality (this is Foucault's example): it might be politically important to affirm that one is homosexual, just as it might be politically necessary to refuse to respond to the injunction to define oneself.

17. Foucault, "The Social Triumph of the Sexual Will," 157.

18. Ibid., 160. Thus Foucault can say that "gay culture will be not only a choice of homosexuals for homosexuals—it would create relations that are, at certain points, transferable to heterosexuals" (160).

19. One might think that the PACS or the "domestic partnerships" of certain European countries or American cities fit more logically within the Foucauldian point of view than does the struggle for gay marriage, even if it is clear that Foucault supported this whole set of struggles.

20. Foucault, "Sex, Power, and the Politics of Identity," 164; translation modified. Foucault specifies that it's not a question of creating "our *own* culture," for that would already be to program the forms of inventiveness, but rather of realizing "cultural creations" (something that in his eyes happens less by way of "gay novels" than by way of new "modes of life").

21. Foucault, "Friendship as a Way of Life," 139; translation modified.

22. Foucault, "Sex, Power, and the Politics of Identity," 172–73. On "resistance"

as the possibility of "saying no," but also as the possibility of creation, see ibid., 167–68.

23. Foucault, "The Social Triumph of the Sexual Will," 159–60.

24. Foucault, "Sex, Power, and the Politics of Identity," 170.

12. Among Men

1. At the beginning of the 1980s Foucault frequently expressed his desire to move to the United States, especially to San Francisco.

2. Foucault, "Friendship as a Way of Life," 137–38; translation modified.

3. "Sex, Power, and the Politics of Identity," 165, 169–70. Foucault indicates that he borrows the expression "s&m subculture" from "our friend Gayle Rubin," the American anthropologist and theoretician. He also affirms in this interview that "drugs should become an element within our culture" (165; translation modified).

4. Paul Rabinow, Hubert Dreyfus, Leo Lowenthal, Charles Taylor, Robert Bellah, Martin Jay, "Discussion with Michel Foucault," April 21, 1983, transcript in the archives of Paul Rabinow. A part of this conversation was published as "Politics and Ethics: An Interview," but the passages in question here are not reproduced in the published version.

5. "The work of intellectuals can never be linked to a certain kind of government or political structure, but, quite the opposite, must always be critical in their regard. . . . It's a negative form of interest, systematically negative. This is, I think, the only politics that an intellectual qua intellectual can defend" (ibid.).

6. Ibid.

7. In another interview, after having described the "s&m subculture of San Francisco" with great praise, Foucault responds to a question about whether or not such a subculture runs the risk of being exploited commercially: "We can never be sure [that exploitation won't take place]. In fact, we can always be sure *it will happen*, and that everything that has been created or acquired, any ground that has been gained will, at a certain moment be used in such a way. That's the way we live, that's the way we struggle, that's the way of human history. And I don't think that is an objection to all those movements or all those situations. But you are quite right in underlining that we always have to be quite careful and to be aware of the fact that we have to move on to something else, that we have other needs as well. The s&m ghetto in San Francisco is a good example of a community that has experimented with, and formed an identity around, pleasure. This ghettoization, this identification, this procedure of exclusion and so on—all of these have, as well, produced their countereffects. I dare not use the word *dialectics*—but this comes rather close to it" ("Sex, Power, and the Politics of Identity," 166–67).

8. Foucault, "The Social Triumph of the Sexual Will," 161–62.

9. Ibid., 161. See also "Friendship as a Way of Life," 138–39.

10. On Dumézil's way of talking about his life during World War I, see Eribon, "Georges Dumézil, un homosexuel dans le siècle," 31–32.

11. Dumézil, Mythe et épopée.

12. See the anthology edited by Taylor, Lads. See also Fussel, The Great War and Modern Memory, esp. chap. 8, 270–309. There is also the magnificent trilogy of novels by Pat Barker, in which Sassoon and Owen figure as characters: Regeneration, The Eye in the Door, and The Ghost Road.

13. Foucault, "Friendship as a Way of Life," 138; my emphasis.

14. Rich, "Compulsory Heterosexuality and Lesbian Existence." For Rich, as for Faderman, any kind of relation two women enter into is a means of resisting masculine domination, resisting the violence of "compulsory heterosexuality." Rich goes so far as to suggest—as will Luce Irigaray—that male homosexuality is nothing other than an extreme case of male homosociality, and that consequently gay men are the ultimate incarnation of the oppression of women, and of lesbians in particular. As Sedgwick has so pertinently commented, this way of opposing gay men to lesbians is found more frequently among gay men and lesbians than among their opponents, who hate them both and lump them together in order to combat them (Epistemology of the Closet, 36–37).

15. See Marcus, "Quelques problèmes de l'histoire lesbienne," 35–43, esp. 36–37 and the bibliography (43).

16. Foucault would often insist on friendship as a possible relation for two people of different ages, and it would seem that he was personally very interested in this possibility, one that the normative idea of the couple generally does not make available. (See the fine remarks he makes on this subject in "Friendship as a Way of Life," 136–37.) One might even wonder if the question of people's ages, of the relations that are possible between an older and a younger man, was not a determining feature of Foucault's thinking about gay culture.

17. Eribon, Michel Foucault et ses contemporains, 125–26.

18. I don't mean "misogyny" in the sense of "hatred of women," but more specifically in the sense of a nearly exclusive preference for single sex situations, the desire of gay men to be together in the absence of women. (The same desire, in inverse form, can be found in lesbian circles.) This preference was, for Foucault, irrelevant when it came to supporting the feminist movement, which was an entirely different matter. This kind of "misogyny" is still characteristic of today's gay male culture, even if it is clear that the gay men of the 1990s have less difficulty thinking in terms of "gay and lesbian" culture.

19. Foucault, "Friendship as a Way of Life," 136; translation modified.

13. Making Differences

1. Foucault, "What Is Enlightenment?," 315.

2. Ibid. In his preface to *Ethics*, Paul Rabinow has emphasized the importance of this opposition between an impossible emancipation (*affranchissement*) and the possible work of exceeding, or over-stepping, or crossing-over (*franchir, franchissement*). See *Ethics*, xxxii-xxxiii.

3. Foucault, "Sex, Power, and the Politics of Identity," 167.

4. Foucault, "A propos de la généalogie de l'éthique," 4:617. [Translator's note: A version of this text is published in *Ethics* under the title "On the Genealogy of Ethics: An Overview of Work in Progress," 253–80. The text is based on conversations that were conducted in English and was first published in English in 1983. When a French translation of the conversations was published in 1984, Foucault made revisions. There are notable variations between the two versions, as this passage makes clear. Eribon cites the 1984 French version. *Ethics* republishes the earlier English version.]

5. See "On the Genealogy of Ethics," 262. The reference is to aphorism 290 of *The Gay Science*, 232–33.

6. Foucault, "What Is Enlightenment?," 311–12. Baudelaire's pages on dandyism can be found in *The Painter of Modern Life and Other Essays*, 26–29.

7. Hadot, "Réflexions sur la notion de 'culture de soi.'" In *The Use of Pleasure* and *The Care of the Self*, Foucault refers to Hadot's work, notably to his *Exercises spirituels et philosophie antique*.

8. See Deleuze, *Negotiations*, 94–95.

9. See Foucault, "On the Genealogy of Ethics," 256, and "A propos de la généalogie," 4:615.

10. See Foucault, *The Use of Pleasure*, 23.

11. Foucault, "On the Genealogy of Ethics," 278. [Translator's note: I have changed the word order of the English text to correspond to the French text that Foucault revised. See "A propos de la généalogie," 4:630.] Foucault adds, "The idea that from one's own life one can make a work of art is an idea that was undoubtedly foreign to the Middle Ages, and reappears at the moment of the Renaissance." In Foucault, *The Use of Pleasure* (17) he adds a reference to Greenblatt, *Renaissance Self-Fashioning*.

12. See Foucault, *The Use of Pleasure*, 11.

13. Deleuze, *Negotiations*, 151.

14. Foucault, "Ariane s'est pendue," 1:771. This is Foucault's review, first published in *Le Nouvel Observateur* dated March 31–April 6, 1969, of Deleuze's *Difference and Repetition*.

15. [Translator's note: Eribon is referring once again to the full preface from 1961, to be found in *Dits*, 1:159–67. The verse from Char that Foucault cites can be found in Char's *Fureur et mystère*, in "Partage formel" (section xxii).]

Addendum: Hannah Arendt and "Defamed Groups"

1. When I speak of "French readings of her work," I do not mean to refer to those interpretations offered by university scholars and researchers, but rather to the image of Arendt's work that has been propagated, popularized and, yes, vulgarized, by various mediagenic essayists and by certain generalist cultural journals.

2. Arendt, "Reflections on Little Rock," 231–46. The article was first published in *Dissent* 6, no. 1 (1959). For the history behind this article and its reception, see Young-Bruehl, *Hannah Arendt*, 308–18.

3. See Young-Bruehl, *Hannah Arendt*, 315–17.

4. Arendt can be seen making the same point with great clarity in a text that predates the one on Little Rock by about fifteen years, titled "Our Foreign Language Groups." A longer version is available as "Foreign Affairs in the Foreign-Language Press."

5. See, on this subject, Canovan, *Hannah Arendt*; Benhabib, *The Reluctant Modernism of Hannah Arendt*; Bohman, "The Moral Cost of Political Pluralism"; Kaplan, "Refiguring the Jewish Question." Important French works include Courtine-Denamy, *Hannah Arendt*, and Leibovici, *Hannah Arendt, une Juive*.

6. Here I am obviously not speaking of the works of Sylvie Courtine-Denamy or Martine Leibovici, who have provided us with rigorous commentaries of Arendt's thought, situating it carefully in its historical and intellectual context. Rather I am referring to the politico-ideological appropriations of her work, in which it is reduced to a few decontextualized citations on the idea of a "common world" that is somehow incompatible with "particularist" claims. This is obviously exactly the opposite of what Arendt says.

7. See Bohman, "The Moral Cost of Political Pluralism," 57–58.

8. Canovan, *Hannah Arendt*, 227.

9. Arendt, *The Human Condition*, 57.

10. Arendt, *Qu'est-ce que la politique?*, 112. See also the commentary by Leibovici, *Hannah Arendt*, 289–90.

11. Rich, "Conditions for Work," 205, 212.

12. See Benhabib, *The Reluctant Modernism of Hannah Arendt*, 4. See also Young-Bruehl, "Hannah Arendt Among Feminists," 307–22.

13. Cited in Canovan, *Hannah Arendt*, 213.

14. See Arendt, *The Origins of Totalitarianism*, 79–88.

15. Cited in Arendt, *The Origins of Totalitarianism*, 86.

16. See ibid., 81–82.

17. See ibid., 65–68.

18. Ibid., 83. One might wonder if this text is not one of the hidden sources for Foucault's *La Volonté de savoir*, especially for the moment in which he describes the nineteenth-century invention by psychiatry of the personage of the "homosexual," an invention that happens by way of the incorporation as a perversion of what had up until then been thought of as a crime (*HSI*, 43). Arendt's volume was translated into French in 1973, and Foucault's book was published in 1976.

19. On "worldlessness," see Arendt, "On Humanity in Dark Times," 3–31. See also Leibovici, *Hannah Arendt*, 180–344.

20. Arendt, "The Jew as Pariah: A Hidden Tradition," 67–90. On Bernard Lazare, see 76–79.

21. Arendt to Jaspers, December 12, 1946, in *Hannah Arendt Karl Jaspers Correspondence, 1926–1969*, 70. See also Arendt's letter to Jaspers of September 4, 1947, ibid., 98–99.

22. See on this topic Bernstein, *Hannah Arendt and the Jewish Question*, 195–97.

23. Arendt, *The Origins of Totalitarianism*, 66.

24. Leibovici, *Hannah Arendt*, 471.

25. Ibid., 472.

Works Cited

Adam, Barry D. *The Rise of a Gay and Lesbian Movement*. New York: Twayne, 1995.

———. *The Survival of Domination: Inferiorization and Everyday Life*. New York: Elsevier, 1978.

Ahlstedt, Eva. *André Gide et le débat sur l'homosexualité*. Göteborg: Acta Universitatis Gothoburgensis, 1994.

———. *La Pudeur en crise: Un Aspect de la réception d' "A la recherche du temps perdu" de Marcel Proust, 1913–1930*. Göteborg: Acta Universitatis Gothoburgensis, 1985.

Althusser, Louis. *The Future Lasts Forever: A Memoir*. Ed. Olivier Corpet and Yann Moulier Boutang. Trans. Richard Veasey. New York: New Press, 1993.

———. "Ideology and Ideological State Apparatuses." In *Lenin and Philosophy and Other Essays*. Trans. Ben Brewster. Pp. 127–86. New York: Monthly Review Press, 1971.

———. *Lettres à Franca, 1961–1973*. Paris: Stock-IMEC, 1998.

Altman, Dennis. *Homosexual: Oppression and Liberation*. 1970. Reprint, London: Serpent's Tail, 1993.

Amnesty International. *Breaking the Silence: Human Rights Violations Based on Sexual Orientation*. London, 1997.

Arendt, Hannah. "Foreign Affairs in the Foreign-Language Press." In *Essays in Understanding, 1930–1954*. Ed. Jerome Kohn. Pp. 81–105. New York: Harcourt Brace and Company, 1994.

———. "The Jew as Pariah: The Hidden Tradition." In *The Jew as Pariah: Jewish Identity and Politics in the Modern Age*. Ed. Ron H. Feldman. New York: Grove Press, 1978.

———. *The Human Condition*. Chicago: University of Chicago Press, 1958.

———. "On Humanity in Dark Times: Thoughts About Lessing." Trans. Clara and Richard Winston. In *Men in Dark Times*. Pp. 3–31. New York: Harcourt, Brace, and World, 1968.

———. *The Origins of Totalitarianism*. New York: Harcourt, Brace, Jovanovich, 1973.

———. "Our Foreign Language Groups." *Chicago Jewish Forum* 3, no. 1 (fall 1944): 23–34.

——. *The Origins of Totalitarianism*. New York: Harcourt Brace Jovanovich, 1973.

——. *Qu'est-ce que la politique?* Paris: Seuil, 1995.

——. "Reflections on Little Rock." In *The Portable Hannah Arendt*. Ed. Peter Baehr. Pp. 231–46. New York: Penguin, 2000.

Arendt, Hannah, and Karl Jaspers. *Hannah Arendt Karl Jaspers Correspondence, 1926–1969*. Ed. Lotte Kohler and Hans Saner. Trans. Robert and Rita Kimber. New York: Harcourt Brace Jovanovich, 1992.

Austin, J. L. *How to Do Things with Words*. 2nd edition. Cambridge, Mass.: Harvard University Press, 1975.

Barbedette, Gilles, and Michel Carassou. *Paris Gay 1925*. Paris: Presses de la Renaissance, 1981.

Bard, Christine. *Les Garçonnes: Modes et fantasmes des années folles*. Paris: Flammarion, 1998.

——. "Lectures de La Garçonne." *Les Temps modernes* 593 (April–May 1997): 78–95.

Barker, Pat. *The Eye in the Door*. London: Viking, 1993.

——. *The Ghost Road*. London: Viking, 1995.

——. *Regeneration*. London: Viking, 1991.

Barré, Jean-Luc. *Jacques et Raïssa Maritain: Les Mendiants du ciel*. Paris: Stock, 1995.

Barthes, Roland. *Roland Barthes by Roland Barthes*. Trans. Richard Howard. New York: Hill and Wang, 1977.

Bartlett, Neil. *Ready to Catch Him Should He Fall*. London: Serpent's Tail, 1990.

——. *Who Was That Man? A Present for Mr Oscar Wilde*. London: Serpent's Tail, 1988.

Baudelaire, Charles. *The Painter of Modern Life and Other Essays*. Trans. and ed. Jonathan Mayne. London: Phaidon, 1995.

Beauvoir, Simone de. *A Transatlantic Love Affair: Letters to Nelson Algren*. New York: The New Press, 1998.

Bech, Henning. *When Men Meet: Homosexuality and Modernity*. Trans. Teresa Mesquit and Tim Davies. Chicago: University of Chicago Press, 1997.

Bell, Alan P., and Martin S. Weinberg. *Homosexualities: A Study of Diversity among Men and Women*. New York: Simon and Shuster, 1978.

Benhabib, Seyla. *The Reluctant Modernism of Hannah Arendt*. Thousand Oaks, Calif.: Sage Publications, 1996.

Benstock, Shari. "Paris Lesbianism and the Politics of Reaction, 1900–1940." In *Hidden from History: Reclaiming the Gay and Lesbian Past*. Ed. George Chauncey, Martin Duberman, Martha Vicinus. Pp. 332–46. New York: Meridian, 1990.

——. *Women of the Left Bank, Paris 1900–1940*. London: Virago, 1987.

Bernstein, Richard J. *Hannah Arendt and the Jewish Question*. Cambridge, Engl.: Polity Press, 1995.

Bersani, Leo. *Homos*. Cambridge, Mass.: Harvard University Press, 1995.

——. "Is the Rectum a Grave?" *October* 43 (winter 1987): 197–222.

———. "Trahisons gaies." In *Les Études gay et lesbiennes*. Ed. Didier Eribon. Pp. 65–72. Paris: Éditions du Centre Pompidou, 1998.

Bersani, Leo, and Ulysse Dutoit. *Caravaggio's Secrets*. Cambridge, Mass.: MIT Press, 1998.

Bérubé, Allan. *Coming Out Under Fire: The History of Gay Men and Women in World War Two*. New York: Plume, 1991.

Bohman, James. "The Moral Cost of Political Pluralism: The Dilemmas of Difference and Equality in Arendt's 'Reflections on Little Rock.' " In *Hannah Arendt: Twenty Years Later*. Ed. Larry May and Jerome Kohn. Pp. 53–80. Cambridge, Mass.: MIT Press, 1996.

Bory, Jean-Louis and Guy Hocquenghem. *Comment nous appelez-vous, déjà? Ces hommes que l'on dit homosexuels*. Paris: Calmann-Lévy, 1977.

Boswell, John. *Christianity, Social Tolerance, and Homosexuality: Gay People in Western Europe from the Beginning of the Christian Era to the Fourteenth Century*. Chicago: University of Chicago Press, 1980.

———. *Same-Sex Unions in Premodern Europe*. New York: Villard Books, 1994.

Bourdieu, Pierre. *Distinction: A Social Critique of the Judgement of Taste*. Trans. Richard Nice. Cambridge, Mass.: Harvard University Press, 1984.

———. *Homo Academicus*. Trans. Peter Collier. Cambridge, Engl.: Polity Press, 1988.

———. *The Logic of Practice*. Trans. Richard Nice. Stanford: Stanford University Press, 1990.

———. *Masculine Domination*. Trans. Richard Nice. Stanford: Stanford University Press, 2001.

———. *L'Ontologie politique de Martin Heidegger*. Paris: Minuit, 1988.

———. "Le Paradoxe du sociologue." In *Questions de sociologie*. Pp. 86–94. Paris: Minuit, 1981.

———. "Quelques questions sur la question gay et lesbienne." In *Les Études gay et lesbiennes*. Ed. Didier Eribon. Pp. 45–50. Paris: Éditions du Centre Pompidou, 1998.

———. "Remarques provisoires sur la perception sociale du corps." *Actes de la recherche en sciences sociales* 14 (April 1977): 51–54.

———. "Sur le pouvoir symbolique." *Annales* 3 (May–June 1977): 405–11.

Bourdieu, Pierre, et al. *The Weight of the World: Social Suffering in Contemporary Society*. Trans. Priscilla Parkhurst Ferguson, et al. Stanford: Stanford University Press, 1999.

Brassaï. *Le Paris secret des années trente*. Paris: Gallimard, 1978.

Bray, Alan. *Homosexuality in Renaissance England*. New York: Columbia University Press, 1982.

Brossard, Nicole. *"Amantes" suivi de "Le Sens apparent" et "Sous la langue."* Montreal: L'Hexagone, 1998.

Brown, Peter. *The Body and Society: Men, Women, and the Sexual Renunciation in Early Christianity*. New York: Columbia University Press, 1988.

Burleigh, Michael, and Wolfgang Wippermann. *The Racial State: Germany 1933–1945*. Cambridge: Cambridge University Press, 1991.

Butler, Judith. *Bodies That Matter: On the Discursive Limits of "Sex."* New York: Routledge, 1993.

——. *Excitable Speech: A Politics of the Performative*. New York: Routledge, 1997.

——. *The Psychic Life of Power: Theories of Subjection*. Stanford: Stanford University Press, 1997.

Canovan, Margaret. *Hannah Arendt: A Reinterpretation of Her Political Thought*. Cambridge: Cambridge University Press, 1992.

Cardon, Patrick, ed. "Enquête sur l'homosexualité en littérature: *Les Marges* 1926." In *Cahiers Gai Kitsch Camp*. No. 19. Lille: Cahiers Gai-Kitsch-Camp, 1993.

Carpenter, Humphrey. *W. H. Auden*. London: Allen and Unwin, 1981.

Chauncey, George. "Christian Brotherhood or Sexual Perversion? Homosexual Identities, and the Construction of Sexual Boundaries in the World War One Era." *Journal of Social History* 19 (1985): 189–211.

——. "From Sexual Inversion to Homosexuality: Medicine and the Changing Conceptualization of Female Deviance." *Salmagundi* 58–59 (autumn 1982–winter 1983): 114–46.

——. *Gay New York: Gender, Urban Culture, and the Making of the Gay Male World 1890–1940*. New York: BasicBooks, 1994.

——. "Genres, identités sexuelles et conscience homosexuelle dans l'Amérique du XXe siècle." Trans. Didier Eribon. In *Les Études gay et lesbiennes*. Ed. Didier Eribon. Pp. 97–107. Paris: Éditions du Centre Pompidou, 1998.

Chauncey, George, Martin Duberman, Martha Vicinus, eds. *Hidden from History: Reclaiming the Gay and Lesbian Past*. New York: Meridian, 1990.

Clerc, Catherine. *La Caricature contre Napoléon*. Paris: Promodis, 1985.

Cocteau, Jean. *The White Book*. Trans. Margaret Crosland. San Francisco: City Lights, 1989.

Contat, Michel, and Michel Rybalka. *Les Écrits de Sartre: Chronologie, Bibliographie commentée*. Paris: Gallimard, 1970.

Courtine-Denamy, Sylvie. *Hannah Arendt*. Paris: Belfond, 1994.

Cressole, Michel. *Une Folle à sa fenêtre: Chroniques de "L'Autre Journal," 1990–1991*. Lille: Cahiers Gai-Kitsch-Camp/Question de genre, 1996.

Crompton, Louis. *Byron and Greek Love: Homophobia in 19th-Century England*. Berkeley: University of California Press, 1986.

D'Eaubonne, Françoise. "FHAR, la fin d'un mouvement." *La Revue h* 3 (winter 1996–1997): 23–36.

——. "Le FHAR, origines et illustrations." *La Revue h* 2 (autumn 1996): 18–30.

Delay, Jean. *La Jeunesse d'André Gide.* 2 vols. Paris: Gallimard, 1956–1957.

Deleuze, Gilles. *Foucault.* Trans. and ed. Sean Hand. London: Athlone, 1988.

——. *Negotiations 1972–1990.* Trans. Martin Joughin. New York: Columbia University Press, 1995.

Deleuze, Gilles, and Félix Guattari. *Anti-Oedipus: Capitalism and Schizophrenia.* 1972. Reprint, trans. Robert Hurley, Mark Seem, and Helen R. Lane. Minneapolis: University of Minnesota Press, 1983.

Deleuze, Gilles, and Claire Parnet. *Dialogues.* Trans. Hugh Tomlinson and Barbara Habberjam. New York: Columbia University Press, 1987.

Dellamora, Richard. *Apocalyptic Overtures: Sexual Politics and the Sense of an Ending.* New Brunswick: Rutgers University Press, 1994.

——. *Masculine Desire: The Sexual Politics of Victorian Aestheticism.* Chapel Hill: University of North Carolina Press, 1990.

D'Emilio, John. "Capitalism and Gay Identity." In *Making Trouble: Essays on Gay History, Politics, and the University.* Pp. 3–16. New York: Routledge, 1992.

——. *Sexual Politics, Sexual Communities: The Making of a Sexual Minority in the United States, 1940–1970.* Chicago: University of Chicago Press, 1983.

Derrida, Jacques. *Feu la cendre.* Paris: Éditions des femmes, 1987.

——. "Signature Event Context." Trans. Samuel Weber and Jeffrey Mehlman. *Limited Inc.* Evanston: Northwestern University Press, 1988.

——. *Spectres de Marx.* Paris: Galilée, 1987.

Dickens, Charles. *Our Mutual Friend.* New York: Knopf-Everyman, 1994.

Dover, Kenneth James. *Greek Homosexuality.* London: Duckworth, 1978.

Dowling, Linda. *Hellenism and Homosexuality in Victorian Oxford.* Ithaca: Cornell University Press, 1994.

Duberman, Martin. *Stonewall.* New York: Plume, 1994.

Duflot, Jean. *Entretiens avec Pasolini.* Paris: Belfond, 1970.

Dumézil, George. *Mythe et épopée.* Paris: Gallimard, 1967.

——. Preface to *Homosexualité et initiation chez les peuples indo-européens* by Bernard Sergent. Pp. 9–12. Paris: Payot, 1996.

Dunning, Eric. "Sport as a Male Preserve: Notes on the Social Sources of Masculine Identity and Its Transformation." In *Quest for Excitement: Sport and Leisure in the Civilizing Process.* Ed. Norbert Elias and Eric Dunning. Pp. 267–83. Oxford: Basil Blackwell, 1986.

Ellmann, Richard. *Oscar Wilde.* New York: Knopf, 1988.

Eribon, Didier. *Faut-il brûler Dumézil? Mythologie, science et politique.* Paris: Flammarion, 1992.

——. "Georges Dumézil, un homosexuel au XXe siècle." *Ex Aequo* No. 4 (February 1997): 31–32.

——. *Hérésies: Essais sur la théorie de la sexualité.* Paris: Fayard, 2003.

——. *Michel Foucault*. Trans. Betsy Wing. Cambridge, Mass.: Harvard University Press, 1991.

——. *Michel Foucault, 1926–1984*. Paris: Flammarion, 1989; revised and augmented edition, Paris: Flammarion [Champs], 1991.

——. *Michel Foucault et ses contemporains*. Paris: Fayard, 1994.

——. *Une Morale du minoritaire: Variations sur un thème de Jean Genet*. Paris: Fayard, 2001.

——. "Traverser les frontières." In *Les Études gay et lesbiennes*. Ed. Didier Eribon. Pp. 11–25. Paris: Éditions du Centre Pompidou, 1998.

——, ed. *Dictionnaire des cultures gays et lesbiennes*. Paris: Larousse, 2003.

——, ed. *Les Études gay et lesbiennes*. Paris: Éditions du Centre Pompidou, 1998.

Faderman, Lillian. *Odd Girls and Twilight Lovers: A History of Lesbian Life in Twentieth-Century America*. New York: Penguin, 1992.

——. *Surpassing the Love of Men: Romantic Friendship and Love Between Women From the Renaissance to the Present*. New York: William Morrow, 1981.

Fanon, Franz. *Black Skin, White Masks*. Trans. Charles Lam Markmann. New York: Grove Press, 1967.

Fassin, Éric. "L'Illusion anthropologique: homosexualité et filiation." *Témoins* 12 (May–June 1998).

——. "Ouvrir le mariage aux homosexuels." *Le Monde diplomatique* (June 1988).

——. "Politiques de l'histoire: *Gay New York* et l'historiographie homosexuelle aux États-Unis." *Actes de la recherche en sciences sociales* 125 (December 1998): 3–8.

Felman, Shoshana. *The Literary Speech Act: Don Juan with J. L. Austin, or Seduction in Two Languages*. Ithaca: Cornell University Press, 1983.

FHAR. *Rapport contre la normalité*. Paris: Champ Libre, 1973.

Fillieule, Olivier. "Mobilisation gay en temps de sida." In *Les Études gay et lesbiennes*. Ed. Didier Eribon. Pp. 81–96. Paris: Éditions du Centre Pompidou, 1998.

Folsy, John. *The Trials of Oscar Wilde: Deviance, Morality and Late Victorian Society*. New Haven: Yale University Press, 1997.

Forster, E. M. *Maurice*. New York: Norton, 1987.

Foucault, Michel. *Aesthetics, Method, and Epistemology*. Ed. James D. Faubion. Trans. Robert Hurley et al. Volume 2 of *Essential Works of Foucault, 1954–1984*. Series ed. Paul Rabinow. New York: The New Press, 1998.

——. *Les Anormaux: Cours au Collège de France (1974–1975)*. Paris: Seuil/Gallimard, 1999.

——. "A propos de la généalogie de l'éthique: Un Aperçu du travail en cours." In *Dits et écrits, 1954–1988*. Eds. Daniel Defert and François Ewald. 4 vols. Paris: Gallimard, 1994, 4: 609–31.

——. *The Archaeology of Knowledge and The Discourse on Language*. Trans. A. M. Sheridan Smith. New York: Pantheon, 1972.

——. "Ariane s'est pendue." In *Dits et écrits, 1954–1988*. Eds. Daniel Defert and François Ewald. 4 vols. Paris: Gallimard, 1994, 1: 767–71.

——. "The Confession of the Flesh." Trans. Alain Grosrichard. In *Power/Knowledge: Selected Interviews and Other Writings 1972–1977*. Ed. Colin Gordon. Pp. 194–228. New York: Pantheon, 1980.

——. "Des caresses d'hommes considérées comme un art." In *Dits et écrits, 1954–1988*. Eds. Daniel Defert and François Ewald. 4 vols. Pp. 4:315–17. Paris: Gallimard, 1994.

——. *Death and the Labyrinth: The World of Raymond Roussel*. Trans. Charles Ruas. New York: Doubleday, 1984.

——. *Discipline and Punish: The Birth of the Prison*. Trans. Alan Sheridan. New York: Vintage, 1979.

——. *Dits et écrits, 1954–1988*. Eds. Daniel Defert and François Ewald. 4 vols. Paris: Gallimard, 1994.

——. "The End of the Monarchy of Sex." Trans. Dudley M. Marchi. In *Foucault Live (Interviews, 1961–1984)*. Ed. Sylvère Lotringer. Pp. 214–25. New York: Semiotext(e), 1996.

——. "Entretien avec Michel Foucault." Interview by Alessandro Fontana and Pasquale Pasquino. In *Dits et écrits, 1954–1988*. Eds. Daniel Defert and François Ewald. 4 vols. Pp. 3:140–60. Paris: Gallimard, 1994.

——. *Ethics: Subjectivity and Truth*. Ed. Paul Rabinow. Trans. Robert Hurley et al. Volume 1 of *Essential Works of Foucault, 1954–1984*. Series ed. Paul Rabinow. New York: The New Press, 1997.

——. "La Folie, l'absence d'oeuvre." In *Dits et écrits, 1954–1988*. Eds. Daniel Defert and François Ewald. 4 vols. Pp. 1:412–20. Paris: Gallimard, 1994.

——. "La Force de fuir." In *Dits et écrits, 1954–1988*. Eds. Daniel Defert and François Ewald. 4 vols. Pp. 2:401–5. Paris: Gallimard, 1994.

——. *Foucault Live (Interviews, 1961–1984)*. Ed. Sylvère Lotringer. New York: Semiotext(e), 1996.

——. "Friendship as a Way of Life." Trans. John Johnston. In *Ethics: Subjectivity and Truth*. Ed. Paul Rabinow. Trans. Robert Hurley et al. Volume 1 of *Essential Works of Foucault, 1954–1984*. Series ed. Paul Rabinow. Pp. 135–40. New York: The New Press, 1997.

——. "Le Gai Savoir: Entretien avec Michel Foucault par Jean Le Bitoux." *La Revue h* 2 (autumn 1996): 40–53.

——. *Histoire de la folie à l'âge classique*. Paris: Gallimard [Tel], 1972.

——. "History and Homosexuality." Trans. John Johnston. In *Foucault Live (Interviews, 1961–1984)*. Ed. Sylvère Lotringer. Pp. 363–70. New York: Semiotext(e), 1996.

——. *The History of Sexuality. Volume 1: An Introduction.* [*La Volonté de savoir*]. Trans. Robert Hurley. New York: Vintage, 1990.

——. "*Il faut défendre la société.*" *Cours du Collège de France, 1975–1976.* Paris: Seuil/Gallimard, 1997.

——. "L'Intellectuel et les pouvoirs." In *Dits et écrits, 1954–1988.* Eds. Daniel Defert and François Ewald. 4 vols. Pp. 4:747–52 Paris: Gallimard, 1994.

——. "Interview de Michel Foucault." In *Dits et écrits, 1954–1988.* Eds. Daniel Defert and François Ewald. 4 vols. Pp. 4: 656–67. Paris: Gallimard, 1994.

——. "Interview with Michel Foucault." In *Power.* Ed. James D. Faubion. Trans. Robert Hurley et al. Volume 3 of *Essential Works of Foucault, 1954–1984.* Series ed. Paul Rabinow. Pp. 239–97. New York: The New Press, 2000.

——. Introduction to *Le Rêve et l'existence* by Ludwig Binswanger. In *Dits et écrits, 1954–1988.* Eds. Daniel Defert and François Ewald. 4 vols. Pp. 1:65–115. Paris: Gallimard, 1994.

——. Introduction to Rousseau's *Dialogues.* In *Aesthetics, Method, and Epistemology.* Ed. James D. Faubion. Trans. Robert Hurley et al. Volume 2 of *Essential Works of Foucault, 1954–1984.* Series ed. Paul Rabinow. Pp. 33–51. New York: The New Press, 1998.

——. *Language, Counter-Memory, Practice: Selected Essays and Interviews.* Ed. Donald F. Bouchard. Ithaca: Cornell University Press, 1977.

——. "Lives of Infamous Men." In *Power.* Ed. James D. Faubion. Trans. Robert Hurley et al. Volume 3 of *Essential Works of Foucault, 1954–1984.* Series ed. Paul Rabinow. Pp. 157–75. New York: The New Press, 2000.

——. *Madness and Civilization: A History of Insanity in the Age of Reason.* Trans. Richard Howard. New York: Vintage, 1973.

——. "Madness Only Exists in Society." Trans. Lysa Hochroth. In *Foucault Live (Interviews, 1961–1984).* Ed. Sylvère Lotringer. Pp. 7–9. New York: Semiotext(e), 1996.

——. *Maladie mentale et psychologie.* Paris: PUF, 1962.

——. "Médecins, juges et sorciers au XVIIe siècle." In *Dits et écrits, 1954–1988.* Eds. Daniel Defert and François Ewald. 4 vols. Pp. 1:753–66. Paris: Gallimard, 1994.

——. *Mental Illness and Psychology.* Trans. Alan Sheridan. Foreword by Hubert Dreyfus. Berkeley: University of California Press, 1987.

——. "My Body, This Paper, This Fire." Trans. Geoff Bennington. In *Aesthetics, Method, and Epistemology.* Ed. James D. Faubion. Trans. Robert Hurley et al. Volume 2 of *Essential Works of Foucault, 1954–1984.* Series ed. Paul Rabinow. Pp. 393–417. New York: The New Press, 1998.

——. "Nietzsche, Freud, Marx." In *Dits et écrits, 1954–1988.* Eds. Daniel Defert and François Ewald. 4 vols. Pp. 1:564–79. Paris: Gallimard, 1994.

——. "Nietzsche, Freud, Marx." Trans. Jon Anderson and Gary Hentzi. In *Aesthetics,*

Method, and Epistemology. Ed. James D. Faubion. Trans. Robert Hurley et al. Volume 2 of *Essential Works of Foucault, 1954–1984*. Series ed. Paul Rabinow. Pp. 276–78. New York: The New Press, 1998.

——. "Nietzsche, Genealogy, and History." In *Aesthetics, Method, and Epistemology*. Ed. James D. Faubion. Trans. Robert Hurley et al. Volume 2 of *Essential Works of Foucault, 1954–1984*. Series ed. Paul Rabinow. Pp. 369–91. New York: The New Press, 1998.

——. "Non aux compromis." In *Dits et écrits, 1954–1988*. Eds. Daniel Defert and François Ewald. 4 vols. Pp. 4:336–37. Paris: Gallimard, 1994.

——. "Of Other Spaces." Trans. Jay Miskowiec. *diacritics* 16, no. 1 (1986): 22–27.

——. "On the Genealogy of Ethics: An Overview of Works in Progress." In *Ethics: Subjectivity and Truth*. Ed. Paul Rabinow. Trans. Robert Hurley et al. Volume 1 of *Essential Works of Foucault, 1954–1984*. Series ed. Paul Rabinow. Pp. 253–80. New York: The New Press, 1997.

——. *The Order of Things: An Archaeology of the Human Sciences*. New York: Vintage, 1973.

——. "A Preface to Transgression." Trans. Donald F. Bouchard and Sherry Simon. In *Aesthetics, Method, and Epistemology*. Ed. James D. Faubion. Trans. Robert Hurley et al. Volume 2 of *Essential Works of Foucault, 1954–1984*. Series ed. Paul Rabinow. Pp. 69–87. New York: The New Press, 1998.

——. "Politics and Ethics: An Interview." In *The Foucault Reader*. Ed. Paul Rabinow. Pp. 373–80. New York: Pantheon, 1984.

——. *Power*. Ed. James D. Faubion. Trans. Robert Hurley et al. Volume 3 of *Essential Works of Foucault, 1954–1984*. Series ed. Paul Rabinow. New York: The New Press, 2000.

——. "Prisons et asiles dans les mécanismes du pouvoir." In *Dits et écrits, 1954–1988*. Eds. Daniel Defert and François Ewald. 4 vols. Pp. 2:521–25. Paris: Gallimard, 1994.

——. "La Psychologie de 1850 à 1950." In *Dits et écrits, 1954–1988*. Eds. Daniel Defert and François Ewald. 4 vols. Pp. 1:120–37. Paris: Gallimard, 1994.

——. "La Recherche scientifique et la psychologie." In *Dits et écrits, 1954–1988*. Eds. Daniel Defert and François Ewald. 4 vols. Pp. 1:137–58. Paris: Gallimard, 1994.

——. "Sade, Sergeant of Sex." Trans. John Johnston. In *Aesthetics, Method, and Epistemology*. Ed. James D. Faubion. Trans. Robert Hurley et al. Volume 2 of *Essential Works of Foucault, 1954–1984*. Series ed. Paul Rabinow. Pp. 223–27. New York: The New Press, 1998.

——. "Sex, Power, and the Politics of Identity." In *Ethics: Subjectivity and Truth*. Ed. Paul Rabinow. Trans. Robert Hurley et al. Volume 1 of *Essential Works of Foucault, 1954–1984*. Series ed. Paul Rabinow. Pp. 163–73. New York: The New Press, 1997.

——. "Sexual Choice, Sexual Act." Trans. James O'Higgins. In *Ethics: Subjectivity and*

Truth. Ed. Paul Rabinow. Trans. Robert Hurley et al. Volume 1 of *Essential Works of Foucault, 1954–1984*. Series ed. Paul Rabinow. Pp. 141–56. New York: The New Press, 1997.

——. "Sexualité et vérité." In *Dits et écrits, 1954–1988*. Eds. Daniel Defert and François Ewald. 4 vols. Pp. 3:136–37. Paris: Gallimard, 1994.

——. "Sexuality and Solitude." In *Ethics: Subjectivity and Truth*. Ed. Paul Rabinow. Trans. Robert Hurley et al. Volume 1 of *Essential Works of Foucault, 1954–1984*. Series ed. Paul Rabinow. Pp. 175–84. New York: The New Press, 1997.

——. "The Social Triumph of the Sexual Will." Trans. Brendan Lemon. In *Ethics: Subjectivity and Truth*. Ed. Paul Rabinow. Trans. Robert Hurley et al. Volume 1 of *Essential Works of Foucault, 1954–1984*. Series ed. Paul Rabinow. Pp. 157–62. New York: The New Press, 1997.

——. "So Is It Important to Think?" In *Power*. Ed. James D. Faubion. Trans. Robert Hurley et al. Volume 3 of *Essential Works of Foucault, 1954–1984*. Series ed. Paul Rabinow. Pp. 454–58. New York: The New Press, 2000.

——. *The Use of Pleasure, Volume 2 of The History of Sexuality*. Trans. Robert Hurley. New York: Vintage, 1986.

——. "What Is Critique?" Trans. Kevin Paul Geiman. In *What Is Enlightenment? Eighteenth-Century Answers and Twentieth-Century Questions*. Ed. James Schmidt. Pp. 382–98. Berkeley: University of California Press, 1996.

——. "What Is Enlightenment?" Trans. Catherine Porter. In *Ethics: Subjectivity and Truth*. Ed. Paul Rabinow. Trans. Robert Hurley et al. Volume 1 of *Essential Works of Foucault, 1954–1984*. Series ed. Paul Rabinow. Pp. 303–19. New York: The New Press, 1997.

——, ed. *Herculine Barbin, Being the Recently Discovered Memoirs of a Nineteenth-Century French Hermaphrodite*. Trans. Richard McDougall. New York: Pantheon, 1980.

——, ed. *Herculine Barbin, dite Alexina B.* Paris: Gallimard, 1978.

——, ed. *I, Pierre Rivière, having slaughtered my mother, my sister and my brother . . . A Case of Parricide in the 19th Century*. [No translator indicated.] Harmondsworth: Penguin, 1978.

Foucault, Michel, and Arlette Farge, eds. *Le Désordre des familles: Lettres de cachet des Archives de la Bastille*. Paris: Gallimard-Julliard, 1982.

Freud, Sigmund. *The Ego and the Id*. Trans. Joan Riviere. Ed. James Strachey. New York: Norton, 1962.

——. *Five Lectures on Psycho-Analysis*. Trans. James Strachey. New York: Norton, 1977.

——. *Three Contributions to the Theory of Sex*. Trans. A. A. Brill. New York: Dutton, 1962.

Furbank, P. N. *E. M. Forster: A Life*. 2 vols. London: Abacus, 1993.

Fussel, Paul. *The Great War and Modern Memory*. New York: Oxford University Press, 1975.

Gallerand, Régis. *Homo sociatus: Mobilisations et gestions identitaires dans les associations gaies*. DEA thesis in Political Science. Université de Paris I, 1993–1994.

Garcia Canal, Maria Inés. *El Loco, el guerrero, el artista: Fabulaciones sobre la obra de Michel Foucault.* Mexico: Plaza y Valdés, 1990.

Genet, Jean. *Poèmes.* Paris: L'Arbalète, 1946.

Gérard, Fabien S. *Pasolini ou le mythe de la barbarie.* Bruxelles: Éditions de l'université de Bruxelles, 1981.

Gide, André. *Corydon.* Paris: Gallimard, 1924.

——. *Corydon.* Trans. Richard Howard. New York: Farrar, Straus and Giroux, 1983.

——. *Dostoevsky.* [No translator indicated.] New York: New Directions, 1961.

——. *The Fruits of the Earth: Les Nourritures terrestres and Les Nouvelles Nourritures.* Trans. Dorothy Bussy. New York: Knopf, 1957.

——. *If It Die . . .* Trans. Dorothy Bussy. Harmondsworth: Penguin, 1977.

——. *The Immoralist.* Trans. Richard Howard. New York: Vintage, 1996.

——. *Journal 1887–1925.* Ed. Éric Marty. Paris: Gallimard [Pléiade], 1996.

——. *The Journals of André Gide.* 4 vols. Trans. Justin O'Brien. New York: Knopf, 1947–1951.

——. *Oscar Wilde: In Memorium.* Trans. Bernard Frechtman. New York: Philosophical Library, 1949.

——. *So Be It, or The Chips Are Down.* Trans. Justin O'Brien. New York: Knopf, 1959.

Girard, Jacques. *Le Mouvement homosexuel en France, 1945–1981.* Paris: Syros, 1981.

Goffman, Erving. *The Presentation of Self in Everyday Life.* New York: Anchor, 1959.

——. *Stigma: Notes on the Management of Spoiled Identity.* New York, Touchstone, 1986.

Gombrich, Ernst. *Art and Illusion.* London: Phaidon Press, 1960.

Gombrich, Ernst, and Didier Eribon. *Ce que l'image nous dit: Entretiens sur l'art et la science.* 1991. Reprint, Paris: Diderot, 1998.

Grand-Carteret, John. *Derrière "Lui": "L'Homosexualité en Allemagne," suivi de "Iconographie d'un scandale, les caricatures politiques et l'affaire Eulenburg" par James D. Steakley.* Preface by Patrick Cardon. Lille: Cahiers Gai-Kitsch-Camp, 1992.

Green, Julien. *The Transgressor.* Trans. Anne Green. New York: Pantheon, 1957.

Greenblatt, Stephen. *Renaissance Self-Fashioning: From More to Shakespeare.* Chicago: University of Chicago Press, 1980.

Guibert, Hervé. *La Mort propagande.* Paris: Deforges, 1977.

Habermas, Jürgen. *The Philosophical Discourse of Modernity.* Trans. Frederick Lawrence. Cambridge, Mass.: MIT Press, 1987.

Hadot, Pierre. *Exercises spirituels et philosophie antique.* Paris: Institut d'études augustiniennes, 1981.

——. "Réflexions sur la notion de 'culture de soi.'" In *Michel Foucault philosophe: Rencontre internationale, Paris 9, 10, 11 janvier 1989.* Paris: Seuil 1989.

Hahn, Pierre. *Nos ancêtres les pervers: La Vie des homosexuels sous le second Empire.* Paris: Olivier Orban, 1979.

Halperin, David M. "Homosexuality." In *Gay Histories and Cultures: An Encyclo-*

pedia. Ed. George E. Haggerty. Pp. 450–55. New York: Garland Publishing, 2000.

———. "Homosexuality's Closet." *Michigan Quarterly Review* 41, no. 1 (winter 2002): 21–54.

———. "How to Do the History of Male Homosexuality." *GLQ: A Journal of Lesbian and Gay Studies* 6, no. 1 (2000): 87–124.

———. *One Hundred Years of Homosexuality and Other Essays on Greek Love*. New York: Routledge, 1990.

———. *Saint Foucault: Towards a Gay Hagiography*. New York: Oxford University Press, 1995.

Hanna, Martha. "What Did André Gide See in the Action Française?" *Historical Reflections* 17 (1991): 1–22.

Hay, Harry. *Radically Gay: Gay Liberation in the Words of Its Founder*. Ed. Will Roscoe. Boston: Beacon Press, 1996.

Heidegger, Martin. "Pourquoi nous restons en province." In *Écrits politiques, 1933–1966*. Pp. 149–53. Paris: Gallimard, 1995.

Herbart, Pierre. "André Gide." In *Inédits*. Pp. 77–98. Paris: Le Tout sur le tout, 1981.

Herdt, Gilbert, and Andrew Boxer. *Children of Horizon: How Gay and Lesbian Teens Are Leading a New Way Out of the Closet*. Boston: Beacon Press, 1996.

Herzer, Manfred. "Kertbeny and the Nameless Love." *Journal of Homosexuality* 12, no. 1 (1985): 1–26.

Hewitt, Andrew. *Political Inversions: Homosexuality, Fascism and the Modernist Imaginary*. Stanford: Stanford University Press, 1996.

Hirigoyen, Marie-France. *Le Harcèlement moral*. Paris: Syros, 1998.

Hirschfeld, Magnus. *Le Troisième Sexe: Les Homosexuels de Berlin*. 1908. Reprint, ed. Patrick Cardon. Lille: Cahiers Gai-Kitsch-Camp, 1993.

Hirshman, Albert. *Bonheur privé, actions publiques*. Paris: Fayard, 1983.

Hoare, Philip. *Serious Pleasure: The Life of Stephen Tennant*. London: Penguin, 1990.

Hocquenghem, Guy. *L'Amphithéâtre des morts*. Paris: Gallimard, 1994.

———. *L'Après-mai des faunes*. Paris: Grasset, 1974.

———. *Homosexual Desire*. 1972. Reprint, trans. Danielle Dangoor. Preface by Jeffrey Weeks. Introduction by Michael Moon. Durham: Duke University Press, 1993.

Hollinghurst, Alan. *The Swimming Pool Library*. London: Chatto and Windus, 1988.

Hull, Isabel V. *The Entourage of Kaiser Wilhelm II, 1888–1918*. Cambridge: Cambridge University Press, 1982.

Hyde, H. Montgomery. *The Trials of Oscar Wilde*. London: William Hodge, 1948.

Iacub, Marcela. "Le Couple homosexuel, le droit et l'order symbolique." *Le Banquet* 12–13 (September–October 1998): 111–24.

Isay, Richard A. *Being Homosexual: Gay Men and Their Development*. New York: Avon, 1989.

Isherwood, Christopher. *Christopher and His Kind, 1929–1939*. New York: North Point Press, 1976.

Josselin, Jean-François. *Quand j'étais star*. Paris: Grasset, 1976.

[Jouhandeau, Marcel]. *De l'abjection*. Paris: Gallimard, 1939.

Kaplan, Morris B. "Refiguring the Jewish Question: Hannah Arendt, Political Equality, and Social Difference." In *Sexual Justice: Democratic Citizenship and the Politics of Desire*. Pp. 151–76. New York: Routledge, 1997.

Kardiner, Abram, and Lionel Ovesey. *The Mark of Oppression: A Psychological Study of the American Negro*. New York: Norton, 1951.

Kennedy, Hubert C. *Ulrichs: The Life and Work of Karl Heinrich Ulrichs, Pioneer of the Modern Gay Movement*. Boston: Alyson, 1988.

Kissen, Rita M. *The Last Closet: The Real Lives of Gay and Lesbian Teachers*. Portsmouth, NH: Heinemann, 1966.

Kris, Ernst, and E. H. Gombrich. *Caricature*. London: Penguin, 1940.

Leibovici, Martine. *Hannah Arendt, une Juive: Expérience, politique et histoire*. Paris: Desclée de Brouwer, 1998.

Lepape, Pierre. *André Gide, le messager*. Paris: Seuil, 1997.

Lewin, Kurt. *Resolving Social Problems: Selected Papers on Group Dynamics*. New York: Harper, 1948.

Lindon, Mathieu. *Je t'aime: Essais critiques*. Paris: Minuit, 1993.

Livingston, Jenny, dir. *Paris Is Burning*. Film. 1991.

Lucey, Michael. "Balzac's Queer Cousins and Their Friends." In *Novel Gazing: Queer Readings in Fiction*. Ed. Eve Kosofsky Sedgwick. Pp. 167–98. Durham: Duke University Press, 1997.

——. *Gide's Bent: Sexuality, Politics, Writing*. New York: Oxford University Press, 1995.

——. "Practices of Posterity: Gide and the Cultural Politics of Sexuality." In *André Gide's Politics: Rebellion and Ambivalence*. Ed. Tom Conner. Pp. 47–71. New York: Palgrave, 2000.

Lynch, Frederick R. "Nonghetto Gays: An Ethnography of Suburban Homosexuals." In *Gay Culture in America: Studies from the Field*. Ed. Gilbert Herdt. Pp. 165–201. Boston: Beacon Press, 1992.

Maccubbin, Robert Purks, ed. *'Tis Nature's Fault: Unauthorized Sexuality during the Enlightenment*. Cambridge: Cambridge University Press, 1987.

MacKinnon, Catharine. "Feminism, Marxism, Method and the State." *Signs* 7, no. 3 (spring 1982): 515–44.

Marcus, Sharon. "Quelques problèmes de l'histoire lesbienne." Trans. Jean-Yves Boulard. In *Les Études gay et lesbiennes*. Ed. Didier Eribon. Pp. 35–43. Paris: Éditions du Centre Pompidou, 1998.

Marcuse, Herbert. *Eros and Civilization*. Boston: Beacon Press, 1966.

——. *One-Dimensional Man*. Boston: Beacon Press, 1964.

Marshall, Bill. *Guy Hocquenghem*. London: Pluto, 1996.

Martin, Claude. *André Gide ou la vocation du bonheur, Volume 1, 1869–1911*. Paris: Fayard, 1998.

Martin, Luther H., Huck Gutman, Patrick H. Hutton, eds. *Technologies of the Self: A Seminar with Michel Foucault*. Amherst: University of Massachusetts Press, 1988.

Martin, Rux. "Truth, Power, and the Self: An Interview with Michel Foucault." In *Technologies of the Self: A Seminar with Michel Foucault*. Ed. Luther H. Martin, Huck Gutman, Patrick H. Hutton. Pp. 9–15. Amherst: University of Massachusetts Press, 1988.

Marty, Éric. *André Gide: Qui êtes-vous?* Lyon: La Manufacture, 1983.

Mauger, Gérard. "Un Nouveau militantisme." In *Michel Foucault, "Surveiller et punir": La Prison vingt ans après*. Special issue of *Société et représentations*. No. 3 (November 1996): 51–77.

Mayer, Hans. *Les Marginaux: Femmes, Juifs et homosexuels dans la littérature européene*. Paris: Albin Michel, 1994.

McIntosh, Mary. "The Homosexual Role." *Social Problems* 16 (1968): 182–93.

Mendes-Leité, Rommel. *Bisexualité, le dernier tabou*. Paris: Calmann-Lévy, 1996.

Merle, Robert. *Oscar Wilde ou la "destinée" de l'homosexuel*. Paris: Gallimard, 1955.

Merrick, Jeffrey, and Bryant Ragan Jr., eds. *Homosexuality in Modern France*. New York: Oxford University Press, 1996.

Monette, Paul. *Becoming a Man: Half a Life Story*. London: Abacus, 1994.

Mosse, George L. *The Image of Man: The Creation of Modern Masculinity*. New York: Oxford University Press, 1996.

Newton, Esther. *Mother Camp: Female Impersonators in America*. Chicago: University of Chicago Press, 1979.

Nietzsche, Friedrich. *The Gay Science*. Trans. Walter Kaufmann. New York: Vintage, 1974.

Nordau, Max. *Degeneration*. Introduction by George L. Mosse. Lincoln: University of Nebraska Press, 1968.

Nye, Robert A. *Masculinity and Male Codes of Honor in Modern France*. New York: Oxford University Press, 1993.

Oosterhuis, Harry. "Male Bonding and Homosexuality in German Nationalism." In *Homosexuality and Male Bonding in Pre-nazi Germany*. Ed. Harry Oosterhuis and Hubert Kennedy. Pp. 241–63. New York: Harrington Park Press, 1991.

——. "Political Issues and the Rise of Nazism." In *Homosexuality and Male Bonding in Pre-nazi Germany*. Ed. Harry Oosterhuis and Hubert Kennedy. Pp. 183–90. New York: Harrington Park Press, 1991.

Oosterhuis, Harry, and Hubert Kennedy, eds., *Homosexuality and Male Bonding in Pre-nazi Germany*. New York: Harrington Park Press, 1991.

Painter, George D. *André Gide: A Critical Biography*. London: Weidenfeld and Nicolson, 1968.

Pater, Walter. *The Renaissance*. Ed. Adam Phillips. Oxford: Oxford University Press, 1998.

Peck, Dale. *Martin and John*. New York: Farrar, Straus and Giroux, 1993.

Peniston, William A. "Love and Death in Gay Paris: Homosexuality and Criminality in the 1870s." In *Homosexuality in Modern France*. Ed. Jeffrey Merrick and Bryant Ragan Jr. Pp. 128–45. New York: Oxford University Press, 1996.

Pinell, Patrice. *Une Épidemie politique: La Lutte contre le sida en France, 1981–1996*. Paris: PUF, 2002.

Pinell, Patrice, and Pierre-Olivier de Busscher. "La Création des associations de lutte contre le sida." In *Sida et vie psychique: approche clinique et prise en charge*. Ed. Serge Héfez. Pp. 316–23. Paris: La Découverte, 1996.

Plon, Michel, and Élisabeth Roudinesco. *Dictionnaire de la psychanalyse*. Paris: Fayard, 1997.

Pocock, J. G. A. *The Machiavelian Moment: Florentine Political Thought and the Atlantic Republican Tradition*. Princeton: Princeton University Press, 1975.

Pollak, Michael. *Les Homosexuels et le sida: Sociologie d'une épidémie*. Paris: Métailié, 1988.

——. "Un Sujet inclassable." *Un Sujet inclassable: Approches sociologiques, littéraires et juridiques des homosexualités*. Ed. Rommel Mendes-Leité. Pp. 11–13. Lille: Cahiers Gai-Kitsch-Camp, 1995.

Pollard, Patrick. *André Gide: Homosexual Moralist*. New Haven: Yale University Press, 1991.

Prieur, Annick. "Le Mariage homosexuel est-il concevable? L'exemple de la Norvège." In *Les Études gay et lesbiennes*. Ed. Didier Eribon. Pp. 72–79. Paris: Éditions du Centre Pompidou, 1998.

——. *Mema's House, Mexico City: On Queens, Transvestites, and Machos*. Chicago: University of Chicago Press, 1998.

Prieur, Annick, and Rune Sander Halvorsen. "Le Droit à l'indifférence: Le Mariage homosexuel." *Actes de la recherche en sciences sociales* 113 (1996): 6–15.

Proust, Marcel. *Against Sainte-Beuve and Other Essays*. Trans. John Sturrock. London: Penguin, 1988.

——. *A la recherche du temps perdu*. Ed. Jean-Yves Tadié. 4 vols. Paris: Gallimard [Pléiade], 1987.

——. *Correspondance*. Ed. Philip Kolb. 21 vols. Paris: Plon, 1970–1993.

——. *Remembrance of Things Past*. Trans. C. K. Scott Moncrieff, Terence Kilmartin, and Andreas Mayor. 3 vols. New York: Vintage, 1982.

Pucciani, Oreste. "Le 'Dialogue infernal' de Genet et Sartre." *Europe* 808–9 (August–September, 1996).

Raulet, Gérard. *Marcuse: Philosophie de l'émancipation.* Paris: PUF, 1992.

Reade, Brian, ed. *Sexual Heretics: Male Homosexuality in English Literature from 1850 to 1900.* New York: Coward-McCann, 1970.

Régnier, Henri de. "Souvenirs sur Oscar Wilde." *La Revue blanche,* December 15, 1895. Reprinted in *Pour Oscar Wilde: Des écrivains français au secours du condamné.* Pp. 82–86. Rouen: Librarie Élisabeth Brunet, 1994.

Reich, Wilhelm. *The Invasion of Compulsory Sex-Morality.* New York: Farrar, Straus and Giroux, 1971.

——. *The Mass Psychology of Fascism.* Trans. Vincent R. Carfagno. New York: Farrar, Straus and Giroux, 1970.

——. *The Sexual Revolution: Toward a Self-Regulating Character Structure.* Trans. Therese Pol. New York: Farrar, Straus and Giroux, 1974.

Rey, Michel. "Parisian Homosexuals Create a Lifestyle, 1700–1750." Trans. Robert A. Day and Robert Welch. In *'Tis Nature's Fault: Unauthorized Sexuality during the Enlightenment.* Ed. Robert Purks Maccubbin. Pp. 179–91. Cambridge: Cambridge University Press, 1987.

Reynolds, David S. *Walt Whitman's America: A Cultural Biography.* New York: Vintage, 1995.

Rich, Adrienne. "Compulsory Heterosexuality and Lesbian Existence." In *Blood, Bread, and Poetry: Selected Prose, 1978–1985.* Pp. 23–75. New York: Norton, 1986.

——. "Conditions for Work: The Common World of Women." In *On Lies, Secrets, and Silence: Selected Prose, 1966–1978.* Pp. 203–14. New York: Norton, 1979.

Riggs, Marlon T., dir. *Tongues Untied.* Videorecording. 1989.

Rivers, J. E. *Proust and the Art of Love: The Aesthetics of Sexuality in the Life, Times, and Art of Marcel Proust.* New York: Columbia University Press, 1980.

Rosario, Vernon. *The Erotic Imagination: French Histories of Perversion.* Oxford: Oxford University Press, 1997.

Rotello, Gabriel. *Sexual Ecology: AIDS and the Destiny of Gay Men.* New York: Dutton, 1997.

Roudinesco, Élisabeth. *La Bataille de cent ans: Histoire de la psychanalyse en France, t. 2, 1925–1985.* Paris: Fayard, 1994.

Rowbotham, Sheila, and Jeffrey Weeks. *Socialism and the New Life: The Personal and Sexual Politics of Edward Carpenter and Havelock Ellis.* London: Pluto Press, 1977.

Russo, Vito. *The Celluloid Closet.* New York: Harper and Row, 1981.

Said, Edward. *Culture and Imperialism.* New York: Vintage, 1994.

Sartre, Jean-Paul. *Anti-Semite and Jew.* Trans. George J. Becker. New York: Grove Press, 1960.

——. *Being and Nothingness.* Trans. Hazel E. Barnes. New York, Washington Square Press, 1966.

——. *Black Orpheus.* Trans. S. W. Allen. Paris: Présence africaine, 1963.

——. *Critique of Dialectical Reason, Volume 1: Theory of Practical Ensembles*. Trans. Alan Sheridan-Smith. Ed. Jonathan Rée. London: NLB, 1976.

——. "De la vocation d'écrivain." In *Les Écrits de Sartre: Chronologie, Bibliographie commentée*. Ed. Michel Contat and Michel Rybalka. Pp. 694–98. Paris: Gallimard, 1970.

——. "Entretien." *Gay Pied Hebdo* No. 13, April 1980.

——. *The Family Idiot: Gustave Flaubert, 1821–1857*. 5 vols. Trans. Carol Cosman. Chicago: University of Chicago Press, 1981–1993.

——. "Qu'est-ce qu'un collaborateur?" In *Situations III*. Pp. 43–61. Paris: Gallimard, 1949.

——. *Saint Genet: Actor and Martyr*. Trans. Bernard Frechtman. New York: George Braziller, 1963.

——. "Textes politiques." In *Situations X*. Paris: Gallimard, 1976.

——. *What Is Literature?* Trans. Bernard Frechtman. In *What Is Literature? and Other Essays*. Cambridge, Mass.: Harvard University Press, 1988.

——. *The Words*. Trans. Bernard Frechtman. New York: George Braziller, 1964.

Schiltz, Marie-Ange. "Parcours de jeunes homosexuels dans le contexte du VIH: la conquête des modes de vie." *Population* 52, no. 6 (Nov.–Dec. 1997).

Schlumberger, Jean. *Madeleine et André Gide*. Paris: Gallimard, 1956.

Schmidgall, Gary. *The Stranger Wilde: Interpreting Oscar*. New York: Abacus, 1994.

——. *Walt Whitman: A Gay Life*. New York: Dutton, 1997.

Scott, Joan Wallach. "The Evidence of Experience." *Critical Inquiry* 17 (1991): 773–97.

——. *Only Paradoxes to Offer: French Feminists and the Rights of Man*. Cambridge, Mass.: Harvard University Press, 1996.

Sedgwick, Eve Kosofsky. *Between Men: English Literature and Male Homosocial Desire*. 2nd edition. New York: Columbia University Press, 1992.

——. "Construire des significations *queer*." In *Les Études gay et lesbiennes*. Ed. Didier Eribon. Pp. 109–16. Paris: Éditions du Centre Pompidou, 1998.

——. *Epistemology of the Closet*. Berkeley: University of California Press, 1990.

——. "Gender Criticism." In *Redrawing the Boundaries: The Transformations of English and American Literary Studies*. Eds. Stephen Greenblatt and Giles Gunn. Pp. 271–302. New York: Modern Language Association of America, 1992.

——. "How to Bring Your Kids Up Gay: The War against Effeminate Boys." *Tendencies*. Pp. 154–64. Durham: Duke University Press, 1993.

——. "Queer Performativity." *GLQ: A Journal of Lesbian and Gay Studies* 1, no. 1 (1993): 1–16.

Sibalis, Michael. "The Regulation of Male Homosexuality in Revolutionary and Napoleonic France, 1789–1815." In *Homosexuality in Modern France*. Ed. Jeffrey Merrick and Bryant Ragan Jr. Pp. 80–101. New York: Oxford University Press, 1996.

Steakley, James. *The Homosexual Emancipation Movement in Germany.* Salem, N.H.: Ayer, 1975.

Stein, Edward, ed. *Forms of Desire: Sexual Orientation and the Social Constructionist Controversy.* New York: Routledge, 1990.

Symonds, John Addington. *The Letters of John Addington Symonds.* Ed. Herbert Schueller and Robert Peters. 3 vols. Detroit: Wayne State University Press, 1969.

——. *Male Love: A Problem in Greek Ethics and Other Writings.* Ed. John Lauritsen. New York: Pagan Press, 1983.

——. *The Memoirs of John Addington Symonds.* Ed. Phyllis Grosskurth. Chicago: University of Chicago Press, 1984.

——. *A Problem in Modern Ethics.* London, 1896.

Tadié, Jean-Yves. *Marcel Proust: A Life.* Trans. Euan Cameron. New York: Penguin, 2000.

——. *Proust: Le Dossier.* Pp. 86–92. Paris: Pocket, 1998.

Tamagne, Florence. *Recherches sur l'homosexualité dans la France, l'Angleterre et l'Allemagne du début des années vingt à la fin des années trente.* Doctoral dissertation. Institut d'études politiques de Paris, 1997.

Taylor, Martin P. *Lads: Love Poetry of the Trenches.* London: Duckworth, 1998.

Thompson, Victoria. "Creating Boundaries: Homosexuality and the Changing Social Order in France, 1830–1870." In *Homosexuality in Modern France.* Ed. Jeffrey Merrick and Bryant Ragan Jr. Pp. 103–26. New York: Oxford University Press, 1996.

Timmons, Stuart. *The Trouble with Harry Hay, Founder of the Modern Gay Movement.* Boston: Alyson, 1990.

Trumbach, Randolph. "The Birth of the Queen: Sodomy and the Emergence of Gender Equality in Modern Culture, 1660–1750." In *Hidden from History: Reclaiming the Gay and Lesbian Past.* Ed. George Chauncey, Martin Duberman, Martha Vicinus. Pp. 129–40. New York: Meridian, 1990.

——. "Sodomitical Subculture, Sodomitical Roles, and the Gender Revolution in the Eighteenth Century: The Recent Historiography." In *'Tis Nature's Fault: Unauthorized Sexuality during the Enlightenment.* Ed. Robert Purks Maccubbin. Pp. 109–21. Cambridge: Cambridge University Press, 1987.

Vanita, Ruth. *Sappho and the Virgin Mary: Same-Sex Love and the English Literary Imagination.* New York: Columbia University Press, 1996.

Vidal, Gore. *Palimpsest: A Memoir.* New York: Penguin, 1995.

Voeltzel, Thierry. *Vingt ans et après.* Paris: Grasset, 1978.

Weeks, Jeffrey. *Coming Out: Homosexual Politics in Britain from the Nineteenth Century to the Present.* London: Quartet Books, 1990.

——. *Sex, Politics, and Society: The Regulation of Sexuality Since 1800.* London: Longman, 1981.

Weindel, Henri de, and F. P. Fischer. *L'Homosexualité en Allemagne: Étude documentaire et anecdotique*. Paris: La Renaissance du Livre, 1908.

Whitman, Walt. *Leaves of Grass, Complete Poetry and Collected Prose*. New York: Library of America, 1982.

Wilde, Oscar. *The Complete Works of Oscar Wilde*. New York: Harper and Row, 1989.

——. *De Profundis*. In *The Complete Works of Oscar Wilde*. Pp. 873–957. New York: Harper and Row, 1989.

——. *The Letters of Oscar Wilde*. New York: Harcourt, Brace and World, 1962.

——. *Lettres*. Paris: Gallimard, 1994.

——. *Œuvres*. Paris: Gallimard [Pléiade], 1996.

——. *The Picture of Dorian Gray: Authoritative Texts, Backgrounds, Reviews and Reactions, Criticism*. Ed. Donald Lawler. New York: Norton, 1988.

——. *The Picture of Dorian Gray*. In *The Complete Works of Oscar Wilde*. Pp. 17–167. New York: Harper and Row, 1989.

——. *The Portrait of Mr. W. H.* In *The Complete Works of Oscar Wilde*. Pp. 1150–1201. New York: Harper and Row, 1989.

——. *The Soul of Man Under Socialism*. In *The Complete Works of Oscar Wilde*. Pp. 1079–104. New York: Harper and Row, 1989.

Wittmann, Carl. "A Gay Manifesto." In *Out of the Closet: Voices of Liberation*. Ed. Karla Jay and Allen Young. Pp. 330–42. New York: New York University Press, 1992.

Wolff, Charlotte. *Magnus Hirschfeld: A Portrait of a Pioneer in Sexology*. London: Quartet Books, 1986.

Young-Bruehl, Elisabeth. "Hannah Arendt Among Feminists." In *Hannah Arendt Twenty Years Later*. Ed. Larry May and Jerome Kohn. Pp. 307–22. Cambridge, Massachusetts: MIT Press, 1996.

——. *Hannah Arendt: For the Love of the World*. New Haven: Yale University Press, 1982.

Index

DIDIER ERIBON, one of France's leading intellectuals, is the author of numerous books and articles, notably the celebrated 1989 biography *Michel Foucault 1926–1984* and, most recently, *Une Morale du minoritaire: Variations sur un thème de Jean Genet* and *Hérésies: Essais sur la théorie de la sexualité.*

MICHAEL LUCEY is a Professor of French and Comparative Literature at the University of California, Berkeley, and is the author of *Gide's Bent: Sexuality, Politics, Writing* and *The Misfit of the Family: Balzac and the Social Forms of Sexuality.*

Library of Congress Cataloging-in-Publication Data
Eribon, Didier.
[Réflexions sur la question gay. English]
Insult and the making of the gay self / Didier
Eribon; translated by Michael Lucey.
p. cm.
Includes bibliographical references and index.
ISBN 0-8223-3286-8 (cloth : alk. paper)
ISBN 0-8223-3371-6 (pbk : alk. paper)
1. Gays—Social conditions. 2. Gays—Psychology.
3. Homosexuality in literature. 4. French
literature—20th century—History and criticism.
I. Lucey, Michael II. Title.
HQ76.25.E736 2004
306.76'62—dc22   2003025359